MW00561477

ALSO BY JACKSON LEARS

Rebirth of a Nation: The Making of Modern America, 1877–1920

Something for Nothing: Luck in America

Fables of Abundance: A Cultural History of Advertising in America

No Place of Grace:
Antimodernism and the Transformation of American Culture, 1880–1920

ANIMAL SPIRITS

ANIMAL SPIRITS

The American Pursuit of Vitality from Camp Meeting to Wall Street

JACKSON LEARS

Farrar, Straus and Giroux
New York

Farrar, Straus and Giroux
120 Broadway, New York 10271

Printed in the United States of America
First edition, 2023

Title-page illustration by Xenya / Shutterstock.
Illustration on page 9: Poitiers, Médiathèque François Mitterrand;
https://patrimoine.bm-poitiers.fr/digital-viewer/d-4164381.
Illustration on page 325: Library of Congress, Prints & Photographs Division, FSA/OWI Collection [LC-USF34-T01–020908-D].
Endpapers art from *Photographs of British Algae: Cyanotype Impressions*,
Anna Atkins, 1843–53; Gilman Collection, Purchase, The Horace W. Goldsmith Foundation Gift, through Joyce and Robert Menschel, 2005.

Library of Congress Cataloging-in-Publication Data
Names: Lears, T. J. Jackson, 1947– author.
Title: Animal spirits : the American pursuit of vitality from camp meeting to Wall Street / Jackson Lears.
Description: First edition. | New York : Farrar, Straus and Giroux, 2023. | Includes bibliographical references and index.
Identifiers: LCCN 2023001282 | ISBN 9780374290221
Subjects: LCSH: National characteristics, American. | Social values—United States. | United States—Social life and customs. | Animism—United States. | Vitalism. | Spirituality.
Classification: LCC E169.1 .L478 2023 | DDC 306.0973—dc23/eng/20230322
LC record available at https://lccn.loc.gov/2023001282

Designed by Patrice Sheridan

www.fsgbooks.com
www.twitter.com/fsgbooks • www.facebook.com/fsgbooks

1 3 5 7 9 10 8 6 4 2

For Karen Parker Lears

Sine qua nihil

Not unfortunately, the universe is wild—game-flavored as a hawk's wing. Nature is miracle all: She knows no laws; the same returns not, save to bring the different.

—William James, quoting Benjamin Paul Blood

Contents

ANIMAL SPIRITS

Introduction

In the beginning, everything was mixed up with everything else. All living things inhabited a boundaryless world. Identities were fluid, species and sexes interchangeable. All was in constant flux, until a trail of cosmic accidents led to tension and eventual separation between women and men, humans and animals, gods and mortals. Yet even after this fragmentation, earthly creatures continued to inhabit an animated universe, where rocks, trees, plants, and animals were all ensouled with a mysterious force or spirit—what anthropologists would call *manitou*, or *mana*—a force that kept the fragments from flying apart.

This, in rough outline, was the origin tale told by many indigenous peoples throughout the world. It shaped their sense of a cosmos where humans were not unique and superior beings, but participants in a common world undivided by barriers between wildness and civilization. The universal presence of *mana* enabled animals to intervene in human affairs, to serve as messengers from an unseen spirit world or as instruments of divine purpose. What united these perceptions was an animistic outlook that made certain conceptual categories—matter and spirit, body and soul—pliable and permeable. The fluidity of this worldview flowed from the deep but implicit conviction that the universe is alive.

This book traces how animistic thinking survived in the modern Anglo-American world, even while most indigenous peoples were being exterminated or reduced to marginality. The fate of the animated universe is a huge and elusive subject, and my method for finding a way through it is to track the cultural history of a single complex idea—the notion of animal spirits. The phrase has recently returned to contemporary currency, as policy intellectuals have revived John Maynard Keynes's idea that the key to investor confidence is the presence of animal spirits—"the spontaneous urge to action." Buoyed by animal spirits, the ideal Keynesian investors would deploy capital for productive purposes and with any luck would create more of it. Capital, from the Keynesian view, could be conceived as a shimmering magnetic force at the core of economic life. Like the *mana* of indigenous peoples, it was a product of the human imagination that took on a life of its own: it could be conjured into existence, directed toward certain purposes, but rarely controlled completely. Keynes had hit on a fundamental insight that even his devotees have left largely unexplored: the world of finance capital, despite its apparatus of quantified rationality, is governed at bottom by fantasy and fear.

My interpretation follows the idea of animal spirits in two forms: a loosely defined outlook acknowledging the centrality of spontaneous energy in human experience, and a metaphysical worldview—the philosophical successor to animistic thinking that was known as vitalism. The bundle of beliefs and emotions that constituted a modern version of *mana* went by various names—life force, libido, *élan vital*—and the history of these vitalist ideas is part of the history of animal spirits. By following the parallel but often convergent threads of animal spirits and popular vitalism, I hope to illuminate another way of being in the world, one that thrived on the margins and beneath the surfaces of conventional thinking—an alternative to the dominant ethos of human centrality and mastery. One might call it "deep America," in deference to its marginality and invisibility, its absence from most of the official conceptions of what America was (and is) all about. But there have been times, as we will see, when strong vitalist currents have run close to the surface of everyday life. And nearly always they have possessed a subtle, unacknowledged potency, for good and ill.

My own view is that animal spirits—and the currents of vitality they embody—constitute a crucial part of what it means to be human, as well as an essential reminder of the animality humans share with the nonhuman world. Yet I am also aware of how often the celebration of unalloyed vitality has sponsored violence, in vigilante or state-sanctioned forms. This sponsorship has continued to our own time, when the siren song of regenerative war has repeatedly served to justify inflicting destruction on innocent populations. The most profound vitalist thinkers have resisted this temptation and recognized the risks of exalting raw force. That is why Keynes and William James play such an important role in this narrative. They epitomize the most humane and capacious understanding of animal spirits—an understanding that led James to imagine a moral equivalent of war and Keynes to conceive capital investment as an instrument of the common good. Theirs is the version of vitalism that we need to resurrect at this fraught historical moment. The story of animal spirits and popular vitalism has important implications for contemporary public life.

At first this story may seem restricted by its white masculine focus. In the early part of this narrative, down to the end of the eighteenth century, the people who struggle to articulate the idea of animal spirits are nearly always white men and their vitalist discourse is often shaped by their white maleness. But after 1800, white women begin appearing more often, empowered by evangelical Christianity, New World mobility, and various forms of feminism. They make their own contributions to defining animal spirits, and their definitions reflect their own ambitions and longings. People of color, too, eventually appear as subjects in their own right, after long service as objects of white vitalist fantasy. Animal spirits, over the course of my narrative, cross racial and gender boundaries.

The connotations of "animal spirits" change over time, but the phrase nearly always embodies an effort to capture the relationship between the material or organic world and an invisible realm of spirit. Though one can find that melding of matter and spirit in a vast variety of settings ranging from Papua New Guinea to the Bight of Benin, the best place to begin tracking it, for my purposes, is among the indigenous peoples of North America. They were the people whose worldview—strange but also in some obscure ways familiar—confronted Europeans when they began encountering the New World.

Animistic thinking shaped Native Americans' encounters with animals, whom they endowed with spirits. The Cree of northern Canada, for example, imagined a delicate dance of hunter and hunted that required close attention to the animal's spirit as well as its flesh. According to the Cree, animals deliberately presented themselves to the hunter to be killed. When the meat was consumed, the soul of the animal was released to be reunited with flesh in another body that could be hunted again. But animals would not return to a hunter who had mistreated them—by causing undue pain in killing them, by failing to observe proper procedures in butchering and eating them or disposing of their bones, by killing unnecessarily for sport instead of need, and by refusing to share the meat or wasting it.

For the Cree as for other Native Americans, hunting was not the human pursuit of wild animals, alien beings from another world; it was a ritual connecting participants in the same world. A successful hunt was proof of amicable relations between humans and animals, based on mutual trust and linked to a cosmic economy of shared resources. Hunting was not only a search for food but a ritual of reciprocity. And at the core of Native American cosmology, as the ecologist Paul Shepard wrote, was "a pantheon of animal spirits"—beginning, perhaps, with the great aurochs represented on cave walls but ultimately encompassing all creatures.

Still, some creatures were more powerful than others, and none more than the wolf. The Cheyenne, Lakota, and Blackfoot all credited the wolf with teaching them how to hunt. One or two Cheyenne hunters, for example, would mimic a wolf's behavior and don a wolfskin in order to approach buffalo on the Great Plains. Not seeing a large pack of hunters, the buffalo would not be alarmed. Once in close, the hunters would loose their arrows, ensuring a kill. The Koyukon of central Alaska held the belief that they, too, were taught to hunt by wolves. The name of the Tonkawa tribe, who lived in what is now Oklahoma, could be translated literally as "the people of the wolf." Believing they were descendants of a mythical wolf, they refused take up any sort of farming. For them as well as for some other tribes, the killing of a wolf was taboo—the equivalent of killing a family member. In a story told by the Ojibwe, Original Man complained of loneliness and the Creator provided the wolf as his companion. After a time, when man and wolf had seen all things, the Creator separated the two but linked their fate. "What shall happen to one of you shall happen to the other," the Creator said. This was a prescient prophecy, as the wolves in North America were nearly exterminated at about the same historical moment when the Ojibwe, like other Native Americans, met a similar fate.

The history of Native American cosmologies resists reduction to neat binary opposition between hunter-gatherer and agricultural worldviews. It may be, as some scholars have argued, that nomadic hunter-gatherers see the world in terms of fluidity and complementarity, while farmers and pastoralists see it in terms of opposition and duality. The domestication of animals, from this view, may be seen as key to a broader shift in human-animal relations, from trust to domination. Yet elements of the animistic worldview survived among more settled Native American civilizations. One of the most striking is the belief that animals mediate between seen and unseen worlds, which has lasted to the present among the Hopi of the North American Southwest, who have been farming in the same arid region for centuries.

Hopi cosmology postulates the intimate coexistence of temporal and spiritual realms. "When a bowl of *nyookwivi* (mutton stew) is set before you, the *nyookwivi* is of the world. The steam that rises is the *nyookwivi* that belongs to the other world," a Hopi informant told the anthropologist Mark Bahti in 1990. The two worlds occupy the same space. When building a house, the Hopi leave a small patch unplastered so that "the unseen people of the spirit world might plaster it in their world with an equally unseen plaster," Bahti writes. Animals as well as people populate that invisible world, and the animals' spirits, like the people's, are embodied in the katsina dolls and costumes that are used in traditional Hopi rituals. All animals with a significant role to play in the spirit world (and many have one) command respect in the temporal world, whatever their utility or lack of it in everyday Hopi life.

The Hopi spirit world is a place where, according to a Hopi religious leader, things are "just the same, just the same. Only a little different." Animals often "act human"—deer, antelope, and mountain sheep dance to increase their kind, for example. They shed their fur or feathers at will. They are often indistinguishable from humans, and are referred to as if they were members of other tribes, "snake people," "badger people," and the like. When snake people shed their skins, it is said, they look like the Hopi.

Snakes and many other animals serve as messengers, carrying prayers to the spirit world. Eagles beseech the cloud people to create rain-bearing formations. Frogs and turtles are likewise "spirits that can help us" due to their association with water. Turtles and eagles are often "sent home" (sacrificed) so their shells and feathers can be used in sacred ritual. All these practices suggest that the Hopi see the spirit world as more powerful, influential, and permanent than the temporal world. They demonstrate not only what William James called "the reality of the unseen" to the Hopi, but also the power of the unseen to penetrate and inform everyday life. This principle pervaded traditional visions of universal animacy.

For their part, Europeans retained the idea of an animated universe long after they had shifted from hunting and gathering to producing food. Animism informed Greek and Roman mythology, where gods became swans, wolves, and other earthly creatures, as well as popular Christianity, where ritual objects acquired magical power to mediate relations with the supernatural. In animistic belief systems, the animal who is sacrificed is a gift from the cosmos but is also self-given, embodying the reciprocity of eater and eaten. By swallowing the enspirited flesh of a god or godlike creature, humans acknowledge their place in a system where death is no less essential than life. From Ovidian metamorphoses to the Catholic sacrament of the Eucharist, animistic thinking survived in a variety of cultural idioms.

Yet early Church fathers struggled with some success to separate their cult from older animistic ideas. The Christian idea of the Incarnation—word become flesh, God become man—posed particular problems. Theologians redefined it by insisting on the separation between the physical human and the spiritual divine in Jesus, though the whole subject remained murky and contested terrain, especially among the vast unlettered majority. Among orthodox ecclesiastics, there was a gradual pull away from the commingling of nature and the supernatural. The earliest Christian imagery blurred boundaries between humans and animals by, for example, representing three of the four evangelists with animals' heads.

By the ninth century, such hybrids had largely disappeared from orthodox iconography; and by the thirteenth century, feminine earth spirits and wild beasts were beginning to be associated with evil forces. What was passing away was something important—the primal myth "that, beneath the masks of feathers and fur, the animals and plants are a sacred society, rich in marriages, festivals, speech, commerce, the whole range of social intercourse," as Shepard wrote. Monotheism eradicated this vision when it deprived animals of *numen*, or spirit.

The triumph of monotheism in Europe set up an ontological conflict between the Old World and the New. Visions of wildness and hybridity dominated early European travelers' reports from the strange New World across the sea, where beasts were like men and men like beasts, where the inhabitants might be deferential and even noble. But reports persisted of remote places populated by "wild men" with goats' horns and dogs' heads. These were wondrous but also monstrous creatures, from a monotheistic and human-centered point of view. Here as at other, later moments in the history of Anglo-American consciousness, "wild" meant incomprehensible to Western eyes or minds, or simply out of human control. In New World aboriginal consciousness, by contrast, wildness was not projected onto a menacing Other in a howling wilderness but incorporated into the myriad differences that characterized a common world.

The Europeans who waded ashore onto Caribbean islands and the east coast of the Americas carried with them an outlook decidedly different from the worldview of the native populations. The Spanish, despite their church's capacity to assimilate indigenous beliefs, promoted an ethos of dominion over nature—not to mention over the native population. For the English, the distance between New and Old worldviews was widened by the Scientific Revolution and the Protestant Reformation. The merger of Newtonian science and Puritan religion elevated soul over body, active mind over inert matter, in a synthesis of rationalist dualism. Max Weber's formulation, despite its limitations, still holds: among many scientists and laypeople alike, a disenchantment of the world was taking hold—a proto-Cartesian view of human rationality's triumph over inert nature and animal automata. And for educated English Protestants, the deity in charge was an abstract Providence, impersonal and unmoved by Catholic cajolery. Under His aegis, liturgical rituals and artifacts meant to summon the spirit world began to look (and sound) like mere hocus-pocus.

But behind this scrim of no-nonsense empiricism, English minds were a tangled mass of animistic myths and lore. The English settlers headed for North America started out from a land roiling with religious and economic upheaval. In both realms, an animated universe survived and even flourished.

Animistic survivals were most apparent in religious practice. Vestiges of medieval Church magic continued to inspire a broad range of the population, from Roman Catholics and High Church Anglicans to unlettered villagers paying homage to sacred oaks and holy wells. Early evangelical revivalists, too—proponents of "enthusiasm"—began to recognize the benefits of preaching in wilderness settings, where the faithful could feel the presence of God more intimately than in a church or meetinghouse. Even Puritans still saw visions, heard voices, and looked for signs and portents in the natural world. In 1635, the Puritan Rev. Richard Mather, gathering his shipmates on deck to see an enormous porpoise the crew had caught, celebrated the occurrence as a portent of God's favor. For Protestants as well as Catholics, ravens, magpies, and other birds could be interpreters of the cosmos, omens of future events—spring, rain, death. The English settlers' cultural baggage was filled with tales of human-animal metamorphoses, those by not only Ovid but Dante and the twelfth-century French poet and fabulist Marie de France, as well as the upstart John Donne, whose poem "Metempsychosis" describes the progress of a human soul through various plant and animal avatars.

Yet while there was some resonance between Native American and English visions of animacy, the differences were more important than the similarities. Like Native Americans and other Europeans, the English told folktales that featured animals as examples of human traits. But while for Native Americans animals were inspirited creatures, endowed with *mana*, for the English, spirits might inhabit animals in more demonic form, as witches' familiars (the devil's diabolic accomplices), or as the fleshly shapes the devil himself assumed—black dogs, foxes, and the like. English and Indians agreed that animals were good to eat, but while native hunters treated prey with respect and performed rituals of reciprocity, the English declared their dominance, reducing animals to objects of sport and amusement, or to markers of status.

But the English did pioneer the animation of the economic realm. As the historian Eugene McCarraher observes (moving a step beyond Keynes), speculative capitalists promoted "the meretricious ontology of capital, in which everything receives its value—and even its very existence—through the empty animism of money. It proclaims that capital is the *mana* or *pneuma* or *soul* or *élan vital* of the world, replacing the older enlivening spirits with one that is more real, energetic, and productive." While this "empty animism" was more metaphorical than metaphysical, its influence was profound. In the trading houses of the City of London, animal spirits took a new form, playing a central role in motivating investors and keeping the whole business humming—as Keynes would notice, centuries later.

But as this book will make clear, animal spirits were never reducible to their economic role. The history of the term unveils its broad significance as a leitmotif—not only in the citadels of finance but in the broader society as well. Tracking animal spirits reveals the thinness of orthodox dualism. Despite official commitments to the superiority of spirit over flesh, the Elizabethan English (and their American colonists), Anglican and Puritan alike, inhabited a fluid cosmos where ontological boundaries blurred and opposites overlapped.

Indeed the word "spirit" itself reveals significant ambiguities. Its original meaning was bodily: breath. Aristotle's *De spiritu* was all about respiration. Yet even by Aristotle's time an alternative connotation had emerged, especially in Stoic tradition; spirit began to imply soul. What later, dualistic thinkers would imagine to be an exalted, ideal entity (the soul) was paired linguistically with an essential physiological process—the inhaling and exhaling of air.

The phrase "animal spirits" compounds the ambiguity. It is etymologically descended from *anima*, soul—a meaning that has survived for centuries in the notion of a being *animated* by vitality or soulful life. Yet by the late 1500s, "animal" had also come to refer to nonhumans, lower beings lacking soul or even intellect, or else to the portions of human nature that humans had in common with those lower beings. In Shakespeare's *Love's Labour's Lost* (1598), the supercilious Nathaniel dismisses the oafish constable Dull: "His intellect is not replenished, he is only an annimall, only sensible in the duller partes." The tendency to link animality with "the duller partes" was reinforced by Puritans when they equated the "animal man" with the "natural man"—the man or woman who had not been transformed through the saving grace of conversion.

Amid these blurred boundaries, animal spirits played a fluid role in medieval and early modern thought, operating as emissaries between body and soul. The first influential figure to discuss animal spirits was the second-century Greek physician Galen, whose ideas shaped European assumptions about the body for a millennium and a half. According to Galen and his subsequent interpreters, animal spirits were a "subtil, aiery substance" that connected the ventricles of the brain with the sense organs and played a critical part in visual perception. They became rays of light that entered the brain through the eyes but were also emitted from the eyes outward, into the world beyond the perceiving self. Animal spirits thus rendered the air itself an organ of perception, which acted on the crystalline lens in the eye and allowed it both to exude spirit and perceive objects. This elaborate theory survived in fugitive forms for centuries. It is a prototypical instance of the cultural work done by animal spirits—providing palpable form to impalpable processes, linking immaterial with material existence. In this case the sense organ in question (the eye) had already acquired spiritual significance from classical and biblical authors, who agreed that the eye was the mirror, or window, of the soul.

For centuries, the struggle to find a place for the soul (and later the mind) in the body would focus fitfully but frequently on animal spirits, which were defined in a bewildering variety of ways. The question that puzzled most thinkers was: Were animal spirits corporeal or spiritual, visible or invisible? Sometimes it seemed they were everything and anything: within the same treatise, their "subtil, aiery substance" could be characterized as air, light, fire, and liquid—something evanescent, fleeting, and fugitive, but still physical.

By the early nineteenth century, the medical profession had largely discarded animal spirits, but the concept increasingly pervaded the vernacular—even while the kindred idea of philosophical vitalism emerged among Romantic thinkers. Preoccupation with primal vitality took many forms; animal spirits spilled over the boundaries of the self and permeated the cosmos as invisible sources of energy—animal magnetism, mesmerism, electricity. A fascination with Force and Energy as ends in themselves became a kind of secular religion, while financial markets gyrated in tandem with the flow of animal spirits, or at least Keynes's version of them.

Managers and moralists sought to contain the vitalist ferment with numbers, creating the appearance of orderly progress and efficient control. The inadequacy of their efforts is one of the leitmotifs of this book. By no means do I intend to dismiss the value of statistical knowledge, any more than Keynes did. Instead, I follow Keynes in recognizing that while statistics can provide invaluably precise description, they can easily be overvalued and misused as tools of interpretation and prediction. Yet social scientists and policymakers still seek, more insistently than ever, to quantify the unquantifiable sources of vitality—in human beings and throughout the cosmos.

Posed against the background of a dominant ethos devoted to managerial mastery, animal spirits serve as entrée into an alternative way of thinking and being in the world. This animistic worldview has flourished among idiosyncratic thinkers for centuries, but it has begun to acquire new legitimacy in our own time as scientists have rediscovered the uses of animist-derived ideas in physics, botany, geology, and epigenetics. All of these tendencies coincide with an efflorescence of ecological thought and converge on a common wisdom: we inhabit a living cosmos. That is the recognition that animates this book.

But to begin with the first chapter of the story, we must return to the point of departure for most Englishmen who arrived on North American shores in the early 1600s: Elizabethan London.

1

Between Body and Soul

SIXTEENTH-CENTURY LONDON was a dangerous place, where sudden reversals of fortune were commonplace. Waves of plague swept repeatedly through the city, littering the streets with piles of corpses that had been healthy people only days before. House fires were a constant menace, another reminder of the vagaries of fate. As one Elizabethan chronicler wrote, "He which at one o'clock was worth five thousand pounds, and, as the prophet saith, drank his wine in bowls of fine silver plate, had not by two o'clock so much as a wooden dish to eat his meat in, nor a house to cover his sorrowful head." Fire, the giver of warmth and light, was also an agent of calamity. Sex posed equally contradictory possibilities: the act of creating life imperiled its creators; sublime union could result in catastrophic denouement—venereal disease, stillbirths, fatal infections, failed deliveries.

The structures of Elizabethan feeling were fraught with violent contrasts, and the sharpest was between life and death. Reminders of one's personal mortality were everywhere, beginning for Londoners with the dead plague victims in their streets. The plague embodied the perversities of fate—coming and going mysteriously, striking healthy people down swiftly, leaving physicians baffled. "Whence it cometh, wherof it ariseth, and wherefore it is sent," a scornful preacher said, "they confess their ignorance." The medical profession was equally helpless in its treatment of other fatal illnesses; indeed its bleeding and purging remedies often hastened the victims' demise. But even for the lucky ones who survived conventional treatment, life was always precarious and often short.

The physical facts of death were an everyday presence, impossible to ignore. Bodily decomposition bore witness to the transiency of beauty and the inevitability of decay, underscoring the insignificance of mere mortal life. The notion of the dead body as a banquet for worms pervaded common speech. "A plague o' both your houses!" cries the dying Mercutio, "they have made worms' meat of me." It was difficult to forget that flesh, however lovely or vigorous, was always just a few heartbeats away from putrefaction.

Still, there were ways to keep the specter of death at arm's length. Early modern people were used to frequent sickness and early death; they cultivated low expectations and stoical resignation, often with the aid of alcohol. The poet John Taylor's tribute to ale captured its central place in Elizabethan social life: it "doth comfort the heavy and troubled mind; it will make a weeping widow laugh and forget sorrow for her deceased husband . . . It is the warmest lining of a naked man's coat; it satiates and assuages hunger and cold; with a toast it is the poor man's comfort; the shepherd, mower, ploughman, and blacksmith's most esteemed purchase; it is the tinker's treasure, the pedlar's jewel, the beggar's joy, and the prisoner's loving nurse."

More hopeful souls also clung to the redemptive promise of Christian faith. Longings to transcend the vulnerability of a mortal body encouraged the exaltation of an immortal soul. Yet while eternal life offered deliverance from decay, it also included the possibility of endless punishment for sins committed in this life. Wayward believers faced the prospect of a miserable few decades in this world followed by everlasting damnation in the next. Still, there was a way out. Flesh could be redeemed by spirit, and both be reunited after death in the resurrected body. Visions of salvation evoked the promise of eternal wholeness. The question was how to reach that dreamed-of state. Protestants and Catholics disagreed violently, but politics and theology did not necessarily disturb ontology. For most English people, foundational assumptions about the ground of being remained intact; they continued to inhabit an animated cosmos where body and soul blended, where matter was infused with spirit. How those fusions occurred was determined in part by liturgical tradition, but not entirely. There was always a surplus of enchantment in the cultural atmosphere, available for multiple purposes—medicinal, recreational, and even (eventually) financial.

According to the textbook tale, the Enlightenment fostered the transition from enchanted tradition to disenchanted modernity—from a sacred cosmic order based on faith and fear to a rational, secular universe based on Newtonian science, and from a social world stifled by communitarian conformity to one hospitable to individual choice. Enlightenment thinkers, in this tale, were benign rationalists, so committed to the life of reason—to an orderly mind in an orderly cosmos—that they tended to underrate the ungovernable power of passion in human motivation and the unpredictable role of chance in cosmic affairs generally.

For some time now, historians have been complicating this picture. What has emerged is a darker, wilder version of the Enlightenment—a mental habitat more hospitable to occult forces and mysterious vital principles than the textbook version of Enlightenment rationality could ever have been. In this atmosphere, animal spirits shuttled between body and soul, animating the cosmology of divines like Donne and Milton, novelists like Laurence Sterne, and a host of philosophers and scientists who were trying to figure out how visible matter produced invisible thought and feeling. The deeper one probed into these mysteries, the more elusive certainty seemed. The disenchantment of the Anglo-American mind remained precarious and incomplete; patterns of medieval thought persisted in altered form. Enchantment survived enlightenment.

THE AMBIGUITIES OF ENCHANTMENT

Medieval dreams of resurrection melded sacred and secular life, shaping the larger significance of Carnival as well as other festivals. Before the Reformation, English villages joined the rest of Catholic Europe in celebrating the days leading up to Ash Wednesday with a riot of sensuous excess. The annual rituals of Carnival—the parading of giant sausages through the streets, the mock plowing performed by unmarried women—framed food and sex with larger liturgical meaning. Carnival endowed flesh with spirit, prefiguring the posthumous reembodiment of soul in heaven. Meanwhile, here on earth, the fragility of flesh made the experience of the senses all the more piquant and precious.

Everyday devotions enacted theological truths. Catholic preoccupation with Jesus's bodily suffering flowed from the church's doctrine of the Incarnation: "the Word became Flesh, and dwelt among us" (John 1:14). Humanity melded with divinity, and worm's meat became the body of Christ. The interpenetration of body and soul was epitomized in the eucharistic sacrifice—swallowing the God, drinking His blood. The sacrament of the Holy Eucharist, undergirded by the doctrine of transubstantiation, resonated with the sacramental feasting of many indigenous peoples. Despite theologians' efforts to separate Christ's godhood and manhood, the Eucharist kept animistic magic at the core of the Christian faith.

The magic of the medieval church sustained a Christian version of an animated cosmos. Spirit interacted with matter at every turn—investing relics, statues, images, and ritual gestures with magical efficacy. The most common ritual gesture available to the laity was the sign of the cross: it was used by ordinary folk to ward off evil spirits along with more palpable dangers, and by priests to exorcise the devil from persons, animals, and objects, as well as to endow organic or material entities with sacramental significance. Holy water was holy because it was blessed by a priest using the sign of the cross, and such blessings benefited body as well as soul. Water, once consecrated, had medical uses as a tonic for sick cows, sheep, and people. Church rituals, talismans, and amulets ensouled the material world, creating an enchanted path between the self and God. Popular understanding of the Eucharist reinforced belief in the physicality of the divine, which broadened to obscure the boundaries between the visible and invisible worlds, encouraging the faith that sacraments could promote physical as well as spiritual well-being. The common practice of baptizing puppies, kittens, lambs, and foals was based on the belief that baptized babies, of whatever species, "got on better" after the ritual had been performed.

Though orthodox thinkers distinguished between religion and magic, village priests and laity merged the two realms by undermining the distinction between prayers and spells or charms. This fostered the popular assumption that mere repetition of verbal formulas could automatically guarantee their efficacy. The most popular repetitive ritual became the praying of the rosary, originally known as the Marian Psalter—150 "Hail Marys" divided into equal groups by ten "Our Fathers." Prayer beads helped the worshipper keep track. According to Roman Catholic lore, the need for praying the Marian Psalter was revealed to St. Dominic by the Blessed Virgin Mary during the thirteenth-century crusade against the Albigensian heretics, who stressed a radical duality between body and soul. The point of the Marian Psalter was not meditation but repetition of words with (one hoped) magical efficacy.

Theologians opposed magical thinking but accepted the consequences of earlier syncretic strategies, which church authorities had deployed when they preserved the veneration of holy wells, trees, and stones by turning pagan sites into Christian ones and substituting saints for pagan divinities. Sometimes the pagan divinities survived, in all but name. On the eve of the Reformation, English men and women inhabited a material universe pervaded by spiritual forces.

But by the mid-1500s, the more militant English Protestants—popularly known as Puritans—had pushed their protest beyond mere objection to the rule of Rome. They had begun challenging the Catholics' animated universe, dismissing the attribution of magical powers to consecrated objects, scorning the celebration of feast days throughout the liturgical year. In the battle between Carnival and Lent, Puritans sought a permanent victory for Lent—and ultimately achieved it, at least as far as the traditional celebration of fleshly excess was concerned. Carnival celebrations devolved from liturgical feasts to market fairs as Puritanical sentiments spread, even among Anglicans. Yearnings for a kind of spiritual (as well as social) transparency spurred efforts to purify the practice of Christianity—to put plain speech in place of mumbo-jumbo, plain dress in place of excessive display, biblical truth in place of papal decree.

Political change licensed Puritanical frenzy. After 1558, when Elizabeth's succession to the throne secured Protestant rule, militant mobs felt emboldened to smash icons, wreck churches, and burn down monasteries. Disdain for the claims of enchantment took vigorous popular form. At Downhead in Somerset, a man was heard to say his "mare will make as good holy water as any priest can." Disenchanting the priests' supposedly magical power was one of the priorities of Protestant business. Orthodox theologians, Anglican and Puritan, rejected claims for the sacraments' magical efficacy; so, eventually, did Counter-Reformation Catholic theologians, responding to Protestant critiques of Romish superstition. Many Christians of various denominations reasserted the divide between a transcendent God and a fallen world. In subsequent decades, some would embrace René Descartes's philosophical restatement of this dualism: man was the only creature with a "rational soul"; the others were mere automata. It would be hard to find a more disenchanted vision of the universe.

Yet as Keith Thomas and other historians have made clear, the cosmos of the early modern West remained enchanted in many ways, for most people. Even the most militant Protestants (indeed sometimes especially they) inhabited a universe enveloped with spiritual significance; they heard voices, saw visions, and dreamed divinatory dreams. In many English minds, the everyday world of common sense coexisted with another, enchanted one, shimmering and fluid, washing up along the shores of consciousness, seeping into the interior.

This was how the animated universe survived, in fits and starts, in eddies and backwaters. Long after the Reformation, among common folk but also many of the more educated, the nonhuman universe remained enchanted. Animals retained their significance as messengers from the unseen world, who might possess preternatural power for good or ill—dogs had a sixth sense of danger; cats and other creatures could still be witches' familiars; magpies and ravens still served as omens and auguries—and astrology survived as a system of cosmic correspondences that explained otherwise inexplicable occurrences. Among English Protestants, the process of disenchantment was fitful, uneven, and incomplete.

Yet Protestantism was not the only challenge to medieval enchantment. A more potent alternative was what McCarraher calls "the religion of modernity"—the emergent belief system generated by modern capitalism, which involved not the disenchantment but the *misenchantment* of the world in the service of a new deity, money. The nascent capitalist worldview, like its Christian rivals, reflected the upheavals, scarcities, and insecurities of everyday life in early modern London. The desperate search for reliable sustenance ranged well beyond the precincts of poverty. Ambitious young men without a trade were dependent on political preferment, which in turn might be dependent on military adventure, including expeditions to America sponsored by men with mobile capital in search of investment opportunities. The omnipresence of risk facilitated the emergence of a commercial and financial system based on credit—an invisible force that was meant to rationalize risk but also, paradoxically, reinforced it. The presence or absence of credit could generate overnight rise or ruin.

Belief in the possibility of magical self-transformations was one of many religious features accompanying the rise of capitalism. The capitalist religion of modernity, as both its creators and critics realized, invoked divine sanctions for commerce and incorporated the fetishistic appeal of commodities. But the most fundamentally religious dimension of capitalist misenchantment was the mysterious power of money to reconstitute the essence of value—to transform it from something comparatively stable to something fluid and ever-changing.

The liberal philosopher John Locke celebrated money's transformative powers when he distinguished between use value and monetary value, declaring his preference for the latter because it "altered the intrinsic value of things." Money possessed the power to beget more money, especially when it took the impalpable form of credit—a concept that revealed its religious roots in its etymological descent from *credo*: "I believe." Finance capital, trading in invisible assets, was a faith-based enterprise; fortunes were made and lost on the basis of fantasy, rumor, and fear. Centuries before Keynes was born, speculative capitalists were demonstrating the accuracy of his insight.

To be sure, there were other sorts of capitalists at work in the early modern world as well, notably the sort devoted to calculation, efficiency, double-entry bookkeeping, and disciplined achievement as a way of life—Weber's ideal type of early modern man, whose Protestant ethic was turning into a spirit of capitalism. Some finance capitalists undoubtedly resembled the Weberian type in certain ways, but many cultivated a more emotionally charged ethos, one more attuned to the fluctuations of the emerging business cycle.

While the notion of animal spirits captured the emotional turbulence at the core of capitalism, it also illuminated alternative visions of universal animacy—some rooted in sacramental tradition, others resonating with newer forms of enchantment. The English Reformation was a time (and place) of religious searching, along and outside the borders of orthodoxy. Few seekers left a more revealing record than the poet and preacher John Donne.

Donne's poems evoked a vibrant state of being—above and below theological controversy—where flesh and spirit merge in ecstatic union. T. S. Eliot glimpsed this synthetic vision in his classic essay "The Metaphysical Poets." According to Eliot, these poets *felt* their thought "as immediately as the colour of a rose." Donne, for Eliot, was an especially strong example of this immediacy. "A thought to Donne was an experience," Eliot wrote, "it modified his sensibility." But from Eliot's view, Donne was among the last of his kind. The capacity to fuse thought and feeling, Eliot thought, had fallen victim to a "dissociation of sensibility" in the later seventeenth century. In fact, that fusion had survived, and Donne was a key figure in its survival.

A BRACELET OF BRIGHT HAIR ABOUT THE BONE: JOHN DONNE

Donne was born in 1572 to a prominent Catholic family and brought up amid long-standing resentment of Protestant persecution. One of his great-great-great-uncles was the martyred Thomas More, and his uncle Jasper Haywood was a Jesuit priest who had been banished from England for sedition. Donne's father, a successful ironmonger who kept his Catholicism to himself, died when John was four. His mother soon remarried a physician with friends at Court, who was also a camouflaged Catholic. Recalling his youth, Donne acknowledged his own "hydroptique immoderate desire of humane learning and languages," which was its own form of "voluptuousness." He entered Oxford at twelve, accompanied by his brother Henry, who was a year younger. (Precocious enrollments were not unusual at the time.) Four years later the boys were withdrawn by their family, so they could avoid taking the required Oath of Allegiance to the Protestant crown. Like other literate young men with connections at Court, Donne took to reading law at Lincoln's Inn.

Early on he discovered his passion for poetry. "Though like the Pestilence and old fashion'd love," he wrote, "Ridlingly it catch men." A big part of its appeal, for Donne, was the opportunity it provided to celebrate the melding of romantic and erotic experience—and also to imbue sentimental conventions (or what would later become sentimental conventions) with larger philosophical significance. In Donne's early lyrics, his biographer John Stubbs writes, "matters of the heart become matter." Lovers are emotionally entangled through things left behind after lovemaking—trinkets, keys, and the like. In popular romances, this became a familiar device, but for Donne it had a larger significance, connecting with his lifelong conviction that matter could be infused with spirit.

Donne's poetry posed a powerful counterpoint to the separation of disembodied, analytical mind from inert, manipulatable matter, partly by exploring the limits of the quantitative thinking that underwrote those dualities. Mathematically literate, Donne was aware of the advances in that discipline during his lifetime toward the expansion of a symbolic mathematical language. Yet he was also aware that mathematical symbols, despite their apparently objective existence in the world, were in fact humanly fashioned cognitive structures that frame our perceptions of the world and shape our orientation to it.

Not everything is best apprehended through numbers, as Donne realized, and his poetry illuminates the areas of human experience that resist quantitative measurement. "The Computation" deploys hyperbole to show how inadequately numbers convey an anxious lover's impatient wait for his inamorata: by the end, the "years, since yesterday" amount to 2,400; every hour has seemed like a hundred years. This trope, too, becomes a sentimental convention, but the idea behind it has a place in the subsequent history of philosophy. Donne's poem anticipates (by three centuries) the philosopher Henri Bergson's experience-centered notion of time as "duration." The quantification of time was a key example of the modern effort to objectify subjective experience, using the apparent precision of numbers to create the impression that the immeasurable had been successfully measured. From Donne to Bergson, devotees of animal spirits and their vitalist fellow travelers would challenge the quantifiers' claim.

For all its intellectual ambition, Donne's poetry could also celebrate the pleasures of the flesh for their own sake. In "To His Mistress Going to Bed," he lovingly describes each article of clothing as the woman removes it, concluding with an exuberant apostrophe:

Full nakedness, all joys are due to thee.
As souls unbodied, bodies unclothed must be,
To taste whole joys.

Yet from early on, celebrating the pleasures of the flesh was also compensation for pain incurred elsewhere. Poetry, Donne wrote in 1593, was a "cherishing fyre which dryes in mee / Griefe which did drowne mee." He was grieving over the death of his brother Henry, who had been arrested for harboring a fugitive Jesuit and imprisoned at plague-ridden Newgate, where he died within weeks. John blamed the rigidity of the Catholic resistance for placing his brother at the mercy of the merciless Protestant state. The poet had begun to realize that there was no career path forward for a young Catholic who sought a place at Court. One way to signal his fealty to the Protestant regime was to volunteer for one of Elizabeth's many military missions against the Spanish, an assault on Cádiz. It turned into an ordeal of fetid nights belowdecks, oppressive days on deck in still, relentless heat, and fitful fights with the

Spanish that left scorched bodies flailing helplessly in the sea. Still, it was a politically useful signal of Donne's break with the Roman Catholic Church—a good career move, with no harm in repeating it. He volunteered for a similar mission to the Azores in 1597.

Donne's break with Catholicism left him metaphysically at sea. He had grown skeptical of all doctrinal claims, suspicious that there were political motives behind them—as indeed there often were, on both sides of the Protestant-Catholic divide. Court life was a never-ending round of self-interested jostling for advantage—a vision of hell, as far as Donne was concerned. In his poems he tried to refine his notion of patriotism, distinguishing between "a rotten state" and "England, to whome we owe, what we be, and have."

Yet, soon after he returned from the Azores, he attached himself to that rotten state, by securing a court position as secretary to Thomas Egerton, Lord Keeper of the Seal. Among other responsibilities, Egerton headed the government effort to imprison, torture, and execute leading Catholics who refused to bend a knee to the new regime. Donne served (however indirectly) as a cog in the machinery of that systematic suppression. Though Donne always opposed torture, he blamed the Roman Catholic minority for their refusal to accept what he had come to believe was legitimate political authority.

He was also engaged in a private search for the best path to eternity—a Protestant quest that revealed a shift in his sensibility, though not in his fundamental beliefs. His quest was epitomized by "The Relic." The poem revealed a complex blend of Catholic and Protestant impulses, along with other divisions that haunted early modern minds—flesh and spirit, body and soul, life and death. Addressed to a departed lover, "The Relic" begins in a graveyard, with a reminder that cemetery space was limited in London and existing graves were often disturbed to entomb new occupants:

When my grave is broke up again
Some second guest to entertain . . .
And he that digs it, spies
A bracelet of bright hair about the bone,

Will he not let us alone,
And think that there a loving couple lies,
Who thought that this device might be some way
To make their souls, at the last busy day,
Meet at this grave, and make a little stay?

Donne imagines a sympathetic gravedigger, who believes that he has uncovered the remains of a "loving couple" lying together. The "bracelet of bright hair," he assumes, is a clever "device" that links the couple's bodies after death and allows their souls to find each other at this very spot on "the last busy day" of the resurrection. The gravedigger refrains from disturbing the grave, and the poem proceeds to envision how in a time of "misdevotion" the grave becomes an object of pilgrimage, the bracelet a venerated relic. True devotion, Donne implies, would be directed not to the bracelet but to the actual miracle of the love it represented. Despite his embrace of this Protestant sentiment, the ex-Catholic in Donne remained fascinated by a relic's power to meld bodies and souls.

While Donne's personal religious synthesis would be years in the making, his employment with Egerton evoked more immediate emotional turmoil. He lived in Egerton's house with the status of a senior servant, but he took meals with the family and they treated him as a social equal. Among those at the table was Ann More, a wellborn fourteen-year-old girl who was staying with her aunt, Egerton's second wife. Both he and she were entranced, and before long they were conducting a furtive courtship in the nooks and crannies of the labyrinthine Egerton mansion. When Ann moved back to her parents' country estate, returning to London only for brief and occasional visits, Donne was engulfed by erotic longings, depression, and drift.

Ultimately he pressed his suit, and Ann responded. Two lovers champing at the bit of paternal disapproval could not be held back by mere convention. On December 19, 1601, the seventeen-year-old Ann and Egerton's twenty-nine-year-old secretary—an ex-Catholic with no prospects apart from Egerton's patronage—were secretly married. When

Egerton learned of the union, he was enraged and dismissed Donne immediately. The young couple were thrown back on their own resources, the most abundant of which was their love for each other.

Donne's marriage reinforced his reinvention of himself, and transformed his conception of love from promiscuity and predation to tenderness and devotion. His poems praising enduring sexual love and blissful monogamous unions were unprecedented, and popular. Married love, Donne felt, was love without nervousness, without the anxious fretting induced by jealousy and suspicion. It was like a waking up, a sunrise. "For love, all love of other sights controules, / And makes one little room, an everywhere," he wrote. The couple's first child was named Constance, and in "The Extasie," the poet holds his lover fast on a "Pregnante Bank" while the day and the river run by. The poem meditates on the interdependence of body and soul, which in Donne's medieval psychology are linked through the action of spirits produced by the blood.

As our blood labours to beget
Spirits, as like souls as it can,
Because such fingers need to knit
That subtle knot, which makes us man
So must pure lovers' souls descend
T'affections, and to faculties,
Which sense may reach and apprehend,
Else a great prince in prison lies.
To our bodies turn we then, that so
Weak men on love revealed may look;
Love's mysteries on souls may grow,
But yet the body is his book.

The union of bodies necessarily accompanies the union of souls, revealing a glimpse of the mysteries of love to "weak men" who haven't a clue what it's all about. The role of spirits in this process is foundational. Donne did not explicitly refer to *animal* spirits, but the provenance was clear: he was describing a Christian version of what physiologists since

Galen's time had called animal spirits. As, years later, Donne told his congregation at St. Paul's in London: "In the constitution and making of a natural man, the body is not the man, nor the soul is not the man, but the union of these two makes up the man; the spirits in a man which are the thin and active part of the blood, and so are of a kind of middle nature, between soul and body, those spirits are able to do, and they do the office, to unite and apply the faculties of the soul to the organs of the body, and so there is a man." As the crucial links between body and soul, Donne's spirits were at the heart of what it meant to be human. The "extasie" he experienced with Ann was an awakening into full humanity.

Yet practical demands increasingly intruded on their idyll. For years Donne tried and failed to secure a place at court, while Ann continued to bear children—twelve in all, four of whom survived to adulthood. By 1609, when he was about to turn forty and had been only occasionally employed for eight years, he had fallen prey to chronic melancholy. The omnipresence of death in plague-ridden London intensified his fear of posthumous punishment, especially given his insistent memories of his flesh-fueled "idolatrous" youth; he was haunted by visions of his "profane mistresses" stalking by, and by visions of hell that recalled the burnt bodies leaping from a burnt ship off Cádiz. For the next five years he kept a journal recording the fearful wandering of his soul, among various eternities.

Still, he continued to write poetry celebrating the melding of matter and spirit. In 1611, before he left for a temporary assignment on the Continent as an assistant to the diplomat Robert Drury, Donne addressed "A Valediction: Forbidding Mourning" to Ann, who was pregnant and staying on the Isle of Wight with her sister. After invoking the romantic convention that souls could be together while bodies were apart, Donne turned to a strikingly material image to represent how the couple would transcend their separation:

Our two souls, therefore, which are one,
Though I must go, endure not yet
A breach, but an expansion,
Like gold to airy thinness beat.

The blending of matter and spirit surfaced most clearly in a poem Donne wrote in 1612 to commemorate the second anniversary of the death of Drury's daughter Elizabeth.

She of whose soul, if we may say, 'twas gold,
Her body was th'electrum, and did hold
Many degrees of that; we understood
Her by her sight, her pure and eloquent blood
Spoke in her cheeks, and so distinctly wrought,
That one might almost say, her body thought . . .

Who with God's presence was acquainted so,
(Hearing, and speaking to him) as to know
His face in any natural stone, or tree,
Better than when in images they be . . .

The "electrum" was an alchemical term for an alloy of gold and silver, which (the alchemist hoped) was en route to becoming pure gold—an analogue to Elizabeth's thinking body, which was better able to see the face of God in stones and trees than in man-made images. Elizabeth, Donne imagined, inhabited an animated universe. Since he had never met the girl, the poem was clearly a projection of Donne's own spiritual yearnings.

Entering the priesthood seemed a last-ditch move, but soon he was desperate enough to make it. He continued to fall short of steady employment. In May 1614 his three-year-old daughter, Mary, died, followed by seven-year-old Francis in November. What was left of his family needed more than favors from his rich friends. Donne finally decided to become a priest, though to friends and enemies alike, he was still the poet of erotic love whose marriage was tainted by scandal.

Donne's hopes for a new phase of family life would not last long. In August 1617, Ann died of a "raging fever" after giving birth. Like so many women of that era, she remains mute and nearly invisible to us—except as the object of Donne's (often powerful and moving) tributes. She remains an off-stage figure, rather than a player in her own right.

As Donne became a prominent preacher, with a broad and heterogenous London congregation, he occasionally succumbed to orthodox formulas. "Every man is a little *Church*," he once said, "and in every man, there are two sides, two armies, the flesh fights against the Spirit." And on another occasion, he announced that "marriage is but a continual fornication sealed with an oath." Since this utterance occurred at a wedding, one can only speculate on the ambivalence he had begun to feel toward sex, especially in his chosen celibate state.

Yet Donne was always drawn to melding flesh and spirit, erotic experience with intense religious feeling. One of his "Holy Sonnets" addresses the face of Christ crucified, remembering what "I said to all my profane mistresses . . . so I say to thee, To wicked spirits are horrid shapes assigned / This beauteous form assures a piteous mind." And in another, addressed to the Trinity, he wrote: "Batter my heart, three-personed God . . . / Take me to you, imprison me, for I / Except you enthrall me, never shall be free, / Nor ever chaste, except you ravish me." The conditions of chastity and ravishment are opposites and remain opposites even as they fuse together; Donne was a connoisseur of paradox, especially in religious matters. After he had joined the priesthood, he wrote less poetry but remained committed to the intimate merger of body and soul. In his Easter sermon of 1623, he declared, "All that the soule does, it does in, and with, and by the body." His preaching, which one listener called a "sacred Art and Courtship," was empowered by sublimated sexual energy. And to witness him preach, as Stubbs writes, was "to share in an ecstasy." This was altogether appropriate for a man who believed that bodies and souls would be reunited on the last day, and that the physical universe was a miracle of divine creation.

Donne's version of Christianity joined the physical and spiritual realms in a fluid, volatile cosmos. God was the blazing, boiling energy at the core of Donne's universe, which was filled with fragments coming together in friction-filled unity. Key fusions were performed by animal spirits, which constituted "a kind of middle nature, between soul and body," as Donne said. Everything was in a constant state of liquefaction, including our hearts when they responded to God's mercy. Yearning and melting were bound together—a metaphorical convergence that recalled the transports of medieval mystics but also foreshadowed evangelical Protestants' accounts of their own conversion experiences.

Donne wanted to describe not only what a flower looked like but how it felt. At the same time he defined spiritual vitality as participation in the perpetual motion that characterized the natural world. In the modernist aesthete Walter Pater's admonition to "burn always with this hard, gem-like flame," one hears echoes of Donne, for whom blood was always seething and sublimating into spirit.

Donne straddled two widely separated worlds: his outlook was rooted in the animated universe of the medieval church and foreshadowed the modernist vitalism of Bergson and Pater—as well as the yearnings for restored wholeness that gave rise to Eliot's poetry. It is possible to trace a vitalist lineage between the seventeenth and twentieth centuries. After Donne, one of the earliest examples of that tradition was John Milton. According to recent scholarship, his mature cosmology was an idiosyncratic version of "animist materialism." He rejected the orthodox view that God had created the universe ex nihilo. Instead he embraced the notion that everything was a part of "one first substance"—a belief held by many of his contemporaries. This led to a vitalist account of creation:

Thus God the heav'n created, thus the earth,
Matter unformed and void: darkness profound
Covered th' abyss: but on the wat'ry calm
His brooding wings the Spirit of God outspread,
And vital virtue infused, and vital warmth
Throughout the fluid mass, but downward purged
The black tartareous cold infernal dregs
Adverse to life . . .

The theological consequences of this vision were profound, especially for Milton's notion of body's relationship to soul. "Instead of being trapped in an ontologically alien body," the critic Stephen Fallon writes, for Milton the soul became "one with the body." Spirit and matter were "two modes of the same substance: spirit is rarefied matter, and matter is dense spirit." The corporeal world was neither inert nor mechanical, but "animate, self-active, and free." We can detect the subsequent history of this vitalist vision, partly by tracing the fate of the crucial connectors between body and soul, animal spirits, through epochs conventionally labeled Enlightened, Romantic, and Modernist.

Yet through the centuries, vitalism never became a dominant current of thought. Its most successful rival was Christian dualism, often in traditional orthodox forms but also increasingly in some version derived from the ideas of René Descartes. He acknowledged the existence of animal spirits but denied them reason or will, treating them as subtle and elusive components of the bloodstream—what he called "extremely small bodies which move very quickly, like the jets of flame that come from a torch. They never stop in any place." This formulation preserved Galen's idea that animal spirits were an essential component of human physiology, but its emphasis on the constant motion, speed, and ephemerality of animal spirits left a spiritual aura hovering over these allegedly corporeal entities. Still, Descartes's underlying dualist doctrines proved most decisive in shaping Western thought: his assumptions that only humans possessed a "rational soul," that nonhuman animals were mere machines operating out of inner necessity, and that vivifying spirit was forever divorced from inert matter.

In his time, Descartes's chief critics were mechanistic materialists such as Thomas Hobbes and Pierre LaPlace, who shared his emphasis on the inertness of matter but denied the existence of a rational soul and indeed of any invisible spirits of any kind. Human beings, from this view, which survived and resurfaced in the nineteenth and twentieth centuries, were governed by the same material forces as the rest of nature. In the face of this challenge, Cartesian dualists protected traditional ideas about God by sequestering mind and soul from the physical workings of the universe. This boundary lay at the heart of Protestant and Catholic orthodoxy for centuries.

Yet as early as the late 1600s, a few defenders of the Christian faith were creating an intellectual hybrid—an animistic materialism, which (like Donne's and Milton's views) prefigured vitalism even while it resonated with surviving vernacular ideas of an animated cosmos. The

French priest and philosopher Pierre Gassendi endowed matter with energy and direction by melding the dancing atoms of Lucretius and Epicurus with divine Providence. God, in Gassendi's scheme, creates a world of mobile atoms whose nature He wills to "always include a force by which they can be moved." The nature of this primal implant, this source of force at the atomic level, remained obscure—which is why other thinkers sometimes invoked animal spirits to embody it.

SOMETHING MORE: BEYOND INERT MATTER

During the late 1600s, even the most prominent men of science kept one foot planted in an animated universe. For Thomas Willis, the Anglican clergyman and Cambridge professor who coined the term "neurology," the entire universe was a bodying-forth of a soul, alive and self-actualizing, not designed from without but generated from within by "moving animal spirits." Willis's colleague Ralph Cudworth postulated a teleological force, driving toward greater complexity and variety in an organized fashion, operating immanently in natural things and "*Magically* and *Sympathetically*" producing the diversity of forms that makes up the natural world. Isaac Newton himself combined precise observation and measurement with the postulation of mysterious invisible forces, notably gravity.

Throughout the eighteenth century, Enlightenment thinkers in all areas of inquiry were beset by the growing suspicion that "*there must be something more* than dead matter," as the historians Jonathan Sheehan and Dror Wahrman have shown—some vivifying principle that pervaded the cosmos, linking humans with other animals and the rest of creation. The nature of this vital force became a subject for free-ranging speculation. By the mid-eighteenth century the notion of animal spirits was losing scientific legitimacy, while in popular culture it was being refashioned into belief in a more diffuse and pervasive power that animated the material world as well as the individual person. The encompassing name for this power was animal magnetism, which merged in the vernacular with the practice of mesmerism and the awareness of electricity. As these ideas and practices multiplied, a ferment of vital force enveloped religious and financial affairs, sparking eruptions of emotional energy in evangelical revivals as well as stock market bubbles and panics.

Revivalistic religion provided a burgeoning new arena for frenzied entrancement. By the early 1700s, Protestant Dissenters had rejected ritual and declared the only legitimate prayer to be spontaneous; in subsequent decades, evangelical revivalists on both sides of the Atlantic upped the emotional ante. During the 1730s and '40s, the evangelist George Whitefield became the first transatlantic celebrity, perfecting a theatrical preaching style that produced thousands of conversions and provoked the ire of conservative Anglicans.

Like Donne's, Whitefield's preaching style took strength from sublimated sexual energy. But to his critics, Whitefield evoked female sexuality, not male. "Hark! He talks of a Sensible New Birth—then belike he is in Labour, and the good Women around him are come to his assistance," the *Anglican Weekly Miscellany* remarked. "He dilates himself, cries out, and is at last delivered." Under patriarchal eyes, Whitefield's histrionics embodied effeminate emotional excess—what the orthodox had long derided as "enthusiasm" and Jonathan Swift had mocked as mere manipulation of animal spirits, an emotional confidence game. Revivalist preachers evoked "tears, trembling, groans, loud outcries, agonies of body" among the assembled faithful, as Whitefield's admirer Jonathan Edwards reported from Massachusetts; such transports culminated for the converted in "a kind of ecstasy."

Meanwhile, in the City of London, other forms of excitement floated freely: coffeehouses proliferated in Exchange Alley, serving as betting parlors and stock exchanges, dealing in rumors, libels, and stray bits of military intelligence (battles could be bet upon). New financial practices—options trading, short selling—involved placing bets on whether certain asset values would rise or fall by a certain future date. Speculative "projectors" relied on an excited public imagination to endow their projects with dramatically increasing value; if the excitement subsided or grew fearful, the project's value fell. The spread of speculative investment detached value from any material foundations and made it seem as much a product of imagination as of calculation.

Yet while religion and finance were awash in animal spirits, neither religious nor financial apologetics resorted to the concept, even though it could have captured the intense psychic energy that characterized both business and belief. To admit that energy openly, to give it a local habitation and a name, was a subversive gesture, revealing unwelcome possibilities: that the transcendent transports of religious conversion were rooted in mere emotional excitement, and that the apparent rationality of finance capitalism was a thin crust covering a bubbling mass of fantasy.

For Christians or capitalists to acknowledge the role of animal spirits in their enterprises would undermine their claims to legitimacy; they sought to contain surges of emotional energy with an overriding ethos of control. Evangelical moralists insisted that the proof of a true conversion was not only that it was accompanied by "a kind of ecstasy" but that, after the ecstasy subsided, the believer embraced a strict regimen of self-discipline. Apologists for commercial trade, led by Adam Smith, tended to ignore speculative investment as a means of wealth creation and instead constructed a business world powered by steady work and prudent habits, where animal spirits were absent. Still, the idea of animal spirits, despite its disappearance from religious and economic discourse, would persist in the vernacular and on the intellectual margins, in romantic literature and early evolutionary biology. The sense that "*there must be something more* than dead matter" survived. While the medical profession began to reject animal spirits as a physiological fact, the wild card was still available to be played.

Even the harshest medical critics of the concept of animal spirits wanted to preserve some connection, however mysterious, between body and soul. In *The English Malady* (1733), the physician George Cheyne aimed to trace the bodily sources of the malady in question, nervous debility—which turned out (in his telling) to be a disease of civilization, promoted by the intemperance and overindulgence of the fashionable classes of London.

Contrary to the claims of his predecessors, Cheyne wrote, animal spirits or their absence had nothing to with nervous disorders; indeed the very notion of animal spirits lacked any empirical base. Microscopic observation by Anton Leeuwenhoek ("the best Observer doubtless") and other scientists had demonstrated that nerves were not hollow tubes that could contain either air or fluid (the two supposed vehicles for animal spirits): Nerves "appear solid, transparent, and with broken Reflexions, even when dry, like crack's Glass-Wire, Horn, or any other solid Substance, without any apparent Cavity." Cheyne could only conclude that the concept of animal spirits was outmoded nonsense, "of the same Leaven as *the substantial Forms of Aristotle,* and the *celestial System of Ptolemy.*"

Still, Cheyne was a devoted Newtonian, and like the Master he refused to reduce life itself to a mechanically interlocking system of material components. Cheyne believed that "in *Substances* of all Kinds, there may be Intermediates between *pure, immaterial Spirit and gross Matter,* and that this intermediate, material Substance, may make the Cement between the human Soul and Body." Indeed, he concluded, this intermediary may be "the same (for ought I know)" as the "infinitely *fine and elastic Fluid or Spirit*" postulated by Sir Isaac himself in his *Opticks* (1705) as a force for energizing the "Aether" that sustains and surrounds all life. This was not a reversion to animism tout court but a new way of seeing, an animistic materialism that allowed room for indeterminacy and uncertainty, but not Providence, and certainly not a knowable one. Cheyne, like Newton, was willing to acknowledge that there were some things in his system that were inexplicable, and might well remain so.

Despite Cheyne's dismissal of animal spirits, defenders of the concept as a physiological fact did not yield the field altogether. Cheyne's contemporary Richard Mead, who was also his chief rival in ministering to the medical needs of London Society, argued in *Medical Precepts and Cautions* (1755) that an "extremely subtile fluid of the nerves, commonly called animal spirits" could be the instrument of madness, both melancholy and mania. Animal spirits "make that great engine of the blood's motion, the heart, contract with greater or lesser force," activating a circular, interactive relation between body and mind. The passions affected physical health, and physical health (or sickness) affected the passions—thus patients with dropsy, said Mead, became unaccountably sanguine about their economic affairs.

Overindulgence in rage or sadness could bring about mental disease, and "to asswage these swelling surges of the soul is the business of philosophy"—but alas, Mead noted, even the Stoics had proved unequal to the task of healing soul-sickness. It was up to the medical men to step in, he announced, concluding with a secular sermon on moderation in sensual pleasure, urging the cultivation of fortitude and self-command with the ultimate goal of achieving tranquility. This was not the first nor the last time self-command would be recommended as an antidote to unruly emotions and as a path to tranquility.

Such a strategy seemed especially necessary amid the economic conditions emerging in early eighteenth-century London, where animal spirits energized frenzied finance—though financiers were only occasionally willing to acknowledge the importance of unruly emotions in creating (or destroying) asset values. They sought reassurance, however faint and fitful, in numbers. The ubiquity of quantification made the irrational seem rational. Yet above the turmoil of the markets hovered the mysterious power of money and its even more mysterious instrument—invisible, odorless, tasteless credit. The capitalist religion of modernity was taking hold, promoting strange new ways of assessing human worth.

2

The Madness and Mildness of Money

WHAT PROTESTANTS CALLED the Glorious Revolution of 1688 was a revolution in finance as well as political power. When William of Orange became King William III of Great Britain and Ireland, he brought Dutch financial innovations to England. The government increasingly financed its operations (mainly wars with France) by borrowing from private creditors—in particular the Bank of England, which was founded in 1694. Paper began to displace gold and silver as the chief medium of exchange—not only banknotes but shares in the capital stock of corporations that were themselves traded on what became known as the stock exchange. Signifiers of value were becoming less substantial, more susceptible to gusts of subjective feeling.

TRADING IN THE AIR: THE FANTASIES OF FINANCE

When it came to immaterial transactions, the Dutch showed the way: they were pioneers in short selling and options trading. In 1722, a commercial writer described conditions in Amsterdam, where "one very often trades several sorts of merchandise in the air, whether by selling what one does not possess, or buying what one has no intention to accept." Trading "in the air"—betting on what one imagined an asset price would be at some future date—had by that time also become a way of life in the City of London. It was another way of detaching value from any solid foundation, actual or apparent, just as paper banknotes had done by displacing metal currency. And if one fell short of paper, observed an anonymous poet who called himself "a Money'd Man," the indebted investor could "Some Project or another find, / Where *Words* may do, and *Words* are *Wind*." The more insubstantial money became, the more exciting were the possibilities surrounding it, as the new profession of "stock jobbers" pumped up stock prices by spreading rumors and feeding fantasies.

Many dreams of instant wealth focused on the South Sea Company, which was founded in 1711. As the Victorian journalist Charles MacKay wrote in *Extraordinary Popular Delusions and the Madness of Crowds* (1841), the company's success depended on "visionary ideas" about "the immense riches of the eastern coast of South America."

> Everybody had heard of the gold and silver mines of Peru and Mexico; every one believed them to be inexhaustible, and that it was only necessary to send the manufactures of England to the coast, to be repaid a hundredfold in gold and silver ingots by the natives. A report, industriously spread, that Spain was willing to concede four ports, on the coasts of Chili [*sic*] and Peru, for the purposes of traffic, increased the general confidence; and for many years the South Sea Company's stock was in high favour.

When these cheerful prospects all proved illusory, the speculative bubble finally burst in 1720. One of the investors was Isaac Newton, who had stood aghast as the company's share prices soared. As the mathematician reportedly said, he could "calculate the movement of the heavenly bodies, but not the madness of people." Rational calculation could not comprehend the emotions that animated speculative finance. The "Money'd Man" marveled at how completely wealth had become decoupled from familiar markers of worth:

How from all Corners of the Nation
The Wise, Fools, Cits, and Folk of Fashion
Repair promiscuous to the Alley
To lose or gain more Money daily:
Say how, and by what means, a Lord,
On sudden, turns out not worth a T__d;
While, from a Dunghill to a Coach,
A Rascal *rises in a Touch.*

One of the earliest and most acute observers of this chaotic scene was Daniel Defoe, the novelist and political pamphleteer who was also an avid and frequently feckless speculator in the financial markets. Defoe's life reveals how a Protestant ethic of disciplined achievement could serve as a counterweight (though not always an effective one) to the undisciplined emotions that characterized the spirit of financial capitalism. He was born in London in 1660, the son of a pious Presbyterian tradesman: his father was a tallow chandler, a freeman of the City of London, and a member of an ancient livery company. From early youth, Defoe gradually became familiar with the latest fashions in finance, even as his commitments to fortitude and diligence were reinforced by adversity: the Plague, the Great Fire, and the persecution of Dissenters like himself by the Anglican establishment. Defoe's earliest mentors were articulate and disciplined Dissenters—Samuel Annesley, the family pastor, who read twenty chapters of scripture a day; and Charles Morton, whose academy Defoe attended and who included the vitalist Catholic Gassendi on the curriculum. Both Annesley and Morton remained articulate defenders of their Presbyterian faith despite constant harassment from secular and religious authorities. According to Defoe's biographer Paula Backscheider, they embodied virtues the novelist attributed to his own creation, Robinson Crusoe: "invincible patience recommended under the worst of misery, indefatigable application and undaunted resolution under the greatest and most discouraging circumstances."

Yet despite being inspired by these characteristically Protestant virtues, when it came to finance Defoe was an undisciplined young rogue whose affairs were falling apart before he was thirty. He came of age at a time, the late 1600s, when wars with Spain and France obstructed English merchants' access to European and American markets, and left them with idle capital. They began to put it into a flurry of joint-stock companies that were floated to buy some commercial privilege from the Crown, or into simple wagers, often on the outcomes of military operations. As Defoe recalled: "there was not less gaged [wagered] on the second siege of Limerick [August–October 1691] than two hundred thousand pound." Defoe himself had an incurable propensity for speculative projects, which involved everything from diving bells to civet cats (for perfume) to a ship he bought from pirates that turned out to be "weake and Leakey." Like many of his fictional characters, he kept engaging in schemes that failed, kept trying to reform, and kept backsliding. He was too willing to give people credit, too indifferent to collecting what was owed him, too careless about records, and too litigious. As he sank more deeply into debt, he continued to live beyond his means and kept borrowing money he could not repay. Finally, in October 1692, he was imprisoned for bankruptcy. He was thirty-two years old, with a young family, five servants, and debts of more than £17,000.

Defoe quickly managed to deal and write his way out of debtors' prison, but his political pamphleteering soon got him charged with seditious libel. The libel in question was *The Shortest Way with Dissenters* (1702), a Swiftian satire of Anglican hostility toward nonconforming believers. Irony, it turned out, was no defense. Defoe was fined more than a hundred pounds, confined to Newgate prison until he could provide surety for seven years' good behavior, and sentenced to stand three times in the pillory, where prisoners were usually pelted with garbage and insults.

But among neighborhood Dissenters Defoe became a local hero, pelted only with flowers. And he had no trouble securing surety. He was soon on the streets of London again. Still, his times in prison had intensified his feeling of isolation from respectable social life. He was no longer a convivial blade about the City; he was a professional writer, paid by the word. His method was straightforward: once he secured a contract with a publisher, within a few days he began to deliver pages to be set up in type. Plagiarism and repetition were constant temptations, and Defoe succumbed to both. He also continued to feel the allure of speculative "Projects and Undertakings," which kept him in debt to the end of his days, in 1731.

Defoe was uniquely equipped to write about the subjective experience of speculative finance, from the inside. His writings provide a fragmented but compelling account of emotional life in the Vatican of early capitalism, the City of London. With compelling personal detail, he captures the visceral urges beneath transactions tricked out in the guise of quantitative rationality. In 1706, in one of the early numbers of *Defoe's Review,* he described "the Infinite Mazes of a Bankrupt before he comes to the *Crisis*" with precision born of painful memory: "what Shifts, what Turnings, and what Windings in Trade, to support his dying Credit; what Buying of one, to raise Money to pay for another, What Discounting of Bills, Pledgings and Pawnings; what selling to Loss for present Supply; What Strange and Unaccountable Methods, to buoy up sinking Credit!" That same year, when Parliament was debating a bill "to Prevent Frauds Committed by Bankrupts," he weighed in to urge leniency, arguing that "Men whose Affairs are declining, are not always *the exactest People* in their Books . . . Omissions, Mistakes, and forgotten Articles are never so frequent, as when men, knowing they are *playing a losing game*, grow desperate." Two decades later, in *The Complete English Tradesman* (1727), he was still describing the prolonged desperation induced by the slide toward bankruptcy, recalling "the miserable, anxious, perplexed life, which the poor Tradesman lives under before he Breaks . . . how harass'd and tormented for money . . . how many little, mean, and even wicked things will even the most religious tradesman stoop to in his distress, to deliver himself even such things, as his very soul would abhor at another time; and for which he goes, perhaps, with a wounded conscience all his life after?" The last words may have captured the plight of Defoe himself, his conscience permanently wounded by his departures from the straight and narrow path in pursuit of ready money—the Protestant ethic repeatedly succumbing to the spirit of finance capitalism.

Yet when Defoe was not inhabiting the soul of a harassed debtor on the brink of bankruptcy, he could sound as sanguine as Adam Smith about the benign effects of trade on national health. "If the Pulse of the Trade beats true and strong, the Body is sound," he wrote in *The Complete English Tradesman* (1727). His *Essay upon Projects* (1697) revealed an understanding of probability theory, which by then was becoming known in English intellectual life. Yet unlike many contemporary social scientists (who believe they can quantify subjective experience), Defoe separated the secret logic of the aggregate from the unpredictable vagaries of the individual. This move underwrote his vision of the investor (or "projector") as a creator of wealth whose idiosyncratic imagination was the prime mover of economic growth. From Defoe's view, banks had a responsibility to oil the workings of commerce by extending credit to visionary entrepreneurs (as twenty-first-century business ideologues have learned to call them). The fluid metaphors seemed inescapable: the oil of credit promoted other forms of liquidity.

In recognizing the centrality of credit to the emerging capitalist economy, Defoe had hit upon the most pervasive and elusive power in the early modern world. For him, in effect, credit was to the body economic as animal spirits were to the individual body: a mysterious but essential vital force, an evanescent liquid evaporating into thin air.

> This substantial Non-Entity called CREDIT, seems to have a distinct Essence (*if nothing can be said to exist*), from all the Phaenomena in Nature; it is in itself the lightest and most volatile Body in the World, moveable beyond the Swiftness of Lightning; the greatest Alchymists could never fix its Mercury or find out its Quality; it is neither a Soul nor a Body; it is neither visible nor invisible; it is all Consequence, and yet not the Effect of a cause; it is a Being without Matter, a Substance without Form—a perfect free Agent acting by Wheels and Springs absolutely undiscover'd; it comes without Call, and goes away unsent; if it flies, the whole Nation cannot stay it; if it stays away, no Importunity can prevail for its Return . . . it has the effectual Power

> of Transmutation—for it can turn Paper into Money, and Money into Dross—While it lives with a Merchant, he can trade without a Stock, draw Bills where he has no Effects, and pay Bills without Money—; if it forsake him, his Trade dies, his Money won't circulate, the Vitals of his Management stagnate . . . This is the Wheel within the Wheel of all our Commerce, and all our publick Transactions.

While Defoe's hyperbole recalled traditional reflections on the elusiveness of Fortuna (and the turbulent powers of Potentia), he also captured the perversities and paradoxes at the heart of the emerging financial system. "Why do East India Company's stock rise, when Ships are taken? Mine Adventures raise annuities, when Funds fall; loose their vein of Oar in the Mine, and yet find it in the Shares; let no Man wonder at these Paradoxes, since such strange things are practiced every day amongst us?" The decoupling of wealth from any material foundation was stunning and deeply puzzling. The only explanation Defoe could suggest was: "Great is the Power of Imagination!"

The centrality (and dangers) of imagination in finance were becoming apparent in the early 1700s on both sides of the English Channel. Consider the career of John Law. He was a Scottish adventurer who transformed the French financial system and created a vast real estate scheme centered on the Louisiana territory that became known as the Mississippi Bubble. It burst in March 1720, five months before the South Sea catastrophe. "It's a shame really that he did not place limits on his boundless imagination for he has something great about him," Eleanor de Mezieres, one of Law's aristocratic patrons, said of him after his disgrace. "He has perished for too grand a conception of himself." The focus on powerful, even boundless imagination illuminated the impulse behind "the spontaneous urge to action" that Keynes would associate with animal spirits two centuries later.

Most of the time Defoe could only step back and wonder at the consequences of the tradesman's imagination. "Trade is a Mystery which will never be discover'd or understood," he announced. "It has its Critical Junctions and Seasons, when acted by no visible Causes, it suffers Convulsive Fits, Hysterical Disorder, and most unaccountable Emotions . . . today it obeys the Course of things, and submits to Causes and Consequences; tomorrow it suffers Violence from the Storms and Vapours of Human Fancy, operated by exotick Projects, and then all runs counter, the Motions are eccentric, unnatural and unaccountable—a sort of Lunacy in Trade attends all its Circumstances, and no man can give a rational Account of it."

The perception of "a sort of Lunacy in Trade" was what many generations of stock jobbers, economists, financiers, brokers, and business apologists would struggle to counteract. They sought to stabilize the inherent instability of capital markets in a template of numbers, formulas, and research—or at least to create the impression that they had done so. Law's career was an early case in point. He was nothing if not a reckless gambler, with other people's money to boot. But as the founder of the Royal Bank of France, the lender of first resort for a cash-strapped government, he projected a persona embodying mastery and poise. As a French observer noted, "The bank[er] is impressive, calm, and cold. He never fails in the smallest article of conduct. He may not lose his head, while the punters are free to do so and often do so."

The City of London during the early 1700s was populated mostly by punters, many of whom lost their heads regularly. Efforts to stabilize finance had barely begun. But the need for them became apparent in August 1720, when the South Sea Bubble burst and angry, ruined investors filled the streets of London, thirsty for revenge against the men who had bilked them. "Sell" orders wiped out bankers' cash reserves and spread ruin across fashionable London society. The Better Sort embraced the banner of sauve qui peut. "The madness of stock-jobbing is inconceivable. The wildness was beyond my thought," said the son of Robert Harley, who was founder of the South Sea Company and (for a while) a patron of Defoe.

The novelist himself was untouched by the South Sea collapse. To defray his ever-present debts, and with uncharacteristic prescience, Defoe had signed his own South Sea stock over to creditors in 1719. When the crash came, the writer struck a disingenuous tone of moral disapproval toward the "City gamblers" who had brought this ruin on themselves and on many innocent credulous people besides. Resorting to familiar moral tropes, he declared himself for contentment and against ambition, denounced mob madness, and discerned providential justice in the sight of "Extravagant gamesters" brought low. Still, he also performed more substantive service to the polity: he did all he could as a journalist to restore investors' confidence and reestablish public credit, including the credit of the South Sea Company. With this in mind, he refused to join the witch hunt against the company (and his sometime patron Harley). He also perceptively noted the role of newspapers in promoting the bubble, chiding his journalistic colleagues for their uncritical repetition of promoters' claims.

During his last decade, Defoe tried to sustain this stance of detachment from the allure of the market. He embraced a role as dispenser of homely wisdom on the importance of prudent business habits, the comforts of family life, and the insidiously transformative powers of money. "What makes a homely woman fair?" he asked in a poem of 1720. "About five hundred pounds a year." Yet he was still hounded by creditors, some seeking payment for debts more than thirty years old. Despite his celebration of simplicity and sincerity, the spirit of finance capitalism lingered on in his life like a guest who would not leave.

The divisions in Defoe's mind reflected debates across a broad swath of Western intellectual life. During the late seventeenth and early eighteenth centuries, as the political theorist A. O. Hirschman argued, thinkers in Britain and on the Continent struggled to make sense of the emotions unleashed by early modern capitalism (though the word did not exist yet). The struggle was a preliminary effort to stabilize the sorcery embedded in emerging market societies—the apparently magical capacity of money, increasingly mere marks on a piece of paper, to transform the possessor's condition from poverty to wealth, dowdiness to beauty, shame to respectability. Finance capital in particular carried a potentially magical charge: it was no accident that when King Louis XV of France hired John Law to manage his fiscal affairs, he fired all the court alchemists. Money could beget money more easily than gold could be made from dross. The ease with which money might accomplish its transformative alchemy fired the passion to possess it. But that passion could be tamed, at least rhetorically, into something more socially acceptable: economic interest.

STABILIZING FINANCIAL SORCERY: FROM PASSION TO INTEREST

How could society's rulers maintain public order amid the manic pursuit of private gain? The Italian philosopher Giambattista Vico inaugurated a new sort of intellectual alchemy when he argued that passions and vices could be transformed into civic happiness: ferocity could stimulate military defense; ambition could energize politics; avarice could animate commerce. The trick, said Vico's countryman Niccolo Machiavelli, was "*to set affection against affection and to master one by another*"—to balance countervailing passions and fashion a stable social order where flesh and spirit could coexist in productive harmony.

The founders of the American republic, among other Enlightenment intellectuals, broadened the connotations of the word "interest" (already in wide commercial and legal use) to make it a generic term for those passions that were assigned the countervailing function. Gradually, during the latter decades of the eighteenth century, interest was conflated with economic advantage; avarice was divested of unsavory associations and promoted (as Hirschman observed) "to the position of the privileged passion given the job of taming the wild ones." Alexander Hamilton, arguing against term limits for the U.S. presidency, claimed that desire for private wealth would counterbalance ambition for political power and encourage the president to leave office to pursue his financial interests, rather than running repeatedly for reelection. Traditional mistrust of unbridled accumulation melted away as avarice was sanitized into interest and interest became the new paradigm used to explain human action. Interest, it was assumed, partook of the best of both passion and reason: the passion of self-love was constrained by reason, and reason was given direction and force by passion.

The mob scenes in London and Paris after the bubbles burst were quickly forgotten by Enlightenment intellectuals seeking to legitimate the life of trade. A world governed by interest, they claimed, would be characterized by predictability and constancy, since avarice did not wax and wane like other passions. Commerce tied people together; it did not pull them apart. This stability was inherent, apologists for trade assumed, even in paper transactions based on the invisible power of credit. In this emerging economic discourse, value was becoming more subjective, a product of imagination rather than calculation; wealth was created not by accumulating precious metals but by satisfying human wants.

This was a benign vision, more humane and socially useful than merely piling up gold bars, but it depended on a sanitized vision of commerce. Operating within an interdependent web of consumer desires and commercial obligations, the tradesmen imagined by eighteenth-century intellectuals became steadfast, single-minded, methodical, and self-disciplined. In "the industrious professions," David Hume observed, "love of gain prevails over love of pleasure." The trader was a peaceful, inoffensive fellow, and moneymaking was a uniquely calm passion, innocent and doux—harmless, innocuous. The douceur of commerce became an article of faith among its Enlightenment apologists.

None was more influential than Adam Smith. He was born in Kirkcaldy, Scotland, probably in 1723. The son of a solicitor who died before his birth, Smith was baptized as an infant into the (Presbyterian) Church of Scotland and retained a Protestant ethic of disciplined achievement (if not Protestant beliefs) all his life. His mother was determined that he be well educated, and after attending a local academy he entered the University of Glasgow at the age of fourteen. At Glasgow he encountered the charismatic presence of Francis Hutcheson, the philosopher who taught that human morality arose from an inner moral sense, which inclined its possessor to choose right over wrong. Smith later rejected the notion of a moral sense because he believed that morality was rooted in "immediate sense and feeling," and a moral sense—unlike human sympathy—could not be felt, only postulated. But he remained powerfully influenced by Hutcheson's earnest cast of mind.

Smith's move from Glasgow to Balliol College, Oxford, proved a deep disappointment. Professors held lifetime sinecures and, with no incentive to attract students, made little pretense of bothering to teach. Yet they summoned enough energy to seize Hume's *Treatise of Human Nature* from Smith and punish him for reading such a heretical book, which dismissed the conventional claims of both religion and rationality. Oxford professors were nothing if not conventional. Still, despite the mediocrity of its faculty, Oxford did offer the rich resources of the Bodleian Library, and Smith spent many hours roaming its stacks.

He also continued reading Hume, and developed heretical views of his own. All scientific theories, he wrote in a youthful essay, were "mere inventions of the imagination" designed to reassure us that the universe made sense by providing provisional explanations of otherwise baffling phenomena. Every theory was forever subject to revision—there was no last word. Like Hume, Smith was cultivating a skeptical attitude toward both reason and religion, concluding that both were human inventions designed to allay anxiety and uncertainty—and that dogmatic religion was the more dangerous of the two. By manipulating terror and cowardice, the young Smith charged, religious orthodoxy promoted "the lowest and most pusillanimous superstition" and retarded human impulses toward self-improvement. The intellectual kinship between Smith and Hume, who was ten years older, was already becoming apparent. The men did not meet until 1750, but they remained warm friends until Hume died in 1776. Smith wrote an account of Hume's death that scandalized defenders of orthodoxy by praising the skeptic Hume for dying as bravely as any believer.

Hume and Smith, both lifelong bachelors, shared similar commitments to prudence and moderation in personal finance as well as a common faith in the douceur of commerce. Both challenged the emphasis on self-love in Bernard Mandeville's description of social life, *The Fable of the Bees* (1714), which told the story of a great "grumbling hive" of bees whose commercial prosperity and imperial power was based on vanity, pretension, deception, and greed: "all trades and places knew some cheat, / no calling was without deceit." When some morally sensitive bees persuaded Jove to make their great hive an honest one, the hive soon collapsed, as thousands of bees were left with no means of livelihood. For Mandeville, the lesson was plain:

Then leave complaints: fools only strive
to make a great an honest hive
to enjoy the world's conveniencies,
be famed in war, yet live in ease,
without great vices, is a vain
Utopia seated in the brain.
Fraud, luxury and pride must live,
while we the benefits receive.

Hume and Smith, in contrast, focused on the centrality of sympathy rather than cupidity. Recoiling from Mandeville's famous claim that "Private Vices" could yield "Public Benefits," Smith argued that Mandeville reduced all virtue to disguised vice. For Mandeville, Smith wrote, virtue always "falls short of that complete self-denial which it pretends to, and instead of a conquest, is commonly no more than a concealed indulgence of our passions." Hume was equally intent on presenting a view of human motives that resisted reduction to the vicious and transcended mere selfishness. As he wrote: "whatever other passions we may be actuated by . . . the soul or animating principle of all of them is sympathy"—by which he meant a kind of contagious fellow-feeling.

As Dennis Rasmussen observes in his account of the men's friendship, Hume's version of sympathy as contagion was passive and mechanistic compared with Smith's fuller and more active notions of projection and identification. Smith described occurrences when "we feel emotions on behalf of others that they do not or cannot feel themselves," such as the insane or the dead. He was a subtler psychologist than Hume, and a more important figure in the emotional history of capitalism.

He was also readier than Hume to acknowledge the potential drawbacks of commercial society. Smith deplored endless toil in pursuit of objects that provide only fleeting satisfaction. Though he celebrated the emerging nation of shopkeepers, Smith remained keenly aware of the emotional stress of commercial life, which he thought was exacerbated by the "impertinent jealousy," "mean rapacity," and "interested sophistry" of merchants.

Discerning the degrading effects of the division of labor, Smith even questioned the conventional history of humanity as an ascent from barbarism to civilization. Intelligent barbarians, he observed in *The Wealth of Nations*, had to perform varied occupations. "Invention is kept alive, and the mind is not suffered to fall into that drowsy stupidity, which, in a civilized society, seems to benumb the understanding of all the inferior ranks of people," Smith wrote. "The man whose whole life is spent performing a few simple operations, of which the effects too, are, perhaps, always the same, or very nearly the same, has no occasion to exert his understanding, or to exercise his invention in finding out expedients for removing difficulties which never occur . . . he becomes as stupid and ignorant as it is possible for a human creature to become." Smith began to glimpse what a later generation would learn to call the hidden injuries of class, which were emotional and rooted in social relations rather than simply in economic deprivation. He saw how inequality in commercial society encouraged emulation and admiration of the rich and feelings of invisibility and even shame among the poor. This was hardly an unembarrassed rhapsody to unfettered trade and its consequences.

Still, Smith, for all his sharp perceptions, ultimately provided an exceptionally bland view of everyday life under early modern capitalism, a view that was easily assimilable to free market apologetics in subsequent decades. It is no accident that this quotation from *Wealth of Nations* appears prominently on the Web page of the Liberty Fund, a libertarian think tank:

> By preferring the support of domestick to that of foreign industry, [the individual] intends only his own security; and by directing that industry in such a matter as its produce may be of the greatest value, he intends only his own gain, and he is in this, as in many other cases led by an invisible hand to promote an end which was no part of his intention. Nor is it always the worse for the society that it was no part of it. By pursuing his own interest he frequently promotes that of the society more effectually than when he really intends to promote it.

By the time Smith published these words in 1776, the invocation of an invisible hand or its equivalent was a familiar rhetorical move in natural history as well as social, economic, and political thought. Enlightenment thinkers were keenly aware of the foundational (or antifoundational) role of chance in the cosmos—the capacity of fortune to undermine rational order and systems. Still attracted to system-building, they had to abandon brittle taxonomy and find subtler ways to accommodate serendipity. One was probability theory, which refocused attention on (comparatively) predictable aggregates rather than wayward individuals. Another was the concept of self-organization—often more a rhetorical device than a coherent idea—a claim that, somehow, apparently chaotic conditions could give rise to flexible forms of order in organisms, governments, and indeed whole societies.

Smith was more precise than many devotees of self-organization, some of whom could only claim (as Ralph Cudworth had done) that biological order arose "*Magically*" out of the operations of vital force. Smith was no free-market fundamentalist; he acknowledged the need for taxation, bank regulation, and other government interventions in business life. Still, he argued that collective good came not from any public source but from the individual pursuit of self-interest—even while, against Mandeville, he assumed that self-interest lacked any taint of vice. Smith's reasoning was that men employ capital as close to home as they can, so they can keep closer tabs on it; and they endeavor "to direct that industry, that its produce may be of the greatest possible value." The last stage of the process, the transformation of private into public wealth, was left largely unarticulated—except by passages like this one from Smith's *Theory of Moral Sentiments*, which revealed a kind of invincible innocence:

> The rich . . . divide with the poor the produce of all their improvements. They are led by an invisible hand to make nearly the same distribution of the necessities of life, which would have been made, had the earth been divided into equal portions among all its inhabitants, and thus without intending it, without knowing it, advance the

interests of the society, and afford means to the multiplication of the species.

While Smith's invisible hand was one of many instruments of self-organization imagined by eighteenth-century thinkers, his particular version of the trope met a peculiarly urgent ideological need, at least for moral philosophers like himself—the need to provide moral legitimacy for the life of trade, to make commerce seem like more than an amoral scramble. To do that, one had to address the serendipitous swerves of investment capital that left gentlemen destitute and ruffians rich—unless one ignored them. Smith mostly chose the latter option. By the early 1770s periodic frenzies and panics were affecting more and more ordinary tradesmen, not just City investors. Yet Smith paid little attention to the role of finance capital in deflating or inflating asset values; he presented commerce as at bottom simply an expression of "the uniform, constant, and uninterrupted effort of every man to better his condition." When all else failed there was the anodyne of steady work—an impulse toward individual gain with desirable collective consequences.

Smith's benign view of trade reflected his own isolated, insulated, and placid life. A beloved professor at Glasgow for many years, later tutor to the young Duke of Buccleuch, eventually a bestselling author draped in academic honors, he never lacked for employment or patrons. He lived a life of steady work, recognition, and reward—protected enough from practical demands that he embodied the quintessential otherworldly professor. Smith was "the most Absent Man that ever was," a friend recalled. Once he took a piece of bread and butter, rolled it in his hands, put it in the teapot and poured hot water on it; when he poured himself a cup a few minutes later, he said it was the worst tea he'd ever tasted. Smith did not cut too dashing a figure in London intellectual circles. Samuel Johnson's biographer James Boswell called him "as dull a dog as he had ever met with," while Johnson himself dismissed Smith as a "a professed infidel with a bag-wig." Smith, for his part, recoiled from Johnson's weird recitation of the Lord's Prayer at inopportune moments.

Smith's social insulation may have helped him to create a calm, bland picture of commercial society. But the absence of any real conflict, social or personal, in Smith's vision also depended on his own intellectual assumptions—especially his conception of the human self as a being governed by sympathy. He presented a tamped-down version of emotional experience under early capitalism, oddly bereft of extremes. Compared with Defoe's account of a desperate debtor's life in the early 1700s, Smith's vision of early capitalism is almost unrecognizable. While he was writing his *Theory of Moral Sentiments* in the 1750s, he was groping toward a conception of human nature that would definitively refute Mandeville's *Fable*, which imagined a society of self-love and masked vices. By the time the *Theory* was published in 1759, Smith had fully elaborated his argument for the centrality of human sympathy in social relations. This would be his gentle, genuinely virtuous alternative to Mandeville's faux-virtuous self. Smith's alternative self inhabited a society where tranquility was the norm, where emotions oscillated across a narrow range between vexation and contentment. *The Theory of Moral Sentiments* proved a primer for emotional moderation and an introduction to a society where animal spirits were assumed to be no longer needed as either metaphor or physiological fact.

The Theory of Moral Sentiments depended on the assumption of a self divided between the observer—an "impartial spectator"—and the observed, whose conduct comes under the scrutiny of the impartial spectator. For Smith, the impartial spectator was an internalized conscience or superego that constituted the "Highest Tribunal" by which our actions could be judged. Despite this emphasis on an internal seat of judgment—"the man within the breast"—Smith understood the central role played by social relations in shoring up our sense of an independent moral self. A sociable man who valued the opinion of his peers, he produced a social construction of virtue, defining it as acting "so as to deserve applause" from the impartial spectator we imagine within us, but also from the non-imaginary others who exist in the world. The desire for praiseworthiness and the approval of others was the key source of virtue and a powerful force for moral progress, Smith believed. Yet the man within the breast remained a crucial figure, too. If others judged us harshly for no good reason—if they depended on false accusations, for example—we could still fall back on the judgments of "the man within" to secure Smith's summum bonum: "tranquility of the mind."

While Smith celebrated ambition, enterprise, spirit, and keenness rather than mere regularity in the performance of duty, he always elevated tranquility and contentment over vanity and striving; his Presbyterian temperament recoiled from anything that resembled the pursuit of fashion or social status. Though explicitly religious references faded from *The Wealth of Nations*, in *Theory of Moral Sentiments* Smith linked the cultivation of tranquility to our awareness of a higher law and our expectation of "a world to come." Tranquility arose from obedience to God's law, but obeying God's law was not mere conformity to rule; the practice of decency to others had psychological as well as theological justifications. This was Smith's breakthrough moment in the emotional history of capitalism. Moral sentiments, he recognized, were rooted in natural affections—the human capacity for sympathy, which in turn stemmed from our ability to imagine other people's hardships and project ourselves into their pain.

Yet Smith's account of social life was surprisingly pain-free. "By the constitution of human nature," he wrote, "agony can never be permanent; and, if [the agonized person] survives the paroxysm, he soon comes, without effort, to enjoy his ordinary tranquility." The assumption that tranquility is ordinary and agony extraordinary reminds one, again, of Smith's insulated life. In the world he imagines, the worst feelings that befall a tradesman are "discouragement" and "vexation," both states of mind that were likely caused by the "frequent visits and odious examination of the tax-gatherers." Such conventional prejudices reveal why Smith is so easily appropriated by business apologists unfit to shine his boots.

Smith had no need or desire for animal spirits to animate his Scottish Presbyterian version of the Protestant ethic. The key to achieving his ultimate goal of "exact propriety and perfection" was ruling one's passions through self-command. This was not a mere matter of prudence, which, unlike propriety, inflamed passions by suppressing them. What

Smith had in mind was something subtler, akin to what Freud would call sublimation: anger, restrained by Smith's impartial spectator, mellowed into indignation.

Yet Smith appreciated the fire of passion and its kinship to the concept of spirit, as he identified the desire for applause (or at least one version of it) to be the source of human virtue. Desire for moral approval could promote unselfish, even heroic conduct; just as anger, tempered by calm, could become measured indignation. Even while he recommended science as "the great antidote to the poison of superstition and enthusiasm," Smith was no dour rationalist. He elevated sincerity over casuistry, feeling over rules. But that was partly because the rules were so fully embedded in everyday life that no proper bourgeois noticed them. Smith's world was an ordered one where babies napped at two and tea was served at four. And all was securely anchored in an ethos of self-command.

It would be hard to find a sharper contrast than the one between Smith's world and Laurence Sterne's in *Tristram Shandy*—which, like *The Theory of Moral Sentiments*, was published in 1759. In Smith's imagined society, animal spirits were unnecessary and altogether absent; in Sterne's, animal spirits were essential to physical and mental health but only fitfully available and all too easily dispersed or dissipated. Smith imagined a world devoid of animal spirits and in no need of them, where a supple ethos of self-command kept everyone in benign equipoise; Sterne imagined a world deficient in animal spirits and in dire need of them, where a brittle ethos of self-command left his characters longing for vital experience even as they clung to collapsing frameworks of rational control.

Smith and Sterne offered rival visions of selfhood—or more precisely, manhood. Smith's fusion of sympathy and self-command reflected the growing eighteenth-century respect for the "man of feeling" who possessed "the gift of tears." It suggested a more capacious notion of manliness than the one embodied in traditional patriarchy, a softer male self, more open to conventionally feminine virtues. Sterne's characters, in contrast, epitomized the lingering and lurching of the patriarchal ethos in a world where male authority was becoming detached from its traditional sources in dogmatic religion and landed wealth. Staking out the rivalrous claims of control and chaos, Smith and Sterne explored the antipodes of psychic life available in a modern commercial society.

THE DISPERSAL AND SURVIVAL OF ANIMAL SPIRITS

Laurence Sterne was an Anglican preacher, who comes across in his sermons as a tolerant and humane man, profoundly aware of the predominance of chance in human life and death. He urged charity as a bulwark against the vagaries of fate and the instabilities of fortune. He also invoked a traditional Christian vision of Divine Providence, by contrasting a life that seems perverse and nonsensical to us here on earth with a life that is actually governed by wisdom known only to God. He was an orthodox enough believer to embrace the latter option.

But *Tristram Shandy* was anything but orthodox. Sterne's novel was a kind of summa of the developing vitalist worldview—or at least an explicitly masculine version of it. Animal spirits are practically characters in themselves; and the human characters embody a wayward vital force that suggests Sterne's respect for unpredictable, unmediated experience over scientific, aesthetic, or religious forms. The book has long been a playground for critics celebrating its modernity and postmodernity. Sterne departs constantly from novelistic conventions (to the extent that novelistic conventions existed in 1759): there is no coherent narrative or plot, but rather a series of meandering and sometimes baffling digressions. And the book is peopled by figures who seem strange indeed by comparison with the characters created by Sterne's contemporaries, the stout fellows of Henry Fielding or the imperiled maidens of Samuel Richardson. Sterne's characters are fragmented, scattered, indecisive. They are also given to pompous intellectuality and absurd theorizing—particularly Tristram's father, Walter, who displayed an "infinity of oddities" that "baffled, Sir, all calculation," as his son says. Or they are gripped by "hobby-horses," such as Tristram's uncle Toby is by his obsession with fortifications—and the rebuilding of those in place at the Battle of Namur, where he was wounded in the groin.

The placement of the wound is significant. It puts Uncle Toby's physical manhood in question, underscoring his position outside the patriarchal ethos that dominates the book. Unlike Walter and other blustering patriarchs, Uncle Toby is an appealing and even admirable man of feeling whose character gestures toward a masculinity more capacious than conventional criteria of manliness allow.

Uncle Toby's wound also resonates with larger themes. Sterne is preoccupied by the fraught relations between flesh and spirit. *Tristram Shandy* is unabashedly sexual and scatological. Elaborate medical theories are unmasked to reveal they have little or no relation to the bodies they purport to describe. Exalted abstractions are always pulled down by physicality; things—rocks, window sashes, hot chestnuts—are always falling on (male) genitals. Like Donne's "The Ecstasy," *Tristram Shandy* is at pains to show that the most exalted expressions of the human mind and soul can be traced to bodily origins; there is no such thing as detached intellect. The characters' intellectual ambitions are often absurd, but their absurdities animate individuality, resilience, exuberance.

Except, perhaps, for the eponymous hero. He attempts to tell his life story, but is constantly digressing; he does not even manage to get himself born for 200 pages. To be sure, he begins early, at the moment of his conception—which turns out to be a botched job when his father's animal spirits prove unable to flow alongside the homunculus toward its destination in the womb. This is consistent with Sterne's male perspective—the woman is the passive receptor of the animal spirits produced by the man—but he may also be playing a little subversively with common assumptions about procreation.

Tristram opens the subject on a note of intellectual camaraderie with the reader: "You have all, I dare say, heard of the animal spirits, as how they are transfused from father to son, etc. etc. . . . nine parts in ten of a man's sense of his nonsense, his successes and miscarriages in this world depend on their motions and activity, and the different tracks and trains you put them into, so that when they are once set a-going, whether right or wrong, 'tis not a halfpenny matter—away they go clattering like hey-go mad; and by treading the same steps over and over again, they presently make a road of it, as plain and smooth as a garden-walk, which, when once they are used to, the Devil himself shall not be able to drive them off it." Animal spirits, in this view, established what twenty-first-century neurologists might call neural pathways that allow for habitual, repetitive action—what the eighteenth century might have called manly resolution. Tristram lost his chance for such traits, and indeed for any sort of satisfying life, when his mother asked his father if he'd remembered to wind the clock. Or so his father believes. "My Tristram's misfortunes began nine months before he ever came into the world," Walter announces.

Tristram, sharing his father's implicit misogyny, declares that his mother's inquiry about the clock was "a very unseasonable question at least—because it scattered and dispersed the animal spirits, whose business it was to have escorted and gone hand in hand with the homunculus, and conducted him safe to the place destined for his reception." The immediate consequences were catastrophic for Tristram as he developed in the womb, "his own animal spirits ruffled beyond description . . . a prey to sudden starts, or a series of melancholy dreams and fantasies, for nine long months together." By the time he was born, "what a foundation had been laid for a thousand weaknesses both of body and mind, which no skill of the physician or the philosopher could ever afterward have thoroughly set to rights."

The long-term results of the scattering of animal spirits were ontological as well as physical. "I have been the continual sport of what the world calls Fortune," says Tristram, "the ungracious duchess has pelted me with a set of as pitiful misadventures and cross accidents as ever small Hero sustained." The misogyny here is deep-dyed: before Tristram is even born, he has already been the victim of two capricious females, his mother and the "ungracious duchess," Fortune. One of the prenatal "cross accidents" endured by the "small Hero" involves the many knots that had to be untied before the man-midwife's bag could be opened at his mother's delivery. Due to his mother's ill-timed question, Tristram complains, "the few animal spirits I was worth in the world, and with which memory, fancy, and quick parts should have been conveyed—were all dispersed, confused, confounded, scattered, and sent to the devil."

Much of *Tristram Shandy* is devoted to demonstrating the silliness of Walter Shandy's ideas, but his idea of animal spirits is not included in the general indictment. On the contrary: the book's central theme—the bodily origins of spiritual beliefs and aspirations—depends on the assumption that animal spirits are at work in the world in either metaphorical or physiological forms. Walter, speculating on the physical location of the soul, rules out the brain, because people can lose parts of their brain and still go about their business; he also eliminates "a puddle or a liquid of any kind" inside the body, because such an exalted being as the soul could not live like a mere tadpole.

But if Sterne's characters shift their gaze from soul to mind, fluid metaphors become more acceptable. Dr. Slop, the man-midwife, thinks Mrs. Shandy's difficulties in labor are God's mercy, as they allow him time to undo the knots obstructing his access to his instrument bag. Sterne's narrator (Tristam) observes that "the thought floated only in Dr. Slop's mind, without sail or ballast to it, as a simple proposition, millions of which . . . are every day swimming quietly in the thin juice of a man's understanding, without being carried backwards or forwards, till some little gusts of passion or interest drive them to one side." It is a brilliant account of the way many minds work: maintaining a pond stocked with conventional assumptions ("simple propositions"), any of which might be blown into assertive consciousness by breezes of circumstance.

Fluid metaphors could also be pressed into more exalted service. "The Author's Preface," which occurs 150 pages into the novel, uses images of saturation and liquefaction (reminiscent of Donne) to characterize the process of poesis. The author imagines wit and judgment being "poured down warm as each of us could bear it—scum and sediment and all (for I would not have a drop lost) into the several receptacles, cells . . . and spare places of our brains" till the whole lot is saturated and filled to the brim—"Bless us!—What noble work we should make!—how should I tickle it off! And what spirits I should find myself in, to be writing for such readers!" He concludes by conjuring the utopia that would ensue from such a general flow of spirits: "What confusion!—what mistakes!—fiddlers and painters judging by their eyes and ears—admirable!—trusting to the passions excited—in an air sung, or a story painted to the heart—instead of measuring them by a quadrant." This is the closest Sterne's narrator comes to articulating an aesthetic of animal spirits; it combines empirical observation ("judging by their eyes and ears") while elevating spontaneous composition or performance ("trusting to the passions excited") over quantitative precision ("measuring them by a quadrant").

Sterne's distrust of quantitative measurement was especially keen with respect to time. Early on in the novel he imagines a "hypercritic" who insists that the passage of time in the novel does not make sense. The time it takes the reader to get from Uncle Toby's ringing of the bell (to summon the servant Obadiah to fetch Dr. Slop) and Dr. Slop's rap at the door is no more than two minutes, thirteen seconds and three fifths, says the hypercritic, and this is impossible since Dr. Slop lived at least a half an hour away. "I would remind him that the idea of duration, and of its simple modes, is got merely from the train and succession of our ideas," says the narrator. Like Donne (and Bergson), Sterne insisted that time was a subjective experience of flow, not fully susceptible to measurement by numbers.

Tristram's visit to Montreuil, whose cathedral was a major tourist attraction, gives Sterne an opportunity to enlarge his critique of quantification; the aesthetic of animal spirits pointed to a more satisfying way of being in the world. Tristram, sipping wine at a café, ponders the options for a tourist like himself. He has read much about the Montreuil cathedral—its history and dimensions, the width of its transept, the depth of its nave. It is all very stable and solid and quantifiable. Then he spots Janatone, the innkeeper's beautiful daughter. He decides to observe her rather than tour the cathedral, choosing the fleeting experience of her immeasurable transient loveliness over the cathedral's solidity and stability and precisely measured greatness.

Sterne's aesthetic of animal spirits, despite its range and force, is limited by gender conventions. Janatone radiates vitality, but passively, as the object of male admiration rather than a character capable of her own subjective experience. Still, even though *Tristram Shandy* is hobbled by a crumbling patriarchal ethos whose absurdities the author recognizes and satirizes, the book remains an extraordinary exploration of animal spirits. Never again would the idea receive such extended and explicit attention in imaginative literature.

As British intellectual life migrated to North America in the latter decades of the eighteenth century, the notion of animal spirits remained part of the migrants' cultural baggage. Animal spirits grew increasingly immaterial and emotional rather than physical, yet they continued to play a role as a link between body and soul. "People are said to be cured of the bite of the Tarantula by musick; which by quickening the animal spirits raises in the blood such a ferment as drives out the poison," observed an anonymous author in the Springfield (Mass.) *Federal Spy* in 1794. Animal spirits were manipulatable emotions with unpredictable consequences: "I have seen a beggar gain an alms by a heavy and affecting groan, when a speech of Cicero's composing, spoken without Cicero's art, would not have gained it . . . The groan struck the animal spirits sympathetically, and being continued to the imagination, raised up a thousand sudden conjectures and pre-occupations in his favor, and a thousand circumstances of distress, which he who uttered it perhaps never felt nor thought of." Acknowledging that the beggar's groan may have been a genuine expression of misery, the *Federal Spy* also evoked a secular version of Swift's sardonic remarks on religious enthusiasm. Beggars, like preachers, could play confidence games with the sympathetic emotions extolled by Adam Smith. It apparently never occurred to him that commercial society might systematically foster duplicity in the name of sympathy.

As commerce expanded on both sides of the Atlantic, some observers began to suspect that animal spirits might have some relation to the mysterious power of money. A British essay, reprinted in four American newspapers between 1785 and 1806, announced that "a wonderful connexion and sympathy have lately been observed between the breeches pocket and the animal spirits, which continually rise or fall as the contents of the former ebb and flow; insomuch that, from constant observation, I could venture to guess a man's current cash by the degree of vivacity he has discovered in conversation. When this cutaneous reservoir is full in flesh, the spirits too are elate; when it is sunk and drained, how flat, dull and insipid is every word and action." One could see this pattern in poets' effusions and politicians' pronouncements: "this barometer of state rose or fell" as "current silver contracted or expanded itself within its secret cell . . . It is impossible to record a tenth part of the wonderful effects this latent force of life and spirits has produced upon the animal economy."

The force in question was money, which "has made youth and beauty fly into the arms of age and impotence; given charms to deformity and detestation; transformed Hymen into Mammon, and the god of love into a satyr: it has built bridges without foundations, libraries without books, hospitals without endowments, and churches without benefices." What concluded as a conventional assault on the corrosive powers of cash had nevertheless captured the confusions of an emerging commercial society, where the increasing use of credit was beginning to transform money—even the mere expectation or imagination of it—into a powerful emotional and social force.

This attraction to invisible sources of energy spread from the financial world to scientific and philosophical circles, where thinkers began to imagine a universe animated by a single life force. A vernacular philosophy of vitalism began to emerge, a kind of intellectual working out of the impulses unleashed in evangelical revivals and frenzied stock trading. Vitalism endorsed a sensibility that connected Protestant churches in the wild with the City of London, and released animal spirits into a ferment of cosmic forces—mesmerism, electricity, and, most capacious of all, animal magnetism.

THE EMERGENCE OF THE VITALIST FRAME OF MIND

Amid the economic and political upheaval of the 1780s and '90s, older ways of representing vitality persisted as newer versions appeared. Notions of a vital principle shifted their focus from internal to external sources that were still capable of animating subjective experience. This was consistent with many existing theories, which held that animal spirits flowed beyond the individual organism, mingled with the ether, and became a "gelatinous fluid"—less substantial than fire or even light—that linked all sentient life-forms.

By 1800, other vitalist idioms were proliferating. In Enlightened as well as Romantic minds, the universe was pervaded by mysterious invisible forces—Newton's gravity, Benjamin Franklin's electric fluid, Anton Mesmer's animal magnetism (which was conveyed by "mesmeric fluid" and could transform human consciousness into a will-less trancelike state). This was the intellectual atmosphere that gave rise to the emergent new philosophy of vitalism, which incorporated animal spirits as one ingredient in a stew of ill-defined powers that sometimes took liquid form, but always remained invisible. They showed themselves only through their alleged effects on material objects as well as on human bodies and minds.

Among early popularizers of vitalist ideas, Mesmer was the most influential and controversial. His theoretical assumptions were sweeping and vague. "He maintained to all who would listen to him," MacKay wrote, "that the magnetic matter, or fluid, pervaded all the universe—that every human body contained it, and could communicate the superabundance of it to another by an exertion of the will. Writing to a friend from Vienna, [Mesmer] said, 'I have observed that the magnetic is almost the same thing as the electric fluid, and that it may be propagated in the same manner, by means of intermediate bodies. Steel is not the only substance adapted to this purpose. I have rendered paper, bread, wool, silk, stones, leather, glass, wood, men, and dogs—in short, everything I touched, magnetic to such a degree that these substances produced the same effects as the loadstone on diseased persons. I have charged jars with magnetic matter in the same way as is done with electricity.'" This mishmash of magnetic and electric fluids (which were invisible) with magnetized matter (which was not) was characteristic of the discourse surrounding animal magnetism. So was the universal availability of the invisible fluids and forces that constituted sources of vitality.

A sometime medical student, Mesmer claimed he could use animal magnetism to cure everything from arthritis to scrofula, to the mysterious headaches and lassitude that accompanied what we now call depression. A full-time rogue and committed social climber, he deployed animal magnetism in his sumptuous Paris salon to send aristocratic ladies into paroxysms of panting ecstasy, followed by calm recovery from their ailments. Sitting around a vessel that contained iron rods protruding from magnetized water, the patients held hands and pressed their knees together, and applied the rods to the afflicted parts of their bodies. But this was only the beginning, MacKay reported:

> Then came in the assistant magnetisers, generally strong, handsome young men, to pour into the patient from their finger-tips fresh streams of the wondrous fluid. They embraced the patients between the knees, rubbed them gently down the spine and the course of the nerves, using gentle pressure upon the breasts of the ladies, and staring them out of countenance to magnetise them by the eye! . . . Gradually the cheeks of the ladies began to glow, their imaginations to become inflamed; and off they went, one after the other, in convulsive fits. Some of them sobbed and tore their hair, others laughed till the tears ran from their eyes, while others shrieked and screamed and yelled till they became insensible altogether.

Then Mesmer stepped into the midst of this delirium—richly robed and holding a white rod. He calmed those still conscious with an imperious glance and restored the insensible to consciousness by stroking them with his hands and tracing figures on their breasts and abdomen with his long white rod. They awoke calmly and acknowledged his power over them, reporting that they felt hot or cold vapors passing though their bodies, depending on how he waved his wand or fingers.

Such scenes would change dramatically in subsequent decades. As Mesmer fostered the movement that bore his name and it spread across the Atlantic to the New World, the rituals became less physical, a matter of manipulating mental powers rather than curing bodily ailments, with men as well as women submitting to the mesmerists' power—though an erotically charged relationship persisted between male mesmerist and female client. The settings became less opulent, the clientele more democratic. American mesmerists dispensed with the ornate trappings, the iron rods, magnetized water, and handsome male assistants; they pared down the mesmeric ritual to a one-on-one encounter in a Victorian parlor. But like Mesmer himself, they continued to assert that they could manipulate the vital force at the heart of the universe. For decades mesmerism remained a key component of vernacular vitalism on both sides of the Atlantic.

Mesmer invoked scientific authority, while most of the transatlantic medical establishment dismissed him as a crank. The only genuine power at work in mesmerism, the doctors charged, was the power of the human imagination—the same power, they might have noted, that was igniting frenzied finance. Yet the medical profession could claim few therapeutic accomplishments on the basis of its own largely mechanistic assumptions, and belief in the objective existence of animal magnetism flourished, reinforced by confused but pervasive awareness of electrical and magnetic force.

These cosmic energies underwrote popular vitalism—melding the material and immaterial realms, posing challenges to dualistic orthodoxy. "Electricity defied the logic of Cartesian dualism," the historian James Delbourgo writes, "by putting mind and body into startlingly direct communication." Electric fluid created a kind of "spiritual fire," according to some observers, while others believed mesmeric fluid was even stronger—it was "the medium of passion, the very stuff of life," said the French poet Théophile Gautier. Such forces could provoke an awe bordering on the religious, and like animal spirits, they were often described in terms that merged the invisible and ethereal with the visible and palpable. As Archibald Spencer, who introduced Benjamin Franklin to electricity, said in 1743: "electric fire" was "a subtle fluid, a weightless but material entity that exerted a force on material bodies." Decades later, Joseph Macrery expanded the claim for electricity, asserting that "all the phenomena of life and motion, are owing to the energy of a subtil, active fluid, called the electric fluid." Like grace or credit, electricity was an invisible and apparently boundless power that could be harnessed to transform one's life. Small wonder it flowed into vitalist currents that broadened the stream of scientific thought.

By the 1790s, animal spirits were receding from physiology but the language used to characterize what they embodied—spontaneous energy—remained similar to what it had been for centuries. In *A Discourse on the Principle of Vitality* (1790), Benjamin Waterhouse of the Harvard medical school noted that philosophers have long realized "that things change, and that nothing is truly lost; that the sum total of matter in the Universe remains perfectly the same." The most poetic expression of this idea was Ariel's song to Ferdinand in *The Tempest*:

Full fathom five thy father lies;
Of his bones are coral made;
Those are pearls that were his eyes;
Nothing of him that doth fade,
But doth suffer a sea-change
Into something rich and strange.

But Waterhouse was less interested in poetry than philosophy. As he wrote, philosophers have reasoned that since "it was the work of OMNIPOTENCE to create something out of nothing, the same Omnipotence is required to reduce anything back to nothing." Hence they postulated a "*moving principle*," which "they called the *Anima Mundi*, or *Soul of the World*." What form did it take? Was it water (Thales), fire (Heraclitus), air (Anaximenes)? Magnetism, electricity, some chemical attraction?

Waterhouse's answer ran something like this. An irritability or susceptibility to irritation within plants and animals combines with a "certain something," a Vis Vitalis in animals and a Vis Actuosa in humans, and the combination is (crucially) affected by heat from without. Along with heat, vitality requires the respiration of atmospheric air, which contains a vivifying principle. This creates "an oscillation, a concussion, or excitement of the nervous energy" that gets the bodily fluids flowing again and is itself animated by "that portion of the subtil electric fluid, which pervades all bodies and animates every particle of matter." No one, Waterhouse believed, could discount the sun as the origin of vital energy, especially when one took into account the many swallows, snakes, and even flies thawed out and restored to life after being frozen in ice.

But this was not merely a physiological matter, at least not for humans. The search for a vital principle involved "the union of soul with body," which (Waterhouse believed) "is the most abstruse contemplation that can exercise the mind of man!" The ultimate question, which he attributed to Voltaire, bedeviled every thinker who sought to meld flesh and spirit: "What is that unknown fluid, which is quicker and more active than light, and flies in the twinkling of an eye, through all the channels of life, produces memory, sorrow, or joy, reason or frenzy, recalls with horror what one would wish to forget, and makes of a thinking being, an object of admiration, or a subject of pity and tears?" Only the "First, Divine Cause" knows, Waterhouse concluded, as he strained to distance himself from Voltaire's atheism.

In some ways that struggle was beside the point; vitalism transcended conventional categories of belief and unbelief. Most vitalists tried to preserve a sharp distinction between religion and science, but as the psychiatrist George Makari writes, they "would often land between the two worlds, a wild, unmapped place where brain and soul, spirit and flesh, and Nature and God seemed to touch." Gradually they moved away from a belief that animal spirits were the immaterial connectors between body and soul, and toward a notion of thinking matter, which defined animal spirits as a sentient principle underlying all nature.

These ideas persisted into the early nineteenth century, when vitalist tendencies linked scientists and poets, sustaining their common belief in an animated universe. Erasmus Darwin, Charles's grandfather, advanced the notion of a vibrant cosmos where living organisms, including humans, could be the result of a gradual process; nature could be a kind of self-renewing machine; and humans had sentient self-development in common with the rest of brute creation. "Go, proud reasoner, and call the worm thy sister!" Darwin wrote in *Zoonomia* (1794).

Some Romantic poets embraced a similar animistic perspective. The Fairy who dictates *Europe: A Prophecy* to William Blake undertakes to show him "all alive / The world, where every particle of dust breathes forth its joy." And in Blake's *Milton*, "even the gorgeous clothed Flies that dance & sport in summer / Upon the sunny brooks and meadows; every one the dance / Knows in its intricate mazes of delight artful to weave."

But such moments were idiosyncratic. More typical was a view of Nature animated by the vestigial presence of a God who was no longer believed in, at least not in any recognizably orthodox sense.

This was William Wordsworth's perspective. To risk oversimplifying a rich and complex oeuvre, one might say that when Wordsworth celebrates nature as a realm of embodied Spirit, he restricts the ability to see that Spirit to poets. Not just famous poets like himself, but the mute inglorious ones among the lowly folk he encounters on his solitary rambles—such as the pedlar in "The Ruined Cottage":

. . . he was a chosen son
To him was given an ear which deeply felt
The voice of Nature in the obscure wind
The sounding mountain and the running stream
. . . In all shapes
He found a secret and mysterious soul,
A fragrance and spirit of strange meaning.

While Wordsworth gestured toward a vitalist ontology, he confined the vitalist vision to a poetic elite and he usually invoked a more ethereal conception of meaning in Nature—one often more compatible with winds and breezes than rocks and trees:

Ye motions of delight, that through the fields,
Stir gently, breezes and soft airs that breathe
The breath of Paradise, and find your way
To the recesses of the soul!

Wordsworth epitomized a broad transatlantic movement with philosophical and scientific as well as literary significance. While he lamented the ravages of science on nonhuman nature—"we murder to dissect"—other Romantics confronted the impact of Cartesian rationalism on human ways of thinking and feeling. Samuel Taylor Coleridge challenged Descartes by insisting on subjective experience as the foundation of individual identity and displacing *cogito ergo sum* with *sum qui sum*—"I am that I am." Like Erasmus Darwin (and, decades later, Henri Bergson), Coleridge envisioned a generative creative principle pervading existence at all levels from the cosmic to the individual.

Scientists shared such ideas. The most famous—now notorious—scientific vitalist was Jean-Baptiste Lamarck, who in 1802 appropriated the word *biologie* to describe the study of living beings and postulated an intrinsic *pouvoir de vie* that animated them. Plants and animals enacted this life force, composing themselves, elaborating and complicating their organization across generations. This process unfolded over an "incalculable series of centuries," Lamarck wrote. All plants and animals developed and transformed as a result of the movements of fluids within them. The more complex animals added will to the mix, forming "habits" and "ways of life" in response to circumstance.

This was an essentially *historical* view of nature, in keeping with the broader sense of history emerging during the late eighteenth and early nineteenth centuries: material changes actuated by internal energies, rather than by God. History was a way of knowing the natural world, as well as apprehending the nature of past human societies—a focus on purposeful actions in a web of interdependent contingencies.

For Lamarck, the habits adopted by humans and higher animals led to changes in their bodies—including their brains, which, like any organ, differed according to the uses and exercise it got. "The brain of a man of labor, who spends his life building walls or carrying burdens," was not "inferior in composition or perfection" to those of our greatest thinkers, said Lamarck: it simply had not been exercised in the same way. By the early nineteenth century, for Lamarck and his followers, any living being was an agent, capable of constant, self-generated motion and the transformation of its material parts.

For decades if not centuries, these ideas have been consigned to the dustbin of failed science. Yet as Jessica Riskin and other historians of science have begun to show, Lamarck and many of his colleagues in the faculty of the Jardin des Plantes shared a common conception of nature as fluid, dynamic, and constantly developing through the interaction between organism and its environment—a conception strikingly compatible with the recently emergent field of epigenetics. Charles

Darwin himself, Riskin argues, was a good deal more of a Lamarckian than contemporary neo-Darwinians have acknowledged. He was torn between the mandate to banish agency from nature and the impulse to make agency synonymous with life. In key passages of his *Origin of Species*, Darwin postulated an innate power of self-transformation within organisms. Later in the same book he labeled this tendency "*generative variability*." It could be seen, for example, in the wayward development of animal traits across generations, despite breeders' attempts to control them. The tendency to vary could not be equated with development in a particular direction and still less with teleological schemes of progress. Adaptation was a haphazard process, dependent in part on contingent circumstances that changed over time—on history, in other words.

Yet animated naturalism remained a minority tradition. By the later eighteenth century, Anglo-American Protestants were turning toward another version of animal spirits, the one engendering the evangelical revival. Revivals played a major role in fashioning the blend of emotional intensity contained by ethical discipline that helped to create the emerging ideal of bourgeois selfhood. This project depended on achieving an equipoise between complementary impulses toward ardent feeling and systematic control. The figure embodying the bourgeois ideal—the self-controlled, self-made man—was entering intellectual history at about the same time Tristram Shandy was being conceived. The ideal's reified manliness served as a willed cultural counterpoint to the effeminacy moralists feared as a consequence of commercial life, as well as to the centrifugal forces at the heart of market society. The notion of self-made manhood celebrated a character so perfectly formed that no financial quake could shake it, no seduction swerve it from its path of righteousness. This was how, as Max Weber said, a certain kind of Protestant ethic provided psychic sanctions for systematic accumulation.

Yet this was not the whole story. There were powerful vitalist countercurrents in the emerging Protestant sensibility, emanating from its molten emotional core. As M. H. Abrams demonstrated decades ago, literary Romantics like Wordsworth promoted a "natural supernaturalism" for Protestants who could no longer embrace the orthodox version of the spiritual world. But fervent believers revealed an even stronger attachment to a more volatile and palpable version of vitalism. The historian Brett Grainger has recently explored evangelical vitalism in early America, revealing it to be a blend of European philosophy, African American folk beliefs, Protestant piety, and Romantic nature worship. Its central tenet equated the living God with an immanent power that animated, directed, and gave meaning to everything in the universe. From the evangelical vitalist perspective, the soul could be likened to "a small drop in the vast sea"; trees could be personified as holy protectors; and God could be worshipped more sincerely in a budding grove than in a meetinghouse or church. African American Christians wove European vitalism and African animism together in distinctive fusion. They prized the magical powers of twisted roots and deformed creatures, cultivated reciprocal relations with the nonhuman creation, and treated animals as more than mere commodities. The free black woman (and Methodist preacher) Zilpha Elaw was visited by a vision of Jesus; she was afraid to believe it was happening until her cow "bowed her knees and cowered down on the ground" out of reverence for Christ. White Methodists were also powerfully affected by these impulses: Thomas Coke, John Wesley's right hand, sought communion with God by "ingulphing" himself in the "quiet vegetable creation"; Hannah Syngh Bunting, a Philadelphia Sunday school teacher, equated birdsong with "the creation's state of unceasing prayer." The woods were where one went to experience the "sweet meltings" described by the peripatetic preacher Francis Asbury during his periods of solitary prayer in the forest. Donne would have recognized the melting metaphor if not the wooded setting.

What Donne would probably have found more puzzling was a pamphlet called *Electricity, or Ethereal Fire, Considered* (1802), written by an itinerant electrotherapist from upstate New York. It identified electricity as "the very soul of the universe . . . the accelerating, animating, and all-sustaining principle both of the animate and inanimate creation." Evangelical Protestants found the soulful properties of electricity appealing. Throughout the eighteenth century, scientists and philosophers had entertained the idea of an animate ether, which became popular with Protestants fretting about the fraught relation between soul and body. Catholics had the Incarnation and the sacraments, especially the Eucharist; Protestants had the animate ether and—eventually—the "ethereal fire" of electricity. By the late eighteenth century, evangelicals began to speculate on its mystical agency, remembering the links between God and light in Genesis.

Some found more palpable connections between electricity and divinity. During the buildup to the revival near Cane Ridge, Kentucky, in 1801, Colonel Robert Patterson reported that the spirit came upon the converted "like an electric shock, as if felt in the great arteries of the arms or thighs; [the spirit] closes quick into the heart, which swells, like to burst." Charles Grandison Finney, who became the most popular revivalist of the antebellum era, remembered that during his own conversion, the indwelling of the Holy Spirit felt "like a wave of electricity going through and through me." For decades, electricity remained a powerful metaphor for the emotional intensity of vital religion. Not until nearly mid-century did the carapace of moral precision contain the molten core of evangelical ardor.

Meanwhile, vitalist impulses periodically pushed Protestants in interesting theological directions. In 1806, a poem in an evangelical magazine described Christ as the "enkindler" of the "vital flame," the secret force that sparks and sustains biological life and universal motion. For Protestants preoccupied with will and control, it must have been a profound challenge to believe in a dormant fire that existed in all things, waiting to be kindled. Like animal spirits, electricity, and mesmerism, the notion of the vital principle as a flame enkindled by Christ suggested powerful connections between the natural and supernatural worlds. Evangelical vitalism resonated with the metaphors of dissolution and liquefaction articulated by believers from Donne to Asbury. In this cosmic conjunction of the divine and the human, however fleeting, body and soul could become one.

Yet in the characteristic pattern that pervades Protestant history, revivalist fervor repeatedly cooled and congealed into listless conformity. The Protestant faith of the young American republic was no exception. A faith that was once on fire would become formal, cold, and dead, and would periodically have to be relit by another revival. This involved the rekindling of vital force.

The rekindling process was always understood as a renewed indwelling of divine grace—but that meant many things to many sects. Pentecostals and other socially marginal congregations sought to sustain the physical manifestations of charismatic spirit, to keep the fire burning constantly. But for more mainstream Protestants, the animal spirits excited by conversion were ultimately contained by a code of respectable conduct; the true Christian was characterized by sober cheerfulness rather than agitated enthusiasm. Even emotionally fervid evangelical Christianity could eventually sanctify the steady pursuit of self-interest. From this prudential moral universe, as Adam Smith implicitly recognized, animal spirits had to be banished. But they still flickered on the fringes of respectable society—and even, sometimes, flared up in the middle of it.

3

Toward a Pulsating Universe

AFTER 1800, ANIMAL spirits began to flow outward from the self to the world. They seeped into the eddies and rivulets of vernacular philosophy, swelling a vitalist alternative to dualist orthodoxy, rationalist or religious. In this emerging way of thinking, spontaneous force continued to animate individual lives, linking body with soul; but it also came to seem to animate the cosmos, situating sentient beings in a pulsating universe. The world was beginning to look less static and hierarchical, less easily reduced to taxonomies. It was thrumming with invisible currents of energy, to which antebellum Americans attached various labels—animal magnetism, mesmeric fluid, electricity. Whatever they were called, these forces posed a vitalist challenge to the assumption that nature was stable, measurable, and predictable. They reopened the possibility of a universal animacy.

Yet vitalism never displaced dualism as a dominant mode of thought. Defenders of binary hierarchies dominated classrooms and pulpits, creating a consensus of conventional wisdom. They associated animal spirits, like animal instincts, with frivolity and exuberance but never with higher things. Orthodox Christians, like philosophical idealists, tended to be dualists who elevated spirit over matter; freethinkers and atheists tended to be monists who reduced spirit to matter. Neither believers nor unbelievers had much use for the vitalist notion that matter and spirit merged in a force animating all life.

The Protestant majority settled into a dualistic metaphysics composed of faith and facts, transcendent spirit and inert matter—leavened by Scottish moral philosophers' emphasis on the importance of human sympathy in creating a basis for ethics. It was, in many ways, a more explicitly religious version of Adam Smith. Vitalist perspectives remained a marginal strain in popular philosophy, sometimes present in the places where ultimate questions were discussed, more often slipping through a crack in the door, an exotic stranger. The perspective that commanded the widest assent remained dualism. So before surveying the vitalist outliers, it will be helpful to explore the dualist consensus—which passed for common sense among most respectable Americans.

EVANGELICAL RATIONALITY: THE COMMON SENSE OF THE YOUNG REPUBLIC

As the American republic took shape in the early 1800s, most educated Protestants wanted to be anything but strange or exotic. They were eager to blend their religious beliefs with main currents of secular thought—the Enlightenment devotion to scientific rationality, the liberal commitment to individual autonomy. Melding biblical faith and modern progress, Protestant thinkers created a synthesis that lasted much of the nineteenth century, a worldview that could be called "evangelical rationality." Since this is not a phrase that fits easily with contemporary assumptions, it is worth a brief explanation.

The label "evangelical" encompassed a much broader range of beliefs in the nineteenth century than it does today, when it is usually coupled with fundamentalist Protestantism. Nineteenth-century evangelicalism was a sensibility that existed in various denominations—Methodists and Baptists to be sure, but also Presbyterians and Low Church Episcopalians. It sanctioned believers' ability to choose salvation by embracing Jesus, as well as their postconversion responsibility to cultivate individual moral responsibility and personal holiness; it fostered a spiritual atmosphere of missionary zeal, fired by millennial expectation. It encouraged emotional expression, but that took a variety of forms—ranging from the shouts of backcountry folk to the sedate sympathies of the urban man of feeling.

Barely literate people shared an evangelical sensibility with the better educated, who were more likely to become devotees of evangelical rationality. What was rational about evangelical rationality was its assumption that God had created an orderly, predictable universe, knowable through empirical methods. The evangelical rationalist outlook evaded philosophical subtleties and elided contradictory beliefs, allowing Americans to imagine a world—and more specifically a nation—ruled by an omnipotent God but populated by free people fashioning their own future.

The earliest evangelical rationalists were men who came of age amid the social hierarchies of the New England colonies—a deferential public life, governed by an alliance of political and religious elites. But they conducted their adult careers amid the democratic ferment of the new American nation—a fractious polity, characterized by increasingly open challenges to established authority in politics and religion. Their intellectual tasks were especially urgent in the religious realm: to remain true to their orthodox upbringing, evangelical rationalists had to beat back an assault from "French infidelity" and then face what amounted to a vitalist challenge from revivalists, who assailed the coldness and deadness of Calvinist orthodoxy. This involved creating a creed dedicated to reason but also willing to acknowledge the importance of feeling as an element of faith and morality. Among educated Protestants, evangelical rationality became the basis of informed belief—an ethos that blended piety, progress, and (ultimately) profit.

The evangelical rationalist consensus was the creation of many people, but among the most prominent was Timothy Dwight (1752–1817)—Congregational minister, conservative Federalist, cofounder of the Connecticut Wits, and president of Yale College. The grandson of Jonathan Edwards, Dwight clung throughout his life to remnants of Calvinist orthodoxy. But he did not deny humans' ability to seek their own salvation. On the contrary, he urged Protestant seekers to take advantage of the "means of grace" that included reading the scriptures, discussing theological issues with other believers, and listening to sermons from ministers like himself.

Dwight was also a postmillennialist: he believed that the Second Coming of Christ would occur after human beings had established a thousand-year reign of peace and prosperity: the Kingdom of God on Earth. This belief emphasized the importance of human will in promoting progress toward the millennium; it reinforced an ethic of mastery that underwrote secular ideologies of success. Dwight combined his millennial expectations with a cosmology derived from the natural philosophy of the English minister William Paley—a clockwork universe, set in motion by a watchmaker God. Paley's clockwork universe was thoroughly deanimated, devoid of mysterious signs and miraculous events, ultimately subject to human understanding through observation and measurement. Dwight, like other evangelical rationalists, wedded Paleyite cosmology to Protestant Christianity—unwittingly creating common ground between himself and men like Ethan Allan and Thomas Paine, the freethinkers and deists he despised.

The capacity to merge divergent streams of thought carried Dwight into prominence as a public figure, a man of the cloth who could make pronouncements on secular as well as religious matters. His synthesis of faith and reason made him an American clerical counterpart of Adam Smith—a precursor of later American college presidents who installed Scottish commonsense philosophy as the crown of the curriculum, and promoted evangelical rationality as the currency of educated opinion. "Common sense" became a phrase to conjure with in the early nineteenth century, the Scots' comforting counterweight to the corrosive skepticism of George Berkeley and David Hume, as well as the colloquial definition of assumptions that came to represent reality itself—what Antonio Gramsci called the "common sense" of the entire society.

Dwight's near-blindness prevented him from reading widely and engaging with the finer points of theological debate. The consequence was that his views were superficial, accessible, and popular. They became the basis of an outlook that dominated respectable thought for decades—a worldview with little room for vague ideas of vital force, and still less for animal spirits.

THROUGH A GLASS DARKLY: THE WORLDVIEW OF TIMOTHY DWIGHT

As president of Yale from 1795 until his death in 1817, Dwight established a reputation for vanquishing unbelievers, as his student Lyman Beecher recalled. "He preached incessantly for six months" against "the Tom Paine school," on the theme "Is the Bible the word of God?" Eventually, Beecher said, "all infidelity skulked and hid its head." Soon after that triumph, the college was swept up in the Second Great Awakening—the firestorms of revival that burned across the countryside during the first six decades of the nineteenth century, creating hundreds of righteous communities in an unsettled frontier society.

In contrast with most evangelical revivalists, Dwight's preaching style was frosty and conservative. What he and his colleagues hailed as "revival" among Yale students was a model of decorum. Those who accepted Christ as their savior felt a quiet surge of elation and quickly bent a knee to acknowledge a power outside themselves. Dwight made revivalism acceptable to an educated, genteel population, unaccustomed to bending a knee before anyone.

Part of his appeal was nationalistic as well as religious. To Dwight the Second Great Awakening was a sign that the Kingdom of God on Earth was beginning here, now, in America. The fledging United States would become the Redeemer Nation of the world. The thought had crossed the minds of other prominent Protestants, including Edwards. But a belief that had earlier been fitful and indirect became explicit and triumphalist in Dwight. He was a founding father of American exceptionalism, the faith that America was divinely ordained to remake the world in its image.

Dwight's ideas became foundational to a new, enlightened orthodoxy that lasted for decades, sustaining a hegemonic ethos with scant sympathy for animal spirits or vitalist philosophy. For many educated Protestants, this evangelical rationality successfully papered over fundamental cultural tensions, between belief and unbelief, piety and profit, individual freedom and omnipotent Providence. This precarious synthesis was short on intellectual consistency, long on moral duty. Dwight was one of its major architects.

This involved a fraught relationship with the memory of his grandfather. When Timothy was a boy, Edwards was revered in the Dwight household as an orthodox martyr to liberalizing forces in his congregation; no doubt less attention was paid to his more idiosyncratic intellectual positions. He was a radical conservative, or a conservative radical. Perhaps his most challenging ontological doctrine was his idea of continuous creation. Edwards believed that all humanity and indeed the entire universe rested on "the immediate continued creation of God." God creates all things, he wrote, "out of nothing at each moment of their existence." The obverse of this was that the universe depends "at each moment" on God's willingness to keep creating it. Were He to withdraw His hand from beneath it, in effect, the entire world would collapse into nothingness. This was the notion behind Edwards's notorious sermon, "Sinners in the Hands of an Angry God"—the precarity of all existence, the thinness of the crust separating everyday life from the chaos below. His text was "Their foot shall slide in due time" (Deuteronomy 32:35). An existentialist sensibility linked Edwards with Martin Heidegger, William James, and other twentieth-century thinkers. And Edwards's notion of continuous creation, despite its Calvinist theological framework, resonated with later ideas of a scintillating, vibrating universe.

Young Timothy Dwight (the fourth) knew next to nothing of his grandfather's theological innovations. What he did know was that he himself was the grandson of two of Northampton's leading citizens, Edwards and his champion, Colonel Timothy Dwight (the second). It was a serious, bookish family. The boy Timothy began his formal preparation for college at eleven with Rev. Enoch Huntingdon of Middletown, Connecticut, and entered Yale at thirteen, the youngest member of the class of 1769. During his first two years, young Timothy's discipline wavered, as he succumbed to the seductions of cards and dice. He became a reckless gambler, until a Yale tutor and family friend took him aside toward the end of his sophomore year and told him to shape up.

Timothy took the advice all too seriously. Lamenting lost opportunities for scholarly work, he struggled to make up squandered time by embarking on a rigorous course of independent study—arising earlier than necessary, parsing one hundred lines of Homer before breakfast. His asceticism paid off academically but put him on the road to physical and emotional collapse. By age twenty, after he was appointed a tutor at Yale, he had become a compulsively driven young scholar, adding a restrictive diet to his ascetic regime. Convinced that overeating caused sluggishness, which hampered his studies, Dwight restricted himself to twelve mouthfuls of vegetables at each meal. This, he believed, was how he would fulfill his highest aspiration: to vindicate and elaborate the theological doctrines of his grandfather. But problems soon arose. If he kept reading for an extended period, he found himself afflicted by severe headaches that forced him to rest. When these attacks become more frequent, his eyes became useless for days at a time; soon he suffered fits of nausea, too. Finally he collapsed altogether, a physical and mental wreck, and left academic life for a long recuperation in Northampton.

He emerged from invalidism with permanent eye damage, though he turned this handicap to professional advantage by developing an extemporaneous preaching style. One can only conjecture about the emotional work Dwight's poor vision performed for him. Certainly his affliction allowed him to bypass theological conflict with his grandfather by becoming an eloquent preacher, providing the means of grace to anyone who cared to listen seriously.

Dwight was ordained in 1783. His first pulpit was the Congregational Church at Greenfield, Connecticut, and he took to the place immediately. It inspired him to write "Greenfield Hill," a long poem celebrating life in a New England village as an ideal existence among virtuous citizens dwelling together in harmony, simplicity, and faith. These were people of "one blood, one kindred," who shared "one faith, one worship, one praise"—they would eventually engulf the nation, perhaps even the world, with their benign universalism.

Early on he envisioned a broad Protestant consensus. In 1788, he preached the influential "Address to Ministers of Every Denomination," making an ecumenical plea for a big Protestant tent. His version of Protestantism eschewed theological subtlety to promote morality: the best path to a moral life, in Dwight's view, was Protestant Christianity, New England version; Christian truth rested on the revelations of the Bible and these could be plainly discerned by human reason. These convictions lay at the core of the emerging evangelical ethos, a superstructure of faith and morality that Dwight helped establish almost in spite of himself—even while he hesitated to abandon the Calvinism of his youth.

The biggest barrier between Dwight and the evangelical majority was the rampant emotion let loose at the typical revival—the barking, twitching, and rolling-about that took place when common folk were possessed by the spirit. Nothing could have been further from Dwight's chill temperament. In May 1802, when the revivals occurred at Yale, Dwight was proud to report that "nothing enthusiastic, nothing superstitious, nothing gloomy, morose, or violent occurred." The effects of the revivals proved their worth—converted students worked harder, tended to their duties with greater diligence, and conformed more precisely to the proper protocols of respect for their superiors. Such were the effects of Dwight's doctrines of grace—an almost self-parodic conformity to conventional expectations.

Like a good postmillennialist, Dwight had faith that the march of moral progress was inevitable. Despite his fear of barbarians on the western prairies and in the southern swamps, Dwight believed they could be civilized over time, as New England preachers spread their values to the entire nation. He wanted to contain multitudes in an expansive orthodoxy. As Dwight's son Ben later recalled, "it was impossible for him to enter the desk [pulpit] but as the herald of reconciliation."

Still, the reconciliation had to be predicated on what Dwight believed were certain "common sense" assumptions that all educated believers could share. One of the authors of that consensus was William Paley, required reading in Dwight's undergraduate courses. Paley envisioned a calm, predictable cosmos, a fit setting for everyday life in a climate of evangelical rationality, and a far cry from the uncertain cosmos of continuous creation—or indeed from any cosmos animated by pulsating, invisible currents of energy.

The other major contributors to the evangelical rationalist consensus were Scottish moral philosophers—Thomas Reid, Dugald Stewart, and James Beattie, among others, along with Smith. But not Smith's friend David Hume, who served as a straw man for the Scottish philosophers. Their dismissals of him resembled the commonsensical Samuel Johnson's claim to refute Bishop Berkeley's solipsism by kicking a stone. Reid attacked Hume's skepticism by resorting to epistemological and ontological common sense. "If there are certain principles, as I think there are, which the constitution of our nature leads us to believe, and which we are under a necessity to take for granted in the common concerns of life, without being able to give a reason for them—these are what we call the principles of common sense; and what is manifestly contrary to them, is what we call absurd," Reid wrote. Hume's questioning of causality fell into the latter category; the man, from the Scots' view, was simply mad. Beattie derided him (unfairly) as "a man who thinks a horse running toward him at full gallop is an idea in his mind." The alternative to skepticism, for most Scottish moral philosophers, was mainly to assert that what seemed real was real.

This was entirely congenial to Timothy Dwight. He became one of the chief ambassadors of Scottish moral philosophy to the young American republic. For Dwight, Christian faith was married to Christian duty; the presence of virtue was the surest sign of faith. Arid theological dispute was at best a waste of time. The impulse toward logic chopping, the taste for paradox, the quest for a metaphysics of everything were all grievously mistaken. Some mysteries, Dwight wrote, are "so high, and so vast, that we cannot attain to them."

Dwight envisioned Americans Protestants choosing to participate in a vast moral consensus, creating a righteous national community. This millennial dream had powerful political implications. It reinforced Dwight's faith that Americans were creating the Kingdom of God on Earth in their own new nation—and perhaps eventually throughout the world. His poem "America" captured this imperial vision:

Hail land of Light and Joy! Thy power shall grow
Far as the sea, which round thy regions flow
Through earth's wide realm thy glory shall extend
And savage nations at thy sceptre bend.

This exceptionalist interpretation of Providence became a centerpiece of American nationalism and eventually of imperial apologetics as well. So did the corollary and implicitly racist notion that other "savage nations" would eventually bow to America's moral superiority.

Dwight's hatred and fear of North American "savages" surfaced in his *Travels in New England and New York* (4 vols., 1818). One of his major themes was the need to conquer superstition with knowledge—the intellectual progress that, he believed, must accompany moral progress. And in his view the most dangerous superstitions could be found among the Indians. He assumed that their worldview sanctioned cruelty, cannibalism, and nearly every other form of human depravity. Consider how the Indians tortured Robert Rogers ("a corpulent man") by snacking on his flesh while he was still alive; compare this savagery, Dwight said, with the sentimental ideal of a "state of nature" envisioned by such "modern philosophers" as the English radical William Godwin.

The pathetic state of subjugated Indians, according to Dwight, proved the fatuity of Godwin's ideal of a sexually promiscuous utopia, where sin does not exist and human depravity is allowed full rein. Indeed, Dwight wrote, "labor is the only source of those [material] enjoyments which make up what Godwin calls happiness, and . . . without the dominion of law, which alone secures to man the benefits of his efforts, no human being will labor." So much for Godwin's idea that the perfectibility of man could be achieved through the absence of restraint; "among civilized people," disciplined achievement is the only path of ascent, Dwight announced, and "poverty is . . . another name for disgrace." We must civilize the Indians, he concluded, by undermining "their love of glory" and substituting "*the love of property.*"

White people, too, needed civilizing. Moral and intellectual progress did not occur without sustained effort. The key to genuine advance was the primacy of individual character, molded by an ethic of self-command—the ethic recommended by Smith in his *Theory of Moral Sentiments*. Unregulated commerce, such as the sort embodied in itinerant peddlers, could undermine that ethic. "Mere wanderers, accustomed to no order, control, or worship," peddlers focused entirely on gain. "No course of life tends more rapidly or more effectually to eradicate every moral feeling," Dwight wrote.

The idle rich were a threat, as well. Dwight charged that "people of fashion" allowed their children to avoid mental discipline and instead gorge themselves on the overripe fruit of fiction: "A soft, luxurious, and sickly character is spread over both the understanding and the affections, which forbids their growth, prevents their vigor, and ruins every hope of future eminence and future worth." For Dwight, "minds destitute of sound principle and defensive prudence" encouraged "the luscious indulgence of fancy." As a consequence, "the mind, instead of being educated, is left to the care of accident and fashion."

In contrast with such layabouts, Dwight exalted Rev. Habijah Weld of Attleboro, Massachusetts, a man who epitomized self-command. As Dwight marveled, "industry, regularity, and exactness in all his concerns" allowed him to support a large family on very little money. Nor were the Welds damaged by the discipline required to sustain themselves: "Every member of his family was courteous and well-bred. Nothing was seen among them but happiness and good will." This was the New England family in its ideal form, a nursery of cheerful, genteel, and godly children.

The family writ large was the village, and Dwight's favorite remained Northampton. He admitted that "the increase of wealth, the influx of strangers, and other causes of degeneracy" had corrupted some of its inhabitants, but "a general submission to laws and magistrates, a general regularity of life, a general harmony and good neighborhood, a sober industry and frugality, a general hospitality and charity" still prevailed among most Northamptonians. All of these traits underscored the superiority of New England village life over the society of "scattered plantations" that prevailed elsewhere in the republic, especially the South. (Dwight opposed slavery long before there was any hint of a public movement against it.) Not that New England was entirely civilized. Rhode Islanders, for instance, revealed a fondness for horse racing—"the gross amusement [that] turns men into clowns, and clowns into brutes." But with the rise of manufacturing, Dwight reassured his readers, even

Rhode Island would show an increase in wealth, education, and liberal views, and a contraction of brutish leisure.

Despite his provincial prejudices, Dwight popularized a world-view that acquired national scope and persisted into the mid-century decades—an outlook that elevated soul over body, transcendent Spirit over animal spirits. It was such a pervasive point of view that it did not often have to be formally articulated; rather it seeped into all manner of discourse as a tacit assumption. The *Yale Literary Magazine* provided an example in 1840, arguing that "good music . . . seldom produces a high flow of the animal spirits, but rather a sober cheerfulness favorable to serious thoughts and feelings." Real religious emotions also had to be distinguished from animal spirits; "Christian Joy," averred the *New York Evangelist*, was "unspeakable and full of glory . . . not a sudden glow of feeling, a transient emotion partaking more of passion than of sentiment . . . It was in fact a state of mind and not a mere exercise of animal spirits." This was the standard evangelical rationalist dismissal of overly excitable revivalists. From this view, animal spirits were always "mere," associated with sensual appetites and pleasures; the slope was slippery from animal spirits to animal instincts.

Through the antebellum era, animals continued to do a lot of psychic work as a collective negative identity for humans. Success in this life, as well as salvation in the next, required that mere animality be transcended. So *The Merchants' Magazine and Commercial Review* urged in 1854, contrasting a mighty shipping magnate with a lowly sand peddler. The magnate exercises "the all-powerful faculties of an immortal soul," actuating ambition and imagination, and from an office in New York City sends fifty thousand dollars' worth of goods around the world; the sand peddler trundles his cart up and down the streets, surviving "by a sort of animal instinct" and remaining little more than "a sort of living automaton." Such assumptions affirmed the persistence of Cartesian assumptions in popular thought. For many antebellum Americans, the tacit belief survived: animals and automata could at least fitfully be twinned, while humans transcended both.

Dualist hierarchies reinforced respectable tastes; they could be deployed to put disreputable persons in their place, as in the *New-York*

Daily Tribune's criticism of Goethe's biographer George Lewes in an 1856 review. Lewes was the life partner of Mary Ann Evans, better known as the novelist George Eliot. The couple could not marry for complicated legal reasons, and despite their loyalty to each other, respectable majority opinion viewed their relationship as scandalous. That disapproval colored the *Tribune*'s left-handed compliments to Lewes: "He touches no subject, however heavy in itself, which he does not kindle into momentary vivacity by the contagion of his exuberant animal spirits. His spirits are indeed intensely animal, with scarcely any vestige of celestial radiance upon their wings, he himself a capital instance of what a sunny natural disposition will do for a clever man, unaided by any of the profounder instincts." Lewes's limitations, according to the reviewer, allow him to indulge in "puerile twaddle" about the privileges of genius—in Goethe's case, his avid pursuit of random sexual liaisons. No doubt, the *Tribune* conceded, Goethe was a "stupendous genius" of "astonishing personal magnetism," but he was also "a very vulgar sensualist." Since geniuses tend to have overdeveloped imaginative and underdeveloped rational faculties, they are likely to be "diseased men, or to lack harmonious and balanced endowments." Unfit for ordinary social and personal life, the genius is likely to be an "unmitigated nuisance"—precisely because of his excess animal spirits.

Yet the association of animal spirits with vulgar sensuality was contested, as American thinkers imagined new ways to connect body with soul (or mind), and self with world. Nearly all involved some effort to expand the sense of human vitality to encompass the cosmos itself.

THE STIRRINGS OF ANIMAL MAGNETISM

Emerson and Whitman are the best-known promoters of a quintessentially Romantic (and American) intellectual project—the celebration of autonomous selfhood within a vibrant cosmos. Of the two, Whitman was the more consistent vitalist. He referred to "a visible or invisible intention, certainly under-lying all," but his descriptions of this "intention" remained vague, as when he paid homage to a "vital, universal, giant force resist-less, sleepless, calm," without exploring its nature. More enthusiastically than Emerson, Whitman veered toward the newer idioms in his exaltation of the "invisible magnetism, dissolving and embracing all," and his tribute to the underlying vitality of the universe as "the joyous, electric all."

Much of Whitman's poetry depended on notions of a universal magnetic or electric power binding matter to mankind—and mankind to one another. In "I Am He That Aches with Love," Whitman asks: "Does the earth gravitate? does not all matter, aching, attract all matter? So the body of me to all I meet or know." This is the vitalist physical self that animates "I Sing the Body Electric" and surfaces in "Song of Myself" as a potent but painfully sensitive source of energy: "Mine is no callous shell, / I have instant conductors all over me whether I pass or stop, / They seize every object and lead it harmlessly through me. // I merely stir, press, feel with my fingers, and am happy, / To touch my person to some one else's is about as much as I can stand." For Whitman, the quiverings of human desire resonated with the pulsations at the core of the cosmos. What seemed to conservatives to be vulgar sensuality was from Whitman's view a profound relationship between the imperial self and the material world.

Not all Romantic writers embraced Whitman's benign view of the pulsating universe. Poe, among others, explored its darker dimensions. He tracked the new forces unleashed by mesmerism and animal magnetism to explore the murky transition between life and death. Yet he was no idiosyncratic connoisseur of darkness. His preoccupations reflect those of his contemporaries: How did body relate to mind, and both to a cosmos pervaded by invisible currents of energy? How did life differ from death, and what was the dividing line between them? Vitalist thinking—diffuse and unsystematic though it may have been—provided Poe and his contemporaries with a way to perceive traditional dualities as a vibrant unity

Unlike Dwight, these vitalist thinkers paid little attention to the middle range of human institutions that mediated between the individual and the universe—families, communities, polities. Veering toward solipsism, they tended to imagine an autonomous self, adrift in an ocean of cosmic consciousness, even as they hoped to locate sources of union with other selves. This popular philosophy proved appropriate for a new nation with restless citizens, boundless frontiers, and an economic system that resembled "a vast lottery," in Alexis de Tocqueville's words.

Popular philosophers of a vitalist bent aimed to capture this sense of free-floating energy and possibility. They imagined animal spirits prowling the wider world in various aliases and disguises: animal magnetism, mesmeric fluid, electrical fluid, electromagnetic fluid, electricity. Attempts to define these concepts recalled older descriptions of animal spirits as well as Defoe's account of credit; all postulated an invisible, odorless, tasteless source of energy, which was often imagined to take fluid form and create vibrating links between body and soul, individual and cosmos, one individual and another. The last sort of link was a scary one. What worried many nineteenth-century Americans was the possibility that certain (usually male) adepts could manipulate animal magnetism or some other mysterious force to win occult power over their (usually female) subjects. The ghost of Anton Mesmer hovered. Beneath this sexual anxiety lay a fear of the condition that seemed to characterize certain versions of mesmeric trance: a loss of will—the power of choice that kept chance at bay, the cornerstone of the ethic of mastery. Whether the mesmerized person became an automaton or a seer (or both) was an open question.

The vibrant new forces enveloping the universe were not only sexually charged; they also evoked a broader and more diffuse state of arousal—a release of control, a propensity to play. The notion of animal spirits in various forms helped some Americans imagine a more fluid way of being, beyond the static hierarchies produced by dualist thinking. What emerged was an alternative, vitalist ontology based on a recognition that even the most exalted ideas could arise from bodily sources, and that body and mind—or body and soul—were implicated in each other's deepest secrets.

ANOTHER WAY OF BEING

Vitalism captured imaginations on both sides of the Atlantic. In Britain, Percy Bysshe Shelley and other Romantic poets mingled with such respected (if controversial) vitalist thinkers as the freethinking surgeon William Lawrence. In pursuit of the meaning of vitality, Lawrence had discarded the notion of a fluid or force supplied to the cosmos by God, replacing it with the spontaneous impulses toward self-organization that he called sensibility and irritability. Such views were subversive not only in their disavowal of divine agency, but also in their rejection of static structures, their fascination with organic growth, and their assertion that life was a process rather than a thing.

Lawrence's worldview resembled those of many American vitalists who, like their British counterparts, claimed scientific legitimacy for their ideas. Through the early and mid-antebellum decades, medical societies and journals published lectures and articles documenting the search for a vital principle that united all life-forms. Desires for unity proliferated in a new nation where social relations often seemed fragmented, distended, and disorganized. Some authors used traditional language to characterize this unifying force. "The animal spirit is to be regarded as a general term for the vital principle, as it is diffused throughout the body, and as originating from the blood, and as giving, in connexion with organic structure, a general propensity to motion," wrote Elisha North in *The New England Journal of Medicine and Surgery* in 1826. "That there is a hidden or invisible principle that moves the vital organs, and gives them sensibility and excitability . . . cannot be disputed. The old name of animal spirit is . . . a suitable one for the principle."

Other more polemically inclined commentators took on dualism directly. The secretary of the Free Press Association, an organization of deists and freethinkers in New York City, told readers of its magazine, *The Correspondent*, in 1828, that most efforts to explain "the principle of *Vitality*" were "radically wrong, inasmuch as they assume the existence of a separate and substantive being, which they term *the mind*, in contradistinction to *matter*, as if man was composed of two natures, an etherial [*sic*] or spiritual one, and a material one. This I hold to be an illusion. The physiology of man, and the observation of daily experience, prove him to be a *feeling*, not a thinking animal." Though the secretary did not know it, he shared this perception with evangelical Protestants. A new respect for feeling melded believers and freethinkers.

The question of vitality was at bottom a question about ontology—the metaphysics of being, the disputable ground of reality. Such ultimate matters were debated in the language of Protestant Christianity, which was increasingly influenced by revivalistic idioms. They shaped popular notions of selfhood, personal identity, and what it meant to be alive in the world.

From the outset, revivals came in many forms, from the staid affirmations of the existing order in New Haven, Connecticut, to the fits and groans in Cane Ridge, Kentucky. The Second Great Awakening, which began in Kentucky in 1802, culminated in New York City in 1857 amid a major Wall Street panic: more and more businessmen were falling on their knees during each pause in the frantic trading, finding Jesus where one might least expect him. Soon after the panic, the Civil War constituted a bloody coda to this evangelical epoch, an apocalyptic struggle between two sides who prayed "to the same God," as Lincoln said in his Second Inaugural—two implacable foes fired by the same millennial expectancy and missionary zeal. During the post–Civil War decades, the revivalist sea would recede and become at least fitfully more channeled into the rhythms of an urban, industrial society—while the taming of the "Wild West" fulfilled Dwight's dream of civilization triumphing over savagery.

But all through the antebellum decades, most revivals had been shaped by the experience of untamed nature. Most scenes of the Second Great Awakening were set in the American forest. Historians led by Grainger have shown how profoundly the natural settings reinforced a strain of evangelical vitalism—a conviction that one could feel God's presence more intensely in the wilderness, among wild creatures, than anywhere else. And fortunately for revivalists, there was abundant wilderness in early nineteenth-century America.

The faith that nature was animated by God possessed traditional and even scriptural warrant. "In the estimation of the Psalmist," John Harris wrote in the *Millennial Harbinger* (1840), "the creation is a vast temple and often did he summon the creatures and join them in a universal song of praise . . . Thus nature, with all her myriad voices, is ever making affirmation and oath of the divine existence, and filling the universe with the echo of his praise." Animals could join people in praising the miracle of divine creation.

Besides regenerating traditional forms of worship, vitalist beliefs led toward new ways of healing body and soul. This regenerative vision animated a host of itinerant practitioners who combined mesmerism, clairvoyance, and medicine, led by the charismatic Andrew Jackson Davis, "the Poughkeepsie Seer." Practical thinkers were drawn to more straightforward forms of healing. Among them was Catharine Beecher—daughter of the influential revivalist Lyman Beecher, sister of the liberal Congregationalist Henry Ward Beecher, and author herself of bestselling domestic-advice literature. In 1849, Catharine urged a friend to take the Northampton Water Cure under the direction of the famous hydrotherapist David Ruggles. She embraced what Grainger identifies as a key vitalist assumption—"human bodies were surrounded by fields of invisible fluid or ether, which a skilled practitioner could manipulate and heal through the direction of his own superior magnetic field." In Beecher's view, Ruggles was just such a practitioner: he possessed, she said, "a power in *the ends of his fingers* in detecting *the heat of diseased action*—which no physician can approach." Beecher combined belief in two somewhat conflicting entities: a sovereign, personal God and a universe throbbing with impersonal energy. This was not unusual for persons in pursuit of relief from mysterious lassitude.

By the 1830s and '40s, evangelicals and other Americans were embracing hydrotherapy and electrotherapy, two emerging efforts to achieve personal, physical regeneration through direct contact with vital forces available to be tapped from the natural world—the healing medicinal waters produced by certain mineral springs, the electric current or fluid manipulated by adepts in animal magnetism. For decades, mesmerists claimed the regenerative power of animal magnetism. Only gradually did mesmerism become hypnotism—a completely mental procedure, with no mesmeric fluid, invisible or otherwise, required. Idioms and methods proliferated, creating a confusing landscape of "isms" and other labels—all purporting to characterize an invisible force that melded flesh and spirit, individuals and the cosmos. Animal magnetism was the most popular name for that force, and during the antebellum era it was acquiring both scientific and religious legitimacy.

One typical advocate was Edward Hitchcock, a geologist, Congregationalist minister, and eventually president of Amherst College who extolled the therapeutic benefits of both mesmerism and electricity. In his view, both had the capacity to unleash energies that linked nature and the supernatural—a release of primal force that could only enhance human life. And both carried the imprimatur of science. Recent scientific discoveries, Hitchcock asserted, made it "nearly certain that electricity, magnetism, galvanism, and electro-magnetism, are all but modifications of one great power of nature . . . the electric fluid"—which in turn possessed a "very intimate relation" with "the mysterious principle of life." Discovering this vital principle, Hitchcock believed, was a key to experiencing the more abundant life that Jesus had promised through conversion.

The vitalist search for life force inspired a host of vernacular ontologies, speculative efforts to situate human beings in a universe abuzz with mysterious energies. Idioms varied widely, but common themes converged in the concept of animal magnetism. The "animal" in "animal magnetism" had little to do with actual animals, but instead referred, at least metaphorically, to the visceral, physical impact of apparently invisible powers. Animal magnetism was a force like the one Whitman imagined, binding human beings to the world and to one another. Mesmerists often rechristened themselves magnetizers and claimed comparable access to occult powers. For decades they displayed their capacity to summon and direct vital force, in parlors, auditoriums, and theaters throughout the country. Rituals varied but also fell into common patterns.

One of those patterns involved healing. The mesmerist sat facing his (usually female) subject, their hands and knees touching, then started moving his hands an inch or so above the subject's body, producing glazed eyes, panting breath, tingling flesh, and other signs of (usually sexual) excitement. When the subject slipped into a trance, tranquility supplanted excitement. Assuming the breath carried a magnetic charge, the mesmerist blew on the afflicted part of the body. He might also magnetize a glass of water, passing his fingertips over it and letting their supposed electricity suffuse the liquid, while blowing on it to intensify the electric charge and create the magnetic state. Then he poured the water directly on the diseased area. If the subject was very ill, painful symptoms might assert themselves—feelings of suffocation, nervous spasms—until a crisis was reached and the symptoms subsided. Belief in the power of such healing rituals came easily to Protestant Christian Americans, some of whom attributed Christ's miracles to the magnetism emanating from his hands.

The other major element of magnetic or mesmeric performance was clairvoyance—the ability to describe hidden objects or distant places one had never visited, to read a stranger's mind or character, and to diagnose the illnesses of sick people one had never seen. The most common examples of clairvoyance were somnambulant travelers like Loraina Brackett, a blind woman of modest means who spent much of 1837 in Providence, Rhode Island, under the guidance of the physician-mesmerist George Capron, demonstrating her ability to "travel" to New York, Washington, and Saratoga Springs—where she spat out the mineral water, claiming to dislike it. The novelist Nathaniel Hawthorne dramatized this sort of performance in his *Blithedale Romance*, a satire of the utopian experiment at Brook Farm. The mesmerist Professor Westervelt has chosen the character Priscilla as his subject, presenting her to the assembled crowd at the nearby lyceum hall as the Veiled Lady. Though she cannot hear the voices of those in the same room, Westervelt says, if he willed it, "she could hear the desert wind sweeping over the sands as far off as Arabia; the icebergs grinding one against the other in the polar seas; the rustle of a leaf in an East-Indian forest; the lowest whispered breath of the bashfullest maiden in the world, uttering the first confession of her love." These were the sort of performances typically staged to show the power of animal magnetism. They could be as simple as table-turning and hat-moving, but no matter how crude or elaborate, all such demonstrations were meant to show how immaterial forces could be harnessed to affect the physical experiences of healing, seeing, and hearing.

The intellectual rationale for animal magnetism was often vague and elusive. Hawthorne provides his own skeptical perspective by summarizing Westervelt's prefatory remarks before introducing the Veiled Lady: "He spoke of a new era that was dawning upon the world; an era that would link soul to soul, and the present life to what we call futurity, with a closeness that should finally convert both worlds into one great, mutually conscious brotherhood. He described (in a strange philosophical guise, with terms of art, as if it were a matter of chemical discovery) the agency by which this mighty result was to be effected; nor would it have surprised me, had he pretended to hold up a portion of his universally pervasive fluid, as he affirmed it to be, in a glass phial." Hawthorne aptly caught the blend of spirituality and science, immateriality and materiality, in the ontology underlying the practices accompanying animal magnetism.

A more extended version of that ontology was spelled out by "A Practical Magnetizer" in *The History and Philosophy of Animal Magnetism, with Practical Instructions for the Exercise of This Power* (1843). The principles of animal magnetism, in the Practical Magnetizer's account, recalled the classic physiological accounts of animal spirits from the eighteenth century. Summarizing what was alleged to be professional medical opinion, the Magnetizer wrote that "there is an elastic, invisible *ether* pervading all nature, which, under *different modifications*, and in *different bodies*, assumes the character of the electric, the galvanic, and the magnetic fluid . . . a *modification* of this elastic ether is resident in the nerves of the human system, and is the *connecting link* between *mind* and *matter* . . . this ether, or fluid, is called the *Magnetic Medium*." The human system included "a material body . . . a vital or animating principle . . . a mental power, and . . . a soul or spirit . . . the magnetic fluid is the *vital principle*, and the cause of all the strengths and animation of the body."

When inducing a mesmeric trance, the Magnetizer manipulates "the *vital* or *magnetic fluid*" to exclude external sensations, freeing "the *internal sense* (or spirit) . . . from the ordinary influences of the body, (as it will be [freed] after death)" and allowing it to reveal its "spiritual power"—including the clairvoyant capacity to read people's minds (or letters in sealed envelopes), and to see events in the geographic or temporal distance. Despite these spiritual (or mental) consequences, the Practical Magnetizer insisted that the magnetic fluid must be physical; if it were not a physical entity, how could it be "*poured out and exhausted*," or "*lost and regained*," or "*diminished and increased*"?

For its devotees, animal magnetism preserved the physical dimension that animal spirits had possessed in the eighteenth century. Table-moving and hat-turning became popular and entertaining ways to demonstrate "a very simple application of the nervous fluid, animal magnetism, or whatever be the agency, to brute matter," as the *New-York Daily Tribune* reported of "experiments" conducted in 1852. Still, animal magnetism also sustained a spiritual aura, though not always a flattering one. Brigham Young said it was the source of his success in bringing converts to Mormonism, and that was precisely the problem for rationalists and skeptics, who claimed animal magnetism was at the core of religious enthusiasm, ready to be manipulated by Christian as well as Mormon preachers.

Some vitalist thinkers sought to transcend religion altogether. They addressed an audience of Americans weary of denominational conflict, longing for spiritual unity, and responsive to a vision of the universe as abuzz with energy as life in commercial society seemed to be. Andrew Jackson Davis (1826–1910) was one such figure. He disdained parlor tricks and sought larger spiritual truths through mesmerism. And he made a decent living doing it.

THE BEWILDERING MAGNETIC ELYSIUM OF ANDREW JACKSON DAVIS

Davis was born to a poor family in Blooming Grove, New York, near Poughkeepsie. When he was seventeen he heard a local lecture on animal magnetism and soon discovered he had remarkable clairvoyant powers, as well as a capacity for mesmeric healing. Early on he realized that publicizing his powers would be an exit strategy from his hardscrabble life. Like other mesmerists, he became an itinerant entrepreneur, selling his magical powers to credulous audiences on Greene Street in Manhattan and other public venues throughout the Northeast. (Poe was among the audience on Greene Street; he was unimpressed.) Davis may have been as much a humbug as P. T. Barnum or any patent medicine advertiser, but he concealed his duplicity (perhaps even from himself) in clouds of rapturous rhetoric—and some of his visions resonated with contemporary theories of holistic medicine. His confidence games, however fraudulent or sincere, played a major part in providing many Americans with an alternative sense of spirituality, not divorced from the material world but emanating from it—and a way to look beyond Christianity toward what they believed was a more scientific way of understanding the universe.

Davis produced a memoir, *The Magic Staff*, in 1857, when he was still a young man but after he had already established his reputation as the Poughkeepsie Seer. *The Magic Staff* seemed intended to vindicate Davis from charges of humbuggery, not to mention bigamy, adultery, and superstition. It presented his life as a poor boy's stereotypical triumph over adversity, but with supernatural assistance rather than hard work as the key to his success.

Davis's life began, he said, in "a certain isolated, unpainted, unfinished dwelling" surrounded by fields and woods full of copperheads. His father was a weaver turned cobbler turned journeyman shoemaker, with a weakness for strong drink; his mother, "upon whose form the weary weight of 33 years had left its mark," was "simple and childlike," Davis remembered. "The heavy chains of poverty, which her husband could and did wear with only ordinary fretting," combined with his intemperance "to cut deep channels into the very substance of her soul."

Young Jackson grew up in a world of mysterious signs and portents. Once when he and his siblings were playing on the edge of the woods, his brother Sylvanus saw a light in the forest that the others did not, and raced home to tell their mother. She received the news with "inward grief," and when Jackson asked what was the matter, she said: "Sylvanus will soon leave us." He died a few days later. Even after the boy's death his skeptical father still said "Poh!" to his wife's belief in her own clairvoyance.

As soon as the boy Jackson discovered there was such a thing as death, he began to fear it, trembling at the possibility that he might not reawaken when he went to sleep. His mother reassured him, but his father dismissed his anxiety as "nothin' but worms ailin' him." This was a pivotal moment for the boy. "Now, though a very little child, I felt that

I *knew better*, and so, for the first time, I found my mind rejecting my own father's judgment," Davis remembered. "Here was individual sovereignty in a trundle-bed." The growth of his own personal autonomy—eventually in concert with invisible supernatural forces—was a major theme in Davis's memoir. Still, the father won his son's respect from time to time—as when he faced down the White Spook, a local apparition that turned out to be a scarecrow.

Demystification of ghosts and backwoods magic was a leitmotif in Davis's account of his self-development. His fitful but growing respect for his father paralleled the moderation of his own "organ of *marvellousness*"—which phrenologists later confirmed to be "small and secondary." In *The Magic Staff*, he was determined to separate his own experience of the spirit world from any taint of superstition or hocus-pocus. Even as a small child, he boasted, he discovered that his mother and big sister, not Santa Claus, filled his Christmas stocking with doughnuts; this, he wrote, produced a lifelong "vigilant incredulity regarding the existence of *invisible personages*." Of course, the spiritual authorities he would encounter in his later trance states were "*invisible personages*" to anyone but himself, but they carried, he would claim, the authority of mesmeric science.

Even as he sought to distance himself from rural folk superstitions, Davis began to hear messages with no recognizable source. At times these utterances were sweepingly, if obscurely, theological. When he was singing a hymn with the line "In their graves laid low," he heard a voice in his head saying "No!" Having tried the Episcopal church (too much catechism), and the Presbyterian (too many theological contradictions), he soon found himself equally unable to respond to a Methodist revival. "What alarmed me was, the more I desired the further I receded from conversion." The Methodist pastor feared for Jackson's soul, envisioning his eternal damnation in the biblical language of weeping and gnashing of teeth. At that phrase, Davis said, "A soft breathing passed over my face, and I heard in a voice like the gently whispering summer breeze—*'Be—calm!—The—pastor—is—wrong; you—shall—see!'*" The voice suggested the astonishing possibility that "there existed some people who did not believe in a God of implacable wrath!" Davis's voices were leading him from persistent orthodox habits of mind, which had kept the hell fires burning, to a vision of universal salvation in a spirit world to come. What brought this world and the next together, he would eventually assert, was the persistence of "vitalic force"—an invisible, immaterial source of eternal life.

Seeking to fling wide the doors of perception, Davis opened himself to offbeat mental experiences, including the popular craze of mesmerism. When an itinerant phrenologist, Professor J. Stanley Grimes, arrived in town to perform experiments in mesmerism, Davis submitted to his alleged powers and found himself unmoved by such "magnetic buffoonery." (This, ironically, was what Grimes had wanted, as his aim was to debunk mesmerism.) But a few days later, Davis met a local tailor named William Levingston who offered to show Davis what mesmerism could really do. Davis agreed.

The result, for Davis, was the beginning of a career full of astonishing revelations, achieved through clairvoyant trances—induced at first by "operators" like Levingston, later by Davis on his own. Davis's reputation for clairvoyance rested in part on evidence produced by standard mesmeric performances—reading books inside a chest of drawers across the room, or describing houses in distant cities he had never visited—feats that could apparently be confirmed by third parties. But at many crucial moments in his life, Davis also depended on clairvoyant visions that no one else could have seen—real to him, maybe, but not true in any conventionally verifiable sense. Still, they resonated with emerging vitalist notions of the universe and won Davis a wide following. He became a regional celebrity, making a career out of manipulating the credulity of his audience but also, perhaps, cultivating credulity in himself. Credulity, in effect, opened the door to what he was convinced was a revolutionary way of seeing, one that envisioned a spirit land over the horizon and ultimately beyond death itself.

His career began in Levingston's parlor, where Davis submitted to the mesmerist's powers amid a group of curious townspeople: "the mystic magnetic state was induced in less than thirty minutes." As in Calvinism, the passive voice was significant: mesmerized human beings were dependent on a mysterious force more powerful than themselves.

Contact with that force, Davis claimed, empowered him with supernatural insight. "I not only beheld the exteriors of the individuals in that room—clothed with light as it were—but I also as easily perceived their interiors, and then, too, the hidden sources of their luminous magnetical emanations," Davis recalled. This was the beginning of Davis's journey toward a vision of a pulsating universe.

Davis's clairvoyance involved the ability to see the vital force that energized every facet of the universe, down to and including the bodies of the people in the room with him. "Thus I saw not only the real physical structures themselves, but also their indwelling structures and vitalic elements," Davis remembered. "I knew the individuals had garments upon them, because *I could see an element of vitality, more or less distinct, in every fiber of clothing upon their persons!*" His vision ranged far beyond Poughkeepsie. "I saw the many and various forms of the forests, fields, and hills, all filled with life and vitality of different hues and degrees of refinement." At such moments, he inhabited an "I" unbound by space and time, like Whitman's in "Song of Myself": "My ties and ballasts leave me, my elbows rest in sea-gaps, I skirt sierras, my palms cover continents, I am afoot with my vision." Both men courted feelings of boundlessness.

For Davis, the ocean was an especially rich source of revelation: "The various salts in the sea sparkled like living gems; sea plants extended their broad arms, filled with hydrogenous life, and embraced the joy of existence; the deep valleys and dim-lit ravines, through which old ocean unceasingly flows, were peopled with countless minute animals—all permeated and pulsating with the spirits of Nature . . . Oh, the ocean is a magnificent cabinet of beauty and wealth immense, and, by virtue of more recent examinations I am impressed to say that man shall yet possess it!"

Davis's last exclamation—the notion that man would one day "possess" the ocean—marked a further turn in Americans' departure from pagans' and indigenous peoples' notions of an animated universe. Medieval and early modern Catholics as well as later Protestant revivalists had envisioned a universe animated by God, whose powers could be summoned by appropriate prayers or rituals. While Davis claimed clairvoyance reinforced his belief in God, saying it taught him "to revere, obey, and depend upon that Power which directs and controls the universe," he was at heart a humanist. He capped off his vision of universal animacy by placing humans atop it all:

> And—mark this fact!—in each mineral, vegetable, and animal I saw something of MAN! In truth, the whole system of creation seemed to me like *fragments of future human beings*! In the beaver I saw, in embryo, one faculty of the human mind; in the fox, another; in the wolf, another; in the horse, another; in the lion, another; yea, verily, throughout the vast concentric circles of mineral, vegetable, and animal life I could discern certain relationships to, and embryological indications of, Man! . . . all Nature was radiant with countless lights, with atmospheres, with colors, with breathings, and with emanations—all throbbing and pulsating with an indestructible life-essence—which seemed just ready to graduate and leap up into the human constitution! Everything apparently emulated to be Man!

This vision, strained and even a little pathetic in its stridency, pointed toward a progressive humanist form of vitalism that began to flourish decades later—though without the trailing clouds of glory Davis seemed unable to resist. Davis's culminating crescendo reveals how, during the mid-nineteenth century, even vitalist believers in universal animacy were reluctant to relax their commitment to human supremacy. While indigenous peoples imagined a universe animated by *mana*, where human and nonhuman animals coexisted, Davis channeled his vitalist impulses toward a vision of human uniqueness, superiority, and perfectibility.

Still, there was something enchanted about the visions Davis claimed he saw while mesmerized. To move from the influence of his employer, the skeptical storekeeper Ira Armstrong, to that of the mesmerist Levingston was to move from the cut-and-dried realm of utilitarian business to the wondrous world of magnetism. It was hardly surprising, as Davis wrote, that "the unknown attraction [of mesmerism] predominated over my business obligation; and as the fish leaps joyously into its native element, so plunged I with delight into the bewildering magnetic Elysium!" Davis's choice of "bewildering" was significant. The word's original connotations were "being led into the wild." Harnessing animal magnetism could allow a glimpse of spiritual or mental wildness.

Davis began to have visions—as well as continued to hear voices—on his own. In one especially compelling encounter Davis met "a man of ordinary stature but of a spiritual appearance" who said:

> It was demonstrated to me that all the diversified external forces in this, as in other universes, are unfolded by virtue of an elemental or spiritual principle, contained in each, which is their life, or Soul; and this essence, by men, is called God . . . Accordingly I founded a system upon these principles and considerations, which may be called "a medical system of the trinity." In this system I maintain that every particle in the human body possesses a close affinity to particular particles below in the subordinate kingdoms—and that these latter particles, if properly associated and applied, would cure any affected portion of the human frame.

In Davis's account, he asks to become acquainted with the stranger and his system. The stranger says of course, that's why we've met. He carries a cane that turns into "a staff, far exceeding in beauty any I had ever beheld." The stranger says, "Take this"—it signifies "that *the spirit* is the creating, developing, perfecting, expanding, beautifying, organizing, healing, eternal essence in the possession of every being." Davis gratefully accepts it, but when he sets the staff aside to climb over a fence, he gets his clothing caught in a rail, gets embarrassed and angry, scales the fence, and finally asks the stranger to return the staff. Not until you earn it, says he: "in a due season thou shalt return, and then this staff shall be thine; *but thou must first learn not to be under any circumstances depressed, nor by any influences elated*, for these are the extremes of an unguarded impulse, in minds not strong with pure wisdom." There is something slightly absurd about a massive phallic Magic Staff serving as an emblem of self-command; still, for the rest of his memoir, Davis summons the staff mentally whenever he is tempted to violate his ethic of compulsory moderation. His refusal of depression and elation resembled the resolution of evangelical rationalists, who sought a stable self amid the confusions and temptations of commercial life.

Yet Davis was no devotee of commonsense empiricism. Early on he began to claim that his powers could be put in the service of medical healing through the restoring of the steady flow of vital force. "I soon ascertained Disease to be a want of equilibrium in the circulation of the vitalic principle," he wrote, articulating an idea that resembles the non-Western vital principle of *qi*. Positive results quickly followed, according to his account. Davis cured a countryman's deafness, he claimed, by placing the hot humid skin of a fresh-killed rat over each ear every night; he cooled a monstrous "*felon*" (inflammation) on a man's hand by telling him to put a frog's skin on it; and he discovered in a clairvoyant trance that he could cure another case of deafness by applying the oil of thirty-two weasels to the patient's ears. But not enough weasels could be found—and even the credulous country folk began whispering that Davis and his "operator" Levingston might be humbugs.

As his practice of medical healing came under a cloud, Davis succumbed to feelings of depression, fears that he had somehow lost something important, a cane maybe. At that moment he had another vision, as if spelled out on a signboard: "Here is thy magic staff—UNDER ALL CIRCUMSTANCES KEEP AN EVEN MIND." The ethic of self-command stabilized the selfhood of a young man whose confidence games were concealed—probably even from himself—by a thick cloud of spirituality, roiling with vital forces.

Even as Davis hustled all over the Northeast, marketing his self-proclaimed mental powers, he conceived "an unconquerable repugnance to all Yankee speculation and money-getting operations generally," while his Magic Staff endowed him with a "flippant levity" that never touched "that mysterious sub-current of noiseless energy, which ever flowed through my spiritual constitution." This was the sort of "noiseless energy" that kept the universe pulsating; it maintained the resonance between self and world, animal spirits and animal magnetism. And always Davis preserved an "even mind" under the most challenging circumstances—or so *The Magic Staff* purported to show. Accosted by a hostile "ministerial-looking stranger," he was on the verge of replying with heat when he remembered that "fortunately the Magic Staff was in my possession"—and he remained calm, relying on the staff under similar circumstances henceforth.

As his fame grew Davis became a familiar figure out and about in Poughkeepsie, accompanied by his small dog Dickie, a mutt with spirit. Indeed, Davis observed, "that morceau of the Spirit of Nature which animated his little body, *did certainly perceive the presence of invisible beings*—and that, too, sometimes in advance of my own far more exalted impressibility!" On one occasion Dickie directed him to the very spot where his invisible benefactor, the one who gave him the Magic Staff, sought to tell him to "*Seek—the—mountain!—At four o'clock—delay not!*"

Eventually Davis broke Levingston's "magical spell" and, as he remembered, "the luxurious freedom of individual ownership rushed over me like a flood of heavenly joy." Levingston had been a necessary mentor but had ultimately become an obstacle to Davis's self-development. "Individual ownership"—by which he meant self-ownership—was Davis's lodestar. For a while the young clairvoyant set up shop on Greene Street in downtown Manhattan with another operator and a scribe to record his visions—these would eventually become the basis of his magnum opus, a six-volume compendium of his lectures he called *The Great Harmonia: A Revelation of the Seven Mental States, and of the Laws and Effects of Man's Relation to the Spiritual Universe* (1850–1861).

He began treating "physical indispositions" at a distance, healing by mail. Many of his correspondents were women, including one he identified as Katie D——, an affluent New Orleans woman who became his wife after successfully divorcing her bigamous husband. "The God of eternal destinies, the great Positive Mind, keeps your feet in the right path. Believe in him!" he wrote to her, foreshadowing a rhetoric that would become widespread among positive thinkers a half century later. Katie, whom a voice later told Davis to rename "Silona," became a familiar figure at Davis's performances—a lady of fashion amid the "unpolished mechanics and ungloved merchants" in his audience.

Critics continued to cry humbug. When he left Hartford after a stay of several months, the *Courant* published what Davis himself called a "witty burlesque" of his farewell address to his followers, satirizing him as a patent medicine hustler leaving town to devote himself to "selling his pills in other and less over-stocked markets." Davis still insisted on striking a stance above mere moneymaking. When Wall Street traders asked: Do you have "the power to tell, for instance, the state of the flour market at any given time, if you desire to do so?" He said yes he could, but he would not because "all speculation is wrong . . . and the money, thus obtained, is seldom of any value to the world." Instead of consorting with traders he dedicated himself to the general cause of reform—for freer divorce laws, for temperance and peace, against slavery, yet committed to the belief that "the things which are seen are temporal; but things which are not seen are eternal." This became the motto of Brother Brittan, editor of the *Univercoelum*, the reform paper Davis founded. Davis's belief in the reality of the unseen accelerated his steady drift toward his own idiosyncratic version of Spiritualism, one that transcended the effort to conjure communications from the beyond and blended with a broader philosophical outlook.

By this time, the 1850s, Davis was nearly thirty and ready for another career move. He announced that he now had a direct personal line to clairvoyance—no operator needed! "Oh, I am wholly awake! The sable curtain of mystery—so long hanging between my inner and outer world—is rent in twin and forever banished!" The most complete form of personal autonomy, for Davis, involved unassisted access to the unseen.

The Great Harmonia became the *Summa* of his Harmonial Philosophy, which he tried to integrate with Spiritualism—ultimately without success. From the outset of *The Great Harmonia*, Davis rejected dualism. "Matter and Mind have heretofore been supposed to constitute two distinct and independent substances . . . the latter having no material origin," he wrote. "But it is coming to be seen that Truth is a unit, that Nature is everywhere consistent with herself, and that mind is the flower of matter, as man is the flower of creation . . . That which is grain to-day, may tomorrow form a portion of nerve and muscle, and the third day, it may become an element of life; on the fourth, a sparkling thought."

What held everything in the cosmos together was "the fundamental principle of all Life, which is Attraction." Decades later, at the dawn of the twentieth century, positive thinkers would redefine the Law of Attraction as a force that individuals could control to attract wealth to themselves, merely by visualizing it. But for Davis the law was a gravitational affinity that resembled animal magnetism—that made the cosmos and everything in it a universe rather than a multiverse. It also governed "the relations and dependencies between the Body and the Soul." Spirit and Flesh melded amid universal animacy. "Every fiber of the wild flower, or atom of the mountain violet, was radiant with its own peculiar life," Davis said, recalling his early clairvoyant trances.

By the 1870s, Davis was elevating his Harmonial Philosophy over kitchen-table Spiritualism, comparing most mediums' claims to tales of "broom-riding witches; to the shallow doctrines of personal devils and sorcery; and to the fiction age of astrology and the small gods of superstition." As always he insisted he was among the advance guard of scientific progress. Eventually he was forced to admit that the Spiritualist movement was incompatible with the Harmonial Philosophy. He continued to practice what was still called "magnetic healing," even as the orthodox medical profession began to organize more effectively against it. He diagnosed patients by placing his fingertips on the palms of their hands and "sensing" their physical condition. In 1880, when the New York State Assembly passed legislation barring magnetic healers from practicing medicine, Davis encouraged them to follow his example and enroll in the United States College of Medicine in New York City, which encouraged eclectic practices and would allow magnetic healers to acquire medical legitimacy. Under pressure from the medical profession, the state assembly revoked the school's charter in 1883, but still confirmed the degrees it granted that year, including Davis's.

Still a controversial figure in New York spiritualist circles, Davis soon decamped to Boston, where he gradually regained some status as an elder statesman from the spirit world and continued to practice clairvoyant medicine until his death in 1910. Though Davis never lost his faith in the connections between mind and body, his career as an influential exponent of vitalism was over with the coming of the Civil War. Later generations would speak in more secular accents, abandoning all claims to see a land beyond death.

The popularity of Davis's vitalist visions reveals their resonance with main currents in American vernacular thought. Since the early decades of the nineteenth century, most commentators had begun gradually to acknowledge that animal spirits—like animal instincts—were a necessary part of what it meant to be human. Just as God's "Almighty Power" mixes sunshine and shadow in the natural world, many writers observed, so also He allows glumness and glee to alternate in our emotional lives. And neither could survive without the other: "The animal spirits cannot long sustain a tempest of happiness; our most rapturous sensations must weary with enjoyment, and sink, like the overloaded ocean, to languor and to peace. The asperity of sorrow must at last be worn down by time and reflection," as the *Connecticut Spectator* put it in 1814. This notion enlarged the range of acceptable emotions beyond the narrow boundaries set by the utilitarian self, acknowledging oscillations of rapture and languor but assuming they would be tempered by time. As vitalist impulses proliferated in popular philosophy, animal spirits began to seem a crucial component of health and success.

THE CONFLATION OF ENERGY AND CHARACTER

Though animal spirits had ultimately to be tamed or transcended, one could hardly imagine a successful enterprise without them. This included the Christian ministry, one observer noted in 1834, which required the would-be minister to overcome timidity and cultivate "holy boldness." Boldness was widely assumed to be a masculine trait, and invocations of the need for animal spirits (whether or not that exact phrase was used) often seemed primarily directed at a male audience.

This orientation shaped discussions of the role played by animal spirits in maintaining healthy psychic life, as an essential counterpoint to the paralyzing inner turmoil variously known as "the Blue Devils," "the Horrors," and "the Hypo"—a mental state that, judging by contemporaneous descriptions, sounds like what later generations would call manic depressive tendencies or bipolar disorder. This condition was apparently widespread in antebellum America, at least according to some observers. The Rutland (Vt.) *Herald* urged sympathy for its victims, whose ailments were medical, not moral: "When from some inexplicable cause, a mountain's weight is pressing down the animal energies and almost stagnating the blood in their channels [free-flowing circulation remained central to vitalist notions of health], when imagination is quickened into the wildest and most painful activity and involuntarily conjures up the belief that he is being pursued by a legion of little individual Beelzebubs, *driving one half of him* mad with distraction, chilling the other half into stupid indifference and despondency," the *Herald* opined that the sufferer doesn't need homilies, sarcasm, or ridicule. His pain was "a state of the 'inner man' (either mentally, physically, or both united) over which he has no control," and it could no more be joked or argued away than a toothache.

Yet the man oscillating between mania and depression could be well-suited to life amid the restless uncertainties of a commercial society. As the *Herald* observed, he might be a "man of energy and ambition," embarrassed by the "unavoidable casualties" of commercial life, brought low through no fault of his own. When other tradesmen fail in their financial obligations to him, he is haunted by his sense of loss and harassed by his knowledge of wrongs done to him. Yet "men of this stamp (who are invariably of an impetuous, sanguine temperament) are of the greatest value to society and the world. They are the projectors and accomplishers of the most mighty undertakings—pioneers in every difficult enterprise . . . and in them is displayed that indomitable energy of character so universally admired."

The conflation of energy and character was a telling rhetorical move; it implicitly acknowledged the values of an activist, achieving culture where contentment was an excuse for stasis and risk-taking was a necessary condition for success. Increasingly during the mid-nineteenth century, one finds similar arguments made for "the gambling spirit" as a force for great accomplishments—though seldom arguments for gambling itself. Moralists gradually reshaped ideal conceptions of male character: by incorporating concepts like vitality and force, they recognized the increasing necessity of risk-taking in a restless, unregulated market society.

Yet the survival of animal spirits in antebellum thought revealed more than merely masculine concerns; the concept crossed gender lines, reflecting broadly accepted ideas about personal well-being. Through the 1860s, moralists discussed the importance of animal spirits as a source of discipline, determination, and even domestic harmony. As *The New York Times* reported, animal spirits buoyed up Mrs. Myra Gaines during thirty years of trying to get the inheritance she deserved from the wealthy libertine who had fathered her; they combined with "high principle and extraordinary force of will" to sustain the discipline William Hickling Prescott needed to finish his *History of Ferdinand and Isabella* (1837); their absence at home kept "the clubbable man" from his familial duties, as he "lets off at the club all the effervescence of his animal spirits, and keeps for his wife and family the stale, flat, and unprofitable remnant"—hardly a promising prescription for domestic harmony. Clearly these energizing forces provoked mixed feelings, ranging from admiration to anxiety. In the unfolding discussion of them, some elusive but essential principle of vitality was at stake. The pursuit of this principle began animating ministers, mothers, and practical men of affairs. Vitality, it appeared, was necessary for the well-being of both body and soul.

Nothing better shows the pervasiveness of this idea than patent medicine advertising. Throughout the middle decades of the nineteenth century, the revival of animal spirits remained a key component in the regeneration promised by all manner of magic elixirs. In 1839, "Moffat's Life Medicines" offered readers of the Burlington (Vt.) *Free Press* nothing less than new life: "When the spark of life begins to grow dim, the circulation languid, and the faculties paralyzed, these medicines are found to give a tone to the nerves, exhilarate the animal spirits, invigorate the body, and reanimate the man." Sometimes the vendor claimed to harness "the strengthening, life-giving, vitalizing influence of Galvanism," as Dr. Christie's Galvanic Belt, Bracelets, Necklace, and Magnetic Fluid did in 1851. But more often the remedy was ingested. Holloway's Pills combatted dyspepsia, as the company announced in the Stroudsburg (Pa.) *Jeffersonian* in 1858; and dyspepsia was the key to most other bodily maladies: "The stomach being disordered, the whole vital machinery to which it furnishes sustenance and strength will be weakened, and the animal spirits, sympathizing with the bodily debility, will become greatly depressed." Well into the post–Civil War era, advertisers for patent medicines from Hostetter's Stomach Bitters to Tarrant's Seltzer Aperient offered renovation, refreshment, and purification for torpid, run-down systems. And for most, the return of animal spirits was an aim of their therapy and a sign of its success.

Animal spirits, despite their disappearance from physiology texts, remained a key component in the vernacular discourse of health: nurturing them was a way of keeping body and soul in trim. Good humor arose from the gut, as the *Christian Reflector* implied in reflecting on the merits of "Ripe Bread," which has one fifth more nutriment than newly cooked "unripe bread" and "imparts a much greater degree of cheerfulness. He that eats old ripe bread will have much greater flow of animal spirits than he would were he to eat unripe bread." Influences flowed from mind to body as well as vice versa. "The mind is like the appetite—when healthy, well-toned, receiving pleasure from the commonest food; but becoming diseased, when pampered and neglected," announced the Somerset (Pa.) *Herald* in 1847. "Give it time to turn in upon itself, satisfy its restless search for knowledge, and it will give birth to health, to animal spirits, to everything which invigorates the body while it's advancing by every step the capacities of the soul." Through the 1860s, self-help writers argued that intellectual labors provided excitement and ambition "of a nature calculated to cheer the mind, and to give the animal spirits a salutary impulse" as the critic Lindley Murray wrote in the Clarksville (Tenn.) *Chronicle*. No less a sage than Ralph Waldo Emerson saw animal spirits as the key to persuasive power: "A cold, sluggish blood thinks it has not facts enough to the purpose, and must decline its turn in the conversation," Emerson wrote. "But they who speak have no more,—have less. 'T is not new facts that avail, but the heat to dissolve everybody's facts. Heat puts you in right relation with magazines of facts. The capital defect of cold, arid natures is the want of animal spirits. They seem a power incredible, as if God should raise the dead." Well into the nineteenth century, animal spirits preserved—at least in some minds—a miraculous aura.

Emerson's vision of animal spirits as "a power incredible" reflected their long association with the aesthetic dimension of poesis, or creative making, as well as with the realm of the sacred—where through ritual play, as Johan Huizinga writes, "something invisible and inactual takes beautiful, actual, holy form." Nineteenth-century liberal Protestants may have raised an eyebrow at ritual play in religion but not in theater, dance, or humor—arenas where performers were often praised for the animal spirits they brought to their role. Audiences and critics recognized that animal spirits lay at the source of aesthetic playfulness; and play was about, among other things, the transcendence of everyday life—which in a utilitarian society was increasingly hemmed in by vigilant self-scrutiny, the prerequisite for self-command.

Perhaps the most direct way to break through the reign of utility was through laughter. "I am too old for laughter, they tell me," the critic Horace Smith wrote in *Evergreen* magazine in 1840, "but it is by laughing that I have lived to grow old." In Smith's formulation, "animal laughter" was produced by a "healthy and hearty organization [of body and mind]" from which it flowed in copious streams. Less healthy organisms laughed less. Mental and physical health arose in tandem from a certain kind of laughter, not wit or satire but the spontaneous, boisterous hilarity produced by "high animal spirits."

But the links between animal spirits and amoral animality—sheer, unbridled energy—meant that the meanings of animal spirits would remain enveloped in moral ambiguity. Animal spirits were a force for health and well-being, for entertainment, pleasure, and beauty—but they were sometimes just a force, one that needed to be tamed. This view reflected growing concerns with hooliganism and mob violence in cities. The mushrooming of urban populations, the proliferation of (actual or imagined) hard-drinking immigrants in street-corner saloons, the rise of mass politics, the lurches and shudders of a business cycle increasingly based on "trading in the air"—all these developments intensified the ambiguous potential of animal spirits, as both threat and promise. Animal spirits fostered essential vitality but also hovered behind the visions that increasingly haunted the respectable American's imagination—in politics, a mobocracy manipulated by demagogic animal magnetizers; in commerce, a swarm of traders enveloped in oscillations of elation and panic. A universe pulsating with invisible forces manifested itself in the volatility of public life. Wherever one looked, the potential for collective madness loomed. And whatever one's theory of the universe, the immediate source of public unrest was the private anxiety of individuals, rooted in the everyday uncertainties of a paper-money economy.

4

Feverish Finance, Revival Religion, and War

SURVEYING THE NEWSPAPERS of the antebellum decades, one finds scattered but growing complaints about the excessive seriousness of the young republic, the inability of Americans to let go, to have fun. A deficiency of animal spirits led to the absence of play. Men especially seemed to channel all their available energies into moneymaking, though sometimes with a dash of moral ambivalence. The flood of emotional force drained away into trade was intensified by the ubiquity, uncertainty, and invisibility of forces promoting rise or ruin. As the Wall Street wag Frederick Jackson put it, panics called to mind the old riddle about smoke—"a houseful, a hole full, and you cannot gather a bowlful." For good or ill, there was no such thing as an economics profession, and no understanding or expectations of a business cycle. Yet by the 1830s, it was beginning to be clear that lurches from boom to bust were accompanied by comparable swerves in the public mood from overweening confidence to crippling anxiety. A few observers suspected that the economic developments were preceded, even triggered, by the emotional developments.

Such suspicions were reinforced by emerging popular wisdom regarding the role of confidence in economic affairs. It was beginning to be recognized as a crucial invisible force animating the new world of buying and selling—where appearances, apparently, were everything. Self-confidence reinforced one's capacity to inspire confidence in others, and this was increasingly a key to success in commercial life. In 1843, the New York *New Mirror* mused on the importance of timely eating during the day to maintain animal spirits, which helped M. Toutavous, a French importer, to "keep his system alert and lively." He "impresses everyone whom he sees with the idea that he is born to good fortune and has the look of it, and is a good fellow with no distrust of his credit or of himself." The apparently hard realities of competitive commerce were dependent on the vagaries of an evanescent collective mood, which in turn shaped the availability, indeed the very possibility, of that vital force called credit.

During the early 1800s, like more developed capitalist societies on both sides of the Atlantic, the United States became a society where business transactions required engagement with invisible, immaterial entities. The first step down this road was the growing tendency to use paper banknotes rather than metal coins. The banknotes were issued by the Bank of the United States as well as increasingly by state and local banks (especially after Andrew Jackson vetoed the renewal of the bank's charter in 1832); they were easily altered or counterfeited promissory notes that the holder might or might not be able to redeem in hard currency; and their value fluctuated wildly depending on how much confidence the issuing bank could inspire by reputation and actual practice. Banknotes epitomized the immateriality and uncertainty at the heart of the emerging market society.

In 1815, the *Intellectual Regale, or Ladies' TEA Tray* caught the new mutability of money in a first-person jeu d'esprit called "Adventures of a Bank Note" named Change Buck. His chief quality, Change said, was an inclination toward "blowing—this swelling of the cheeks and distortion of the countenance is undoubtedly very graceful, there is sublimity in it, suitable to the union of riches and ignorance, and it is as necessary to an overgrown trader, or stock jobber, as a chaise and country-house are to him who has been in business six months." Paper money was part of the package of manipulated surfaces proving essential to commercial success. Yet the package kept changing. The volatility of paper-credit instruments meant they could ride, or be blown about by, the winds of opinion. No wonder old-school republicans like John Adams and James Madison, who idealized a deferential society characterized by virtuous community and implicit hierarchy, fretted about paper money "destroying that confidence between man and man, by which resources one may be commanded by another," as Madison told the Virginia Assembly early in his career. Paper money portended a world in constant flux, where no one knew where he stood, socially or economically. It was also a world where even the most substantial commodities—a carload of cotton, say—could gain or lose value in accordance with mysterious changes in public emotional temperature.

When stock prices soared to dizzying heights and then collapsed as suddenly, the population's sense of bafflement amid madness was nearly universal. Americans had next to no experience with market volatility, and economic thought was largely the province of clerical economists—the Baptist president of Brown, Francis Wayland; the Unitarian Rev. Orville Dewey, and others. All of these men were heirs of Dwight, defenders of evangelical rationality. Their orderly worldview was less compatible with life under finance capitalism than was the vitalist vision of a pulsating universe.

Amid the feverish fluctuations of the market, the clerical economists produced warmed-over versions of Adam Smith, with the same emphasis on steady work leading to gradual betterment and the same inattention to finance capital. To the extent they acknowledged the possibility of investing in the stock market, they implicitly advised buying and holding sound assets and waiting for dividend checks. But mostly they papered over the vagaries of the market with the rhetoric of Protestant morality. And when panic struck, they contented themselves with conventional denunciations of speculators.

The brittleness of clerical economic thought portended moral and intellectual fault lines in the evangelical rationalist consensus. The dualist hierarchy of spirit over flesh sanctioned an ethic of mastery that reached beyond the self to the wider world. But more than a few men and women found the ethic of mastery oppressive and sought release from it—in drugs, alcohol, and, increasingly, invalidism. What the neurologist George Miller Beard would call "neurasthenia" in *American Nervousness* (1881) was already making inroads among educated and affluent Protestants. Neurasthenics suffered from many ailments, but their common theme was a mysterious passivity, a loss of will. One way out was to seek liberating communion with the currents of vitality that animal magnetizers, mesmerists, electrotherapists, and other healers seemed to be discovering everywhere in the cosmos. All these forces were invisible, odorless, tasteless, and powerful. And they had these characteristics in common with credit, the energy that kept capital flowing, or failed to, that transformed the investor's feelings into instruments of prosperity or panic. Traders and investors, like invalids in search of regeneration, inhabited a pulsating universe—where they could experience jolts of enlivening or exhausting force.

COTTON FEVER

Through the 1810s, land speculation in the West, intensified in the Southwest by a cotton boom, kept American economic expansion at white heat. Dreams of sudden wealth fired the imaginations of planters in the old tobacco states—Maryland, Virginia, North Carolina—where land was leached out and crops weren't bringing what they once had. Even though U.S. participation in the international slave trade had ended in 1808, within U.S. borders the trade began to intensify, as tobacco planters sold off slaves at top dollar to cotton planters in the Mississippi Valley. A commodity futures market did not officially appear until mid-century, but from the outset the cotton prices rose and fell in expectation of future gain.

For eastern planters, selling slaves, no matter how lucratively, could not scratch the speculative itch the way heading west to the Cotton Kingdom could. In eastern North Carolina in 1817, the planter James Graham wrote to his friend Thomas Ruffin: "The *Alabama Feaver* rages here with great violence and carries off vast numbers of our Citizens." At about the same time, James Henry Hammond of South Carolina confessed, "I have been trying to get over my desire for a western plantation, but every time I see a man who has been there it puts me in a fever . . . I must go West and plant."

The language of "fever" revealed the presence of what Keynes would later call animal spirits—not merely a willingness but an eagerness to plunge into an unpredictable investment, leveraging the move by taking on debt. Fever was a bodily, physiological condition, yet it was also emotional, immaterial. Animal spirits revealed the same ambiguous blend of mind and matter. The collapse of cotton prices in 1819 forced heavily indebted planters into desperate straits—selling off land and slaves, facing foreclosure. Yet what became known as the Panic of 1819 was not a single event or even a series of events, and it was not just about cotton; it developed over several years and involved widespread but interrelated events—an industrial downturn spreading from northeast to northwest in 1815–1817; a banking crisis in 1818, when local and state banks discovered they had inadequate reserves to cover depositors' demands; and finally the cotton bust of 1819.

Most people, even the major players, had no conception of these vast interrelationships, this big picture. Their lives were being transformed by decisions made in distant cities, under circumstances they could not control nor even imagine. No wonder they referred to economic troubles in terms borrowed from physical illness—the "fevers" of migration and land investment, the "dropsical fulness" of inflated paper currency, the financial "disease" (as John Quincy Adams called it) for which the only cure was "time and patience." In September the *Boston Patriot* recorded the disappearance of animal spirits from that city, which "presents a dull and uncheery spectacle—silence reigns in the streets and gloom and despondency in every countenance." The departure of animal spirits allowed the triumph of fear, mistrust, immobility.

The land and cotton bubbles began haltingly and gradually to reinflate by the early 1830s, yet a mood of uncertainty persisted—about prices, which could never be predicted accurately, and about motives, which could rarely be ascertained in a commercial world where social encounters were fleeting and anonymous. Antebellum Americans were increasingly wary of confidence men. An emerging advice literature purported to show (in the words of one guide) how to distinguish legitimate tradesmen from sharpers and shavers with their "keen sharp features, rapid eye, and general attitude of the gamester intent on his play." Yet the decision to invest was often based on trust in distant trade partners whom the investor might never see. As the historian Jessica Lepler has observed, by the 1830s confidence was more than trust of individuals; it had become, she writes, "that mysterious invisible energy that keeps all financial bodies snug in their proper orbits." In this it resembled animal magnetism: as the pulsating power at the heart of the commercial universe, confidence generated credit—the capacity to use money without actually possessing it.

As British textile manufacturers began to pay unprecedently high prices for cotton, they created renewed incentives for westward migration, for planting more cotton, for buying more slaves on credit. Under these circumstances, banks performed the classic conjuring trick at the core of commercial society: by extending credit, they could multiply the amount of currency in circulation, at least as long as the people who held the banknotes trusted the promise to pay the amount printed on them. Since nationally bounded banknotes could not be used to pay debts to British companies and banks, American banks supplemented banknotes with foreign bills of exchange—promises to pay pounds sterling in specie. What was called the discount rate covered the cost of shipping the bills, reflected demand for them in various local money markets, and assessed the likelihood that the bill would be paid. The last issue revealed the centrality of confidence to the maintenance of prosperity.

When President Jackson rejected the rechartering of the Bank of the United States in 1832, he called it a "monster," asserting it held "titanic and unnatural power" over commerce. His attack anticipated post–Civil War denunciations of monopoly corporations, but its most immediate effect was to accelerate the spread of state-chartered banks with lower reserve requirements and looser lending policies. Paper banknotes proliferated across the land as never before, and as Lepler writes, "confidence performed the alchemy of transforming paper into gold." Faith in paper fostered the animal spirits of feverish investors.

The problem was that no one could be certain how long the paper would remain golden—just as no one could tell how long commodity prices would continue rising. And uncertainty bred anxiety. In his novel *The Perils of Pearl Street* (1834), Asa Greene described a young clerk who saved enough from his wages to join two partners in a speculation on cotton. In Liverpool, its price was high, and going higher. But the Americans would not know the selling price until the deal was consummated and word came from Liverpool to confirm the sale. Word was that prices were still rising, and when the partners were offered "a very considerable advance" on their cotton, they turned it down, expecting the prices to keep rising. Winds were contrary, and the packet from Liverpool was delayed for a month. "In that time," said the clerk/speculator, "what a mighty change on the cotton market might take place. How prodigiously the article might rise! Or again, how shockingly it might fall! Ah, there was the rub. Had we been certain of its rising, we might have gone to bed and slept comfortably. But the uncertainty kept us awake." In the event, the price of cotton fell "shockingly," and the boys were left berating themselves for not selling when they had the chance.

The sleepless nights and self-blame of speculators were part of a broader pattern of mental unrest that enveloped the emerging world of finance capital. By 1834, the phrenologist Andrew Combe could announce that "sudden changes of fortune, whether good or bad, are known to excite cerebral disease and insanity." Yet two years later, as western land prices continued to soar, the dark side of the boom remained concealed, and in Manitowoc, Wisconsin, among other places, local observers reported that "speculators went to bed at night hugging themselves with delight over the prospect that the succeeding morning would double their wealth." Still, Jackson was worried about the prospect of bank failures arising from inadequate reserves. In July 1836, he issued the Specie Circular, which required that federal lands must be purchased in gold or silver. This was a draconian restriction of credit. At about the same time, the Bank of England tightened credit too; it had furnished loans for U.S. westward expansion, but its directors had grown concerned about their own dwindling specie reserves. New York banks followed suit. Meanwhile, the overexpansion of the cotton market led to stagnation, decline, and the eventual collapse of cotton prices.

In December 1836, amid gathering gloom, a protracted calm over the Atlantic made the Liverpool packets two weeks late, creating a pause in the frenetic money markets. While investors waited for wind, Nicholas Biddle, who headed the institution still called the Bank of the United States, though it was much reduced in power, wrote a letter to John Quincy Adams—the previous president and now U.S. congressman from Massachusetts, with a reputation for probity and prudence. Biddle endorsed the Bank of England and the soundness of British finance generally. When Adams released the letter to the New York papers, it "infused a species of confidence into the public mind, that operates exactly like a strike of galvanism," as the New York *Herald* reported. Galvanism was frequently associated with animal magnetism, and both were used in efforts to regenerate failing bodies and minds. But the regeneration bred by the Biddle letter was short-lived. Fluctuating news from Great Britain created corresponding market fluctuations in the United States, and by New Year's Eve 1836, the *Herald* lamented the ubiquitous sight of "people losing their senses."

The next day, the Unitarian Rev. Jason Whitman confirmed from his pulpit in Portland, Maine, what everyone in his congregation already knew. "The care-clouded countenance and the anxiously hurried step, of almost any man of business you may meet, proclaim, in language that, if not audible, is perfectly intelligible, that times are hard, that money is scarce." The scarcity of money, for Whitman, stemmed from psychic rather than economic sources. The current anxiety displayed by men of business was the contrapuntal mode of the reckless euphoria that preceded it. The hard times stemmed from the unhinged discontent and desire of the speculator: "He begins to grow dissatisfied with his moderate but regular gains, to feel the first faint promptings of a restless haste to be rich . . . Young merchants and merchants, who for years have pursued the even tenor of their way, gradually amassing wealth; have caught the spirit, have felt the restless haste to be rich, have plunged into the current, and have fallen prostrate before the pressure of the times." What was striking about Whitman's account was the central role it assigned to the human imagination—to fantasies of sudden wealth and their calamitous consequences. Smith's ideal tradesman, in patient pursuit of betterment, had somehow become a maniac rushing pointlessly from pillar to post.

By the spring of 1837, fantasy had failed and uncertainty prevailed. No one knew who was solvent and who was not—not even (sometimes) with respect to one's own affairs, let alone those of one's fellow investors. Every transaction was clouded with suspicion. As the political economist Condy Raguet observed: in a panic, "everybody is afraid to trust his neighbor." Fearfulness undermines trust, the basis of credit—the oil that keeps the mechanisms of money production humming. Without oil, the mechanisms seize up, or fly apart.

Again, the crisis unfolded slowly over time, in various rates at various places. No one knew what to call it. "In one word, excitement, anxiety, terror, panic, pervades all classes and ranks," the *National Intelligencer* announced in April 1837. Amid emotional turmoil, "one word" quickly generated four: "excitement, anxiety, terror, panic"—the situation would not sit still. Anxiety spread as rumors of bank and other business failures were printed uncritically in the penny press. The Panic of 1837 was not a single event but a cascading collapse that seemed beyond human control—thus the resort, as in 1819, to biological and meteorological metaphors. One failing businessman, Joseph Shipley, described the panic as a "general wreck," an unpredictable disaster, as he noted the centrality of chance in keeping Baring's and other major financial houses afloat. What most observers shared was a sense of the invisibility, even unreality of the forces at work in unraveling the social fabric. As the Unitarian Rev. Andrew Preston Peabody noted with some bafflement in May 1837, solid goods—specie, real estate, merchandise—have not disappeared; but "credit, a mere creature of public faith and general good will, is undermined and crushed." It was easy for some ministers to revert from something as evanescent as credit to the familiar language of individual sin, and greedy speculators were an easy target. But many clergymen moved from moral to psychological grounds, warning their congregations against spreading uncorroborated rumors and free-flowing hysteria. "Increase not a general panic by unreal terrors," said Peabody.

Terrors, real and unreal, swept through masses of people, and mass panic sometimes had dramatic individual consequences. Solomon Andrews, a cotton speculator in flight from bankruptcy, absconded from Mobile in the middle of the night and was captured on a steamboat headed north, where he was charged with defrauding his creditors. His lack of a poker face, his open, abject fear, suggested to witnesses that he was not all right in the head—"Andrews is a very timid man and his fear [of a violent mob of creditors] very easily alarmed," said one. Even if they managed to escape vengeful creditors, absconding debtors were often overcome with a "load of disappointment and remorse," as a judge put it, summarizing a deathbed letter from one of them. Another, Theodore Nicolet of New Orleans, descended into "a mire of debt and fear" before committing suicide.

Despite newspapers' claims that the panic was universal, some groups were more susceptible than others. "The merchants are the most excitable class of men in the world," observed the New York patrician Philip Hone: emotionally they were either "in the garret or in the cellar." The stock market merely reflected these mercurial mood swings; indeed it was "the mercury in the thermometer of public opinion"—and public opinion, as Hone and other elite Americans agreed, was perversely unpredictable. On May 6, 1837, a delegation of New York merchants returned from Washington after a failed plea for help to President Martin Van Buren. As Hone recorded, "under strong excitement," they organized a meeting to plan their next move. Hone worried: "It is a dangerous time for such a meeting—combustibles enough are collected to cause an awful conflagration. Men's minds are bent upon mischief; ruin and rashness. Distress and despair generally go together, and a spark may blow us up." Yet it would be a mistake to take such fretfulness as precise empirical description. Hone's language often betrayed his class blinders, as Lepler observes. Describing a run on a New York savings bank, Hone labeled depositors' behavior "madness" when in fact it was perfectly reasonable from the point of view of individual self-protection. These sorts of assumptions afflicted elite assessments of economic crises throughout the nineteenth century, when "the madness of crowds" was too easily invoked to dismiss understandable desperation among ordinary people.

In June 1837, panic began to subside in London. Investors moved beyond "despondency" toward "a much more tranquil feeling," *The Times* of London reported. Traders began to bestir themselves, asset prices to increase. But *The Times* warned that this surface recovery did not mean that hard times were over.

And indeed they were not. For years, real estate prices continued to stagnate; overextended individuals and institutions continued to fail. In 1842, when the state of Illinois defaulted on its debts, the novelist James Kirke Paulding invoked what had become the conventional narrative of emotional rise and fall. The people of Illinois, he said, "had been precipitated from the summit of hope to the lowest abyss of debt and depression. It was the feverish anxiety, the headlong haste, the insatiable passion for growing rich in a hurry, that brought them and other states where they are now shivering on the verge of bankruptcy." When Charles Dickens visited the United States in spring 1842, he found gloom, despondency, and desolation everywhere. Five years earlier, the Philadelphia lawyer Sidney George Fisher had dismissed fears of panic: "The Capitalist is the most easily frightened of beings," he scoffed. By 1842, Fisher was forced to agree with Dickens. Economic and psychological conceptions of depression remained tightly intertwined. Amid widespread confusion, a growing sense of collective guilt and punishment for greed began to afflict the population.

Clerical economists—the closest antebellum Americans could get to professional economists—offered little explanation and no relief. Indeed they exacerbated public anxiety by resorting to formulaic moralism. They were at pains to distinguish speculation from legitimate commerce. Words like "mania" and "delirium" surfaced frequently in their discourse, as did "magic." They knew a rival religion when they saw one. Orville Dewey marveled that some credulous people came to look toward "speculation itself . . . as if it were a god, or some wonder-working magician" who drew their minds away from "sober industry" and fostered overweening passion.

For the clerical economists, speculation posed a direct threat to the human sympathy that Adam Smith had declared to be the very basis of commerce. The Princeton Presbyterian Henry Boardman charged that the speculator "must necessarily regard everyone around him with a jealous eye . . . They are his opposers, almost his enemies. What they gain, he loses; and he must lay his plans so as to make them lose, that he may pocket their losses." Playing a zero-sum game, he becomes a "shrewd, cold-blooded operator"—the very opposite of a man of feeling. The consequences could be public as well as personal. Yielding to "the delirium of speculation," said Boardman, "is like withdrawing the balance wheel from a massive piece of machinery. Its movements, before harmonious and regular, become spasmodic and untractable, until in the end it may destroy itself and everything within its reach." Here again, the machine of material prosperity seemed dependent on immaterial forces—fantasies, longings, fears.

But the critique of speculation did nothing to raise the spirits of a population mired in depression. What finally did the trick was war. To judge by newspaper accounts and the general tone of public discourse, the war against Mexico of 1846–1848 restored a sense of national pride and revived the spirits of a dispirited populace. Perhaps equally important, as the historian Alasdair Roberts observes, the war reintegrated the United States into international financial markets. Worrying about another outbreak of speculative fever, a Whig journal warned Easterners that the West was full of "bold and restless spirits . . . ready for any movement that can minister to their reckless manner of life and love of danger and change." Yet the East was full of these sentiments as well, and the trick to sustaining them, as newspapermen like James Gordon Bennett realized, was to turn them toward war as well as commerce. Here was something new: war in the service of emotional regeneration.

American motives for war differed from those of Europeans, Bennett's New York *Herald* observed in August 1845. While the European masses were ready to turn to violence to claim rights denied them by corrupt aristocratic governments, American enthusiasm for war "springs from directly opposite causes," the *Herald* claimed. "We are restless, fidgety, discontented—anxious for excitement—eager for war, not because we are starving, but because we are too well fed, not because we are ground into the dust by the iron hoof of the oppressor, but because we are perfectly free, and call no man master." Whether "we" were all that well-fed after years of depression was open to question, as was the assumption that "we" were "perfectly free." But Bennett's larger point was worth considering: a society that had not been attacked, the majority of whose population was not in desperate rebellion against autocracy, had to come up with novel reasons for fighting. Apart from territorial conquest, which was plainly on elite agendas, popular pro-war sentiment was kindled by desires to escape boredom.

The notion of war as entertainment was indeed novel. It was also disturbing, at least to a few observers, who subjected war mania to criticism and parody. The New York *Journal of Commerce* took the latter option in summer 1845 in an editorial titled "LET US GO TO WAR" that claimed to be advocating war with Britain. "The world has become stale and insipid, the ships ought to be all captured, and the cities battered down, and the world burned up, so that we can start again. There would be fun in that. Some interest—something to talk about." At least to a few observers, waging war merely for fun and excitement seemed a contemptible enterprise for a nation that claimed to be a beacon of hope to all mankind.

Yet all through the fall and winter, war fever spread. By the end of April 1846, Congress was poised to declare war (it happened two weeks later), and Herman Melville reported from Lansingburgh, New York, that "people here are all in a state of delirium about the Mexican War. A military ardor pervades all ranks. Militia Colonels wax red in their coat facings, and 'prentice boys are running off to the war by scores." Despite the New York city newspapers' assumption that Americans were well-fed and eager only for excitement, times were still hard. Especially in the rural districts, young men had few prospects and no outlets for energy. War met both those needs. Not for the last time in U.S. history, military adventure promised relief from lassitude—economic and psychological.

By the time the U.S. Army had defeated the Mexican forces a couple of years later, celebrants of American nationality were agreed on the meaning of victory: it showed that Americans were not a mere nation of shopkeepers, but rather a people of "indomitable energy," hardihood, and manifest destiny. Antiwar sentiments had survived outside the South and West, especially among antislavery Whigs and abolitionists who worried that the war would whet southern planters' appetite for a slaveholders' empire. This sentiment resonated with Christian distrust of war, even among military men. General Caleb Cushing, quoted in the *Anti-Slavery Bugle*, asked a pertinent question about the nearly universal and centuries-old ritual of regeneration through violence: "Are we not also, in the sanguinary wars which from time to time convulse the world, the self-immolated victims of our own headlong passions and unreasoning animal instincts?" But in general, enthusiasm for the sheer vitality—the animal spirits—unleashed by war won out over the fear of unreasoning animal instincts.

Like war, politics became a way for men to satisfy their yearnings for release from depression and anxiety, as well as for spontaneous excitement amid the repetitive rhythms of an emerging capitalist society. Beginning in the late 1820s, the franchise spread beyond the property-owning class to include a broad population of white males. Public life became increasingly charged with furious popular energies, elections became the scene of drunken riots, and conviviality became a component of political success. But commerce was still the main arena for the flow of animal spirits. And the arena was becoming more capacious than ever.

CAPITALISM AS A WAY OF LIFE

By mid-century, market metaphors were seeping into descriptions of body and society. In 1848, for example, an advertisement for Wright's Indian Vegetable Pills in the Tarboro (N.C.) *Press* compared freely circulating (undepreciated) money to freely circulating (uncorrupted) blood—one was necessary for economic health, the other for physical health. In 1850 the *Water-Cure Journal* was describing human physiology in monetary metaphors. "Now, every human being has a given amount of *capital* put into his possession by his Maker; that capital is his vital energy—his life-force," the *Journal* announced. "This life capital may be wisely or foolishly expended . . . It requires years of labor and toil, as well as rigid economy, to replace the capital soon expended in rioting and drunkenness. So it is with the life-force. If by any process of self-indulgence or over-exertion this power is too rapidly expended, pain and distress result: and often years of time will be required to regain what has been lost, even if the most strict obedience be paid to the laws of life and health." The emphasis on conservation of energy complemented metaphors of flow and circulation: one needed to preserve energy to move it. The larger warning was clear: improvident wastrels could exhaust their biological as well as financial resources.

Bodily metaphors reflected bodily reality. In the emerging world of industrial capitalism, various kinds of labor affected the flow of animal spirits and vitality generally, in various ways. Romantic vitalism influenced the young Karl Marx, who reshaped it to suit his developing critique of political economy. As the historian Dipesh Chakrabarty observes, Marx often turned to vitalist idioms—when he said, "Labor is the yeast thrown into it [capital] which starts it fermenting"; or when he described labor power as a "commodity that exists in [the laborer's] vitality," which the capitalist purchases and deploys for profit. When the worker receives his wages, "capital has paid him the amount of objectified labor contained in his vital forces." Capital feasted on life; no wonder Marxists and later antimonopolists would rail against capitalist vampires, sucking the lifeblood from individuals and communities. At the same time, Marx—like Keynes—understood that capitalists required their own fund of animal spirits, not just what they could suck from workers. "It is precisely the genius of capitalism that relies upon the instincts, enterprise, and sometimes crazy ideas (the animal spirits invoked by both Marx and Keynes) of individual entrepreneurs operating in particular times and places," David Harvey writes in *The Enigma of Capital.* Animal spirits animated risk-taking, for labor as well as capital. From the Marxist perspective, the worker's "vital forces" were never entirely domesticated to the needs of capital; they remained a source of unpredictable, perhaps revolutionary energy.

Few respectable Americans paid much attention to the animal spirits of the working class, except as a source of disruption to be managed. But by the 1850s one begins to see glimmers of a more humane approach. As the proliferation of industrial sweatshops caught affluent observers' attention, a few noticed steep variations in the quality of the workers' experience. Some skilled trades enhanced the worker's vitality; others sapped it. This drain on animal spirits, *The New York Times* thought, should be acknowledged on payday. The paper argued that "the effect of his labor upon the animal spirits and the physical and mental development of the laborer must be considered in connection with his pecuniary rewards. This consideration should measure the wages of the employee"—but it did not.

Consider the plight of the tailor, the *Times* suggested, compared with the blacksmith or shoemaker. "All active occupations offer some vent of the animal spirit," but the tailor's sedentary work is "dull and monotonous," provoking him to protracted bouts of dissipation. For the blacksmith, "the ringing rivalry of muscles at the anvil keeps the nervous system in a glowing state of excitement"; but for the tailor, "labor with the needle is weary, close and depressing." The needle trades contrasted with the shoemakers' lot as well. The tailor's work "is a constant drain on his fixed capital of life and vigor, while the shoemaker's daily toils tend rather to the increase than the diminution of his stock in trade; yet the tailor receives no larger wages, no extra compensation for the wear and tear of his working powers." An oversupply of unemployed tailors allowed sweatshop owners to ignore such humane considerations, the *Times* concluded, in a burst of unwittingly Marxian analysis.

By mid-nineteenth century, most Americans—black and white, enslaved and free—were becoming caught in the coils of a full-blown market society. Slave owners, especially those in the rapidly expanding cotton belt, devoured their enslaved workers' vitality in pursuit of profit, even more relentlessly than northern factory owners squeezed the vital force from their own employees. Workplaces, northern and southern, revealed an emerging capitalist agenda: managing workers, enslaved and free, to maximize productivity and profit. This was as true on the plantation as in the factory. Industrial and agricultural capitalists invested in palpable products—guns, wheat, cotton, locomotives—but to get started and eventually succeed they needed the impalpable power of finance capital. Bankers were at the center of the developing market society—extending credit to planters, merchants, industrialists; oiling the mechanisms of commerce.

In the project of getting and securing credit, a free flow of animal spirits proved to be essential, though dangerous. The danger arose from the madness induced by dreams of overnight wealth. As Kit Kelvin wrote in *The Knickerbocker* in 1849: "In the inordinate hope of success our vision is blinded; our ear deaf to the voice that would warn us . . . A fearful leprosy permeates our organism. It is madness! Shudder at the idea as we may, we all have it, a mental element innate." This "mental element" produced the Mississippi scheme, the South Sea scheme—and now, Kelvin sighed, we confront the consequences of the California gold rush: "Mania's haggard face is staring at us through our windows—we meet it in the streets. While it tempts the rich man to an increment of wealth, it lures the poor laborer from his spade . . . throws the golden apple in the path of the husband, and robs the wife of a protector and supporter. Seriously, what is to be the result of the vast Gold Mania of 1848?" For every "bird of passage" who succeeds, "a score meet with indescribable anxiety, disappointment, sickness and death. And yet this untamable spirit . . . is one of our essentials. It is the parent of all our noble and formidable projects and executed designs, those massive battlements of our country which frown upon all inaction . . . I would not deprecate it; rather would I cherish it." The Gold Mania, from this view, was another example of the "gambling spirit" that produced heroic achievement and great deeds in general; this became a familiar threnody in odes to risk. Kelvin merged risk and caution by endorsing "an intermediate state of feeling," a path of moderation. "Shall we follow it," he asked, "or shall we plunge headlong into that gurgling flood that knows neither a master nor a friend?" The alternative to moderation was engulfment in indifferent chaos.

The emotionally charged atmosphere of nineteenth-century commercial life threatened the possibility of slippage from mania or even mere excitement to insanity—which was implicitly defined as a complete inability to engage with everyday reality. As early as 1851, Edward Jarvis, M.D., was attributing this malady to the emotional turmoil induced by the proliferation of new ways of doing business: "There are many new trades and new employments; there are new schemes of increasing wealth, new articles of merchandise, and speculations in many things of new and multiplying kinds. All these increase the activity of the commercial world . . . The consequent inflation or expansion of prices . . . makes many kinds of business more uncertain, and many men's fortunes more precarious. This increases the doubts and perplexities of business, the necessity of more labor and watchfulness, greater fear and anxiety; and the end is more frequently in loss, and failure of plans, and mental disturbance." Prolonged self-surveillance took a heavy emotional toll—one that was nevertheless unavoidable, the price we pay for civilization. Jarvis's argument is in outline the one Freud would make eighty years later in *Civilization and Its Discontents*: the benefits of modernity required a mounting burden of instinctual renunciation.

"Are We a Happy People?" *Harper's Monthly* asked in January 1857, concluding that the answer was no. "We exhaust our energies in the hard drudgery of our daily labor, and when we seek pleasure, which we rarely do, it must be highly spiced to arouse our jaded appetites. Like the dull German baron, who took to jumping over the chairs to get up his vivacity, the American is forced into equally eccentric efforts to stir his animal spirits. When he takes to pleasure it is violent, spasmodic, exciting, and exhausting. We do not know that we have any sport that can truly be called national, unless it be that of heating ourselves into excitement, and cheering our animal spirits by the burning embers of a neighbor's house." From this view, drudgery in office or factory dampened workers' inner spark and left them frantic to reignite it.

This kind of pattern may have characterized flush times, when the verve of investors and traders—if not exhausted workers—was in copious supply, but in hard times verve was running short for everyone. And by summer 1857, hard times were just around the corner. Railroad stocks peaked in July. On August 11, the failure of N. H. Wolfe Company, the largest and oldest flour company in New York, frightened investors into a long sell-off. Selling accelerated on August 24 when the Ohio Life Insurance and Trust Company, a bank with large mortgage holdings, went belly-up, revealing not only the corrupt practices of its directors but also the dependence of the railroad industry and western land markets on bad loans, overextended credit, and poor management. By the end of September, all the banks in Philadelphia suspended specie payment, provoking bank runs across the nation.

Through the fall, investors' confidence plummeted. By early October, the historian James Huston writes, "men, especially in banking circles, seemed utterly possessed by some demonic force." Since British and French capital had invested heavily in American land and railroads, the crisis soon spread across the Atlantic. The emperor of France, Napoleon III, published a letter observing that "*without either real or apparent cause, the public credit is injured by chimerical fears, and by the propagation of soi-disant remedies for an evil which only exists in the imagination.*" He pleaded with his prime minister to "[g]ive heart to those [who] vainly frighten themselves." In New York, the patrician gentleman George Templeton Strong agreed with Napoleon: "The remedy for this crisis must be psychological rather than financial. It is an epidemic of fear and distrust that everyone admits to be without real ground *except* the very sufficient ground that everyone is known to share them." Newspaper editors advised depositors and investors to fight "FEAR" and "unreasoning panic," to keep their heads cool.

That was easier said than done. In a familiar cycle, fearful depositors withdrew funds in specie, and banks consequently had less credit available to extend to would-be borrowers. On October 12, a note-holding mob in lower Manhattan stormed banks, which survived until the next day, when 20,000 to 30,000 New Yorkers swarmed through Wall Street, demanding metal currency in exchange for their banknotes. Eighteen banks failed, and the rest suspended specie payment the next day. Reflecting on the consequences of the crash for working people, Mayor Fernando Wood observed: "Truly it may be said that in New-York those who produce everything get nothing, and those who produce nothing get everything." This would be a major theme in post–Civil War polemics against finance capital, appearing for the first time at this antebellum moment.

The interpretation of the crisis anticipated future developments in other ways as well, especially as panic began to subside, for reasons as mysterious—to most people—as those that had initially provoked it. Explanations fell into existing channels but sometimes broke new ground. Moralists fixated on familiar targets: the "ravenous intensity" of men in pursuit of money, the indulgence in "fast living," and in some quarters the behavior of the banks themselves, as a group of southern Democrats reviled "these vampyres [who] ply their trade of drawing aliment from the pores of the business community—in which they generate moral pestilence with its accompaniment of horrors." Yet sometimes moralism was mixed with psychology. This struck a new note, however confused. Senator Louis T. Wigfall of Texas, for example, announced that "poverty is a crime. A man who is poor has sinned . . . there is a screw loose in his head somewhere." This was aimless, contradictory drift.

More skillful orators avoided it. Rev. Henry Ward Beecher was one. In *A Discourse on the Present Fearful Commercial Pressure*, a sermon he delivered at the end of 1857, he merged psychology and morality with apparent ease. He began by marveling that our strapping young nation, in the flush of young manhood, now "trembles and staggers, as if it would lie down in faintness. What is the *matter? It is want the* [sic] *of air.* The city cannot breathe. What then *is* this commercial air which is so needful to life and activity. It is the faith of man in man. It is natural trust. It is *confidence.*" Like Strong and Napoleon, Beecher believed that the problems were mental and emotional rather than material—crippling fear, "wanton *cowardice.*" Even the worldly pastor felt the need to swivel from a medical to a moral idiom when confronted with a Wall Street panic. Perhaps he was influenced by the religious atmosphere in New York City—perhaps the most marked novel feature of the Panic of 1857, which coincided with the first great urban revival in U.S. history.

REVIVALISM, WAR, AND THE DRAINING OF ANIMAL SPIRITS

By the 1850s, evangelical Protestants—led by Methodists—had embraced a creed expansive in contrast with orthodox Calvinism's. It foregrounded a doctrine of free will—one could choose conversion and did not have to wait for it—along with free grace and the pursuit of perfection. An appropriate creed for an activist society, Methodism sustained the vitalist strain of feeling that had animated revivals in the North American forest, even as its churches began to appear in cities. "The Evangel of Christ is the all-embracing theme. It is the vital force in earth and in heaven," Rev. Gilbert Haven said. "The Cross is the center of the spiritual, and therefore of the material universe." Spirituality and materiality could interpenetrate in the Methodist cast of mind.

By the 1850s, Methodism was at the center of an interdenominational evangelical ethos, which had become regnant in areas of American culture where religion had barely been present a half century earlier. Ecumenical, undogmatic evangelicalism made its presence felt in cities by promoting the YMCA and other civic organizations and by focusing the responsibility of churches for taming the barely civilized masses in the West, not to mention assorted ruffians and urchins in eastern slums. The task was made more urgent by the rising tide of immigration, which flooded major cities with unchurched and Catholic newcomers. For evangelical Protestants, urban America was becoming missionary territory.

Nowhere was this clearer than in New York. By the 1850s, established Protestant churches in lower Manhattan found themselves casting about for new members as their congregations moved uptown. One strategy was hiring lay ministers to attract businessmen who otherwise had no time for religion. But how? Jeremiah Lanphier would answer that question. An intermittently successful cloth merchant who found Jesus at Finney's Broadway Tabernacle, Lanphier closed his business and embraced missionary work when the North Dutch Reformed Church on Fulton Street hired him as a lay minister. He did his best to promote the church with local businesses, hotels, and schools, but nothing really worked until he hit on the tactic that suited his own desire for peaceful opportunities to talk with God.

On September 23, 1857, he started a weekly noon prayer meeting that coincided with the lunch hour, when businesses were closed. Knowing his harried audience, he passed out handbills that read: "[Wednesday] prayer meeting from 12 to 1 o'clock. Stop 5, 10 or 20 minutes, or the whole time, as your time admits." For the first half hour, no one showed; Lanphier prayed alone. Another man appeared at 12:30, four more by 1:00. Lanphier kept advertising. A week later, there were twenty participants; and two weeks later, forty. They asked to meet daily. That was October 7; on October 10, the stock market crashed, and attendance at the prayer meetings soared. In January 1858, Lanphier had to add another room to hold the swelling crowd, and in February another. By the end of March, every church, theater, and auditorium in lower Manhattan was filled during the lunch hour with businessmen on their knees. Savvy churchmen knew how to use the penny press to spread the Word; the *Herald* and the *Tribune* vied with each other in presenting sensational news of the great Wall Street Revival. But the financial crisis kept the fires burning. As the Presbyterian Rev. James Waddell Alexander (one of Lanphier's mentors) announced, God had been pleased "by the ploughshare of his judgments to furrow the ground for the precious seed of salvation." The crash, from this revivalist's view, was a heaven-sent opportunity.

The revivals themselves were hardly the raucous outbreaks that had occurred in the backcountry. A "still, solemn, and tender" atmosphere usually prevailed; it was "more like a communion than a prayer meeting," said Alexander. In April 1858, the *Christian Register* praised the absence of emotional excitement and sectarian strife in the revival, yet also celebrated the tearful testimony of a Unitarian Universalist woman in response to the question "What Shall I Do to Be Saved?" Intense emotion remained a key part of the evangelical appeal: "heart earnestness" was the key to salvation; the believer accepted Christ through the affections, not the intellect.

The joyous affirmation of direct religious experience linked evangelical revivalists with idiosyncratic believers from Mary Baker Eddy to William James. The emphasis on personal experience as the basis of faith democratized religious authority and encouraged women to take leadership roles. Most notable among them was Phoebe Palmer, who soon became famous for holding prayer meetings in her New York parlor, where Christians could feel the thrill of "immediate sanctification by faith." Yet Palmer warned converts against "selfishly seeking 'ecstatic enjoyment'"; an invisible but crucial boundary remained between genuine religious experience and mere excitement. Animal spirits alone were insufficient for true religion. Part of the problem was their volatility: conversion was for life, salvation for eternity. Animal spirits were of the moment, and difficult to sustain over time, especially under challenging circumstances.

This became apparent with the rise and fall of animal spirits during the Civil War. Before men actually started to kill one another, white southerners and white northerners alike gave the impression that they were brimming over with enthusiasm for battle. In May 1861, a Confederate soldier reported from a Gulf Coast encampment to his hometown newspaper in Fayetteville, Tennessee: "Ten days have passed since our arrival and no perceptible diminution in animal spirits—All of us enjoy the novelty of our position and go through the routine prescribed as if to the manner born."

Union recruits were equally game. The Firemen Zouaves of New York City provided a stylish example. Zouaves were regiments (most Union, a few Confederate) that adopted the distinctive uniform and drilling practices of the French soldiers serving in the North African colonies. When the 11th New York Regiment, locally known as the Firemen Zouaves, marched from Devlin's Store to embark on a troop ship moored at the foot of Canal Street, *The New York Times* reported, "the men were in the highest animal spirits, and all seemed happy at the prospect of soon having a set-to with the Secessionists." Boarding to the tune of "The Red, White, and Blue," many sang along and "all seemed elated at the prospect of a speedy departure. Hurried adieus were made; women were weeping, and strong men were embracing each other with an affection absolutely touching." Such scenes occurred often, north and south of the Mason-Dixon Line, during the early weeks and months of the war.

Yet the actual experience of combat must have made it hard to sustain high spirits; within weeks of their rollicking departure, the Firemen Zouaves took horrific casualties at Bull Run, where they were tasked with protecting the retreating Union army's rear. One can only imagine the range of emotional expressions such an experience would evoke, but it would exclude the naïve bravado of untried troops. The troops were no longer untried.

The political ambiguities surrounding the war further undermined many participants' capacity to sustain fervor. As several generations of historians have made clear, the war was not reducible to the kinds of clear-cut oppositions that fire up raw recruits. It was not simply a conflict between unionists and secessionists, nor even between pro-slavery and anti-slavery ideologues. Elite policymakers held confused and contradictory goals, and many common soldiers' motives became or remained muddled over time.

Planter elites' desire to protect and even expand slavery lay at the root of war. But a deeper source was the persistent resistance to slavery by enslaved people themselves, who constantly challenged the slaveholders' regime by running away, refusing unfair demands from overseers, and sabotaging the productive apparatus. They also sometimes rose in open rebellion.

The specter of slave insurrection provoked the southern ruling class to adopt authoritarian measures—to suppress open debate about slavery throughout the South and even within the U.S. Congress, to demand strict fugitive slave laws and a territorial slave code. Since slaveholders had the power to use federal law to advance their own class interests, white northerners feared that a monolithic, authoritarian Slave Power ultimately posed a threat to northern white men's liberties. "Most Yankees hardly embraced blacks or abolitionists," writes William Freehling. "Yet racist Northerners would fight the Slave Power to the death to preserve their white men's majoritarian rights." To be sure, many white northerners (including Lincoln) came to abhor slavery and demand its abolition. But sectional conflict was not primarily about ending racial injustice. As Eric Foner observes, most debates about slavery "were only marginally related to race."

Nor were most ordinary white southerners, despite their own racism, enlisting in a war to defend slavery—or even the racial caste system that supported it. Though some were no doubt influenced by white supremacist ideology to identify with the planter elite, few were keen on fighting for its interests. As Edward Ayers shows with respect to the Shenandoah Valley of Virginia, as the war wore on, few white southerners mentioned slavery or secession; they were defending their farms against "yankee marauders," not protecting slavery or the right to secede. "What are you fighting for anyhow?" Union soldiers asked a Confederate prisoner, a ragged Virginian private who obviously owned no slaves and knew little about states' rights. "I'm fighting because you're down here," he said.

The war, as wars do, took on a life of its own. Ideological clarity faded amid reports of carnage from the front, except among political and intellectual elites. North and South alike were drained by mass death. When the corpses piled up at Shiloh and Fredericksburg, Cold Harbor and Petersburg, both sides found it hard to sustain animal spirits. Grim determination was a more appropriate mood.

Enslaved black people, in contrast, seized the opportunity to embrace emancipation—by running away and eventually by enlisting in the Union army. They were fighting quite literally for freedom, as well as for their own dignity. Both aims no doubt inspired sustained commitment; neither was easily attained. Assumptions of white superiority were deeply embedded, north and south. In 1855, for example, "Thirty Thousand Disenfranchised Citizens of Philadelphia" presented a memorial to the U.S. Congress. They were "colored citizens" who were denied the vote but who claimed to possess $2,685,623 of real and personal estate, to have paid $9,776.42 for taxes during the past year, and $896,782.27 for house, water, and ground rents. "Here, then, is an addition to the wealth of the state, which requires something more than brute instinct to produce." The poignancy of the last line is striking; the "colored citizens" wanted recognition of their full humanity, which required ascension above "brute instinct." Yet most white people, north and south, were unwilling to grant it. As one self-described "yankee" reported on the "Southern Rebellion" to the Burlington (Vt.) *Free Press* in 1862, "the negroes of the South are a very inferior race—of ready animal instincts, but feeble mental and moral power." Full humanity for black people merely fluttered at the edges of the Union cause. As the war dragged on, only one thing was clear: this was not the kind of quick and easy conflict that could sustain a burst of animal spirits beyond its initial explosion.

A NEW ASCENDANCY OF SPIRIT

When the war finally ended, animal spirits returned to the discourse of mental and physical health, associated with the possession of a certain kind of temperament. Those who "are said to have a fine 'flow of animal spirits,'" the Wheeling *Daily Intelligencer* noted in 1869, "have an exalted degree of sensibility; their whole organism seems elastic and buoyant, they enjoy almost everything and life itself is a perpetual pleasure. To exist is to be happy." It would be hard to find a better description of the personality type William James would later characterize as "once born"—at ease in what seems (to the once-born) to be a benign, harmonious cosmos. This temperament would characterize the devotees of positive thinking who followed in the footsteps of the Poughkeepsie Seer.

The war had introduced subtle changes on the fringes of respectable thought. The claims of spirit began to be reasserted more forcefully in the wake of bodily carnage. Movements that had sought to link matter and spirit before the war—phrenology, spiritualism, mesmerism—began increasingly to ascend into the realm of pure spirit after the war was over.

Mesmerists discarded fluids and other material manifestations of the forces they conjured, transforming their trade into the purely mental practice of hypnotism. Some hypnotists still claimed to assert their own will to induce trance in a patient, but many followed the Englishman James Braid, who coined the term "hypnotism" and introduced the practice. Braid claimed only to be setting the stage for subjects to induce their own trance states, through concentrating on a candle, a dripping faucet, or (what became most familiar) a watch fob or pendulum. Thus was mesmerism etherealized, deprived of its magnetic fluids, its sexual charge, and its dependence on submission to another's will. Similar moves toward respectability characterized the later history of other mid-nineteenth-century popular sciences. Spiritualists sought scientific legitimacy, forming the Society for Psychical Research (of which William James was a member). Phrenologists challenged binaries but still subordinated body to soul. While they were materialists in their insistence on tracing thoughts and sentiments to specific "organs" in the brain, they remained committed to raising the human gaze upward and transcending animal instinct.

This sort of strategy distanced its devotees from the sweaty prurience surrounding animal magnetizers and other mesmeric healers. Consider the career of Mary Baker Eddy (1821–1910), the founder of the Christian Science church. A chronic invalid for years, after she turned forty Eddy sought help from Phineas Quimby of Portland, Maine, a "mesmeric healer, who had assumed the title of doctor," as Eddy's *New-York Tribune* obituary reported. Quimby was the son of a blacksmith and had trained to be a clockmaker but was swept away from that path when a French mesmerist named Charles Poyen came to town. By the time Eddy (then Mrs. Patterson) visited him, the *Tribune* noted, Quimby "had passed from the mere mesmeric treatment to conversing with his patients and persuading them their sickness was a delusion . . . he not only helped [Mrs. Patterson] but convinced her he was a mediator between her and God. She asked him to teach her the principles of [his] philosophy and he gave her his notes."

Quimby was a regional celebrity, whose ideas can be pieced together from those notes and local newspapers. "His theory is that the mind gives immediate form to the animal spirit, and that the animal spirit gives form to the body as soon as the less plastic elements of the body are able to assume that form," according to the Bangor *Jeffersonian* in 1857. "He says that in every disease the animal spirit or spiritual form, is somewhat disconnected from the body, and that it imparts to him all its grief and the cause of it, which may have been mental trouble or shock to the body, as over fatigue, excessive cold or heat. This impresses the mind on the body, and the mind, reacting on the body, produces disease. With this spirit form Dr. Quimby converses and endeavors to win it away from its grief and when he has succeeded in doing so it disappears and reunites with the body." Mrs. Patterson became an acolyte of Quimby's, pronouncing herself cured in numerous newspaper articles, eventually taking his ideas and running with them as she became Mary Baker Eddy, the founder of Christian Science.

En route to respectability as a religious leader in the post–Civil War years, Eddy distanced herself from Quimby and the increasingly disreputable practice of animal magnetism—which still depended on the magnetizer touching and stroking the patient, inducing "crisis" followed by calm. The practice sustained an erotic charge throughout. "I denounced it after a few of my first students rubbed the heads of their patients and the immorality of one student opened my eyes to the horrors possible in animal magnetism," she said. Eddy herself was accused of employing "malicious animal magnetism" by assembling her pupils to direct "evil thoughts" against discontented former followers. Meanwhile, a follower of Eddy's sued the malcontents for using malicious animal magnetism against the founder herself. Apparently animal magnetism, like animal spirits, embodied morally neutral energy that could be used for good or evil. Eddy ultimately found that she was better off deploying the vaguer language of Spirit or God.

Part of the pattern of post–Civil War intellectual life was the emergence of challenges to vitalism in new monistic forms. While Eddy eventually claimed there was nothing but mind, some scientists began to assert that there was nothing but body. They challenged the very notion of a vital principle. "Is Vitality Vital?" *Scientific American* asked in 1874. Surveying various failed attempts to locate a physical source for vitality, the author concluded, "As indicating a force inherent to and wholly peculiar to living matter, something sui generis, so to speak, [the term 'vitality'] is evidently doomed." This assertion marked the beginning of a positivist turn, toward the insistence that vitality was immeasurable and therefore no longer deserved any status as a scientific term.

The positivist view acquired legitimacy in many scientific circles after the Civil War, but the vernacular philosophy of vitalism persisted. Animal spirits continued to flow in new and sometimes surprising directions. Though no one could have known it in the 1870s, times were coming when fundamental moral values would be reconfigured and familiar hierarchies overturned. And animal spirits would play a crucial role in that transformation.

5

The Reconfiguration of Value

DURING THE POST–CIVIL WAR decades, the idea of animal spirits floated in a sea of contradictory cultural currents. One of the strongest was the increasing authority of rationalist and dualist hierarchies, often underwritten by positivist science. What were considered enlightened views of human nature shifted away from a Christian emphasis on a common soul of man, made in the image and likeness of God—to rigid taxonomies based on supposedly inherent physical traits, above all, race. This was the pattern identified by Max Horkheimer and Theodor Adorno as the dialectic of Enlightenment: rational methods could be put in the service of irrational ideologies and prejudices; separation from inherited tradition could create new forms of coercion. Scientific racism reinforced hierarchical distinctions between animality and humanity, wildness and civilization, by assuming they were rooted in irrefutable observation and measurement. Positivist certainty reasserted a mechanistic vision of the nonhuman world and an explicit rejection of vitalism.

The rise of positivism was evident in the transformation of biological thought. By the beginning of the twentieth century, biologists had turned their science into a mechanistic, antihistorical enterprise. Evolution was compatible with vitalism, but natural selection as a mechanism for evolution was not—at least not the way it was conceived in the early twentieth century, when biologists generally accepted the popularizers' conflation of natural selection with "survival of the fittest," defining "fitness" as the organism's ability to pass on its genes to the next generation.

As Charles Darwin was remade into a mechanist, Jean-Baptiste Lamarck became a joke: a romantic vitalist strawman to contrast with a real scientist. The German biologist August Weismann epitomized the new attitude. He attacked a caricature of Lamarck by ridiculing the inheritance of accidental deformations (severed tails, twisted limbs, etc.) and ignoring the fundamental point of agreement between Lamarck and Darwin: that the habits and circumstances of species reshape their organisms over time. Weismann debunked purposefulness in nature even as he insisted that variations were not random but directed by utility and movement toward greater fitness. This is the Providentialist version of Darwinism that has persisted to our own time.

Thus were the ideas of Providence and progress married to the strict adaptationist program, which became the core of the twentieth-century neo-Darwinian synthesis. Weismann helped shape that synthesis by creating the "Weismann Barrier" between inheritable traits in what he called the genetic "germ plasm" and non-inheritable characteristics acquired by the body during the course of its life—a muscular physique, for example. This was an idea that appealed to modern geneticists like James Watson and Francis Crick: for them, it meant that bodily changes could not inscribe themselves in DNA. This anti-Lamarckian version of heredity became conventional wisdom, based on the (allegedly) complete inability of the organism to influence genetic material passed on to the next generation. The positivist version of Darwinian evolution offered a potent argument for pushing the vitalist tradition toward the margins of biological thought—which in fact is what happened during the twentieth century, though recent developments suggest that a more complex and dynamic understanding of genetics is beginning to emerge.

Despite the triumph of positivism among professional biologists, in broader vernacular discourse vitalist assumptions survived and flourished. Explaining their resilience requires surveying the intellectual landscape that lay outside the laboratory, especially a new and widespread fascination with the human body and how it worked. The positivist focus on the physical basis of identity had unintended subversive consequences. Pop-science body-talk ("The Body as an Engine," etc.) reinforced a wider and more self-conscious awareness of physical existence among urban populations, for whom the flesh became something to be tended to as carefully as the spirit had once been. Within the respectable bourgeoisie in general as well as a growing army of clerks and "typewriters," bodily experience, direct engagement with the natural world, became less of a taken-for-granted part of everyday life. Sedentary occupations spread. The swivel away from the body at work provoked an embrace of it at play. Among the white-collar classes in particular, the decades following the Civil War were characterized by a growing awareness of bodily needs, desires, and pleasures—as well as a greater emphasis on the sheer physicality of health, beauty, masculinity, and femininity.

This secular resurrection of the body underwrote a reassertion of its claims against those of soul or mind. Devotees of bodily health implicitly but increasingly challenged hierarchical dualities of body and soul, spirit and matter. In Europe, body-worship blended with imperial and eventually fascist agendas for revitalization; in the United States, it reinforced a belated bid for overseas empire and a cult of the strenuous life. On both sides of the Atlantic, the new respect for the body altered personal as well as political life. Middle-class men and women, freed from farmwork but often tied to office routine six days a week, began to hop on bicycles by day and go dancing by night; their more privileged contemporaries donned tennis togs, football uniforms, or boxing gloves. A mania for sport swept the middle and upper classes.

Yet this insistent physicality had a paradoxical side effect: it helped sustain and refashion the claims of spirit. Behind the fascination with the body and what it could do lay a deeper fascination with the invisible force that enabled it to do anything at all—the vital principle at the core of human life, and indeed all life. The sources of bodily vigor were physical, to be sure (diet, exercise, temperance), but they retained a mental dimension as well. Alongside the new fascination with the strengths of the body there was a new fascination with the strengths of the mind, or at least an intensifying focus on certain mental forces that could influence physical life—"positive thinking," as it came to be called.

THE RESURRECTION OF THE BODY

As early as 1868, journalists were congratulating Americans for pursuing a healthy way of life. The Philadelphia *Telegraph* observed that for twenty-five years "a gradual and sure revival of the physical and sensuous, and demolition of the ascetic, the coarse, and the vulgar" had been occurring. The lumping of the ascetic with the coarse and vulgar was a characteristic Protestant rhetorical move, a disdaining of Catholic extremes of ascetic self-denial and aesthetic self-indulgence in favor of physical and spiritual moderation. These assumptions were symptomatic: the secular resurrection of the body was very much a product of changes in urban Protestant practice. In the cities, the *Telegraph* noted, churches had not only learned to tolerate the fine arts; they had transformed themselves "from theological barns into reformatory parlors" that encouraged well-being in this world as well as salvation in the next. Churches added reading groups but also gyms: medicine balls, dumbbells, and "Indian clubs" became standard equipment for urban pastorates eager to become centers of muscular Christianity.

The new attention to this-worldly wellness had benefited both sexes, but especially "American ladies," who had learned "that waspish intellectuality and a swelling forehead pale with an overload of knowledge, cannot compensate for the absence of a healthy bust, a fine flow of animal spirits, lungs that can sing, and limbs that can walk." As Calvinism loosened its demands on the mind, the body could break free from endless self-scrutiny to unselfconscious exuberance.

Still, there were threats to this healthy program, no longer from churches but from everyday business life. No assessment of "the way we live now" in the post–Civil War era was complete without a gesture toward the pervasiveness of the commercial spirit—which was frequently assumed to be at odds with bodily health, especially for businessmen themselves. In the midst of another Wall Street panic in October 1873, the Troy (Mo.) *Herald* quoted a local lecturer, Professor W. T. Thurmond:

"The American people are great utilitarians. The question 'will it pay?' is ever uppermost," he said. "A monomania seems to exist on the subject of money." The result was frenetic activity everywhere: "The animal spirits of our people are constantly effervescing, running over. There is abundant action. Perhaps deeper study, more thought, would give greater consistency and permanency to our free institutions." Precious animal spirits were effervescing into thin air, the mere exhaust from the perpetual-motion machine of Americans' monomaniacal money lust.

The consequence was a joyless way of life, some charged, as they sharpened the antebellum critique of commerce to suit the intensified pace of industrial and financial life after the war. "Fun, mirth, real animal spirits are dead amongst us," the English writer Henry Barton Baker complained in *Frank Leslie's Popular Monthly* in 1878 (after five years of economic depression), "no brightness remains in us, and we are a mere agglomeration of negatives." This nullity was epitomized in "the old-young man of the present day, with his cynicism, his intense realism which strips the very flesh off humanity and gloats on its skeleton, who believes in nothing save himself, and that the whole duty of man is summed up in Iago's creed: 'put money in thy purse.'" Such callow striplings "have not the vices of their great-grandfathers, but nor have they their virtues; they do not *publicly* sin against the proprieties, but neither do they ever sin against their own interests." The benign liberal notion of self-interest had shrunk to fit a narrow utilitarian creed focused entirely on individual gain; bonds of sympathy loosened as tradesmen took to "trading in the air." Or so some observers feared.

Educators, clergymen, and other moralists increasingly came to believe that the soul sickness induced by money mania was accompanied by bodily sickness as well. The furtive, bloodshot eyes and sallow skin of the speculator were outward and visible signs of the moral malady within. Body and soul, in this emerging view, were interdependent—though over time, body became more immediate and insistent in its claims. Protestant ministers democratized and Americanized the muscular Christianity of the Anglican clergyman Charles Kingsley, spreading it from the playing fields of Eton to the backstreets of the Lower East Side in organizations like the Young Men's (and eventually Young Women's)

Christian Association. The celebration of physical energy brought renewed recognition of the role of animal spirits in business success; bodily vigor could animate entrepreneurial as well as military adventures. A vitalist strain could be absorbed into the emerging America of imperial ambition, periodic panic, and unprecedented concentration of wealth. Body and mind could be merged, as body and soul had been.

A key result of that emerging cultural synthesis would be the revitalization of elite white men. Whether its idiom was religious or secular, the resurrection of the body focused at first on the character formation of the male upper class. Football, baseball, and other team sports blossomed on campus, as did calisthenics and other exercise regimens. In 1890, the Harvard professor Charles Eliot Norton told readers of *Harper's*: "The dependence of health and vigor of mind upon health and vigor of body is now the fundamental proposition in every rational scheme of education." There was no greater difference between the student life of today and that of the preceding generation, Norton said, than the attention given to care of the body—most dramatically revealed in the centrality of sports and the "strong feelings" aroused by them. Five years later, Harvard's president Charles William Eliot was celebrating "the pleasures of animal existence" for the *Independent* magazine: "It must be admitted that men are, in this life, animals through and through, whatever else they may be." This was certainly evident in the young men of Harvard. Yet there was still the necessity of maturation beyond the strictly animal stage, Eliot later observed: "It is a happy thing to have in youth what are called animal spirits—a very descriptive phrase; but animal spirits do not last even in animals; they belong to the kitten or puppy stage."

What became the prevailing wisdom was articulated by Henry Wade Rogers, the president of Northwestern University, in 1893. The decades since the war, he said, had seen the transformation of American students from young hooligans and loutish pranksters into "well-behaved men and women"; this was in part because "students work off their excess of animal spirits on the athletic field and in the gymnasium." Despite the argument that college sports promoted campus rowdyism, the collegiate athletic scene was generally held to be as benignly transformative as the bicycle, which, as *The San Francisco Call* predicted in 1896, might even "cure our American nervousness"—the mysterious lassitude and "lack of nerve force" that the neurologist George Miller Beard had christened "neurasthenia" in 1880 and that had plagued "brain workers" for decades. Physical regeneration might well breed psychic and even moral regeneration, promoting "a desirable step in the evolution and dignity of our National temperament," the *Call* concluded.

The most effective instruments of regeneration were the Protestant voluntary associations, led by the YMCA. Spurning denominational controversy and didactic entreaties, they met the malleable youth on his own turf: his pagan joy in his own bodily energy. As a writer in *The Outlook* observed in 1905: "The ordinary youth exhibits his paganism most obviously by his animal spirits. The association, instead of trying to suppress his paganism, "sets to work to direct it" in the gymnasium. That building "writes in stone and wood, brick and steel, an article of [the association's] distinctive creed: 'we believe in the body.'" The consequence of this belief was nothing less than "a new interpretation of Christianity . . . which concerns not merely what a man calls his soul, but his whole life." Muscular Christianity, it turned out, was far more than just another effort to reform errant boys—girls soon became part of its agenda too—and far more than merely a shrewd adaptation of Protestant values to a secular, urban environment. It involved a fundamental reordering of priorities and beliefs.

The resurrection of the body was part of a broad challenge to hierarchical binaries in general: civilization and wildness, work and play. In these stirrings we see the beginnings of a reconfiguration of value (if not quite the kind of seismic shift Nietzsche referred to as a transvaluation of value). It involved a half-conscious, fitfully articulated revaluation of those "others" outside the fraternity of respectable white males: animals, children, women, dark-skinned people, even (sometimes) criminals. This did not mean admission to full equality, but rather admiration for what respectable white males feared they lacked: animal spirits.

At bottom the reconfiguration of value involved a revaluation of animal life—and particularly wild animal life, the kind civilized people were supposed to tame. It is not coincidental that the "wild card" was introduced into poker by Americans at about the same time—the 1870s and after—that wildness in nature was being systematically tamed and paradoxically revalued as something precious that was about to disappear. In poker, the wild card could be whatever the player who was dealt it wanted it to be to strengthen his hand; it was not a disruptive force to be controlled (like other forms of wildness) but an escape hatch from the constraints posed by the regular rules—a portal of entry into a realm of pure potential, where anything could happen. It would be hard to find a more appropriate symbol for an era when Americans were beginning to feel their sense of boundlessness constrained by new forms of organization, even as they glimpsed new vistas of limitless possibility.

In revaluing wildness, the wild card recast the qualities traditionally associated with brute creation—animal passion, animal instinct, animality in general. Before the late nineteenth century, British Victorians and their American contemporaries used the animal world as a screen for projecting conventional values—against wildness, for domesticity, for obedience. But by the 1880s and '90s, the meanings of animality became significantly more complex, portending what ultimately became a decisive shift in cultural values. This required the dismantling of what, for a long time, had seemed to be common sense.

THE COMPLICATION OF ANIMALITY

The mid-Victorian world picture was deceptively simple. As the historian Harriet Ritvo observed some years ago, the notion of an animal kingdom created an imaginary domestic commonwealth where the best animals were industrious and docile, and the worst declined to serve or even challenged human supremacy. The impact of Darwin on this scheme was minimal. In *The Descent of Man* (1871), he made what one might have thought a subversive claim: "there is no fundamental difference between man and the higher animals in their mental faculties." Yet Anglo-Americans, even those who considered themselves Darwinians, continued to assume human superiority. Indeed, in the wake of Darwin's discoveries, nonbelievers found themselves embracing human centrality even more tightly. With God gone, the source of human preeminence lay within. As Ritvo writes: "Ironically, by becoming animals, humans appropriated some attributes formerly reserved for the deity"—the capacity, for example, to become the unmoved mover, the sole source of development in the universe. The divinization of the human fired the Promethean vision of technological progress as expanding mastery over the earth and its creatures. There was little room in this scheme for an unpredictable, animated universe. Positivistic science demanded a predictable, mechanistic one, where wildness was firmly under the control of human beings with the requisite expertise.

At about the same time that *Scientific American* was declaring the idea of an autonomous vital principle "doomed," Thomas Henry Huxley, the positivist apostle of Darwinism, was reasserting the Cartesian view of the "lower animals" on an American lecture tour. "Are Animals Automatons?" was the question at issue. Huxley acknowledged the changes in terminology between Cartesian philosophy and modern neurology: "Descartes said that the animal spirits were stored up in the brain, and flowed out from the motor nerve. We say that a molecular change takes place in the brain that is propagated along the motor nerve." But the fundamental Cartesian assumptions of automaticity, he believed, remained sound with respect to animals. As Huxley said: "though they feel as we do, yet their actions are the results of their physical organization . . . they are machines, one part of which (the nervous system) not only sets the rest in motion, and co-ordinates its movements in relation with changes in surrounding bodies, but is provided with special apparatus, the function of which is the calling into existence of those states of consciousness which are termed sensations, emotions, and ideas." This "generally accepted view," Huxley summed up, "is the best expression of the facts at present known."

Yet he refused to grant humans an absolute separation from the rest of the animal kingdom. Our consciousness is just as mechanically based as theirs, Huxley insisted, and "our mental conditions are simply the symbols in consciousness of the changes which take place automatically in the organism; and that, to take an extreme illustration, the feeling we call volition is not the cause of a voluntary act, but the symbol of that state of the brain which is the immediate cause of that act. We are conscious automata." So in the end, Huxley affirmed both wide separation and deep attachment between animals and humans: "the brutes, though they may not possess our intensity of consciousness, and though, from the absence of language, they can have no trains of thoughts, but only trains of feelings, yet have a consciousness which, more or less distinctly, foreshadows our own."

Huxley's admission that "they feel as we do" suggested the emergence of an inchoate challenge to human-centered hierarchy. Rising concern about cruelty to animals was rooted not only in Victorian sentiment but also in empirical observation that suggested animals' behavior was not as easily explained as Huxley thought. Among the observers was Charles Darwin himself, who wrote "never use the words *higher* or *lower*" in the margins of his copy of Robert Chambers's *Vestiges of the Natural History of Creation*, and who resisted efforts to reduce all animal behavior to a reductive scheme of natural selection. In 1883, he noted that some animal instincts "one can hardly avoid looking at as mere tricks, and sometimes as play: an Abyssinian pigeon when fired at, plunges down so as to almost touch the sportsman, then mounts to an immoderate height; the bizcacha (Lagostumus) [a South American rodent] almost invariably collects all sorts of rubbish, bones, stones, dry dung &c, near its burrow." Darwin admitted that there were many self-destructive or apparently pointless "instincts," which could be explained by natural selection only if they were reduced to "the grossest utilitarianism." But from Darwin's time down to the present, most of his popularizers have proven to be gross utilitarians. Darwin could have retranslated Marx's statement "Je ne suis pas un Marxiste" to say: "I am not a Darwinist."

Darwin and some of his contemporaries were less formulaic and more circumspect about explaining animal behavior than most of their successors have been, down to the present. As early as 1869, in the *North American Review*, George Cary satirized a mechanistic understanding of "the mental faculties of brutes" by reducing it to absurdity. A dog cannot wag its own tail to show satisfaction when his master holds up a piece of meat, he wrote, "for satisfaction is an attribute of mind, and if a dog may experience this emotion, where is there any limit to his possible emotions? Neither can the dog really know that it is meat which his master is offering him, or that his master is offering him anything at all, or in fact that he has any master, or that there is any such thing as a man or a dog; for to know is to have a mind, and who shall fix the possible limits of human development?" The tone of impatience would persist into subsequent decades, as thoughtful people remained unconvinced by positivism's parsimonious view of mental life.

Those who took appearances seriously, and looked carefully at animals, were often astonished at what they saw. Alongside the positivist insistence on the automaticity of animal behavior, a newer tendency emerged to see animals as an idealized Other—a spontaneous, vital counterpoint to humans' neurotic anxieties, petty rivalries, and thoughtless cruelty. "The pride and beauty of a brute are never based on the enduring misery of another brute," wrote the English artist and essayist Philip Gilbert Hamerton in *Chapters on Animals* (1877). "The brute creation has its diseases, but on the whole it is astonishingly healthy. It is full of an amazing vitality" that humans might well ponder. "The gladness that we seek, how often vainly, in all artificial stimulants . . . the brute finds in the free coursing of his own uncontaminated blood. Our nervous miseries, our brain-exhaustion, are unknown to him . . . Human happiness may be deeper, but it is never, after earliest infancy, so free from all shadow of sadness or regret." Animals' unshadowed happiness was of a piece with "their absolute incapacity for sharing our higher intellectual vitality." They were unlike us in fundamental ways, Hamerton insisted, and he drove the point home by further insisting that "none of us can imagine the feelings of a tiger when his jaws are bathed in blood and he tears the quivering flesh."

To dismiss such creatures as automata was arrogant, but it was equally arrogant to assume that we could get inside their heads and experience the world as they did. "This impossibility of knowing the real sensations of animals—and the sensations are the life—stands like an inaccessible and immovable rock right in the pathway of our studies," Hamerton wrote, admitting that "it is much easier to imagine the sensations of a farmer than those of his horse. The main difficulty in conceiving the mental states of animals is, that the moment we think of them as *human* we are lost." We could not pretend to cross the unbridgeable gulf between species.

Still humans kept making the effort. As the *Westminster Review* observed in 1880, the discoveries of Darwin raised the question "Do the lower animals, in sharing with man vitality and all its accompaniments pain, disease, and death, share with him also that indefinable unknown quality or essence denominated mind?" To be sure, animals' mental presence was elusive by comparison with their physical presence—especially the big ones. The French explorer Paul Du Chaillu said there was "no grander sight in nature than an infuriated or mischievous elephant dashing through the forest," *The Salt Lake Herald* reported in 1883, then paused to ponder: "Compared with such mountains of flesh, how utterly helpless we would be, but for the superior intelligence which makes us monarchs of all we survey!" The last phrase was almost self-parodically strained and unconvincing. It was not at all clear why puny man deserved the monarchical authority with which he had crowned himself.

Smaller animals also raised questions of kinship, if not kingship. Their appeal was largely but not entirely physical—they were energetic, playful, and full of animal spirits. As the *Wichita Daily Eagle* observed in 1887, just as the fox terrier was always readier for a walk than his master, "throughout the animal world we notice that delight in the use of muscle and limb, which in man scarcely survives his majority, which in them lasts far into maturity." This was why "we apply the phrase 'animal spirits' to a boy who is full of life and energy and who enjoys a run over the hills." Animals and children were thought to share the same spontaneous joy in physical existence; and observations of their play could be used to challenge positivist assumptions. Few qualities—one would think—could have been further from automaticity than spontaneity.

Spontaneity was kin to unpredictability and incongruity, and the consensus view held that all were components of good humor. This was a big reason that humans kept pets, who had long provided companionship (and entertainment) for people, on farms and in cities. By the 1890s the neurasthenia epidemic made them even more valuable as a tonic for nervous invalids. So Olive Thorne Miller, an author and lecturer on birds, wrote in *Our Home Pets.* Antic monkeys, saucy parrots, frisky squirrels were all skillful entertainers, dispellers of depression. "Keep the doctor and the drugs in the background," Miller advised, "abolish sighs and long faces, bring in the pets, and make trial of the cheerful thought cure."

While invalids were adapting pets to new therapeutic purposes, zoologists, ethnologists, and their popularizers continued to dismantle the barrier between human and animal intelligence. "The more exact and extended our knowledge of animal intelligence becomes, the more remarkable does its resemblance to human intelligence appear," wrote Edward Payson Evans in 1898. (Evans was a professor of German literature and journalist who wrote frequently on popular science.) "The attempt to discriminate between them by referring all operations of the former to instinct and all operations of the latter to reason is now generally abandoned," he acknowledged. But while old dualities of mind and matter were crumbling, one side or the other still seemed to be granted causal priority. Those with positivist inclinations, including Evans, came down on the side of mechanical determinism—the tyranny of biological and economic circumstances over conscious agency. "If we could trace all the complex incitements and impulses which lead the assassin to lift his arm and strike the fatal blow, we should doubtless find the necessity of the action as absolute and inevitable as the movement by which the decapitated frog raises its leg to scratch an irritative drop of nitric acid from its side," Evans wrote. Prenatal influences and hereditary tendencies, social and moral environment, and early education combine to form a secular doctrine of predestination "that loses nothing of the awful character by being transferred from the province of theology to that of physiology." From this view, humans and animals alike were caught in the same net.

While Evans's determinism avoided the Cartesian fetish of human uniqueness, it reduced humans and animals alike to mere automata. This was too bleak for most Americans, who either clung to religious or secular claims of human superiority, or became convinced that animal consciousness—like the human version—was more than a matter of mere brain chemistry. Among those who held that conviction, popular nature writers took the lead. Along with a lot of precise observation they sometimes embraced anthropomorphism, provoking the ire of John Burroughs (perhaps the most popular nature writer of all) and his friend Theodore Roosevelt. That manly pair maintained an ethos of mastery, dismissing the devotees of animal consciousness as mere sentimental "nature fakers" who falsely projected human traits onto nonhuman creatures.

Recent developments have superseded their hard-nosed stance. Among contemporary scientists studying animal behavior, anthropomorphism is making a modest comeback, as research reveals the complexity of nonhuman consciousness. No serious researcher wants to project human traits onto animals, but it is no longer taboo to use human experience as a guide to what animal experience might be. The "nature fakers" now look as scientific as the manly men.

Yet not all nature writers were given to anthropomorphic habits of mind. On the contrary: some embraced the trope of the idealized Other. For them, animals were fascinating and admirable precisely in the ways that they differed from humans.

The classic statement of this perspective was Whitman's:

I think I could turn and live awhile with the animals . . . they are so placid and self-contained,
I stand and look at them sometimes half the day long.
They do not sweat and whine about their condition,
They do not lie awake in the dark and weep for their sins,
They do not make me sick discussing their duty to God,
Not one is dissatisfied . . . not one is demented with the mania of owning things,
Not one kneels to another nor to his kind that lived thousands of years ago. . . .

Despite the all-embracing humanism in so much of his work, in this passage Whitman was the consummate anti-humanist outsider, anticipating Modernists like Robinson Jeffers. Other critics of humanity included themselves in their critique. In *School of the Woods* (1902), the Congregational minister William Long—one of Burroughs's and Roosevelt's chief targets—noticed "a splendid thing about all great creatures, even the fiercest of them: they are never cruel . . . When their needs are satisfied there is truce which they never break. They live at peace with all things, small and great, and in their dumb unconscious way, answer to the deep harmony of the world, which underlies all its superficial discords, as the music of the sea is never heard till one moves far away from the uproar along the shore." At some point in his youthful wanderings he realized, Long wrote, "I had never yet met an unhappy bird or animal. Nor have I ever met one, before or since, in whom the dominant note was not gladness of living . . . never a one, great or small . . . to whom life did not seem to offer a brimming cup, and who did not, even in times of danger and want, rejoice in his powers and live gladly, with an utter absence of that worry and anxiety which make a wreck of our human life."

Like Hamerton, decades before, Long was a nervous Anglo-American imagining animal consciousness as a worry-free alternative to an anxious way of life. Yet it was only a short step from a mind full of "gladness of living" to a nearly empty vessel. As Long wrote, "the animal has no great mentality . . . and no imagination whatever to bother him. Your Christian Science friend would find him a slippery subject, smooth and difficult as the dome of the statehouse to get a grip upon." Long's imaginary animal felt no emotional pain because he could not, and rejoiced in his powers because he could not do otherwise. Humans could envy his worry-free existence, but not emulate it.

Projecting too much happiness (or anything else) into an animal's consciousness was a risky business. Far safer, perhaps, to stay with observation and inference—though even here the specter of nature fakery loomed. As Charles Cornish, a classics teacher at St. Paul's School in London, wrote in *Animals at Work and Play* (1904), "they do, in fact, share with ourselves many of the pleasant emotions excited by sweet smells and sounds, not for what they may suggest but for their own sake, and enjoy amusements, exercise, and emulation, imagination, love of beauty, pride in accomplishments, 'hobbies'—such as the mania for collecting art treasures, love of society, family pride, and personal affection." Burroughs and Roosevelt would no doubt be rolling their eyes, but one thinks of the social rituals of dolphins and whales and elephants, or the playfulness of Darwin's bizcacha and Abyssinian pigeon, and the many other sorts of animal behavior that elude reduction to strict adaptationist explanations.

Long himself returned to "the question of animal reason" in *Harper's* in 1905, and this time he directly challenged the Cartesian breach between human and animal consciousness. He began by referring to his own recurring experience, wrapping it in Romantic conventions. On awakening to the sound of the robin's sweet song, he feels "the simple gladness of being alive." "That first moment is like a little child's whole life"—thoughts and sense impressions appear, disappear, vanish again. Amid these fitful currents of thought and feeling, "it would be a very wise man—and he has not yet appeared—who would draw the line and say: 'This is thought, and that is no thought. This belongs to man alone, and that to the man and the robin.'" But Long wanted to do more than merely blur the boundaries between man and robin. He had a larger argument to make, and it pivoted on the recognition that consciousness was neither as straightforward nor as unified as reductionist psychology taught.

The key to this claim was the emergence of the concept of the unconscious mind, and of psychoanalysis as an accepted part of American public discourse. The Americanization of the unconscious turned it from a roiling cauldron of aggressive and erotic impulses to a benign reservoir of high-minded energy. The key thinkers in this transformation, apart from popularizing positive thinkers, were psychoanalysts such as James Jackson Putnam, who sought to build a bridge between religion and psychic science with secular idealism.

This was where Long was coming from, but he took the Americanized unconscious (which Americans often called the subconscious) in unfamiliar directions, toward the forging of another link between human and animal minds. "If the subconscious self be indeed a subtle and mysterious manifestation of mind on its highest levels, then [we] are not moved far away but brought nearer to the animal mind, which seems at times to have knowledge outside the realm of senses, which receives warnings and premonitions of danger, and which communicates with its fellows by silent, telepathic impulses." The existence of a "subconscious self" in humans opened up connections of hitherto unexplored complexity between human and animal minds. One conclusion was clear: "instinct is not the animal, and reason not the man." The inherited dualities no longer held; nor did the dismissal of animals as mere machines. "With the animal's instinct are other things that we must consider—something which looks like will, and emotions of love, fear, courage, and self-denial, which are undeniably like those in our own hearts, however much they differ in degree. Since we share so much in common of the physical and emotional life, it is hardly more than to be expected that the animal himself, apart from his instinct, should share something of our rational faculties."

The phrase "looks like" was critical. It anticipated the current revival of anthropomorphism as a stance for perceiving animals—one that recognizes the distance between us and them even as it tries to understand certain kinds of behavior with a sympathetic imagination. The perspective is provisional; we know what the behavior looks like but not necessarily what it actually is. And we may never know. This point of view was one that many Americans found reasonable by the early twentieth century.

The revaluation of animal consciousness betokened the spread of dawning doubts into a reconfiguration of value. The Anglophone imperial gaze had depended on conventional assumptions of hierarchy, often ratified by scientific racism, to maintain the gazer's sense of mastery over various subaltern groups. But by the 1880s and '90s, even as white domination was being consolidated in the extermination of Native Americans, the establishment of Jim Crow, and the acquisition of overseas empire, the imperial gaze had begun to turn back in on itself, revealing troubling truths about the gazer. He was soft, effete, morbidly self-conscious, perhaps in need of the very qualities possessed by the allegedly inferior subaltern—energy and spontaneity, physical grace and force. As Americans moved from the nineteenth century toward the twentieth, conventional hierarchies of value were shaken and familiar boundaries blurred, as supposedly primitive humans were assumed to share traits with children and animals. What they all had most in common was an abundance of animal spirits, which the "overcivilized" imperialist often lacked. Elite white men sought to extract the imaginary secrets of subaltern vitality, without ever relaxing their rule. Primitivist fantasy served the purposes of imperial domination. "Imperial primitivism" can serve as a shorthand term for this cultural mind-set.

Behind imperial primitivism lay a muddle of reconfigured hierarchies. The rise of respect for animal consciousness combined with widespread racist assumptions to place beasts on a par with "primitive" humans. "It is an arbitrary line which separates the intellect of animals from that of men," the prominent Boston surgeon Henry Jacob Bigelow announced in 1900. "There can be little doubt that an intelligent dog has at least the same thoughts, emotions, and suffering under vivisection as a Bushman or a Digger Indian would experience, and if the humanity which would shudder at the vivisection of a being with human speech and human features is callous to the vivisection of an animal without them, the friend of the animal should go to his assistance." Kindness to animals was more than mere sentiment, Bigelow suggested; it was rooted in the recognition that pain was experienced by all sentient creatures, whatever their race or species.

Besides their overflowing vitality and their capacity to feel pain, animals and subaltern races were alleged to have other qualities in common as well. "Bird music" resembled "the music of primitive man," wrote E. P. Evans in *Popular Science Monthly* in 1893, in that both lacked harmony. "If the harmony or concord of sweet sounds, as distinguished from melody or the simple suggestion of sweet sounds, does not enter into bird music, the same may be said of the music of primitive man and of all early nations. Savages, like feathered songsters, sing in unison, but not in accord." The similarities extended beyond aesthetic matters into what might even be called religious sentiments. "The terror of the dog hurt by the stick was out of all proportion to the pain inflicted, and arose solely from the fact that it was produced by a mysterious cause [the stick]; it was fear intensified by the intervention of a ghostly element, and thus working on the imagination it assumed the nature of religious awe. The case is analogous to that of a big, burly, brutal savage trembling before a rude stock or stone, or a Neapolitan bandit cowering before an image of the Virgin or kissing devoutly the feet of a crucifix," Evans wrote. From the modern perspective, animals and primitives shared the same sort of superstitious fears.

References to animal spirits defined but also complicated familiar boundaries—between humans and animals, adults and children, boys and girls, blacks and whites, street urchins and college boys. In keeping with the popular notion that ontogeny recapitulates phylogeny (the development of the individual recapitulates the development of the human race), children increasingly were seen as little savages whose primitive impulses needed to be tolerated and even encouraged in order for them to achieve full adulthood. Erstwhile savages, meanwhile, were increasingly admired for their childlike spontaneity and exuberance. Primitivist currents flowed in multiple directions, disturbing the dualist hierarchies though not destroying them. And beneath the flurry of primitivism lay a primal fascination with force, channeled and contained by economic, cultural, and political structures—the shifting institutional contours of public life.

THE POLITICAL ECONOMY OF FORCE

During the immediate post–Civil War years, the Republican Party quickly began transforming itself from the party of emancipation to the party of big business. Abandoning freed blacks to the mercy of their former masters, they joined their white southern counterparts in promoting the exclusion of African Americans from U.S. public life. The white male electorate that remained in northern cities was increasingly composed of working-class immigrants exposed to the wiles of urban machines run by barely literate, corrupt bosses. Established Anglo-Saxon cultural elites fretted about the future of democracy, and proposed restricting the franchise to the literate minority (as white disenfranchisers had claimed to do in the South).

Meanwhile, electoral mass politics came into its own as an arena for animal spirits. Audiences could vent them in riotous demonstrations; politicians could embody, evoke, and manipulate them in their audiences. Partisan fury unleashed mob scenes that might well terrify contemporary Americans. In June 1880 the Washington *Star* published "Chicago! The Great Convention." The convention in question was the Republican Party's national quadrennial meeting; its task was to nominate presidential and vice-presidential candidates. The party was torn by factional disputes between supporters of President Grant, war hero and two-term chief executive, and backers of James G. Blaine, a loyal party regular who was known as the "Continental Liar from the State of Maine" to his detractors. One might not think that mere intraparty factional disputes could arouse such fury, but (the *Star* reported): "The adherents of both the renowned candidates vied with each other in roaring like wild bulls, or . . . an immense band of wild Indians sounding their ferocious war whoops at a gigantic scalp dance . . . It was bedlam, and beyond bedlam."

The specter of mob madness was intensified by lurches in the business cycle, which persisted with broader and deeper social consequences. The Gilded Age was bracketed by the Panics of 1873 and 1893; years of depression followed each. As in the past, observers resorted to meteorological and medical metaphors to characterize conditions they really could not understand. Traders, investors, ordinary citizens with a little money in the bank—all gave in, as in the past, to frenzied behavior, mania, and fear. Yet there were new conditions, too. Gilded Age economic expansion depended heavily on the rapidly growing high-tech sector—the railroads. Since this was industrial capital, the contraction of credit for railroads meant reduced wages or layoffs for industrial workers, who began to form unions to protect themselves. From now on, for decades, downturns in the business cycle would renew class conflict. Capital brought state-sponsored violence to its aid; brute force became a regular tactic for the preservation of privilege.

Yet this political economy of force involved more than the assertion of superior power. The railroading of America, as Richard White has called it, was not simply about raw strength; a subtler kind of force was at play as well. The dramatic expansion of the railroads across the continent, as White shows in *Railroaded*, was a classic expression of trading in the air—financing railroads that had no equipment, that had laid down no tracks, that had no existence except on paper. As White describes it, the railroads' influence on settled ways of doing business was profound—comparable to the influence of high-tech companies today. In issuing bonds and persuading investors to buy them, the railroads created a "new virtual world" that was "temptingly easy to manipulate. Numbers and words that were supposed to stand in for things could be changed and still retain their influence; news could be altered or withheld; reports could claim assets that didn't exist and deny trouble that did exist. Altering the numbers and changing the words of this virtual world could prompt actions in the parallel universe where people paid money for bonds." Down to and during the Civil War, most Americans extended or received credit through a system of face-to-face promissory notes, endorsed by the borrower and often by cosigner, too. But by the 1860s and '70s the market in corporate bonds was overwhelming this world of face-to-face transactions by flooding commercial life with "millions of pieces of printed paper" that represented agreements between strangers who might be hundreds of miles apart.

This was how men who posed as captains of industry—Jay Cooke, Daniel Drew, et al.—financed the railroads' advance across the continent. They were captains of finance, not industry. They knew how to raise money by selling bonds: Cooke's brilliantly orchestrated campaigns financed the Union victory in the Civil War; within a few years after the Confederate surrender, Cooke and his contemporaries were deploying similar strategies to build transcontinental railroads. The difference was that war bond buyers were supporting the survival of the Union, a cause with visceral, palpable meaning to them, while railroad bond buyers were speculating on the future prospects of enterprises that barely existed, except on paper. The bonded debt of American railroads rose from $416 million in 1867 to $2.23 billion in 1874—with a pause for the Panic of 1873—to $5.055 billion in 1890. Debt was the other side of credit, and credit was as essential (and as ephemeral) as air.

Cooke's high reputation as savior of the Union helped him attract the capital to create the Northern Pacific Railroad. The Northern Pacific purported eventually to connect Chicago with the Pacific Northwest but during its brief paper existence it ran "from nowhere to nowhere," as Cornelius Vanderbilt acidly observed when Cooke's venture finally crashed on September 18, 1873. This high-profile disaster could hardly have come at a worse time. Ominous clouds had been gathering over Wall Street for days.

The classic pattern of the business cycle was beginning to repeat itself. Banks had overextended credit to reckless borrowers who were unable to meet their obligations to the banks; the banks in turn, having exceeded their reserves, were unable to meet their obligations to their depositors. In what had become (at least to some perceptive observers) a familiar chain reaction, banks and major businesses fell like dominoes as mobs of angry and disappointed depositors milled helplessly in the streets. The nerve center, the originator of the mania, was the New York Stock Exchange. The day Cooke's bank failed, stock traders had already dived into full panic mode, as an anonymous journalist recalled in his *History of the Terrible Panic of 1873*:

> Gradually fevered blood commenced to fire the very brains of those who screamed and howled as though Pandemonium and Babel had formed an alliance, as though a bond of union had been perfected, and high carnival was to be held in their honor. Men grasped one another wildly by the arms; opposing elements jostled and screamed; white hats and memoranda books were slashed through the air by muscles not accountable for their actions; burning brains were cheered by the momentary soother of worldly ills—liquor, and as stocks fell so fell, the drooping, wearied spirits of those who had bulled and struggled in vain.
>
> Shortly after twelve, the presiding officer arose, holding aloft a small slip of paper, and, bringing down his gavel with a vehement jerk, made this announcement: "The Firm of Jay Cooke & Co. Have Suspended!" The wrinkles on many a brow grew deeper; there was a sullen groan, then a prolonged yelling, mixed with cheers; there was whispering of white lips, and a sorrowful, frightened shaking of heads, whilst a score of panic-stricken brokers started towards the once famous banking establishment. In their mad hurry, these stumbled over grimy looking shoe-blacks and persistent news boys, who were announcing, in terms more truthful than grammatical or elegant, "The Cooke's bank are busted!"

Cooke's failure was one of hundreds, but his had special symbolic significance. In many minds, at least, the financial savior of the Union had turned out to be just another confidence man. This was the kind of revelation that could induce real ontological doubt. That was the nature of panics: they ripped the veils of respectability and even reality from the ordinary financial practices of the day; they showed how fortunes based on rumor and fantasy could be brought down by rumor and fear—how insubstantial the whole business could be, how founded on ephemeral emotions. The mob scene on Wall Street on September 19, 1873, made it seem as if a crowd-mind was willing itself into sustained hysteria, imagination run amuck: "Thus, while men rushed wildly from point to point—first to the Fourth National, retailing something that occurred at the Union Trust, then to the Stock Exchange, bulging with what had occurred at both banks, and back again to the banks to empty a budget of romance as to matters transpiring at the exchange—the excitement was steadily maintained," the *History* reported. While ordinary depositors hovered outside banks in uncertainty and anxiety, stock traders were "rendered doubly wild by the announcement of still further failures." In the Gold Room of the Stock Exchange building, men "danced and skipped as though practicing for a prize ballet scene"—a convulsive mirror image of the spontaneous animal spirits that animated risk-taking and underwrote prosperity.

Apart from idiosyncrasies like the ballet in the Gold Room, the Panic of 1873 reenacted many scenes resembling those in previous panics: it provoked similar frenzies and ended in a comparable long-term depression, which lasted until nearly the end of the decade. What was different this time was that the impact of the depression was hardest on industrial workers. These were mostly employees of the railroads and other industries that had been conjured into existence (albeit fitfully and imperfectly) by financiers and industrialists who created a vast web of credit—strong enough to get railroads started and sometimes even completed, but delicate as gossamer and liable to get ripped apart by rumor. When credit contracted, employers cut wages and laid off workers.

The result was that the depression of the 1870s witnessed the outbreak of full-blown class war between labor and capital. In 1877, striking railroad workers challenged the Baltimore and Ohio Railroad's attempt to replace them; they burned boxcars and confronted the men armed by the company to defend scabs and destroy the union. Violence erupted from Baltimore to St. Louis, all along the line. These scenes would be repeated frequently in subsequent decades. Business downturns increasingly had catastrophic social consequences: pitched battles between workers and corporate hired guns or local police, later the national guard or state militia. Federal and state governments put themselves in the service of capital. When the invisible force of credit failed and class conflict intensified, capital had recourse to the more palpable force of state violence.

The cruder uses of force pointed to moral ambiguities at the core of vitalism. Vitality, like animal spirits, was a source of energy that could be channeled in various directions or left to flow. It was not by itself either divine or demonic. When it merged with the celebration of raw power, as it easily could, vitalist thinking acquired a Nietzschean cast. The consequences corroded familiar Christian assumptions—such as the tendency to disapprove the exploitation of the weak by the strong. As Nietzsche wrote, "life itself is *essentially* appropriation, harm, the overpowering of that which is foreign and weak, suppression, cruelty, the imposition of one's own forms, annexation, and at the very least, at the very mildest, exploitation." What Christians condemned, Nietzsche said, was simply "a consequence of the actual will to power, which is precisely the will of life." Exploitation, on this view, was merely a mild expression of the vital principle at work in an unequal world. This sort of thinking exalted a new, amoral sense of self.

BEYOND GOOD AND EVIL

The amorality of vital force surfaced in the discourse surrounding certain public figures. Some were products of the emergent mass politics—"good-natured scoundrels," as the Burlington (Vt.) *Free Press* called Boss Tweed of Tammany Hall in 1871. Tweed, the paper speculated, was Falstaff without the "wonderful wit and versatile intellect" of Shakespeare's character. "Tweed has all that captivating old thief's vulgar qualities, his dishonesty, his lechery, his obesity, his coarse animal spirits, the same disposition to laugh hoarsely as he fattened on the spoils his robber hand has won." Yet he also possessed the "imperturbable good nature" that "seems so characteristic of all the great corrupt in history." These were "men whose countenances always beam with magnetic jollity, whose lips are full of jests, whose hands are as open as they would wish every man's strong box to be." Despite their crimes, they possessed an undeniable appeal peculiar to the new landscape of urban mass politics.

And they were certainly preferable to the clerks in "That Awful State Department," as an Ohio newspaper observed, who cultivated a vaguely mysterious manner, speaking between a whisper and what they imagined was a manly tone, and ended up failing to behave like human beings, still less men. One wanted to ask, "'why in the name of God don't you act like men and be yourselves?' But that would not be diplomatic according to their pedantic notion of the way men should treat men." Given a choice between good-natured scoundrels and tight-lipped bureaucrats, many preferred the scoundrels.

The ultimate good-natured scoundrel was Rev. Henry Ward Beecher (1813–1887), pastor of Plymouth Congregational Church in Brooklyn from the 1850s into the 1880s. By the 1920s he had become the posthumous target of Broadway wits. That was not a typical fate for a clergyman, but Beecher was not a typical clergyman. His career was ultimately clouded by scandal in the 1870s, but for decades before then he was a major public figure, an antislavery activist before the Civil War who was chosen to give the oration at Fort Sumter when the fort was recaptured and the U.S. flag raised over it at the war's end.

The choice was not surprising: Beecher was a magnetic preacher, the supreme embodiment of animal spirits in the American ministry—and the leading Protestant vitalist. Though he never used the term "vitalism," his temperament, ideas, and actions all embodied a vernacular version of that philosophy. His career illuminates its impact on conventional Protestant values in the mid-nineteenth century, and foreshadows its continuing influence well into the twentieth.

Beecher grew up in New England in the long shadow of his father, the dour Calvinist Lyman Beecher. Still, Henry was an ebullient boy, full of mischief and a delight to his adoring sisters. Given the chasm in temperament between him and his father, the ministry seemed a fraught career path for Henry, but he chose it. His first assignment was a Presbyterian church in the malarial swamps of Indianapolis, where he and his pregnant wife, Eunice, moved in 1839. The couple had next to no money and few possessions; Eunice and their babies were often sick; she lost most of her teeth and became prematurely gray. But Henry quickly established a regional reputation as a brilliant orator and prolific writer. Eventually word of him reached the East, and Plymouth Church offered him its prestigious pastorate.

In the fall of 1847, Beecher arrived in Brooklyn. In the emerging media market of New York City, where penny newspapers were on the rise and public lecturers increasingly in demand, he became an instant celebrity—mostly as a result of his arresting preaching style. It involved "emotional soul baring" and "'mental *dishabille*,'" but nonetheless gave an overall impression of "such *manliness*" that more than a few in his congregation (especially the ladies) were swept away by his powerful presence.

Beecher was corpulent and tall, with long flowing hair turning to silver and heavy-lidded eyes that suggested sensuality. In most photographs his shape suggests an eggplant. Still, many women apparently found him irresistible. *Autre temps, autre moeurs.* His manly affect was paradoxically intensified by his rampant emotionality. "The slightest pathos will make his soul run over with tears," observed an early admirer. In everyday conversation, the Unitarian minister Henry Bellows marveled, Beecher "boils with earnestness" and "bubbles with playfulness." Men like Bellows, chafing under Victorian emotional constraints, found Beecher irresistible, too. He combined male and female attributes in a new version of manliness. Yet while his appeal crossed gender lines, Beecher was nothing if not a ladies' man. Ultimately his amours (and one in particular) left him tainted with scandal.

To the extent that he had a theology, Beecher's was liberal. For him, picayune theological debate, false proprieties, and subtle hypocrisies all obstructed the path of Jesus's love—which was the heart of the matter, in his view, for any true Christian. A family friend, Susan Howe, reported to her brother on the new pastor's startling success: "The Unitarians like him because he preaches good works, and calls no doctrine by its name."

When he preached at Williams College, the Brooklyn *Eagle* summarized his message: it was all about "the *doing* of good rather than the *being* of good."

All of this was boilerplate liberal Protestantism, but Beecher gave it a new spin when he delivered his first paid public lecture at the Boston Mercantile Library in 1848. His title was "Amusements" and his thesis was "man was made for enjoyment." One could see this truth, he said, in the catastrophic outcomes of attempts to suppress the human search for pleasure: "You accumulate the pent-up stream only to see it break over the dam with still more sweeping violence . . . You check the flow for a time, but you do not decease the fountain or divert the current to any useful purpose." Beecher's gushing metaphors reflected the vitalist preoccupation with free circulation—of blood, of animal spirits, of energy.

He was also acutely aware of the magnetic power he was able to exert over his audiences. Beecher on stage—he used no pulpit—inhabited a pulsating universe. As he grew more celebrated, even adored by his public, his wife, Eunice, increasingly felt a sense of bereavement when he left home every morning. "The public began to take Henry away from me," she recalled. Soon "Beecher Boats" were crossing the East River from Manhattan every Sunday, ferrying throngs of New Yorkers to hear the young minister preach. A new Plymouth Church, enlarged by Beecher's celebrity, opened its doors in 1850. It was designed according to its pastor's specifications: "It is perfect," Beecher said, "because it was built on a principle—the principle of social and personal magnetism which emanates reciprocally from a speaker and from a close throng of hearers." A wide stage thrust out into the audience; Beecher was surrounded on three sides by his rapt congregation.

This was not just happening in church; Beecher carried his stage presence with him wherever he went. He became used to holding forth, in private conversations and in rooms full of people. On one such occasion, at the home of Chloe Beach (one of Beecher's inamoratas), a Beecher family friend named Mary Hallock Foote got up quietly to slip away. Mrs. Beach turned and said, "Mary Hallock, sit still!" Mary was astonished. "Mr. Beecher was in and out of the house every day," she said, "and still he was sacrosanct. To leave the room where he was in full tide of speech was incredible offense against that homage everyone was supposed to pay him."

Beecher's authority derived from his charismatic leadership of an affluent congregation, his articulation of longings for vitality that were shared by many Americans, and his forceful public stand against slavery. By the Civil War, he was probably better known and more admired than most politicians or other public figures. He was making at least $12,000 a year in salary paid by his congregation (around $400,000 in 2021 dollars), and significantly more than that in lecture fees and book advances. In 1850, Emerson (himself no slouch at collecting lecture fees) bestowed the ultimate compliment on Beecher by labeling him a Transcendentalist, along with the publisher Horace Greeley, the abolitionist Theodore Parker, and the educator Horace Mann—all "men who are self-trusting, self-relying, earnest," and hence (presumably) Transcendentalists.

But Beecher was in a class by himself. Like Parker and other abolitionists, he invoked a higher law to oppose slavery; but unlike them, he also invoked it to push the envelope of Victorian sexual morality. His gospel of love was accompanied by a sanctification of desire—all conveyed in a vitalist vocabulary of psychic abundance and perpetual growth. By the Civil War's end, he was using botanical and evolutionary metaphors for self-development. "The greatest part of a seed is mere bulk, whose office to wrap up the vital principle, or germ. It also is food for the earliest life of that germ," he said in 1865. "So the body carries a vital principle which is hereafter to be developed; and the body is a mere vehicle and protection of this vital principle. The seed cannot give forth the new plant within it except by undergoing a chemical decomposition and absorption. Our savior teaches that this is the law of the evolution of spiritual life in man. Our physical life must expend itself, not necessarily in the immediate act of death, but by ministering to the spiritual element in us." Even if the body was "the mere vehicle and protection of this vital principle," it was also the necessary condition for spiritual growth. It was only a short step from this spiritualized vitalism to a more capacious version.

In 1877, Beecher summed up his vitalist views in a sermon reprinted in *The Christian Union*, the journal he founded and edited. He celebrated "the life force in men," insisting that "this vitality of a Christian soul" was "a force of judgment and discretion" and that "there is no other regulating force like it . . . Nothing is so curative as life-power . . . in all Christian communities there is nothing which makes men so safe as having a life-force in them." The association of life force with safety was a novel rhetorical move, as was Beecher's claim that "if men need regulation it is probably because . . . they have been made artificial, unnatural, by too many rules. Let men have that liberty with which Christ makes the soul free." The liberation offered by Christ released the secular, pagan power of a life force. The marriage of flesh and spirit, denied by centuries of dualists, was once again consummated by the pastor of Plymouth Church, Brooklyn.

Beecher's achievement reached far beyond the confines of his congregation. To audiences throughout the nation, he presented himself as a spokesman for modernity and progress, science and self-improvement, for the accumulation of wealth and the enjoyment of it. And for the status quo in power relations. During the railroad strikes of 1877, Beecher denounced the workers' demands: "It is said that a dollar a day is not enough to live on. No, not if a man smokes and drinks beer. Water costs nothing, and a man who cannot live on bread is not fit to live." The congregation at Plymouth, which included many members of the New York business elite, was no doubt reassured by this moral confidence game.

But even in the early days of Beecher's celebrity, Herman Melville had his number. In *The Confidence Man*, Melville's eponymous antihero ("the cosmopolitan") assumes the persona of Frank Goodman and gets into a conversation over a bottle of wine with a saturnine Alabaman named Charlie Noble. Like Beecher, Frank Goodman surveys human nature with mild approval and dispenses upbeat aphorisms at every opportunity. People are inherently good, and established institutions reflect that goodness. He is especially annoyed by critics of the press (the instrument of Beecher's fame). "In a word, Charlie," Frank exclaims, "what the sovereign of England is titularly, I hold the press to be actually—Defender of the Faith!—defender of the faith in the final triumph of truth over error, metaphysics over superstition, theory over falsehood, machinery over nature, and the good man over the bad." Confronted with the question of temperance, Frank characteristically waffles: "Conviviality is one good thing, and sobriety is another good thing. So don't be one-sided."

The conversation touches on the geniality induced by alcohol and good fellowship, which prompts Charlie to ask: "By the way, talking of geniality, it is much on the increase in these days, ain't it?" "It is, and I hail the fact," Frank replies, launching another paean to progress: "Nothing better attests the advance of the humanitarian spirit. In former and less humanitarian ages—the ages of amphitheatres and gladiators—geniality was mostly confined to the fireside and table. But in our age—the age of joint-stock companies and free-and-easies—it is with this precious quality as with precious gold in old Peru, which Pizarro found making up the scullion's sauce-pot as the Inca's crown. Yes, we golden boys, the moderns, have geniality everywhere—a bounty broadcast like noonlight." All of this celebratory patter is a prelude to Frank's hitting up Charlie for money, which Charlie refuses. Frank, undaunted, continues his wheedling ways until he manages to drive Charlie away.

Melville caught the evasions and omissions in Beecher's creed. A Christian minister who made affluent and powerful people feel at ease with their privilege might well have some explaining to do. But no one demanded any explanation from Beecher until he was publicly accused of committing adultery with a member of his congregation. As the scandal deepened, the Congregational Rev. Joseph Twichell asked Beecher how he could stand the strain. According to Twichell, Beecher said that when he was preaching "he felt strong and dauntless," but that when he was not "he felt—as he expressed it—'like a humbug.'" His critics would have said this was a rare moment of self-awareness.

The scandal had been in the making for years. In 1867, according to two accounts, Beecher either raped or had consensual sex with Edna Dean Procter, a nineteen-year-old editorial assistant at *The Christian Union*. His intimacy with Chloe Beach, a member of his congregation and Eunice's supposed friend, was long-standing and widely known. And his most recent and thorough biographer, Debby Applegate, explores suggestive evidence of his affairs with other women, beginning in Indianapolis. But his affair with Elizabeth Tilton was a thing unto itself. Her husband, Theodore, was Beecher's confidant, protégé, colleague (at *The Christian Union*), and friend. He was also a forthright advocate of secular currents of thought for which the minister could only insinuate his support. Theodore even kept company (and eventually had sex) with Victoria Woodhull, the notorious advocate of "free love." Lacking the legitimacy that clung to Beecher, Theodore devoted himself to speaking and writing in behalf of what he believed was cultural revolution—the end of Victorian sexual and emotional repression.

In the winter of 1866–1867, Theodore left for a four-month lecture tour, asking Henry to look out for Elizabeth; Henry of course complied. Everyone involved (except, perhaps, Henry) seemed committed to what in the twentieth century would become known as a therapeutic ethic of honesty. Elizabeth and Theodore wrote each other extravagant love letters with grandiose expressions of feeling. Elizabeth, meanwhile, vowed to be "perfectly transparent" with Theodore about her feelings for Henry, which were becoming erotically charged. At the mere mention of his name, "my cheek would flush with pleasure," she confided. Theodore kept reading, becoming more and more suspicious and ultimately enraged. The ethic of honesty did not prove therapeutic for him.

Amid charges and countercharges, confessions and retractions of confessions, we will never know definitively what happened between Henry and Elizabeth when they were alone. But Beecher's track record with other women, his furtive (if evasive) admissions, and his unconvincing attempts to claim that his love for Elizabeth was entirely spiritual and therefore blameless—not to mention her confessions, whatever second thoughts she may have had about them—all suggest to Applegate and other scholars that the pair almost certainly had sex. Theodore was convinced, and began to prepare a suit against Beecher for "alienation of affection." Woodhull had caught wind of Beecher's peccadilloes and published a tell-all series in her weekly magazine. By early spring 1874, proliferating rumors, the articles in *Woodhull's*, and the prospect of a trial had begun to tell on Beecher. As Moses Coit Tyler, one of his editors at

The Christian Union, reported: "I found him a gray, haggard old man . . . I had seldom seen eyes and a face expressing greater wretchedness. It was indeed the countenance of a great soul in desolation."

But in the later spring and summer Beecher's friends in the Protestant elite and more particularly in Plymouth Church began to rally around him. In April, Rev. Leonard Bacon denounced Theodore Tilton as a "knave" and a "dog" from the pulpit of the First Congregational Church in New Haven. The Plymouth congregation voted Beecher a substantial increase in salary to provide for his upcoming legal expenses, and did its best to help restore his spirits.

By late summer, Beecher was a changed man. In August 1874, Theodore Tilton sued Henry Ward Beecher in Brooklyn City Court, charging Beecher with willfully alienating his wife's affection and demanding $100,000 in damages. *The New York Times* reported that while Tilton had brought suit against Beecher and would also sue several papers for libel, "Mr. Beecher, so say his friends, laughs at the whole affair, and is in 'better health and spirits than ever.' 'He is laughing and talking all day,' says one correspondent, 'on the piazzas and in the parlors.'" The *Times* was not impressed: "We should be sorry to check this flow of animal spirits, but we are afraid Mr. Beecher may live many years without being able to undo the mischief caused in almost every circle of society by the mass of indecencies poured out by the public in recent weeks." In December, the *Wheeling Daily Intelligencer* provided a follow-up on what had become a national event. Though Beecher claimed he had suffered "the torments of the damned," the paper reported, "he has been able to preserve not only his healthful physical appearance but buoyancy of animal spirits, his equanimity in social life, his capacity for abstract and abstruse thought and research, and his ability to go through with as much work as ever and to perform it just as promptly and as well." Such was the conduct of a "great soul," according to Beecher's admirers, a vital man under duress.

When the trial began, Beecher still looked great. The newspapers, in New York and elsewhere, were puzzled and censorious. Beecher's friend Frank Moulton, who was not religious but who knew the Plymouth Church scene well, had several months before been prompted to perceptive observation by sympathy for Elizabeth Tilton: "We respected her even after her fall," Moulton said, "because we had studied Beecher out and knew him to have a fine mind, a powerful animal nature, and between the two he has got his power. He never could have preached the sermons he has, addressing the weakness of the flesh, but for the animality which drew him into libertinism and was followed by self-reproach. The fact is he has been sifted out of the little principle that he possessed by the flattery of mankind." The last sentence offered the crucial explanation for Beecher's indomitable animal spirits: the sycophancy of his friends. But the focus on Beecher alone, even by someone as sympathetic to Elizabeth as Moulton, underscored her invisibility in the shadow of the Great Man.

As the trial progressed, the *Tribune* reported, Beecher's "great animal spirits, which no amount of work and trouble seem to affect, except momentarily, break out more frequently of late in pleasant and sometimes facetious remarks to friends or court officers than at the beginning of the trial." Finally the verdict—or non-verdict—was announced: the jury could not agree and after three days of deliberation was dismissed. Beecher was neither convicted nor vindicated. *The Nation*, whose editor E. L. Godkin had long found Beecher repellent, announced that Beecher's inappropriate behavior could only be ascribed to a want of moral sensitiveness, which was traceable to the influence of his congregation. "That an excess of animal spirits should at certain crises injure a man in the estimation of right-minded people will probably be somewhat incredible to many of the noisy brethren of Plymouth Church, but they must make up their minds to accept the fact that their modes of expression are repulsive to a very large and respectable portion of the Christian world."

Those "modes of expression" had been revealed during the trial through testimony from various witnesses. Observing it all was George Templeton Strong, himself a conservative Episcopalian who concluded that Plymouth Church offered glimpses of "psychological phenomena" he found difficult to understand. "Verily they are a peculiar people. They all call each other by their first names and perpetually kiss one another." Godkin took the high road, viewing the Plymouth congregation as dupes of Beecher's "purely emotional theology, made up, not of opinions, but of sighs and tears and aspirations and unlimited good-nature." What neither Strong nor Godkin saw was how Beecher's belief in a higher law blended his own need for vindication with the popular belief that humankind was evolving from a lower to a higher state of being—which Darwin himself denied. As Applegate says, Beecher and his congregation might well have believed that ordinary Americans had simply not yet evolved to their own higher plane of consciousness—one that allowed them to endow extramarital affairs with spiritual significance.

Some months after the verdict, in November 1875, the Iola (Kans.) *Register* summed up what might be called the vitalist case for Beecher: "Nothing seems to be able to daunt or check his animal spirits . . . This may be a fault, perhaps, but to this invincible animal force he owes his greatness. He is one of the best poised men in the country—i.e., his body and mind are perfectly fitted to each other . . . Altogether the miracle of the generation is that he could go into such an ordeal and come out of it apparently as young as ever." So the way had been cleared for a new source of human greatness: "invincible animal force." The other criteria were the poised fit of mind with body and the appearance of youthfulness under adversity.

These physical notions of leadership would prove increasingly influential in the decades ahead, as mass politics became more institutionalized and organized, and vigorous young men such as Williams Jennings Bryan and Theodore Roosevelt took center stage. Behind the enthusiasm for youth and vigor was a broader fascination with power for its own sake, with its sources in the cosmos and the polity but also in the individual psyche. In everyday life if not in Sunday sermons, the sacred space once filled by God alone began to include a new, even more abstract entity—sheer energy, impalpable and apparently infinite.

6

The Apotheosis of Energy

AMID THE TUMULT of industrialization after the Civil War, there were more reasons than ever to imagine a universe pulsating with mysterious currents that animated human existence and connected it with a wider, throbbing cosmos. Electrification provided the most pervasive and spectacular example, but one might add X-rays or even what Carl Jung would call a "collective unconscious" that revealed buried affinities between the civilized and savage mind—yet another invisible source of energy.

Henry Adams was the most articulate among many Americans who felt they were inhabiting a new "kingdom of force." As he understood, the fin de siècle reconfiguration of value was at bottom a reconfiguration of the sacred, from Virgin to Dynamo. Adams, who along with William James was the most thoughtful American vitalist, lamented the loss of Mary and all she represented (at least to him): nurturance and forgiveness but also a certain kind of vital force—biologically, even sexually based fecundity. In contrast, the vitality of the dynamo was abstract and technical though the power it embodied (like Mary's) was apparently infinite. By epitomizing energy as an end in itself, the dynamo became

Adams's quintessential symbol of vitalism, completing the reconfiguration of ultimate value from personal God to impersonal Power.

To Adams, recalling the hall of machines at the Paris Exposition of 1900, "the dynamo became a symbol of infinity . . . its value lay chiefly in its occult mechanism," which produced limitless power silently. This was a fantasy—dynamos depended on coal or other fuels that were anything but limitless—but it was a powerful one. Adams's dynamo resonated with long-standing American dreams of boundless possibility, at the precise moment in U.S. history when the sense of boundlessness was being refocused from infinite land to infinite energy. Even the skeptical Adams was sometimes moved to religious awe by technology's empowerment of human beings. The twentieth-century American, he wrote, "the child of incalculable coal power, electric power, and radiating energy, must be a sort of God compared with any former creation of nature." Given this prospect, Adams could conclude that the dynamo was a worthy object of veneration for secular seekers—though he was himself more inclined to venerate the Virgin. In Adams's *Education*, he recalled: "As he grew accustomed to the great gallery of machines, he began to feel the forty-foot dynamos as a moral force, much as the early Christians felt the Cross. The planet itself seemed less impressive, in its old-fashioned, deliberate, annual or daily revolution, than this huge wheel, revolving within arm's length at some vertiginous speed, and barely murmuring—scarcely humming an audible warning to stand a hairsbreadth further for respect of power—while it would not wake the baby lying close against its frame. Before the end, one began to pray to it; inherited instinct taught the natural expression of man before silent and infinite force."

While one could hardly ask for a more explicit redefinition of the sacred, Adams's awe was idiosyncratic. Despite "its occult mechanism," the dynamo was an impersonal machine. Most Americans preferred to pay homage to human embodiments of energy, who radiated psychic power as well as more familiar physical forms of it.

THE UNBOUND PROMETHEUS

Alongside charismatic politicians, another iconic figure emerged toward the fin de siècle—the ruthless entrepreneur, who embodied vital energy in the service of capital accumulation and economic transformation. In 1895, *The Washington Times* identified one such man as "the Savior of Florida." He was Hamilton Disston, "the automatic genius of the swamps," who was by no means self-made. Ham Disston inherited a few million dollars from his father, who had founded a saw company—but Ham increased the fortune with his mammoth land-reclamation projects and the real estate he planted on them. The paper made him sound like a familiar American type—the frontier entrepreneur whose indomitable will drives him to clear forests, drain swamps, and create a thriving commercial civilization from a recalcitrant natural world. William Faulkner's Thomas Sutpen, the obsessive conqueror of the Mississippi lowlands in *Absalom, Absalom!*, is the quintessential literary expression of this character. Like Sutpen, Disston could be cast in a Promethean mold, the sort of titan for whom a $150,000 sugar mill could be a mere "plaything." The *Times* liked Disston's capacity to switch social roles: when in Florida he dressed like a cracker and when at home like a proper Philadelphia gentleman. "He is composed of wire springs, nerves, animal spirits, and electricity" plus "an admixture of good and common philosophy." But above all, the paper concluded, he was a fount of productive energy: "He winters in Florida but never hibernates. He goes there to dig and ditch and drain." This was the kind of persona that American businessmen liked to project—a man engaged in mastering the material world, even if most of his millions came from the astute manipulation of money. Andrew Carnegie and John D. Rockefeller, Sr., were adept at this game.

But above captains of industry in the pantheon of public acclaim were men of genius—not lascivious literati like Goethe but scientists and engineers whose work had practical benefits for all. No one better fit this model than Thomas Edison. He was, some thought, truly sui generis in his brilliance. According to the New York *World* reporter Henry Tyrrell, writing in *Frank Leslie's Popular Monthly*, Edison embodied "a new efflorescence of human genius—a kind of conqueror who stands unprecedented and alone. He has drawn his strengths from the primal elements of nature, and achieved his conquest over the occult but awful forces of the universe . . . his is the godlike power to create." This was the height he had achieved by 1895, when Tyrrell was writing. But Edison had already shown signs of genius when he was a young man working for Western Union. "As a perambulating operator, overflowing with ideas and animal spirits, and restlessly energetic in the exploitations of new experiments," he stopped in towns all over the Midwest and Mid-South. "The ferment of discovery was now working in Edison's veins, militating against the steady, uneventful grind of daily routine." Obsessed with experimental work, he curtailed food and sleep when he most needed them. Marriage brought "sparks of sanity" and moderation. Abstaining entirely from alcohol, coffee, and tea, he remained "a mighty smoker of tobacco." In contrast with the typical millionaire, he created his riches through his own ingenuity and hard work, not by manipulating other people's money; and he sought to disseminate his discoveries, not merely to grasp and guard them.

Edison was indeed sui generis, but he epitomized Promethean fantasies that pervaded Gilded Age America. The unbound Prometheus might broadcast the benefits of his technological breakthroughs for the common good, as Tyrrell claimed Edison did, and he might take his discoveries into the marketplace and make himself very rich, as Edison also did. With men like Edison on the cutting edge of progress, the pursuit of success was infused with a new grandiosity, a new intensity that encouraged the sloughing off of older moral concerns. This was eventually true for women as well as men. As the focus of the success ethic shifted from diligence to ebullience, the very notion of selfhood became more fluid and manipulatable. Willpower began to give way to mind power, self-deprecation to self-praise.

The older success ethic, if it mentioned energy at all, was all about the "energy of will." As the Montpelier (Vt.) *Watchman and State Journal* argued in 1871: "It is energy of will that is the soul of the intellect; wherever it is, there is life; where it is not, all dullness and despondency and desolation." Contrary to popular belief, the *Watchman* claimed, energy of will does not destroy nerves or exhaust animal spirits; indeed, "if the spirits are spent by energy they are utterly wasted by idleness." The deification of will, the horror of waste, never disappeared entirely; William James was enough of a Victorian to make will the center of his "Habit" chapter in *Principles of Psychology*. Yet there is no doubt that the self-help literature of the Gilded Age revealed a subtle change in emphasis, from hard work to high spirits.

Animal spirits became a central theme in this emerging gospel of success. They were a means for reaffirming the celebration of the self, which (some said) had been disdained too long due to inherited puritan habits of mind—particularly the remnants of the doctrine of original sin. "What looks like self-conceit may be after all only the overflow of animal spirits," the Staunton (Va.) *Spectator* observed in 1884, adding that Christians sometimes suffered from a deficit of personal vanity. "Self-Praise," the paper concluded, was not always a bad thing, despite puritanical prejudices against it.

This challenge to rooted assumptions reflected an emerging emphasis on achieving success through manipulation of personal magnetism and psychic power—a strategy that especially characterized professions requiring persuasive skills. In 1889, the *Saturday Review* of London announced that three things were necessary to the young barrister's advancement: "the first was high animal spirits, the second high animal spirits, the third high animal spirits." The statement was widely reprinted in American newspapers. By the early twentieth century, ebullient energy was being prescribed for middle managers as well as established professionals—white-collar workers who depended on their ability to persuade, attract, and influence their colleagues. Much of that ability stemmed from force of will; yet without abundant energy, success advisers agreed, the exertion of will was wasted effort.

Animal spirits melded energy with will, mind with matter. They were part of a broad and deep reaction against positivist conceptions of cosmos and psyche. William James was at the center of this ferment. His radical empiricist perspective took all experiences seriously (including hallucination and despair) as potential sources of knowledge or insight. For him, mind and body existed in a shifting, contingent relation of creative tension and cooperation. Body influenced mind, and vice versa.

In a sense, James was the first positive thinker. Amid his own protracted depressive crisis, swirling around his shaken faith in free will, he fastened on the French philosopher Charles Renouvier's "definition of free will—the sustaining of a thought because I choose to when I might have other thoughts." James decided this capacity sanctioned belief in free will, by which he meant the autonomous capacity to choose. "My first act of free will shall be to believe in free will," he confided to his diary. (This exercise by itself was not enough to pull him out of his depression; an assistant professorship of psychology at Harvard, secured by his mother's intervention, was what ultimately required him to get out of bed in the morning.) He deployed a similar mental strategy to justify religious belief in his essay "The Will to Believe"—which should have been called "The Right to Believe," he later said. In the absence of a convincing refutation of theism, James argued, the would-be believer was justified in embracing religious faith for pragmatic reasons—its revitalizing effects, its capacity to make life dramatic, serious, and meaningful. Like so many of his contemporaries, James was obsessed with energy and how to harness it for personal well-being. Unlike most positive thinkers, though, he defined well-being to include "life's bitterer flavors" as well the sweeter ones. And he never embraced the amorality of the self. James was a popular philosopher, but he swam against the tide of a popular movement. He could never be a full-bore positive thinker.

POSITIVE THINKING AND ITS DISCONTENTS

Despite the similarity of the labels we apply to them, positive thinking and positivist science were radically different styles of thought. Both, to be sure, were intolerant of ambiguity and committed to certainty—equally positive their beliefs were true. But while positivism based its claims on precise observation and measurement of the material world, positive thinking depended for its authority on a mysterious, invisible mental power within.

The big tent for positive thinkers in the late nineteenth century was the movement known as New Thought. It began as an assertion of mind over matter, discipline over desire; Christian Science was the archetype. But toward the end of the century, some of its devotees began moving beyond dualistic ascetism toward a more capacious metaphysics. Eventually New Thought became a popular parallel to Jamesian thought. Both were radically empiricist in their assumptions that "matter and mind were interdependent, equally alive, and capable of growth," as the historian Beryl Satter writes; and pragmatic in their conviction that certain mental practices could have desirable consequences in the material world—their faith in faith.

Despite these affinities, the New Thought movement lacked James's profound awareness of the darker dimensions of the human condition, above all the tragic conflict between the longing for infinite life and the certainty of its ending. New Thought advocates, in contrast, held out the possibility that positive thinking—if properly sustained and focused—could lead to the overcoming of death itself. James was too convinced of the reality of the material world, too respectful of the fragility of bodily existence, to embrace this cosmic optimism. Though James flirted with spiritualism, and even joined the Society for Psychical Research, ultimately he remained committed to the inescapable importance of material life. No one could deny material existence, he said, who has stood beside the coffin of a dead parent or child. He had done both. For him, affirmations of universal oneness failed to compensate for irreparable loss.

New Thought advocates also lacked James's ethical sensitivities. Many of the movement's followers sought release from repressive morality into a world of free self-development, beyond good and evil. For most, clouds of spiritual rhetoric obscured the amoral implications of the-self-as-energy; it was a fluid and evanescent identity, easily accommodated to status quo economic and power relations. The positive thinking side of New Thought celebrated acquisition and accumulation through the manipulation of invisible forces—above all Davis's Law of Attraction, which New Thought transformed in the 1890s from the animal magnetism that keeps the universe from flying apart to a mental force that humans could use to attract health, wealth, and happiness—or if they fell into the wrong habits of mind, sickness, poverty, and sadness. The Law of Attraction underwrote positive thinking by asserting the invisible connections between human beings and the pulsating universe around them. Already one could see in faint outline the ultimate slogan of New Thought, emblazoned on billboards and blaring from loudspeakers at Epcot Center: "If we can dream it, we can do it." Only the "we" nearly always shrank to "I"—the individual who is wholly responsible for his or her emotional and financial state.

New Thought redefined the political economy of force through an ideological sleight of hand, invoking the Law of Attraction to reimagine work as play. Prentice Mulford, an itinerant journalist who became a leading promoter of New Thought, demonstrated the strategy in *Thoughts Are Things* (1889). "To succeed in any undertaking," he wrote, "simply keep it ever persistently fixed in mind as an aim, and then study to make all effort towards it play, recreation. The moment it becomes 'hard work' we are not advancing. I mean by 'play' that both body and mind work easily and pleasantly." Even if the work involved is digging sand or scrubbing floors, the "thought structure" animating that work "is also a magnet. It commences to draw aiding forces to it so soon as made." Indeed, Mulford later wrote: "We are through our mental conditions always drawing things to us good or bad, beneficial or injurious, pleasant or disagreeable. There is possible a state of mind which, if permanently kept, will draw to you money, lands, possessions, luxuries, health and happiness." The contemporary notions of "visualization" and "flow" were present in embryo in Mulford's work, which claimed to foreshadow dramatic social change. If enough people cultivated serenity, utopia would not be far off. "In time to come all the world's physical work will be done in this restful mood, and without hurry or straining to accomplish a certain amount in a certain time. Then all work will become as play," he predicted.

No one can deny the benignity of this vision, nor the palpable role played by positive thinking in meeting all sorts of challenges in life. But the focus on reshaping the material world by readjusting one's thinking had real limitations. This was especially true in the workplace, where the New Thought message tended to be: Think positive and fit in, don't complain. Your mental life will eventually allow you to reshape your material life. As Ralph Waldo Trine advised the readers of *In Tune with the Infinite* (1897), there is no need to change your job if you're dissatisfied; "by the very force we carry with us we can so affect and change matters that we will have an entirely new set of conditions in an old environment." The new job you wanted so badly may turn out to be disappointing, but don't bolt, be careful: "take the attitude of mind that this situation is the stepping stone that will lead you to one that will be still better. Hold this thought steadily, affirm it, believe it, expect it, and all the time be faithful, *absolutely faithful* to the situation in which you are at present placed . . . Never give a moment to complaint, but use the time that would be spent in this way in looking forward and actualizing the conditions you desire." Every moment spent grumbling "is just so much capital stock taken from the bank account of mental force." Positive thinking was the key that unlocked new resources of emotional, physical, and psychic abundance. A copious flow of animal spirits was the clearest expression of that condition.

Animal spirits thus become part of an emerging upbeat synthesis—health, vigor, and financial success all in one package. Unlike earlier success ideologies, this was not for men only. Women played a central role in New Thought and the mind-cure movements that spun off from it. Female positive thinkers took vitalism in some new directions but also trod some familiar paths. Their dominant theme was that women were as capable of mastery as men, and as desirous of freedom, but sometimes expressed their capacities and desires in forms different from men's. Among the most distinctive of these women was Helen Wilmans (1831–1907), by turns a rancher's wife, reform journalist, mental healer, real estate developer, and positive thinker. Wilmans helped shape the shift in New Thought from denial to divinization of matter and desire, in the process challenging etherealized conceptions of womanhood. For Wilmans, Satter writes, "desire, matter, and the animal will formed the heart of healthy female selfhood"—as they did for healthy male selfhood.

The crucial conviction, for Wilmans, was the sanctity of the independent self. "And oh! a wonderful thing is the 'I,'" wrote Wilmans at the outset of her autobiography *A Search for Freedom* (1898). The "I" was "so varied in its phases . . . No two pages in any life history alike, and yet each one so vital, so alive! This aliveness! It is this which gives an autobiography its charm." "Aliveness" was one of Wilmans's touchstone words; so was "freedom"—both were pressed into the service of her reverence for individuality. "When an 'I' shall stand entirely erect, then for the first time the earth will behold a god," she wrote, anticipating Ayn Rand's libertarian self-worship of the mid-twentieth century. The notion of standing erect, resisting the conformities of respectability, preoccupied Wilmans throughout her life. The chief engine of conformity, in Wilmans's world, was Protestant Christianity. Much of her search for freedom involved her struggle to reject the demands of conventional religiosity in the name of an imperial—and by conventional standards amoral—self.

REIMAGINING THE FEMALE SELF: HELEN WILMANS

Wilmans grew up in Fairfield, Illinois, a town with three hundred Protestant souls and no church—though a preacher would occasionally come to town. Aunt Sally Linthecum's Sunday School exercised "complete control of the whole town." Young Helen was restless: "There was always the pressure of some undeveloped force in my brain, and it pushed me forward to—I did not know what," she recalled. She devoured books, but there were few on the premises. *Pilgrim's Progress*, *Fox's Book of Martyrs* ("that I hated and finally destroyed bit by bit on the sly"), and *The Arabian Nights*. This last she read repeatedly, choosing (in effect) imagination over self-immolating duty.

"The aptest word I can apply to myself as a child is 'aliveness,'" Wilmans wrote. "It caused me a pang to kill anything, even the things I was afraid of; as snakes, worms, etc. I seemed to enter with my own feelings into the life of the lower creatures." Through this firsthand study of natural history, she recalled, "I came to think of the law of growth, and man's relation to it. It was also from the study of natural history, aided by the education I had derived from 'The Arabian Nights,' that I began to look upon man as a being of limitless power." But such subversive thoughts were constrained by her upbringing.

Helen grew up a child of small-town privilege. Her father "kept store"; her family did not wear homespun clothes nor homemade shoes; they were "quality folk," quite looked up to, especially by the country folk. "Mother was decidedly a society leader," not to mention "a woman of immense vitality," Wilmans recalled. "I am sure of it simply by recalling her laugh." Alas, from Helen's view, this vital woman was also a devout evangelical Christian. Fairfield eventually built its own church, and a preacher came to town regularly. "Mother soon manifested great interest in the salvation of her soul, and even went so far as to become a sort of assistant in 'bringing other souls to the Savior.' It was at this point," Helen wrote, "that the real wretchedness of my life commenced."

She hated her religious experiences in retrospect even more than she did when they occurred: "I did not fully comprehend how death-dealing they were to the vital principle at that time." As a grown-up vitalist, she grasped the full destructive force of Christian stories about satanic power and eternal punishment. Evil became a palpable, monstrous force in her young imagination—one that eventually drove her to inhabit the benign realm of positive thinking. There was little escape for Helen from the oppressive dread of Satan. When she told her skeptical father about him, he said "damn the devil" dismissively; but he had little influence over the children's religious education—and less authority in general after his business failed. In 1849, when the gold fever broke out in California, he left for the West Coast and died there from a different sort of fever, after a few years of futile prospecting.

Meanwhile, as a teenager, Helen had become a local celebrity, telling stories to rapt gatherings of local children and writing poems for the town newspaper. The steadiest demand was for tributes to babies and young children who had died. There was a constant supply of such subjects in a nineteenth-century farm village. Writing was not easy but Helen had to contribute to the household income. So, "always in some way—by sheer force of animal will, I expect—I got over the difficulties and produced what was required of me, and it satisfied my appreciative audience," she recalled.

Yet she also secretly nurtured an inner certainty, much like the animal spirits of the investor who is convinced his hunch is right. Even as she struggled to crank out poetry, Wilmans wrote, "I felt sure I had something worth more than all the genius in the world . . . it was not vitality, but more than vitality; it was not hope, but certainty; it was not the promise of more life, but the indestructible principle of life itself. It was the perfect assurance of success in any career I might undertake; it was solid ground and rich in the promise of bearing, no matter what kind of seed I planted in it. It was the self-hood of me, the invincible 'I.'" Explicitly rejecting the evangelical promise of "more life," she embraced "the indestructible principle of life itself," grounded in certainty.

The full growth of selfhood required the cultivation of certain mental traits. Most important was "intentness of purpose," which "concentrates the faculties of a person. Such a person becomes a magnet. Knowing this, anyone can become a magnet through the practice of concentration. This power is developed through the study of Mental Science. I seemed to have it naturally when a child. Later in life I think I lost it; but now, with the knowledge of how to regain it, it is coming back in great force." As a woman in her sixties, Wilmans was recovering her childhood capacity for self-centered indifference to the disapproval and eventually even the approval of others. This self-centeredness, she had come to realize, was the key to strong individuality. "I did not know what it was myself any more than the bulb knows of the lily folded within its layers; but I felt the developing force, and was in a great measure obedient to it." When she was a child, Wilmans remembered, she obtained her own way through deception; now she forged boldly ahead. "And what does this mean? I believe it means simply fidelity to my own individual self-hood." For a woman raised to be a Christian, this faith embodied a Nietzschean transvaluation of values. "The very moment a man begins to live from a consciousness of his own strength he sees small use of a personal God; his reasoning powers awake, and little by little he reverses the entire scheme and comes out on top . . . he sees himself the governing power and the creative force of the world, with the Principle of Being at his service and under his command," Wilmans wrote in her memoir, articulating the Promethean perspective that was coming into vogue in the 1890s.

But as a young woman she had been held back from these insights, she later believed, by Christianity. The family moved to Cedar Rapids when Helen was a young teenager, and her mother made sure that they all prayed daily together, morning and night, and kept the Sabbath strictly. Helen accepted all this as a necessary part of life, she later wrote, "but there was an undercurrent of something somewhere that seemed to be insidiously stealing my vitality, until I became so weak I could scarcely climb the stairs in doing the housework." Even worse were her nightmarish visions, conjured up by constant talk of Satan and his work.

Yet those visions led, ironically, to a dawning recognition of the power of human thought. "Upon being put to bed I rarely failed to see strange creatures, part human and part animal, and I was afraid of them. That these forms were real I do not doubt . . . they have taught me one of the greatest lessons of my life; namely, that thought has power to create without the use of the hands, and also without employing any visible means in doing it." This power remained "invisible on the dull plane of sense in which our faculties now preside." But it is one of the "unseen and unexplored forces" long deployed by such traditional adepts as the Indian fakir, and now investigated by modern science.

Indeed, Wilmans wrote, "a machine for photographing thought has recently been invented and stood the test of experiment well." It is unclear which machine Wilmans meant, but there were many possibilities proliferating around the time she was writing, the turn of the century. In the wake of the discovery of X-rays, numerous inventors claimed to have found new ways to reveal "unseen and unexplored forces," including thought itself. Beginning around 1896, the French military officer Commandant Louis Darget claimed he could photograph thoughts in the form of "human radiation," or "V-rays." "V" was for "vital." To catch V-rays on film, Darget devised a "portable radiographer," a photographic plate attached to a headband on a subject's forehead. When the photograph was shot, the radiograph produced blurred images that Darget would interpret in accordance with what they seemed to represent. The attempt to capture and display unseen forces reflected the broad and growing dissatisfaction with the cut-and-dried universe of positivism.

Wilmans's own fascination with invisible forces linked her with earlier devotees of animal magnetism. Along with their common acceptance of the interdependence of matter and mind, she shared with animal magnetizers a fitfully acknowledged preference for the spiritual over the "animal plane." Indeed, she wrote, "there is no real happiness on the animal plane of life; and say what you will, we are still living on the animal plane. We have not ascended above it yet, though some of us are beginning to know that there is a higher plane, and we are striking out for it with all the energy we can command." Despite her attraction to wild nature, she harbored an ambivalence toward the material world and a longing for "higher things"—an outlook that linked her with phrenologists and Christian Scientists as well as other positive thinkers. Animality, for all its appeal, still had to be transcended.

Nowhere was this ambivalence clearer than in her account of her first marriage, to a reasonably successful physician named Baker, who somehow got it into his head that he could make a go of it as a rancher in east-central California, near the Nevada border. There followed three children and twenty years of drudgery for Helen, as she labored to cook and clean up after her feckless husband and twenty or more hired hands. "It was my fate to go through the ordinary animal marriage," she wrote. More concretely, this meant that her "soul [was] ground into the dust daily" during her years as a farm wife. Yet it was precisely this contact with the materiality of the natural world that restarted the vital principle within her: "I became a veritable product of earth, submerged in her fruitful soil—so to speak—where, like some seed or bulb, I took root and began to feel the throbbing pulse of mother earth, quickening the life within me." So—despite her preference for the spiritual over the animal plane—spirit and matter, seed and ground, were still complementing one another in Wilmans's narrative of self-development.

In 1877, after twenty years of backbreaking labor punctuated by occasional flights and extended separations from her husband (but not her children), Wilmans made a decision. Her children were grown, or nearly so; her marriage was loveless; her husband was indifferent to the sore back and blistered hands his chosen way of life inflicted on her. She packed a valise and hitched a ride with a neighbor to the San Francisco area. Having spent down to her last few cents, she found a job on a reform newspaper that was committed to vindicating the rights of labor against the oppressive power of capital. Like Christianity, this leftist critique of capitalism was tolerable at the time but flawed in retrospect, Wilmans decided. In *The Conquest of Poverty* (1899), she wrote: "The slaves of capital are where they are, not because capital oppresses them, but because they will not use their brains"—adding that "they can scarcely be called men." From her mature positive thinker's perspective, the newspaper's staff "were dead to any sense of power within themselves, and were only alive to what they considered their wrongs." But in the early 1880s she still considered herself a labor journalist when she moved to Chicago to take a job with the reform paper the *Express*. The editor became her friend, and when she decided to leave to start her own paper, *Woman's World*, he offered her a promotion to stay. She refused: "On the road to progress it often happens that the warmest friendship may become a tyranny that has to be broken." Her explanation for her departure was "simply the fact that I had reached another stage of growth." Her first article—entitled "I"—according to her account, was the "declaration of individuality" she had been longing to make for years. Gradually she distanced herself from the labor movement. She met and married Charles C. Post; when he became sick with an unspecified illness, she healed him by imagining his recovery—no God required, as in Christian Science—and eventually became a national spokesperson for her version of New Thought, which she called "Mental Science."

In 1897, Wilmans and Post moved to Sea Breeze near Daytona Beach, Florida—an ideal location for a shrewd real estate developer. Wilmans soon demonstrated that she was one. The difference between her and the many male real estate developers surrounding her (including, perhaps, Ham Disston) was that she believed her success came from applying the principles of Mental Science. The mental scientist in her, she claimed, was not really interested in accumulating money.

The "universal reaching out for money," she wrote, "is but an extension of animality into the realm of the human, and no power can lift it to the divine plane the race is now approaching." Yet those who understood Mental Science did possess unique access to an apparently limitless supply of cash, simply by knowing how to tap into it; this was where the rubber met the road, where mind met matter, in positive thinking. Monetary value, as the panicky gyrations of finance capitalists demonstrated, was a product of the human imagination. Why, then, should the money supply not be subject to positive thinking? Why not, indeed? Wilmans suggested this when she wrote: "The supply of money now in circulation and locked up in vaults is equal to the demand of those who come into an understanding of the laws of intelligent demand, and with the increase of those who understand those laws, the supply will increase." Understanding "the laws of intelligent demand" meant first of all divesting oneself of the pervasive cant about work and recognizing that all the "industry" in the world would not have yielded half of the fortune "these positive thought currents, expressed in judicious and courageous action, have yielded me." The trick was to think big. "The man who mentally claims the most, gets the most," discovering that "opulence is an unfailing supply to every demand." This was positive thinking in its most straightforward and influential form: the promise that you could think your way to wealth.

Foreshadowing Franklin Roosevelt, Wilmans announced: "Fear is the only thing of which we should be afraid; it is the only real, live devil; all the others are dead. So now, the one great denial of my life is that of fear. I am not afraid of poverty. I will not pinch down in my money spending. I will not economize, as the word is commonly understood. This is my constant affirmation." Denial of fear kept consumption high, and the machines of production humming. Wilmans was by no means mistaken about this, and her instincts were borne out in the connections Keynes would later make between spending and prosperity. But when she evoked the Law of Attraction to argue, "Every thought a man can have relates him to some external thing and draws him in the direction of it," she ascended into a cloudier realm. Thoughts of Disease, Sin, and Poverty produce the very thing they fear, she insisted; thoughts of Health, Goodness, and Wealth bring us what we yearn for. (Again we can see the origins of contemporary talk about "visualization" and "actualization.")

This sort of positive thinking contained important half-truths, but left out the sheer obduracy of the material world—not to mention the unpredictable but implacable energies of biological life and death.

Thinking about wealth was one thing, thinking about life and death quite another. When Wilmans took her Mental Science in the direction of mental healing, more substantive problems eventually arose. Wilmans's most modest claim for Mental Science was that it constituted a kind of cognitive therapy. Its ontological foundation was the merger of mental and physical life. As she said, "thought is an actual substance generated by the Brain" and "all substance is, fundamentally, mental." All objects existed simultaneously in mental and physical realms—"take a tree," she suggested, somewhat vaguely. Whatever one did with a tree, Wilmans's larger therapeutic point was that you could think yourself out of old, fixed beliefs; you could choose to reject the self-loathing, the sense of helplessness and worthlessness induced by religion. Assuming one agreed about the effects of religion, this was a reasonable therapeutic approach, or at least the beginning of one.

But Wilmans had more grandiose therapeutic aims. She had hit upon a phrase that (she claimed) scientists were using—"correlation of forces"—and she "had found that thought was a force, and bore a direct relation to the thing it was centered upon. I began to experiment with it. Before long I received the absolute assurance that a man is as he believes; that is, the thoughts in which he believes create his body and his external conditions also." Creating external conditions involved thinking your way to prosperity; creating the body required thinking your way to health. As she wrote, "disease is simply a state of ignorance concerning the great truth that life and health are omnipresent." Overcoming disease demanded hope and faith, "for hope and faith do project the life cells into which flows the Vitalizing Principle—the god within; thus rendering us diseaseless incarnations of the great I am." Imagining this diseaseless realm required a rhetoric of cosmic oneness that resisted translation into concrete terms.

Part of Wilmans's reputation (and wealth) depended on her claim that she could heal physical maladies by thought—no laying-on of hands was necessary, no physical contact. She did not even need to be in the same geographical location as the patient. This variation on mesmeric healing (including Davis's) was known by the end of the century as "absent treatment." Wilmans's attempts to recruit patients for absent treatment by mail led her eventually to be charged with fraud by the U.S. Post Office. Her defenders claim that a coterie of rivalrous male real estate operators conspired against her; the charge is plausible. Given the psychological threat posed to patriarchy by a powerful businesswoman, and the routine immunity from prosecution enjoyed by most male medical charlatans at the time, Wilmans may well have been unfairly singled out. Yet she was indeed victimizing sick people with fraudulent claims that she could cure them.

Her lawyers were clever enough to get her cleared on a technicality in 1904, but she was never the same. Her legal battles left her depleted and destitute; her second husband died; and she wanted to die, too. "I am not sick, but I am tired of everything on earth," she wrote to a friend. "I would give anything just to lie down and go to sleep and never to awake again." It was a sad denouement for a positive thinker, perhaps even a tragic one for a woman who had struggled so long and so hard, refusing to admit that there were any limits on human aspiration—and for a while even getting away with it.

As Wilmans's career suggests, when animal spirits became entangled with positive thinking, they lost some of their animating power. Despite all the talk about tapping into a Vitalizing Principle, even as they acknowledged matter and desire, positive thinkers tended to remain on what they deemed a spiritual plane, which they described in abstract language. Animal spirits were most animating when they could actually be observed in action—in the "headlong insouciance and mischievous ardor," for example, of the "wild girl." At such times animal spirits still showed how flesh could be infused with spirit, but in an idiom of exuberant health rather than erotic or mystical longing.

HEADLONG INSOUCIANCE

The sanitizing of animal spirits depended on their association with physical and mental health, with enlightened child-rearing, and with business success. The psychologist G. Stanley Hall led the way in promoting a conception of health more demanding than mere absence of disease. "It is one thing to be well," he wrote, "and a very different thing to be always overflowing with animal spirits and good feeling." Most educators and moralists were less sanguine than Hall about the "always" part: instead of letting animal spirits overflow, they urged the channeling of animal spirits into healthy outlets by both sexes. There was a mildly feminist dimension to most such pleas—let girls do what boys do. In assessing the collective health of all young people, their elders described animal spirits as a precious regenerative resource, possessed by both sexes and in need of full expression.

In 1864 *Harper's Monthly* described a key moment in the history of female consciousness: when Aaron Burr read Mary Wollstonecraft to his daughter Theodosia, particularly Wollstonecraft's assault on over-refinement in girls' education. Wollstonecraft wrote: "The pure animal spirits, which make both mind and body shoot out and unfold the tender blossoms of hope, are turned sour and vented in vain wishes or pert repinings," or else "produce that pitiful cunning which disgracefully characterizes the female mind—and, I fear, will ever characterize it while women remain slaves of power." Wollstonecraft's critique survived. Theodosia became a spirited young woman who steadfastly defended her father from charges of treason, hosted Native American chiefs at his New York estate when he was out of town, married the future governor of South Carolina, and died mysteriously at sea in 1813. She also joined other women (and some men) of her generation in calling for reform of female education. While few could match Wollstonecraft's vehemence, they repeatedly echoed her sentiments—chiefly her preference for spontaneity over precocity. These were the characteristics that distinguished the "wild girl" from the "fast girl," according to the Memphis *Appeal*. The wild girl's wildness stemmed "from sheer excess of animal spirits, the bubbling over of unusual vitality." The fast girl, in contrast, merely seeks notoriety: she "has lost the art of blushing, or rather she has educated herself out of it along with the other weaknesses of childhood." Editorialists lamented "precocious girls" for decades, and by the mid-1880s the mildly feminist argument that girls have animal spirits too had begun to make some headway. "There are nations and families, how fortunate, that have escaped this notion that animal spirits in girls must be murdered, and death take their place in obedience to social behests," the St. Johnsbury (Vt.) *Caledonian* announced with some hyperbole in 1885. "Let the girls then run, and do not check them and make them ashamed to exhibit vitality." That same year, the Washington *Star* noticed a "new feminine style in gait." It was "quick, springy"—"running over with animal spirits and good health." Vigorous women were becoming a national phenomenon. *The Salt Lake Herald* noted, "The metropolitan girl of wealth and fashion is now cultivating natural bloom. The period of esthetic sallowness is past. She now likes to be plump and smooth, with a faint glow in her complexion, and a general semblance of the health hitherto scorned as belonging to milkmaids."

And always the key to health was the opportunity to release animal spirits. "Give the girls exercises at which they can scream and hit and dash and romp and work off excess animal spirits, as is the way with boys," the Maryville (Tenn.) *Times* advised in 1891, "and afterwards they will make better students for it, better tennis players, better riders, and stronger, finer, bigger, handsomer women." But this was not just about physicality; it was about being "keyed to happiness"—the outlook that allowed the poet and New Thought advocate Ella Wheeler Wilcox to enjoy the "Melodies of Existence," as *The Arizona Republican* observed in 1892. "She never calculates 'what if,' but takes for granted the desirable and 'grapples' only when interference really comes . . . This leaves her an immense fund of vitality and animal spirits, and is by herself said to be the cause of her extremely youthful appearance."

By the mid-1890s, it appeared as if the young girls coming home from vacationing in "the West" had all taken their cue from Wilcox. "They are brown as gypsies, rosy as sun-kissed peaches, and have appetites like Comanche Indians, and they are all in such abounding good health that they actually carry about with them an atmosphere of animal spirits that is exhilarating to everybody they come near." By the turn of the century, male observers in newspapers were praising the "outdoor girl" and the "athletic summer girl"—two upper-class social types, "overflowing with animal spirits," who owed their "bubbling vitality" to the rise of sports and country house life. "The woman of the present is not the woman of the past ten or fifteen years; she is a new and entirely alive, more human specimen of femininity," the *Star* concluded.

But none of this increased humanity involved becoming more like men. "The athletic summer girl," according to *The Minneapolis Journal*, "captures all our hearts by her reckless abandon and sinuous grace . . . let her face tan and her muscles grow large and knotty. To these she will point with pride." Yet neither she nor the "cowgirl"—also celebrated as a new model of vigorous femininity—was of "the new woman class—not of the sort that discards her feminine attributes and tries to ape the man, simply a lively, athletic young woman with a superfluity of nerve and animal spirits, with a realization that in affairs where skill is the chief qualification she has an equal chance with her brothers." There is not one who does not "cut a dainty figure on the dance floor." Indeed, the cowgirls at a ranch near Palestine, Texas, were "as pretty a collection of girls as ever set masculine hearts a-flutter," a local newspaper observed. The cowgirls and their cowboy suitors were undoubtedly affluent kids on holiday. We can be pretty sure they weren't herding cows for pay. The revitalization of the young was a class-based project.

But not entirely. When the public conversation turned to young males, the net spread more widely, to include street kids as well as farm boys. Animal spirits were accepted as an essential part of a boy's life, yet they could easily degenerate into "hooliganism" or "hoodlumism," especially in cities. Not expression but management of animal spirits was the key theme in discussions of the "boy problem."

None could deny the influence of "aggressive, fun-loving pluck" in the making of male character. "Well-managed, his animal spirits will give him all the more manly loyalty, and, when true to the right cause, he will be all the more true because so much living sap has gone into his obedience," wrote Samuel Osgood in the Hillsborough (Ohio) *Highland Weekly News* in 1868. But precocity was as much a menace to boys as to girls—especially among the working class: "What is more sad than the sight presented every day in our streets . . . boys who are hardly old enough to be beyond their mother's watch now swaggering with all the airs of experienced bloods, and polluting the air of God's heaven with the vocabulary of hell?" Boys and girls alike were all too eager to cast off childhood ways, squandering precious animal spirits in the process.

But boys were more threatened by girlishness than girls were by tomboyishness. "In the first place," a Vermont newspaper asserted in 1891, "the ideal boy is a boy, not a girl—not a girl-boy, nor fop, nor prig, but a genuine boy, as nature intended him to be. He is full of animal spirits, overflowing with fun, realizing as no one else can the intense delight of living . . . a manly boy. He scorns to do a mean thing." All that was necessary was to point such lads in the proper direction and give them frequent opportunities to work off excess animal spirits—just as one fine spring afternoon in 1898 a Wichita teacher sent Wade B. Cole, who couldn't sit still, outside to run it off: "Without any hesitancy he hurried out, went at it in a business-like way and tore around the yard like a maniac. It had the desired effect, like a safety valve to an engine and solemnly resuming his seat, he studied hard the rest of the day."

By the time young Wade was tearing about the schoolyard, educators and others entrusted with raising the young were pondering more productive channels for excess energy. The very notion of Energy (increasingly capitalized) had acquired a nearly numinous quality. Its invisibility and apparent limitlessness were once considered attributes of divinity. No wonder Henry Adams perceived a slippage from deity to dynamo: before the end, one began to pray to it. So the mastery of Energy, the capacity to direct it to socially useful ends, was the ultimate Promethean task—the assumption of godlike power.

At that imperial moment, the 1890s, the management and direction of physical energy became a national duty. Moral and physical health were twinned. This became the emerging rationale for college sports: "hard play" built character, as President Theodore Roosevelt told the young readers of *St. Nicholas* magazine. "In short, in life, as in a football game, the principle to follow is: Hit the line hard; don't foul and don't shirk, but hit the line hard!" Physical courage, for Roosevelt, was the basis of moral courage; the two realms could be conflated and applied to the behavior of the state. Nations, like individuals, could show resolve, stand tall, or cut and run. These became common tropes of public discourse as the American empire began its rise.

This was not a smooth ascent. On May 5, 1893, soon after the opening bell, National Cordage Company, the rope trust, announced its bankruptcy—hanged itself, said Wall Street wits. Within an hour, traders embark on a frenzied sell-off. As an observer said, "the floor might have passed for a corner in Bedlam." The madness had been in the making for months. Hundreds of railroad bankruptcies revealed the rot at the core of a glamorous high-tech industry. Railroads (like the rope trust) were awash in debt and mismanagement, rickety structures atop a paper-and-air foundation—promissory notes (to repay debt) and unwritten gentlemen's agreements (to restrict competition). The collapse of the rope trust put an exclamation point on the collapse of the railroads, which was already well under way.

The Wall Street Panic of May 5, 1893, touched off a dramatic plunge in the asset values of railroads and their ancillary industries (coal, steel, oil); and, like the Panic of 1873, laid bare the class war that accompanied the rise of industrial capitalism. Once more, strikers protesting layoffs and wage cuts clashed with National Guard troops responding to the call to restore order. Debt-ridden farmers, some close to starvation, flocked into tent meetings to hear Populist orators denounce plutocracy. After three years of depression, most farmers followed William Jennings Bryan into the Democratic Party, embracing his mildly inflationary panacea for economic distress: free and unlimited coinage of silver.

Despite its mildness, free silver struck terror into the hearts of financiers and bankers, for whom the gold standard was the numinous essence of "sound money" and Bryan a dangerous radical. When he accepted the party nomination at the 1896 Chicago convention, he concluded his stirring two-hour speech by warning the bankers: "you shall not crucify mankind upon a cross of gold." *The Washington Post* reported that "a strange and curious magnetism" filled the air, then the crowd "threw forth the fiery lava of its enthusiasm like Vesuvius in eruption." Amid the "cyclonic frenzy," one woman, "standing on a chair, shouted like a savage and danced like a savage." Days earlier, *The New York Times* had already decided that the delegates were little more than "A Wild, Raging, Irresistable Mob." Small wonder that, after Bryan's defeat by William McKinley, relieved investors poured unprecedented sums into capital markets, in the process financing the first great merger wave in American history. Meanwhile, Roosevelt and other advocates of empire were preparing a distraction from any lingering domestic discontent—war with Spain, tarted up as a mission to save the Cubans from their corrupt Spanish overlords.

Imperial adventure had personal as well as political significance. The gradual, halting shift from republic to empire resonated with some Americans' experience at the most basic level. Through the decades following the Civil War, the resurrected male body, toughened by sports and military drill, was gradually assimilated to the needs of the emerging imperial state. Such official spokesmen for manliness as Roosevelt and Hall urged the channeling of animal spirits into conventional military heroism and a broader ethic of mastery—culminating in Roosevelt's Rough Riders, the army regiment that brought cowboys and Ivy League athletes together. The vision of a vanishing but vaguely regenerative frontier pervaded the atmosphere of the fin de siècle, sustaining a mythic promise that appealed to women as well as men. Reports of those "Wonderful Californians" appeared in newspapers from Maine to Kansas and beyond. "Virile, strong, healthy, overflowing with animal spirits, fond of sports, bent on the fullest enjoyment of life, broad-minded, generous, hospitable, chivalrous—all together the most agreeable people in the world," the Wichita *Eagle* announced in 1892.

But agreeableness was not always enough to secure regeneration. At the vernacular level a kind of imperial primitivism asserted itself, though often in veiled or implicit forms—the "outdoor girls" were "brown as gypsies," with "appetites like Comanche Indians." Behind such comparisons was the implicit, half-conscious recognition that supposedly marginal or inferior peoples possessed certain desirable traits that white Anglo-Saxons (especially eastern elites) lacked—an elastic vigor, a reckless exuberance, a readiness to play.

THE REASSESSMENT OF THE PRIMITIVE

Conventional scholarly views of primitive peoples opened up during the decades after the Civil War, widening from a contemptuous view of "Indian Superstitions" to a fuller appreciation of what civilized and "savage" humans had in common. The influential ethnologist Edward B. Tylor reflected this change. In "The Philosophy of Religion Among the Lower Races of Mankind," in the *Journal of the Ethnological Society of London* in 1870, he asked: "Do these savage views represent *remnant* or *rudiment*?" If the former, they are of little interest—if the latter, "they become of immense practical interest." To trace "rude animism" over the centuries, as it is influenced by "advanced intelligence," is to comprehend "not only the historical but the actual position of philosophy and theology." This suggested that, however rudimentary the so-called savage mind, it still had traits in common with the civilized mind—including a tendency to ask some of the same ultimate questions.

So while "the lower races" believed in a universe animated by invisible spirits—for Tylor an archaic notion—they seemed to have modeled their idea of spirits on a more contemporary conception of a soul, seeking a theory to explain "the difference between a living and a dead body:—the fading of light from glazed eyes, the cessation of breath, the stoppage of pulsation, the loss of consciousness and voluntary movement—in a word, of the phenomena classed together under the heading 'Life.'" Thus the allegedly primitive man shared some of the same concerns with modern scientists. Yet he was a man "who scarcely distinguishes his subjectivity," who "hardly knows his inside from his outside"—and who believed that animals have souls like men, and can be sacrificed so that the soul of the dead can reach "its place." He—always "he," for late nineteenth-century scientists—was a bundle of contradictions, but in Tylor's view it was well worth the time to unravel them.

By the 1880s, social scientists were uncovering not only the continuity but the universality of supposedly primitive habits of mind. Anthropologists and scholars of comparative religion followed the path laid out by Max Muller, who found that Zulus have the same folktales as European peasants. The idea of a universal primitive consciousness began to emerge; eventually it became the basis for Jung's notion of a collective unconscious. One pervasive myth was the narrative of higher beings taking animal form; this story, a writer in *The Open Court* observed, "has its roots in the animistic concept of social relations which, as totemism and

Manitou-worship, dominates the childhood of nations." The last phrase suggests the inherent ambivalence built into the recapitulation theory: if nations, like individuals, had a childhood, then they also had maturity and old age; the more advanced a nation, the closer it might be coming to a state of senescence. This fluid conception of human development opened the possibility that what was supposed to be progress might contain the seeds of decline—that earlier stages in the development process might have been characterized by valuable traits, lost en route to modernity. But—here was the crucial move—such traits might be recoverable, if new sources of vital energy could be identified.

Amid widespread fascination with force, an abundance of animal spirits could redeem allegedly inferior races and other despised social groups, transforming them into embodiments of traits that respectable Americans feared were missing from their lives. Consider the Memphis *Daily Appeal*'s account of the execution by hanging of Jere Connolly and George Sherry in Chicago, in 1878: "The two criminals were both of strong, powerful physique and full of animal spirits. Ever since they were sentenced to death they put on a bold front and an air of bravado. This was especially the case with Sherry, whose nerve and self-possession were remarked as wonderful. He was apparently heedless of his impending doom." Here as elsewhere, however fleetingly, personal courage seemed to count more than conventional morality.

Occasionally, race-based constructions of a primitive other were complicated by class divisions. Since the 1840s, Mexicans and other Latinos had been the targets of Anglo scorn, yet they, too, became the objects of ambivalent projection. Among the upper class of Yucatán at an Easter ball in 1888, the *Sacramento Record-Union* reported that "every face wore a look of pure and refined enjoyment, derived from sentiment, rather than excited animal spirits." A lingering distrust of animality required that visceral excitement be sublimated into sentiment.

Yet, at about the same time, the celebration of Latin animal spirits for their own sake was intensifying and leading in some strange directions. The Monroe (La.) *Daily Telegraph* pointed the way when it reported the execution of the Mexican murderer Camillo Gonzales in Brackett, Texas, in 1886. Gonzales

> was a wild beast caged. In a state of liberty he was an impartial and picturesque thief; in prison he was an ill-conditioned ruffian with a curse for his keepers and a kick for all things supernal and infernal. And yet it was a pity that so straight a man should die. Broadshouldered and deepchested, long-armed and thin-flanked, powerful and graceful, he was a picture of human physical possibilities—the highest type of uneducated but splendid brute force, an Adonis of the chaparral . . . Over the brawny breast fell a coal black silken beard; through the heavy mustache, behind sensual thick lips, shone savagely glittering teeth, and on his bull's neck the muscle rose in cords. His copper skin glowed with health and the animal spirits in him found vent perpetually in some outbreak against his captors, his fellow-prisoners or his fate. He was a product of the arrested development of his nation, a simple child of nature, a variegated scoundrel. The face, while very handsome, was Mexican in the extreme, only it had some of that nation's dreaminess.

From this vantage, the "wild beast caged" was not unconverted Natural Man, the tendency to evil within the self; it was a dark-skinned other outside the self. Whether or not this constituted a case of self-purgation through allegorical projection, it would be hard to find a more characteristic expression of imperial primitivism than this encomium to a Mexican murderer—the mingling of individual and national character, the fascination with "splendid brute force," the admiration for a reified and potentially violent masculinity, all within the framework of white legal and political domination. Gonzales, after all, was on the way to the gallows. The paper's tribute to him was the kind of sentiment that, purged of its primitivism and turned inward, would lead young men to embrace Theodore Roosevelt's cult of the strenuous life.

Longings for renewed vitality complicated familiar racist stories of savagery and civilization. One such narrative was based on the belief that even apparently civilized savages were liable to relapse into barbarism at any time. Since the Civil War, this tale had been endorsed by scientific expertise and applied to African American men, as a means of asserting that they could not handle freedom and would inevitably retrogress to savagery—especially in the presence of white female flesh. In the white racist imagination, the Black Beast continued to dwell alongside Sambo. But the discourse of animal spirits, while it was still pervaded with racist assumptions, offered a way of acknowledging black people's vitality without invoking its supposedly sinister side—as in the Washington *Star*'s review of the first musical performance in Washington by "Tom the Colored Boy," who sang Stephen Foster songs and other pseudo-plantation ditties for white audiences: "He is a negro all over, with all the mannerisms of his race; animal spirits high, bursting out into a giggle or some extravagant demonstration of voice or limb upon the slightest provocation, and leading off in the applause of his performance with rollicksome zest." As this account makes clear, animal spirits were compatible with the Sambo stereotype, which had existed for decades.

But the enlistment of African American troops to fight against Spain in 1898 melded black animal spirits with redemptive manliness. This was especially apparent in reports from the recuperation camp for wounded troops at Montauk Point, Long Island. As the New York *Sun* reported, here was "no boisterous fun, no horseplay, no practical jokes, no excess of animal spirits"; indeed there was "something ghastly" about the "general dispiritedness" of the camp until "a troop of colored cavalry" showed up. The "negro regiments," the *Sun* found, were "in better condition than their white comrades . . . and have shown greater powers of rehabilitation." After the black troops' arrival, the camp was animated by singing and storytelling and games of quoits, not to mention "good natured scuffling and boxing," all of which put the white boys on the path to recovery, for "when a man has animal spirits to put up his hands against another he is well on the way to convalescence." At his best, the black soldier epitomized the successful management of animal spirits. "The young negro is ebullient and full of animal spirit and more mutinous than the white man until thoroughly disciplined," but then he is "faithful, brave, and enduring," a Kansas newspaper observed in 1899. Out on Montauk Point, the play of animal spirits revealed an emerging dialectic in U.S. race relations. Even as lynchings multiplied and Jim Crow laws clamped down, black people displayed an elusive vitality that white people wanted and needed.

To be sure, old hierarchies persisted, and not all ethnic groups were equally susceptible to primitivist projections. Native Americans, despite their near annihilation, sometimes still seemed not only a pathetic remnant but also a potential threat. Yet distinctions had to be made, as *The Pittsburg Dispatch* argued when reports of the Ghost Dance cult filtered east in 1890: "When the Indian goes to fighting out of the mere excess of animal spirits inspired by either bad frontier whiskey or race revenge, no sympathy is wasted when he is caught and sharply punished. But the outbreak of a spiritual fever among these remnants of the Aborigines is, seriously, another sort of disease which calls for gentler and more patient treatment." Condescending as it was, this sort of sentiment augured the emergence of a more sympathetic attitude to an aboriginal people who were no longer a threat but merely a remnant.

Other cultic revivals seemed more ominous. In 1903, *The Washington Times* reported that two anthropologists had paid fifteen dollars to two Kiowa Indians on a reservation in Indian Territory (now Oklahoma), "to undergo the tortures of the sun dance" for the purposes of ethnographic research. The official in charge of the reservation was less concerned about the (unspecified) tortures of the sun dance than about "the well-known tendency of even the most highly educated Indians to revert to a semi-barbaric state"; he compared an Indian on a reservation "to a peaceful and sociable tiger in captivity, who is all right as long as he is not necessarily provoked or does not come into contact with what arouses his latent savage instincts, but is a deadly menace when his wild animal spirit is revived; and the inciting of the Indians to perform the ancient sun dance with all its cruel and inhuman features is expected to arouse the Indians as the smell of fresh blood does the tiger." The beast within, apparently tamed, was actually only dozing.

Not all Anglo-Americans projected beastly behavior onto dark-skinned others; some still recognized the potential for it within themselves. Robert Louis Stevenson frequently resorted to animal metaphors in describing Mr. Hyde, the diabolical doppelgänger of the impeccable Dr. Jekyll; the young Frank Norris wrote *Vandover and the Brute* as a Harvard student in the 1890s, the story of a gifted artist brought low by his own bestial other self. William James was one of the few observers to articulate the danger of the lingering beast within in the fraught realm of American race relations.

In 1903 James published "A Strong Note of Warning Regarding the Lynching Epidemic," which began by marveling how thoroughly violence had been banished from everyday bourgeois life: "The average church-going Civilizee realizes, one may say, absolutely nothing of the deeper currents of human nature, or of the aboriginal capacity for murderous excitement which lies sleeping even in his own bosom . . . Methodical diminution of tempting pretexts and provocations, social condemnation of violent acts, the rarity of bad examples, and the fear of the gallows, are the forces which have brought us to this tameness, which is the very triumph of our civilization." But it would be a fatal mistake to get complacent: "the water-tight compartment in which the carnivore within us is confined is artificial and not organic. It will never be organic. The slightest diminution of external pressure, the slightest loophole of licensed exception, will make the whole system leaky, and murder will again grow rampant. It is where the impulse is collective, and the murder is regarded as a punitive or protective duty, that the peril to civilization is greatest. Then, as in the hereditary vendetta, in dueling, in religious massacre, history shows how difficult it is to exterminate a homicidal custom which is once established." Whether these observations were fair to carnivores in general is questionable, but they did capture the darker dimensions of animal spirits when they were harnessed to collective human purposes—from lynch mobs to nations mobilized for war.

James's insights went against the grain of the historical moment. He was a pacifist and anti-imperialist, and though he valued vitality as much as any of his contemporaries, he sought it through a "moral equivalent of war," not war itself. Indeed, war was one of the "homicidal customs" he hoped to minimize if not exterminate. Meanwhile the broader American populace, especially middle- and upper-class white men, were caught up in a wave of popular vitalism that celebrated imperial adventure as a path to personal and national rebirth.

Still, vitalism transcended imperialism, and the idea of animal spirits preserved a complex intellectual significance, beyond the twisted dreams of regeneration through violence. At about the same time that Norris was writing *Vandover*, Thomas Hardy was comparing his heroine in *Tess of the D'Urbervilles* to dozens of animals ranging from leopards to sparrows, all of which suggested her overflowing sensuous vitality, while Helen Wilmans was identifying her own "clawing animal will" as the force that sustained her search for freedom. Vitalist impulses led in many directions, from anarchic self-assertion to the immersion of the self in the healing balm of the racial will, embodied ultimately in the führer. But nobody could see that cataclysm coming in the banquet years before World War I.

7

Another Civilization

THERE ARE TIMES when historical actors themselves can sense a seismic shift under way—a reshuffling of dominant sensibilities and structures of feeling. One of those shifts occurred during the last decade or so before World War I; it was a special, expectant moment. "The fiddles are tuning up all over America," said the Irish painter John Butler Yeats (father of the poet William Butler Yeats). Those years marked a hinge moment in the reconfiguration of value that had been in progress for several decades and would continue long after the war itself had ended—the recovery of the wild, the revaluation of the primitive in the service of imperial vitality. These cultural projects accelerated during the years before the war, converging in a new celebration of Energy, Force, and Power that derived much of its strength from a surge of vernacular vitalism.

Before the war, no one knew they were on the brink of mass carnage, but a few perceptive observers sensed they were inhabiting an era of pivotal transformation. "The present age is a critical one and interesting to live in," George Santayana wrote in 1913. "The civilization characteristic of Christendom has not yet disappeared, yet another civilization has begun to take its place." In the Chicago *Dial*, Charles Moore provided an alternative interpretation of the cultural tremors that were coursing through American society: they did not signify the rejection of religion, he thought, except insofar as it had devolved into mere respectability; rather, they arose from widespread challenges to nineteenth-century science. The refutation of positivist certainty, Moore believed, had brought about the "return of the Gods." As he wrote, "For fifty years or more the Gorgon head of evolution has turned the heart and soul of man to stone. Caught in a mechanical determinism, mankind has lost its freedom—the fluidity which before yielded to all impulses of religion, poetry, and art." But now the emergence of "the new vitalism," particularly in the work of the philosophers Rudolf Eucken and Henri Bergson, was restoring that feeling of fluidity—and with it a sense of spiritual ferment and artistic possibility. The closed universe governed by unchanging natural law was opening, revealing fissures in its conceptual foundation; and in a parallel development, the static precepts of orthodox Christianity and commonsense moral philosophy were weakening. In consequence, "the Gods" (or at least the possibility of belief in them) were drawing new strength from more fluid ontologies and philosophies.

At the center of this ferment was Jamesian radical empiricism—a respect for the knowledge and insight that stem from immersion in the "blooming, buzzing confusion" of sensuous life itself. This outlook resonated with the Romantic impulse to recapture intense, immediate experience, which was resurfacing on both sides of the Atlantic. Yet familiar Romantic conventions acquired a heightened intensity under Modernist auspices. The ontological stakes were higher than they had been in the early nineteenth century; the looming core of emptiness was nearer, the need to flee nothingness stronger. The core motive in many Modernist quests was a craving for action, rooted in a sense that reality was not simply a given but something to be striven for—something pulsating, throbbing, and often (if not always) just out of reach.

This constellation of feelings and thoughts can loosely be labeled vitalism, even if the vitalist thinker in question never embraced vitalism per se as a philosophy or scientific theory. Certainly that was true of James, whose ultimate authority on ontological matters was the American mystic Benjamin Paul Blood. James quoted him appreciatively:

> Certainty is the root of despair. The inevitable stales, while doubt and hope are sisters. Not unfortunately the universe is wild—game flavored as a hawk's wing. Nature is miracle all: she knows no laws; the same returns not, save to bring the different. The slow round of the engraver's lathe gains but the breadth of a hair, but the difference is distributed back over the whole curve, never an instant true—ever not quite.

James built a pluralistic worldview based on a radical empiricist appreciation of multifarious experience. This outlook inspired many young avant-garde intellectuals—the group some historians have called "the lyrical left"—to follow vitalist impulses in new directions, often guided by the aphorisms of Friedrich Nietzsche as well as William James. This path attracted thinkers as diverse as Randolph Bourne, John Reed, and Mabel Dodge Luhan; it led away from conventional morality and toward a wave of bohemian life-worship that peaked on the eve of World War I.

Yet there was a broader current of vitalism that swept up many Americans who considered themselves anything but avant-garde, who sought to inject new energy into existing institutions and familiar forms of moral uplift. Among these more conventional vitalists were prominent figures in Progressive reform. Jane Addams advocated "the subjective necessity of social settlements" as a regenerative experience that would plunge bored young women of leisure into the vibrant life of the immigrant working class; Theodore Roosevelt resurrected the strong body to be an accompaniment to manly virtue, as he addressed elite young men in search of revitalization. Even as he conjured vital energy, Roosevelt corralled it with Victorian notions of masculinity and a conventionally productive ethic of mastery. This was the sort of moderated, managed vitalism that survived World War I and became embedded in corporate and bureaucratic institutions.

The melding of raw force and systematic discipline was at the core of the civilization Santayana saw coming into being in 1913: the taming of Prometheus; the convergence of an unprecedented celebration of vitality with unprecedented structures to contain it—hierarchical organizations, gender conventions, systematic forms of quantitative measurement. Yet scientists as well as artists and intellectuals began to suspect that vital forces might well keep spilling over the structures of containment—as indeed they did, in militarist and fascist movements as well as Modernist experiments in the arts and new conceptions of the cosmos.

SOMETHING NEW COMING ON EVERY MOMENT

By the early twentieth century, obituaries for the concept of vitality had proved to be premature. Clanking schemes of inevitable progress were undone by a spreading attraction to free-flowing energy, from vernacular dance crazes to theoretical innovations in physics and psychology. In urban dives and entertainment palaces, young men and women gyrated to novel rhythms with movements resembling the (actual or imagined) sex acts of various animals—turkeys, bunnies, bears, foxes. Animal spirits, in effect, were unleashed on the dance floor, as well as in other arenas of emergent mass entertainment—adventure fiction, vaudeville, sports. In more cerebral circles, vitalist ideas proliferated, as scientists and philosophers increasingly questioned mechanistic views of the cosmos.

Among the questioners, Nietzsche was the great forerunner. He celebrated instinctual life as a "green" alternative to arid notions of rationality and narrow conceptions of utility. "Empty 'being' but not full and green 'life' is guaranteed me; my original feeling only guarantees that I am a thinking not a vital being, that I am not an animal but at most a cogital," he wrote. And he often succumbed to such oracular pronouncements as "One only acts perfectly when one acts instinctively." His reputation rose after 1889, when he was committed to a lunatic asylum, and especially after 1900, when he died.

Despite his madness but also due to it, Nietzsche's ideas acquired a mystique on both sides of the Atlantic, though often obliquely and in diluted form. George Bernard Shaw's play *Man and Superman* (1903) typified the popular appropriation of Nietzschean vitalism. For the Fabian socialist Shaw, the life force led to higher and higher forms of social organization, and the eventual evolution of man into superman—Shaw's version of Nietzsche's *Ubermensch*. Shaw's progressive optimism shaped his recasting of Nietzsche's pessimistic grand narrative, which concluded not with the Superman with but his opposite, the "last man"—passive, timid, concerned only with comfort and security—the pathetic human residue at the end of the evolutionary process.

Shaw's play unveiled his own idiosyncratic merger of feminism and vitalism. Originating as a modern version of the Don Juan narrative, *Man and Superman* was an awkward blend of drawing room romance and theater of ideas. And the biggest idea was that woman was an embodiment of the life force; exuding erotic attraction, she sought to trap man into perpetuating the species through marriage. In an interpolated episode often staged separately as "Don Juan in Hell," Don Juan himself sets out Shaw's concept of sex as primal energy:

> In the sex relation the universal creative energy, of which the parties are both the helpless agents, over-rides and sweeps away all personal considerations and dispenses with all personal relations. The pair may be utter strangers to one another, speaking different languages, differing in race and color, in age and disposition, with no bond between them but a possibility of that fecundity for the sake of which the Life Force throws them into one another's arms at the exchange of a glance.

Shaw's female lead, the spirited heiress Ann Whitefield, is (he said) Everywoman; her reluctant suitor, the self-styled revolutionary Jack Tanner, is a modern Don Juan and a sort of superman in training. After much badinage, the couple's courtship climaxes in a merger of romantic convention and portentous philosophy. Ann asks: "Why are you trying to fascinate me, Jack, if you don't want to marry me?" and Tanner replies: "The Life Force. I am in the grip of the Life Force." Still, Tanner ponders more mundane questions, such as how he was appointed Ann's guardian in her father's will. She reveals the secret, "in low siren tones": "He asked me who would I have as my guardian before he made that will. I chose you!"

> TANNER. The will is yours then! The trap was laid from the beginning.

ANN. [*concentrating all her magic*] From the beginning—from our childhood—for both of us—by the Life Force.

Still Tanner wavers and Ann grows despondent, announcing: "Well, I made a mistake: you do not love me." This provokes an ambivalent affirmation from Jack.

TANNER. [*seizing her in his arms*] It is false: I love you. The Life Force enchants me: I have the whole world in my arms when I clasp you. But I am fighting for my freedom, for my honor, for myself, one and indivisible.

The most likely candidates for superman were stout hearts like Tanner, but they were also the men most likely to stay attached to the notion of "myself, one and indivisible." And for man to become superman, Shaw implied, he had to immerse himself in the universal energy of the life force, transcending his attachments to familiar notions of unitary, indivisible selfhood. Here as elsewhere, the vitalist creed was hitched to an obsessively masculine project: female sexuality becomes merely an instrument of male ascent.

Still, Shaw's vitalism was about more than his masculine preoccupations; it also reflected the transatlantic obsession with energy in all its forms—technological, psychological, cosmic. Henry Adams among other thinkers was sensing that new discoveries in physics revealed energy to be an invisible, universal vital principle—a master key to unlock cosmic mysteries by dissolving the dualities of mind and matter, flesh and spirit, self and world. As the Scottish biologist John Haldane pointed out in 1898, the return of vitalism was in part a result of the gradual discrediting of rival theories in physics and chemistry that had claimed "to explain some of the most fundamental physiological processes"—cell formation, oxidation, respiration. The question arose: If mechanistic explanation had proved inadequate, might older beliefs still have some truth in them?

This uncertainty opened the door to a revival of *Naturphilosophie*, as the German chemist Wilhelm Ostwald revealed in his Leipzig Lectures in 1901 when he introduced his theory of energetics. Ostwald declared the concept of energy to be a universal solvent of old distinctions. From his view, energy could best be described as "whatever is the result of work, or whatever may be transformed as the result of work." (This was the physicist's "work," not necessarily the Protestant's.) Traditional concepts of metaphysics, substance and causation could be more precisely expressed as "varied manifestations of the fundamental concept of energy. The concept of matter from this point of view becomes superfluous." What we had called matter would be better expressed as "Form-Energy."

Though Ostwald's theory was idiosyncratic, its challenge to materialist assumptions resonated with anti-positivist thought on both sides of the Atlantic. Matter, it seemed, was neither as solid nor as reliable as had previously been thought. This recognition could be liberating but also disturbing. The specter of unreality—of subjectivism and even solipsism—haunted post-positivist science. Activism was a useful escape, but vitalism went further. It constituted a kind of exorcism: the notion that there was an innate force animating the cosmos provided an alternative to dependence on the intellect of the observer. If vital force was "out there" rather than "in here," it was based on something more than the vagaries of subjective mental life.

For educated Christian believers, that "something more" was God. In 1903, the *Independent* reported that an updated version of the old argument from design still won endorsement from the highest scientific authority. In an address to a college Christian association in England, the botanist George Henslow "said that science neither affirms nor denies the creative origin of life. Lord Kelvin, who was presiding, demurred . . . and declared that so far as he could see, science positively affirms the creative power, that science makes everyone feel that he is a miracle in himself." Modern biologists, he said, "are once more coming to the firm acceptance of a vital principle. They have been absolutely forced by science to admit and believe in a directive power." This outlook would resurface in a secular idiom later in the century, when the plant geneticist Barbara McClintock referred to the researcher's need to develop "a feeling for the organism."

In the early twentieth century, vitalist beliefs could reshape humans' conceptions of their place in the universe. D. B. Potter pondered this transformation in *Health* magazine: "Man is ceasing to look upon himself merely as a material machine, which in a mechanical way generates a vaporous something called 'thought.' Man and the world are taking on a more spiritual aspect. The material life is coming to appear like an illusion of human ignorance, which we have passively allowed to dominate us. We seem to see that matter is vibrant with life-force." For Potter, recognizing the vibrancy of matter enhanced the human sense of possibility, revealing to us that "there is no barrier on the road to high accomplishment," from curing disease to preventing old age. Vitalism, from this view, powerfully reinforced conventional faith in progress.

In 1911, the biologist and founder of Scripps Institute William Emerson Ritter posed a timely question in his presidential address to the American Association for the Advancement of Science: "The Controversy Between Materialism and Vitalism: Can It Be Ended?" Ritter thought it could, if his colleagues would accept the third way he proposed: Organicism, a worldview grounded in a sweeping and largely metaphorical view of the evolutionary process. "We need to recognize as we never have that evolution means something new coming on every moment," Ritter said, as well as the likelihood that "evolution is truly a universal principle; that there is not a trait, physical or spiritual, of ours that is wholly finished off and at a standstill. We are . . . in every atom of our existence and at every instant on the move to some extent, up or down, forward or backward." This vision of life was a secular version of Jonathan Edwards's vision of a universe in the process of continuous creation by God. But the emphasis on perpetual motion departed from Edwards's contemplative sensibility, and suited the activist temper of the early 1900s. So did Ritter's twinning of "the sophisticated thinker and the untutored savage" in their shared recognition of the mystery at the heart of the universe and their common recognition of its cause: the unceasing creativity of a universal evolutionary process.

Ritter wanted to find an exit strategy from the stale and mistaken opposition between materialism and vitalism. As he said, "how futile is the attempt of materialism to find the 'cause' of life in any one set of material elements, and how equally futile is the attempt of vitalism to find the significance of the whole in some intangible 'force' . . . Both attempt to explain everything in terms of 'something else,' and this in essence amounts to a denial of the reality of the organic beings we actually see and deal with." But Ritter never really explained what conceptual frameworks organicists would use to understand the beings they observed. Organicism remained more a rhetoric than an organizing principle, and never posed the question that so bedeviled philosophical and scientific vitalists: What does it mean for an organism to be alive?

Outside the academy, popularizers continued to pose it, and contented themselves with open-ended answers. The nature writer John Burroughs, in "The Problem of Living Things," concluded, "There is something that creates and makes matter plastic to its will. Whether we call matter 'the living garment of God,' as Goethe did, or a reservoir of creative energy . . . we are paying homage to a power that is super-material"—but no less real for all that. "The world of complex tho invisible activities which science reveals all about us"—magnetism, radioactivity, the transformation of apparently inert matter into a flash of lightning, the mysteries of chemical affinity—"all point to deep beneath deep in matter itself." Invisibility did not mean unreality.

The fascination with force led ultimately from science to some semblance of religion, as other Americans joined Adams in bending a knee before the new powers. In 1913, the *Tacoma Times* writer Herbert Quick declared "Force" to be "the only thing worth worshipping." This was not, Quick insisted, merely a contemporary fashion: "In all ages and everywhere, by a universal instinct, the human being worships Force." To be sure, there was a time when Force was rivaled by what was thought to be the only other actuality, Matter. But "we now, by the radium discoveries, find that matter seems to be only a form of force. So our minds are brought to confront the apparent proof that there is only one thing real, and that is Force. If so, the blind worship of Force is very close to the intelligent worship of God." It was unclear whether or not this worship involved simply glorifying the omnipotent Other, or humbling one's self before It, as well.

Into this ferment waded Henri Bergson, a philosopher who more than any other addressed the yearnings that animated the revolt against positivist certainty. By seizing the popular idioms of evolution, which had been mostly mechanistic, and infusing them with an energy he called *élan vital*, he imagined a process that allowed for, in fact required, spontaneity and creativity. Without acknowledging formal allegiance to vitalism, he melded idealist and materialist ontologies into a new vitalist synthesis.

Bergson was the consummate anti-mechanist and (as James noted with admiration) the consummate anti-intellectualist. He redefined time as "duration," observing, "Real duration is that duration which gnaws on things, and leaves on them the mark of its tooth . . . We do not think real time. But we live it, because life transcends intellect." Such conceptions seemed to set him against the quantitative imperatives of industrial capitalism—the "standard time" introduced by the railroads, the "scientific management" promoted by Frederick Winslow Taylor. Indeed, Bergson's very definition of "the comic" in his book on laughter was the "idea of regulating life as a matter of business routine . . . something mechanical encrusted upon the living." He was, in effect, the anti-Taylor.

Bergson's notion of duration fed into a sense of experience as flow, which in turn informed his fluid vision of creative evolution—a process not governed by mechanical determinism (as Darwin's popularizers had claimed), but animated from within by an *élan vital*. He used a vitalist master-metaphor to capture his feeling for the indeterminacy and unpredictability of the living organism. "The role of life is to insert some *indetermination* into matter," he said.

Bergson's aphoristic style resembled Nietzsche's, and he had as little regard for consistency. There were times when he appeared to take a balanced view of conflict between intelligence and instinct, as when he said: "*There are things that intelligence alone is able to seek, but which by itself, it will never find. These things instinct alone could find; but it will never seek them.*" But he was also capable of anti-intellectual toss-offs:

"*The intellect is characterized by a natural inability to comprehend life* . . . You must take things by storm: you must thrust intelligence outside itself by an act of will." Above all he had a gift for recasting the pallid idioms of spirituality in language that resonated with the fantasies and longings of the zeitgeist. God, he announced, "is unceasing life, action, freedom. Creation, so conceived, is not a mystery; we experience it in ourselves when we act freely." And "life," he said, "transcends finality as it transcends the other categories. It is essentially a current sent through matter." The last reference was especially resonant: by referring to *élan vital* as an electric current, Bergson paired his concept with the form of force most fascinating to Americans in 1913—electricity—silent, invisible, omnipresent, and apparently limitless.

When cosmic energy descended to the level of the human individual, the consequence was an electric self—or, to use the idiom that still persisted, a self that was overflowing with animal spirits. A piece of fiction published in a Nebraska newspaper in 1884 caught what for decades to come would be the dominant metaphorical association between electricity and health: the doctor in charge of a mental institution tells a visitor, "I believe electricity as a curative element—not the quack nonsense and belts and chains and musical boxes, that only shake the nerve centers, but the real electricity of animal spirits, the tonic of good health." Animal spirits were the source of genuine electricity, the good health that proved contagious. But there were competitors claiming to harness the physical force of electricity for therapeutic ends—mountebanks peddling "quack nonsense." Many pathways, not all reliable, promised to lead the burned-out patient to a new, electric self.

FROM COSMOS TO PSYCHE: ANIMAL SPIRITS ELECTRIFIED

The redefinition of matter as energy made it easier to imagine connections between physical and psychic states. For Ostwald, the key connector was nervous energy, which was produced by the physical energy of sensations, and which in turn generated the psychic energy of thought. Nervous energy, like animal spirits, was a key link between brain and consciousness. Summing up the long-term trend in scientific thought, the *Journal of the American Medical Association* observed in 1914 that "the animal spirits of Galen have become the nervous impulses of today." The question remained: How did they fit into the big picture of relations between body and mind?

The specter of reductionism loomed. Ostwald avoided it by stressing the fluidity of the relationship between physiology and psychology, but the vitalist erasure of mind-body boundaries meant that mind could always be reduced to body, and vice versa. This was especially apparent in the popular science peddled by advertising, such as the "quack nonsense" of claims for the curative powers of electricity. "The Secret of Success Is Nervous Energy" was the headline above an advertisement in the *Los Angeles Herald* in 1906, and below it one learned that the energy could be supplied by a daily charge of electricity from Dr. Samuel Hall's Dry Cell Battery. "The human body is a machine. The nervous system is the motor. Electricity is the power that runs it." This mechanistic idiom, though persistent, was out of phase with the revolt against positivism.

More consistent with the zeitgeist were the mysterious forces pervading such self-help literature as William Walker Atkinson's *Thought-Force in Business and Everyday Life* (1901). This manual for developing "Thought-Force" and "Psychic Force" was based on Atkinson's lectures to his students. The basic argument was straightforward: life is a series of psychic contests in which each man's "Volic Force" struggles for control. "Look around you and you will see that nearly every man who has 'arrived' is possessed of the ability to attract, persuade, influence, or control his fellows," Atkinson advised, before descending into familiar axioms concerning how to cultivate that persuasive power—don't get angry, don't be fearful, cultivate a frank and open manner. A sense of humor also helped in the quest for success, a Kentucky newspaper observed in 1902: "Nothing is a happier incentive to the maintenance of good animal spirits" than a quick sense of humor that finds something to make a jest of even in dark times—this was the sign of a man who can overcome difficulties.

Such prescriptions applied to medical professionals as well as businessmen. "Cheerfulness Counts" in healing, *Cosmopolitan* reminded physicians in 1903: "The sick look with confidence to the well. They demand the hearty dogmatism that comes from overflowing animal spirits. They enjoy the cheerful optimism that comes from a good digestion." This was a default-setting account of the effects of bodily health on the emotions.

William James pushed further. In a lecture called "The Energies of Men," he probed the meaning of "second wind," the rekindling of our mental or physical energy after it has apparently been exhausted. How might this capacity be cultivated? James focused on freighted choice: "A single successful effort of moral volition, such as saying 'no' to some habitual temptation, or performing some courageous act, will launch a man on a higher level of energy for days and weeks, will give him a new range of power." Ideas, beliefs, and spiritual practices could release new energies, too. James and many of his contemporaries feared that their power supply—moral, emotional, intellectual, and spiritual—was in constant need of replenishment.

James's examples of "the energies of men" ranged from Oliver Cromwell and Ulysses S. Grant to an unidentified friend who had taken up hatha yoga, but only one was female—a woman with breast cancer who was keeping herself alive and vigorous through the practice of mind cure. The lecture was addressed to the American Philosophical Society, an overwhelmingly male audience, in 1906; a few years earlier, James had delivered "The Gospel of Relaxation" to the young women of Radcliffe College. His gendering of vitality could not have been more apparent. "The need of feeling responsible all the livelong day has been preached long enough in our New England. Long enough exclusively, at any rate,—and long enough to the female sex. What our girl-students and woman-teachers most need nowadays is not the exacerbation, but rather the toning-down of their moral tensions. Even now I fear that some one of my fair hearers may be making an undying resolve to become strenuously relaxed, cost what it will, for the remainder of her life." While James perceptively criticized the destructive power of the female superego, he also assumed that men needed untapped energy more than women did. His pursuit of vitality, like most others, was shaped by gender conventions.

This gendering process was especially apparent in popular musings on business success. When the landscape architect Frank Waugh visited his son at college, he observed the boy engaging in "a right royal rough housing exercise." At first disapproving, Waugh then waxed nostalgic. "The whole essence of this pleasant game I saw to consist in the play of good animal spirits, engaged in a manly, open, equal personal struggle." This kind of game, he realized, persisted into adult life: "Business, in fact, is the man's rough-house. Here man meets man in an open, friendly, and (normally) equal struggle . . . It is remarkably like a pillow-fight." Politics ("a man's sport") and even religion also required regular roughhousing. Presidents and preachers owed their success to abundant vim.

Where did this leave women? Apart from Helen Wilmans and a few other positive thinkers, they were mostly absent from the literature on vitality and business success. The discourse surrounding animal spirits sometimes insinuated that women's surplus vitality, like men's, always threatened to spill over into the erogenous zone. And in polite society, overtly erotic expression was even more scandalous for women than for men. Hence the need, in self-help literature, for housebroken and gender-specific versions of vitalism—for men a mélange of rough sport, character, and discipline; for women compulsory cheerfulness, which involved stifling spontaneous anger or even sadness.

The "ideal lady typewriter," according to *The Stenographer* in 1896, "should have a bright, cheerful disposition, and when asked to do a thing should, no matter how she may be feeling, she should do it willingly; for business life is full of trials, and what business man cares to have a person with him daily who is sulky and morose?" The question answered itself, but the task could be trying, as Caroline Huling reported in *Letters of a Business Woman to Her Niece* (1906): "Law stenographers are often called upon to take dictated matter that shocks their sensibilities and seems coarse and improper. Such cases must pass unnoticed . . . Remember that you are simply an intelligent machine." "The sensible girl never intrudes her sex or personality upon her employer or his associates. She must be deaf to his profanity, dumb regarding business secrets and blind to his petty weaknesses." The sensible girl's "sex or personality" apparently included conventional feminine traits—an aversion to crude talk, a tendency to gossip, a moral disapproval of "petty weaknesses."

Advice literature encouraged men to be expansive and women, in effect, to suck it up. Emotional pain simply had to be suppressed. The *New York Observer and Chronicle* told the cautionary tale of a young girl who had been fired and didn't know why, as she hadn't broken any rules. Her boss explained: "Your face is constantly clouded and it dampens the spirits of those about you and they lose the company's time in sympathizing with you and your troubles, many of which are imaginary ones." If you get over this "habit of uncheerfulness," he told her, then you can come back.

Women in business were damned if they did and damned if they didn't. "A Business Woman" revealed "how love passed her by" in *Harper's Bazaar*: en route to a successful career, she said, "I became accustomed to stifle my emotions, conceal my dislikes, control my likes, and generally repress any tendency to natural feminine behavior." By "natural feminine behavior," she seemed to imply emotional expressiveness and forthright opinions. Though she was not looking for love, in any case it never found her. Maybe this was because "I allowed myself to be altogether too much of a 'good fellow' among the men I met," she wondered. "I think sometimes I allowed myself to be—well, a little bold." Boldness was mandatory for men, discouraged for women. In much success literature, apart from New Thought, vitality was for men only.

Writers who promoted an electric male self often assumed that its essential feature—vitality—was in short supply. As John James Ingalls wrote in *The Forum*, "Of vital force, his most valuable possession, the American businessman is a perpetual spendthrift. Like his horse, he is trained for speed rather than endurance. He sacrifices the staying power of his ancestors for immediate results." In consequence he has sacrificed their "noble repose" in exchange for "a whole train of nervous and functional disorders." *The Pittsburg* [*sic*] *Dispatch* complained in 1891 that "the great American idol—Push" had inspired self-destructive worship. "There are those who pay their devotion to him after the manner of lunatics," the paper warned. "Their animal spirits ooze out of them with their animal sap and stamina, and the residuum is pig-lead."

Complaints like these persisted into the twentieth century. In 1908, Henry Sedgwick observed in *The Atlantic* that "the typical American becomes a power-house of force, of will, of determination," but he focuses all his attention on "industrial interests" and neglects cultural life altogether. "This neglect betrays itself in feebleness, in monotony, lack of individuality." So we, as a civilization, are faced with a choice: "either to make up our lives to let our religion and our poetry—and all our emotional life—be without passion, or else to use a makeshift in its stead." We have chosen the latter, Sedgwick concluded, with our papier-mâché triumphal arches and our lame mimicry of passion on stage: we have minimized vital emotional energy in order to maximize our industrial energy. The consequence was the impoverishment of our intimate life.

LIBIDO AND ITS VICISSITUDES

Sedgwick's lament was echoed throughout the early 1900s. In 1912, Carl Gustav Jung made similar observations about Americans' misplaced priorities when he came to New York to lecture on the theory of psychoanalysis. This was a crucial moment in Jung's developing break with Freud, when the Swiss psychoanalyst announced his "energic theory of libido." Freud had equated libido with the sex drive, the instinct for preservation of the species, which he distinguished from hunger, the instinct for self-preservation. "In nature, of course, this artificial distinction does not exist," Jung announced. "There we see only a continuous life-urge, a will to live, which seeks to ensure the continuance of the whole species through the preservation of the individual . . . There is no longer any justification for differentiating in principle between the desire to build nests and the desire to eat." For Jung, libido "is not only not concrete or known, but is a complete X, a model or counter, and is no more concretely conceivable than the energy known to the world of physics . . . We shall not be disturbed if we are met with the cry of vitalism. We are as far removed from any belief in a specific life-force as from any other metaphysical assertion. Libido is intended simply as a name for the energy which manifests itself in the life-force and is perceived subjectively as conation and desire."

Yet libido was not limitless, and the American man was focusing his libidinal energy "almost entirely on his business, so that as a husband he is glad to have no responsibilities." This was a serious mistake, and not just for men. "It takes much vital energy to be in love," Jung said, and "in America you give so many opportunities both to your men and women that they do not save any vital force for loving." The ethic of self-control "holds you [Americans] together and keeps you from dissolution, from going to pieces," but you may well break down under the effort to maintain it. "In America there is just such a tragic moment arrived. But you do not know it is tragic. All you know is that you are nervous, or, as we physicians say, neurotic. But you do not know that you are unhappy."

Jung glimpsed the anxiety at the core of American optimism, but overlooked the vitalist impulses that had been proliferating for some time in American literature, arts, and politics—impulses that encouraged the flow of libidinal energies in many directions besides calculating busyness. Theodore Roosevelt embodied much of that energy. He epitomized the conventional version of vitalism that swept through the American public world during these years—the version most easily assimilable to the mainstream culture of Protestant Christianity and masculine mastery. In 1899, a year after his exploits with the Rough Riders and while he was governor of New York, Roosevelt addressed an assembly of mothers and "cautioned his hearers against checking the disposition of their sons to fight, if the provocation is sufficiently good." Punish your boy for cruelty, he said, "though not for what is simply an overflow of animal spirits because he is healthy and full of life." According to TR, this was the origin of the fighting spirit that was needed to right wrongs, and it was sadly lacking among too many Americans. "Because of the lack of courage, there are too many 'nice' people to-day . . . who want to sit at home and are content to confine their warfare against injustice, corruption, and evil influences to the adoption of resolutions," TR complained.

Two years later, after William McKinley was assassinated, Vice-President Roosevelt took his war against mere niceness to the White House. Besotted journalists quickly began to praise him as the epitome of animal spirits in politics. On a trip to Yellowstone Park, "the president was a boy again, full of animal spirits," as he raced through the park on horseback, leading the cavalry that accompanied him on a "merry chase," *The Butte Inter Mountain* reported in 1903. When he returned to the East, his boyish energy was undiminished: "He is full of electricity, sharp shocks, attraction and repulsion," the New York *Sun* declared, "a very human and adventurous character, full of animal spirits, caracoling bravely on his mustang, rattling and brisk, but tempering the cowboy with the field-preacher and emitting in season and out the gospel of the strenuous life."

When the president traveled abroad, the St. Paul *Globe* wondered if he would maintain the cowboy image that fascinated Europeans as well as Americans. "Familiar only with the president's spectacular 'stunts,' [Europeans] will naturally feel aggrieved to learn that he does not habitually gnash his teeth, hobnob always with wild and woolly products of the plains and utter war whoops when his animal spirits get the better of him," the paper predicted. But the American journalists following him, led by Jacob Riis, managed to keep all those assumptions alive, and TR's mystique acquired an international dimension.

The secret of his popularity, wrote the *Indianapolis Journal*, was his capacity to combine relentless energy with reassuring ideas of morality and masculinity. "President Roosevelt has so much vigor and animal spirits that he is saved from coarseness and perhaps from dissoluteness, by the mere force of his education and moral stamina. He is possessed of a temperament and ambition which would be dangerous, were it not for his lofty ambitions and unflinching patriotism." Still, there was no denying that he was a primal force: "Nature permeates him, and he is part of nature."

But this was not the menacing, amoral nature evoked by Emile Zola, Frank Norris, and other naturalistic novelists. "A few years ago a wave of naturalism or animalism, given the misnomer of realism, swept across from the continental reading public to England and America," Annie Russell Marble had declared at the turn of the century, but "this last decade has seen a veritable 'return to nature,' not as the life-restoring panacea of the older poets, but as the life-giving, life-instilling force about us." Roosevelt brought that vital spirit into the political arena, cleansing the Life Force of its amoral and erotic associations. In 1910, Rev. Calvin

Laufer, a Presbyterian minister from central Pennsylvania, revealed how thorough the cleansing had been. He insisted that, while the good nature of the habitually exuberant person could be likened to the "the animal spirits of a boy," it could also be said to embody "that superb brightness which is the result of the immediate indwelling of God's Holy Spirit. On its lower side it is little more than the spirit of mischief or nonsense; on its higher side it is the sublime exhilaration of spiritual communion." Vitalism and Christianity, in short, could be made to cohere.

The creation of beauty provided a similar opportunity for communion of bodies and souls, as the critic Edwin Björkman argued in 1911. Art was not only "the messenger and missionary of a great life-force"—it was "itself such a force," and could "submit to no other mastership than that of life itself—of life in all its fulness and majesty and glory." Submitting to the mastery of life required obeying its most important law, "which demands that all progressive, constructive, creative movement be rhythmical. Thus, by planting in us the sense of beauty—which is at bottom a sense of rhythm so strong that its effects are almost hypnotic—life may be said in a very literal sense to be ever striving to place us 'in tune with the universe.'" The rhythms of beauty were a joy forever; they blended the energies of the individual with the energies of the cosmos.

To descend from the exalted realm evoked by Björkman to the actual practices at play in the popular arts is a bit of a jolt. A vaudeville performance hardly seems to be on the same planet; the life force is there, but in radically different forms, perhaps rhythmical but probably unrecognizable to critics like Björkman. Nothing better epitomized this popular version of vitalism than the nonsense song "Ta-Ra-Ra Boom-De-Ay" and the dance performances that accompanied it. In 1892 the Richmond *Times* described the British singer and dancer Lottie Collins performing "Ta-Ra-Ra Boom-De-Ay" at the Standard Theatre in New York City: "She swaggers, she wriggles, she sways back and forth, she shrugs her shoulders, she whips her hair on the floor, she whoops, she shakes her head, her shoulders, her arms, her hands, her body and her feet. While she sings the chorus she is the personification of resistless motion—a creature who is unable to any longer control the pent up animal spirits which she has contrived to keep in check while she spoke the senseless words of the various stanzas . . . If anyone takes pleasure in seeing the antics of a harebrained schoolgirl, two-thirds intoxicated, depicted on the stage, he will enjoy Miss Collins' attempt to delineate such a character, for she does it to the life." What conservative critics did not realize was that within the next two decades more and more young men and women would be emulating Miss Collins's performance, to the accompaniment of multiplying novel rhythms.

As urban dance halls proliferated, moralists fretted about the "orgy" taking place there nightly. The problem with trying to shut the dance halls down, as a small-town Minnesota paper admitted in 1905, was that young people dancing was as natural as children hopping and skipping, or colts and dogs capering—all were expressions of "Animal spirits, and not to be suppressed—at least so the psychologist and physiologist tell us." Yet dance halls could be dangerous. In the dressing room of one in Chicago, a young woman was found to have committed suicide, just the other night, the paper reported. So communities rightly wondered: What substitute for the dance hall can be found?

The threat of dance halls came not only from the vices that flourished in and around them—drunkenness, drug addiction, prostitution—but also from the dances themselves. "Tango Is Inherited from the Savages," the Anaconda (Mont.) *Standard* announced in 1914, citing a recent lecture by Oscar Duryea, who billed himself as a member of the American Society of Professors of Dancing. "We moderns like these dances because they come nearer savagery than any other dances and because we are at heart merely savages from whom the rougher edges have been worn by civilization," Duryea said. It was clear to him "that civilization has only glossed over their inherent instincts and that their inner selves are finding an outlet for their real inclinations through the dances that are really an outgrowth of the orgies in which their earlier predecessors indulged years ago." The projection of unbridled lust onto "savages" remained a reflex among the respectable.

The persistence of the primitive could be understood as the survival of animal spirits, which (moralists widely agreed) must be regularly released in harmless ways. "Any locomotive boiler will explode if too much pressure is put on the throttle," Rev. Charles Parkhurst warned, as he commended the churchmen of Milwaukee for encouraging dancing. "The girls of Milwaukee are going to dance. Animal spirits that have no vent to govern them are destined to an explosion, and when it comes will it come in a way that is disastrous?" By the early twentieth century, such questions were routinely posed in arguments for the managed release of animal spirits.

Still, there was an indictment to be made, melding morality and aesthetics, focusing on just how "crude and vulgar" the new dances could be. Alice Eis, an Ohio-born dancer back in America after four years abroad, told the New York *Sun* in 1913: "I never could see any excuse for the turkey trot anyway. It is essentially ugly." But, she added, "not until I saw it in New York did I realize how immodest it could be." Yet the pursuit of good health could justify the occasional moral hazard. In the end, Eis was glad that Americans had become obsessed with dancing, "because it is the most healthful exercise and tends to improve the figure and get rid of a great deal of superfluous animal spirits." This became the standard argument for cleansing dance of erotic associations and transforming it into athletic performance, of the sort perfected by Vernon and Irene Castle. By 1913, a writer in *Suburban Life* was asking, "What shall we do with the turkey trot?" and concluding that we had no choice but to accept it. Like other dances it was part of "the universal human expression, by movements of the limbs and body, of a sense of rhythm which is implanted among the primitive instincts of the animal world." The revaluation of the primitive involved recognition of its inevitability. Ignoring or suppressing animal instincts was an exercise in futility; the question was how to manage them.

Yet the vitalist celebration of amoral force continued to point beyond Victorian conventions, in Nietzschean directions, toward a realm beyond good and evil. Besides Adams, Dreiser, Quick, and other worshippers of force, the lyrical left sought its own transvaluation of value. Randolph Bourne, fresh out of Columbia, laid down the gauntlet of the younger generation in the name of the "experimental life"; Max Eastman and other aspiring literati pursued the "wild, free life" available in Greenwich Village; John Reed, fresh out of Harvard, met the Mexican bandit Pancho Villa and transformed him into a revolutionary hero;

Lincoln Steffens learned to spurn moralistic muckraking through psychoanalytic understanding; and Mabel Dodge Luhan (mentored by Margaret Sanger) sought to release the pent-up energy of female sexuality.

All these impulses coalesced during the years leading up to the Great War. The year 1913 became, in effect, the vitalist moment in American cultural history. Never before or since has the exaltation of direct, unmediated experience—"life itself"—acquired so much intellectual legitimacy, nor the chorus of life-worship attracted so many listeners and singers.

8

The Vitalist Moment: 1913 and After

BY 1913, THE current of vernacular vitalism had become a torrent, flooding public and private life, intensifying conflict between generations, sexes, and classes, inspiring new explorations in literature and the arts as well as intellectual and political life. As war clouds gathered, the vitalist wave crested and broke, and it never recovered from the impact of World War I. Yet vitalist impulses survived through the rest of the twentieth century, animating cultural tendencies that were loathsome and menacing as well as benign and necessary.

The innocent culture of life-worship that flourished before World War I was eventually engulfed by mass death. But no one could have been aware of that dark denouement in 1913—certainly not Randolph Bourne. He was a hunchback dwarf with a gift for friendship and polemic, a Jersey boy in flight from suburban blandness, and a recent graduate of Columbia University. He burst onto the intellectual scene as the defender of the younger generation against a conservative cultural critic named Cornelia Comer, who had published "A Letter to the Rising Generation" in *The Atlantic* in 1911. She indicted the youngsters as poorly educated, pleasure seeking, characterless, "agnostic-and-water" layabouts. Bourne responded with a paean to the "great, rich rush and flood of energy" embodied in youth, quickly turning his essay into a book, *Youth and Life*, which appeared in 1911. "It is the glory of the present age that in it one can be young. Our times give no check to the radical tendencies of youth," he wrote, concluding,

> The secret of life is then that this fine youthful spirit should never be lost . . .
>
> Out of the turbulence of youth should come this fine precipitate—a sane, strong, aggressive spirit of daring and doing. It must be a flexible growing spirit, with a hospitality to new ideas, and a keen insight into experience. To keep one's reactions warm and true, is to have found the secret of perpetual youth, and perpetual youth is salvation.

Despite his determined secularity, Bourne's exhortations exuded a religious fervor, a missionary hope. Seldom has the gospel of perpetual youth—in spirit if not years—been more stirringly preached. Still, the second part of the title was more important than the first. Bourne's book represented the apex of untested life-worship.

HIGH TIDE AND GREEN GRASS

The problem with the conventional bourgeois conception of adulthood, Bourne complained, was that it recoiled from direct experience into a brittle world of social and intellectual artifice. This was especially marked among the professional classes: "Most of these professors, these lawyers, these preachers—what has been their training and education, he [youth] says, but a gradual losing of the grip of life, a slow withdrawing into an ideal world of phrases and concepts and artificial attitudes?" The alternative to this fate was the richness of the experimental life, which arose from "a vivid and intense feeling of aliveness which it gives." Bourne claimed—somewhat counterintuitively—that this vividness and intensity depended on an ironic attitude toward life: the conventional paragon of earnestness lives on warmed-over moral formulas handed down from previous generations, he said, but "The ironist is the only man who makes any serious attempt to distinguish between fresh and second-hand experience."

Still, Bourne admitted, even the ironist had his vulnerabilities. "There is but one weak spot in his armor, but one disaster that he fears more almost than the loss of his life," Bourne wrote—"a shrinkage of environment, a running dry of experience." This was a key admission: it revealed the fundamental limitation of vitalist life-worship. If intense experience was the end and aim of life, what happened when the practical demands of daily life began to undermine possibilities for spontaneity and exuberance, when fresh experience began to seem stale or became unavailable? Bourne did not pose Jesus's question, but he could have: "if the salt have lost its savour, wherewith shall it be salted?" (Matt. 5:13) The usual answer, for life-worshippers, was to double down on the quest, seeking ever-new intense experiences. But this could prove exhausting and ultimately unsatisfying—not to mention dangerous, especially in wartime, as Bourne himself would discover when he was confronted by liberal intellectuals' support for U.S. entry into World War I. Bourne died in the flu epidemic of 1918, still a young man at thirty-two but already an apostate from the religion of experience.

Bourne's contemporary and fellow lyrical leftist Mabel Dodge Luhan (1879–1962) lived longer, and sustained her life-worship, in various forms, until she died at eighty-three. A key figure in the revitalized feminist movement of the 1910s, Luhan merged social and sexual radicalism. Her chief inspiration was the birth control advocate Margaret Sanger, who appeared often at Luhan's Greenwich Village salon, mesmerizing the other participants by evoking the unexplored possibilities of female sexual experience. Luhan recalled these episodes in her autobiography: "For Margaret Sanger to attempt what she did at that time seems to me now like another attempt to release energy in the atom, and who knows but perhaps that best describes what she tried to do," Luhan wrote. Indeed, "when she told us all about the possibilities in the body for 'sex expression,' and as she sat there serene and quiet, and unfolded the mysteries and the mightiness of physical love, it seemed to us we had never known it before as a sacred and at the same time a scientific reality."

With a string of husbands and lovers, Luhan explored "the mysteries and the mightiness of physical love" throughout her life.

She was not, however, a relentless activist in the masculine mode. On the contrary, she claimed to cultivate a passive quietude, a perpetual openness to the universe and its surprises. "One must just let life express itself in whatever form it will," she wrote. "That was my only philosophy in those days [the 1910s]. Let it happen. Let it decide. Let the great force behind the scenes direct the action. Have faith in life and do not hamper it or try to shape it." Despite Luhan's sexual radicalism, her version of vitalism remained consistent in certain ways with conventional notions of female passivity.

Her outlook also revealed the links between vitalist sensibilities and avant-garde art. This became apparent in her reaction to the vast exhibit of modernist painting and sculpture that opened on February 17, 1913, at the 69th Regiment Armory. The Armory Show included such venturesome figures as Marcel Duchamp, Pablo Picasso, Paul Gauguin, and Henri Matisse. Many attendees, accustomed to representational work, found the exhibit puzzling and even threatening. Luhan, in contrast, was ecstatic. She had been meeting frequently with the exhibit's planners and reported excitedly to Gertrude Stein: "They have only invited modern artists here who show *any* sign of *life*." That meant people (nearly all men) who were willing to take a pickax to ossified convention and forge new paths forward. "Many roads are being broken—what a wonderful word—'Broken'!" she said. This was a characteristic Modernist utterance, resembling Virginia Woolf hearing "the sound of breaking and falling, crashing and destruction" when she contemplated the avant-garde and its works. Woolf did not pretend to know how it would all turn out, but Luhan was optimistic. "And out of the shattering and petrifaction of today—up from the cleavage and the disintegration," she wrote, "we will see order emerging tomorrow. Is it so difficult to remember that life at birth is always painful and rarely lovely? We can but praise the high courage of the road breakers, admitting as we infallibly must in Gertrude Stein's own words, and with true Bergsonian faith—'Something is certainly coming out of them.'" The "Bergsonian faith" reflected the characteristic progressive belief that breakage and difficulty are mere products of the transition to Something Better. Technophiles and plutocrats would one day appropriate this strategy for their own purposes, and the economist Joseph Schumpeter would summarize it in his own influential phrase, "creative destruction."

Meanwhile Luhan summed up the Armory Show with characteristic self-dramatization, striking a revolutionary pose that was sharply at odds with her motto "Let it happen":

> I felt as though the exhibition were mine. I really did. It became, overnight, my own little revolution. I would upset America; I would, with fatal, irrevocable disaster to the old order of things. It was tragic—I was able to admit that—but the old ways must go and with them their priests . . . I was going to dynamite New York and nothing would stop me. Well, nothing did; I moved forward in my role of fate's chosen instrument, and the show certainly did gain by my propulsion. The force was there in me—directed now.

Luhan's dreams of revolution encompassed economics as well as culture, and she was not alone in making that connection. The vitalist impulse energized the labor movement during this period, chiefly through the intellectual sponsorship of the radical French thinker Georges Sorel, whose *Reflections on Violence* (1906) promoted vitalism for the oppressed masses, not merely the avant-garde bourgeoisie. For Sorel, working-class uprisings were not the pernicious outbreak of the mass mind, but a revolutionary collective expression of an essential intuition. The Industrial Workers of the World (IWW) embraced Sorel's exaltation of direct action—they came closer than any other labor organization to the anarcho-syndicalist ideal of spontaneous protest in behalf of decentralized communal aims.

The Paterson silk workers' strike, organized by the IWW among other unions, provided the occasion for putting Sorel's ideas to work. In March 1913, when the silk workers had been on strike for months, Luhan, John Reed, and others decided to stage a pageant of support in Madison Square Garden. In a series of dramatic scenes, the pageant reenacted the silk workers' growing sense of their own exploitation, their decision to form a union, and their violent confrontations with the bosses. It concluded with the workers and the audience joining together to sing "La Marseillaise." Luhan was ecstatic: "Imagine suddenly teaching 2,000 people of various nationalities how to present their case in a huge, graphic, orderly art form! Imagine planning an event to fill Madison Square Garden, a whole city block, where we used to go see Barnum and Bailey's Circus, with three rings and two bands going at once, and have it audible, visible, and composed enough to be convincing!" The event infused working-class solidarity with the throbbing energies of vitalism. "They were one: the workers who had come to show their comrades what was happening across the river, and the workers who had come to see it," Luhan wrote. "I have never felt such a high pulsing vibration in any gathering before or since." Luhan knew whereof she spoke, having committed her life to the pursuit of pulsing vibrations.

But the euphoria proved impossible to sustain. Gradually, the pageant lost more and more money, while the bosses wore down the workers. After five months, the strike failed. Luhan began to shift her gaze from proletarian to primitivist vitalism. This betokened a broader shift away from labor politics on the lyrical left, though not everyone made the turn. Reed did his best to meld proletarian and primitivist perspectives, as in his profile of Villa: "He is the most natural human being I ever saw—natural in the sense of being nearest a wild animal . . . If he isn't smiling he's looking gentle. All except his eyes, which are never still and full of energy and brutality. They are as intelligent as hell and as merciless. The movements of his feet are awkward—he always rode a horse—but those of his hands and arms are extraordinarily simple, graceful, and direct. They're like a wolf's. He's a terrible man."

But more commonly, primitivist radicals began to look uptown from Madison Square Garden, toward Harlem. The key moment in this transition can be traced to 1913, when a musical show called *Darktown Follies* brought Broadway up to Harlem. As the novelist James Weldon Johnson recalled: "*Darktown Follies* drew space, headlines, and cartoons in the New York papers; and consequently it became the vogue to go to Harlem to see it. One of the song numbers . . . was 'Rock Me in the Cradle of Love' . . . sung by the Negro tenor to the bronze soubrette in a most impassioned manner, demonstrating that the love-making taboo had been absolutely kicked out of the Negro theatre." The white critic Carl Van Vechten could barely contain himself: "Nine out of ten, nay, ten out of ten, of those . . . inexhaustible Ethiopians, those husky lanky blacks, those bronze bucks and yellow girls would have liked to have danced and sung like that every night of their lives, and how they showed it. How they stepped about and clapped their hands and 'grew mad with their bodies,' and grinned and shouted." Van Vechten would go on to make a career promoting black entertainment to white audiences, and would eventually become a major popularizer of the Harlem Renaissance. This was where part of the vitalist impulse was heading: uptown. It would animate white promoters' fascination with black culture down to the present.

Still, Van Vechten's heyday would come later, after the war. What really concentrated the energies of the prewar vitalist moment was not the rhythms of black entertainment but the inspiration of Bergson. Bourne invoked what would become a leitmotif in twentieth-century American intellectual life—the fear of asphyxiation in an airless culture of conformity—when he alluded to Bergson's work as a source of life-giving oxygen, through the melding of science and spirituality. As Bourne wrote in *Youth and Life*, "there has been a spiritual expansion these recent years which has created new atmospheres to breathe. It has been discovered that the world is alive, and that discovery has almost taken away men's breaths; it has been discovered that evolution is creative and that we are real factors in that creation." By the time Bourne wrote those words, an English translation of Bergson's *L'Evolution créatrice* had become a best-seller, and Bergson himself had become an intellectual celebrity.

That became clear in early February 1913, when the French philosopher arrived in New York to give a series of lectures at Columbia University and City College. For the first lecture at Columbia, the hall was filled, and the cars lining up to discharge passengers on upper Broadway created the first traffic jam in American history. As the New York *Sun* reported: "Five hundred women and men, the women outnumbering the men about ten to one, who went yesterday through the rain and slush to Columbia, heard the first of six lectures in French by the philosopher, Prof. Henri Bergson. Hundreds more could not get into the lecture hall. There were all sorts in the audience—distinguished professors and editors, well dressed women and overdressed women—one of whom fainted and created a sensation." A few weeks later, Bergson lectured at City College, where "two thousand students, all of them New York boys and young men, greeted the distinguished visitor with two or three striking forms of the characteristic American 'college yell,' a kind of greeting which the guest of the occasion seemed to understand and to appreciate." Surely there was more going on here than mere celebrity worship. What was it?

Part of Bergson's appeal arose from transatlantic intellectual ferment. He captured the discontent with positivistic and deterministic certainty, and provided a compelling alternative. The philosopher and historian of ideas Arthur Lovejoy summarized the situation as drily as possible in 1909 when he dubbed Bergson "the Metaphysician of the Life-force" and acknowledged that "M. Bergson has thus furnished at least the beginning of a demonstration that the nature of the universe is best understood in terms of process, of development, of the literal coming-into-being of new increments of reality." This was consistent with the Jamesian ethos, and radically inconsistent with older, static ontologies, idealist or materialist.

Apparently abstract ideas, when they entered vernacular use, had consequences for everyday life. If reality itself was in constant flux, then human experience must be as well. Rigid dualism went out the window: the invocation of Life (often capitalized) was a kind of magic wand that awakened disembodied ideas and inert matter from their dogmatic slumbers. It also reasserted human agency against the allegedly iron laws of determinism, as Louise Collier Willcox observed in *Harper's Weekly* while the French philosopher was holding forth in New York. "He offers men again free, creative energy," she wrote. "He shows Life, the great flux, in which consciousness is continually molding, controlling, restraining matter to the highest victory." Life was a flow of "free creative energy," which human beings could direct toward "the highest victory"—over what, remained unspecified. It would be hard to imagine a more bracing (if vague) alternative to a positivist universe unceasingly clanking forward in accordance with inflexible natural laws. Bergson provided a more palatable version of Nietzsche, purged of the German philosopher's overt obsession with power.

There was also something peculiarly American about the Bergson vogue. Americans, especially the educated and affluent ones who flocked to his lectures, wanted to think of themselves as denizens of a dynamic nation. Bergson played to this desire in his farewell interview, which the *New-York Tribune* headlined "Intellectual Bottle of Smelling Salts," calling his ideas an antidote, in effect, to the last fainting vestiges of a bedridden Victorian culture. Bergson no doubt pleased *Tribune* readers by announcing: "There is nothing conservative about Americans. They enjoy nothing that is old, they want everything that is new, whether it is good or bad for them. That is something they will decide for themselves after they have seen or heard about it. They have no patience with anything that is not original. With a people like that there is material for a new race—a race which shall lead the world to a greater understanding of liberty." One could hardly imagine a more flattering homage to Americans' sense of their own exceptional destiny.

Bergson also spoke in an idiom that reinforced the sense of special mission among a rising generation of young Americans, especially on the lyrical left. Walter Lippmann, like Reed a member of the Harvard class of 1910, declared Bergson the "most dangerous man in the world"; this was meant to be high praise. "The world was never so young as it is today, so impatient with old and crusty things . . . This freshness has found its philosopher in Bergson . . . [He] is to thought what Roosevelt is to action: a fountain of energy, brilliant, terrifying, and important," Lippmann wrote. "The reason for his stupendous reputation lies, it seems to me, in this: that Bergson is not so much a prophet as a herald in whom the unrest of modern times has found a voice. He is popular because he says with splendid certainty what thousands have been feeling vaguely." What Bergson said "with splendid certainty" was that the only certainty in a world of creative evolution was constant change. "And if I were interested in keeping churches, constitutions, customs fixed so that they would not change, I should regard Bergson as the most dangerous man in the world," Lippmann concluded. He came close to suggesting (like many prophets of progress since his day) that the mere fact of constant change was more important than where things were actually headed. Stasis alone was the enemy.

Along with the self-consciously young youth of America, Bergson also found an audience among American feminists, who were infusing the suffrage movement with unprecedented energy. In March 1913 they staged a march on Washington that rivaled the Paterson strike pageant in its orchestration of collective vibrancy. "Imagine a Broadway election night crowd surging forward constantly, without proper police restraint, and one gains some idea of the conditions," *The New York Times* reported. Bergson had flattering things to say about feminists, too. He told an interviewer that the current feminist movement was "*the greatest event in the history of the world since the promulgation of the Christian ideal.*" What feminists liked in Bergson, wrote Marian Cox in *The Forum*, was "his insistent demand that we turn away from the intellectualism of life to life itself, and this also is the aim of Feminism . . . Philosophy is becoming more human . . . When subjects of thought are said to become 'human' it is but a synonym for sympathy and harmony with the movement of life; which . . . is the *feminine* element in humanity." What male philosophers distrusted as Bergson's anti-intellectualism, from this view, was merely a sign of their own masculine mind-set—their distrust of any philosophy concerned less with ideas than with "life itself."

For many Americans, Bergson's *élan vital* was an uplifting alternative to the Freudian id. Most of the literate minority of Americans who had heard of Freud's ideas found it difficult to credit them—to believe that "the subconsciousness of every one of us contains nothing but the foul and monstrous specimens which they dredge up from the mental depths of their neuropathic patients and exhibit with such pride," as Edwin Slosson put it. This was part of the reason for the popular fascination with Jung, who became the chief psychoanalytic alternative to Freud. Though Jung's visit to America was overshadowed by Bergson's, his influence paralleled and outlasted the French philosopher's. In his New York lectures and during the years following them, Jung formulated his key departures from Freud—his notion of a collective unconscious, embodied in myriad cultural artifacts from Aztec masks to Tibetan prayer rugs; his definition of libido as a source of undifferentiated psychic energy rather than simply sexual energy; and his therapeutic focus on adult conflicts rather than repressed childhood memories as the origin of neurosis. Most broadly, Jung appealed to Americans by offering a vision of psychic wholeness rather than perpetual conflict. This appealed to the liberationist ethos of Greenwich Village bohemians who wanted more than Freud's "mature reserve" or "ordinary unhappiness," who wanted to harness psychoanalysis to social revolution, to smash the alliance between puritanical repression and capitalistic oppression by creating explosive new art forms and daring new experiments in gender relations.

Both Bergson and Jung contributed to the Americanization of the unconscious—the transformation of the unconscious from a cauldron of uncontrollable urges to a reservoir of energy, to be drawn on in times of need. Bergson especially could be linked with positive thinking, a connection that introduced a fatal blandness, a potential complicity with business bromides, into American interpretations of his work. From Bergson (and Eucken), *The Outlook* asserted in 1913, "Americans have discovered that philosophy is, after all, not merely an academic pursuit to be relegated to the lecture room and the study, but a practical guide that can be used by the business man at any moment of his busy life." The reduction of Bergson to a self-help writer required the melding of Bergsonian and American idioms; the result was a grotesque injustice to the range and originality of his thought. The New York *Post* provided an example:

> To fight hard according to the best light there is in us, to strive for victory but to take no shame in honest defeat, to recognize that the glory and the purpose are in the fighting—when once the French philosopher's conception of "creative evolution" has been translated into familiar, "inspirational" terms, many readers of Walt Mason, of Frank L. Stanton, and of Elbert Hubbard before he gave up philosophy for the advertising business, will be surprised to find they have been reading and thinking in Bergsonian terms all their lives.

All the talk about victory and defeat, glory and fighting, was American (and Rooseveltian) baggage, alien to Bergson's thought—though not, perhaps, to its underlying spirit. Bergson's rejection of fixed truths, his focus on journey rather than destination, on becoming rather than being, opened a fresh approach to the rivalrous claims of science and religion. The *Post* spelled it out: "Because the microscope has not given you the secret of life, it is not necessary to turn to an old-fashioned Power for the explanation. The very bankruptcy of Science is a good enough thing to believe in. A Science that has tried and failed is as satisfactory as a Science that succeeds. Truth simply consists in the perpetual quest after truth." As Lovejoy recognized, this perspective was consistent with the conception of truth-as-process that James had dubbed "pragmatic." It was also far more congruent with the trial-and-error nature of the scientific method than nineteenth-century scientists' claims to certainty had been.

Still, there was a certain vagueness around the edges of the *élan vital* (as there was around all celebrations of raw energy) that left it susceptible to appropriation for vile purposes, including those of militarists and fascists. This was what the French philosopher Julien Benda had in mind in *La Trahison des clercs* (1927), when he attacked Bergson for abetting "the treason of the intellectuals" by rejecting reason. Like other rationalists, Benda assumed that any accommodation with vitalism was the first step on the slippery slope toward soil worship. He seemed unable to acknowledge the possibility that rationality and vitality could ever be reconciled. This was not an arguable case but an emotional preference, what James called "the sentiment of rationality."

Long before Benda's assault, even at the height of the Bergson vogue, some thinkers were finding fault with Bergson's formulations. The heart of the matter, for many, was the equation of evolution with progress—even as its supposed engine changed from clanking mechanism to invisible *élan vital.* Some critics based their objections on what they believed was the highest scientific authority—the Second Law of Thermodynamics, particularly Lord Kelvin's formulation of it.

ENTROPY VS. PROGRESS

William Thomson, later Lord Kelvin, was a Christian who believed that the way to God was through science. He came of age in the mid-nineteenth century, when classical physicists were complicating the Second Law of Thermodynamics—the Law of the Conservation of Matter and Energy—by showing that some energy was lost (or at least made unavailable for further work) in every heat transfer, as in the tendency of heat to move from hotter to colder portions of a warming pan. While he prepared his influential paper on the dissipation of energy, in the 1850s, Thomson recorded his developing conception:

> I believe the tendency in the material world is for motion to become diffused, and that as a whole the reverse of concentration is gradually going on—I believe that no physical action can ever restore the heat emitted from the Sun, and that this source is not inexhaustible; also that the motions of the Earth and other planets are losing vis viva which is converted into heat; and that although some vis viva may be restored for instance to the earth by heat received from the sun, or by other means, that the loss cannot be precisely compensated and I think it probable that it is under-compensated.

For Thomson, the dissipation of energy suggested the eventual "heat death" of the universe—a prospect consistent with his theological conviction that the universe had a beginning and an end. God set it in motion, and will allow it to run down. This was a far cry from his defense of a "vital principle" a half century later, after he had become Lord Kelvin, but the young Thomson still inhabited a world where orthodox Christianity depended on faith in divine creation. Fifty years on, he articulated his beliefs in a different, perhaps even contradictory, vitalist idiom. Meanwhile, other researchers had confirmed the dissipation of energy and labeled it "entropy."

The concept of entropy became a subject of ferocious debate among armchair philosophers and amateur scientists—ferocious mainly because of its actual or imagined theological implications. Consider the scene at the Century Club in Manhattan over dinner in 1891. As A. R. Macdonough reported in *The Century Magazine*: "One evening Roelker of Teutonic build and heroic digestion . . . looked up with a twinkle in his eye from his beefsteak and pint of Chambertin, and discharged this bombshell of a proposition: 'The entropy of the universe tends to zero.' At once there was a commotion, and after ten minutes setting definitions the combat began, raging between divines, astronomers, and poets, till the house doors closed on it, still undecided, at three o'clock in the morning."

The terms of the debate changed gradually. Ultimately some intellectuals—most prominently Henry Adams—became fascinated by entropy, less for its reinforcement of Christian orthodoxy than for its challenge to the emerging secular faith that evolution could be equated with progress. Not even *élan vital* could keep evolution moving forward if the universe was "running down like a clock," as one popularizer put it, and as Adams claimed to believe—mostly to aggravate his progressive colleagues. Since the time span of entropic devolution was hundreds of millions of years, even if one accepted the theory, the attempt to apply it to current human affairs was almost purely fanciful. But the concept of entropy metaphorically captured the apocalyptic fantasies of many elite white men as they viewed the rising tide of democracy and mass culture, which they feared would engulf the "leadership class" in a dead-level ocean of mediocrity. And the determination to refute entropy showed how fragile and tenuous was the belief in ever-expanding energy, perhaps especially among those who most fervently espoused it.

Through the first decade or so of the twentieth century, science popularizers struggled to engage with the concept of entropy. For some it seemed the dark underside of the revolt that enraptured the Bergsonians, the rejection of the neat and tidy nineteenth-century cosmos—"a world of order, perpetuity, and harmony." Before the wide acceptance of the concept of entropy, it was easier to believe that "transformations of energy were always taking place and that their sum total always remained the same, that the universe was passing through a series of constant oscillations from chaos to harmony." But the discovery of the dissipation of energy, as Charles Nordmann wrote in the *El Paso Herald*, "necessarily leads towards a kind of thermic death which will congeal into a hopeless bleak and cadaverous lack of motion." For people who equated life itself with perpetual motion, the specter of "thermic death" was a haunting prospect, even in an unimaginably distant future.

So the early twentieth century was full of efforts to locate "reasons for believing in the eternal duration of the universe" while avoiding traditional theism. "It is very strange to observe," as Nordmann wrote in 1912, that these days it is not religious folk but secular scientists "who believe in a perpetual beginning again of everything, in a world which is constantly rejuvenating itself." Some salvaged eternity by an implicitly dualist sleight of hand, declaring that entropy might apply to physical energy, but not to "the world of thought," which was "constantly accumulating available energy with each succeeding generation." Others were more willing to challenge entropy directly with the help of "the new physics." Writing in *Harper's*, the chemist Robert Duncan declared March 1903 to be "a great historical date in the development of man"—for that was when Curie and Laborde announced the "heat-emitting power of radium bromide," revealing "the transcendent energies that reside within the atom, any atom of matter. The evidence of these atomic energies in the common elements is rapidly accumulating." Duncan claimed these discoveries provided new justifications for religious belief, though not in any orthodox sense. The old conception of the universe, which entropy seemed to uphold, was "God made it and started it at a definite time to run its course"; the new conception, which Duncan espoused, was "The universe *is* God in one phase of Him, and it possesses His attribute of eternal duration." The latter view, he believed, was more common among contemporary scientists and more compatible with "the New Physics." It was also more compatible with Bergsonian vitalism.

Henry Adams clung to the concept of entropy and kept using it as the basis for his critique of evolutionary progress, but other thinkers found more idiosyncratic or subtler ways to challenge the Bergson vogue. The skeptical philosopher Arthur Lovejoy took a stance of bemused detachment. Everyone seemed to feel called upon to write about Bergson, "from ex-presidents and British premiers to the essayists of women's clubs," Lovejoy observed; Bergson's ideas "may be heard on Sunday mornings from the pulpit by the devout, or be absorbed from the Sunday newspapers by the profane." For Lovejoy this furor was simply a matter of recurring intellectual fashion: "The need for a new sort of philosophic *Eleusinia* [initiation into mysteries] is recurrent among the cultivated classes every generation or two; it is a phenomenon almost as periodic as commercial crises. And it cannot be denied that Bergson's is the most Eleusinian of contemporary philosophies,—perhaps the most so since the Hegelian and kindred philosophies of the Romantic period." Four years earlier he had noted in Bergson "a resemblance to features of that a priori and over-imaginative *Naturphilosophie* by which Schelling and Hegel brought so much scandal upon the entire guild of philosophers . . . He is a sort of modernized Heraclitus; but he is thoroughgoing in his "flowing philosophy," whereas Hegel was a Heraclitus afraid of the fire.

Focusing on Bergson's "Eleusinian" qualities, Lovejoy recognized that the French philosopher was not merely a teacher but an initiator into mysteries—what later generations of Americans would call a guru. This was the classic posture of the rationalist dismissing what he deemed irrational. Horace Kallen took a similar stance when he challenged any proposed connections between Bergson intuitionism and Jamesian pragmatism, which he claimed depended on the question of thought's utility. It was a characteristic flattening of James's perspective, which would afflict interpretations of pragmatism for decades to come.

Other critics attacked Bergson from a traditional humanist perspective, confirming Lippmann's claim that Bergson was the sworn enemy of timeless truths and established institutions. "The ancient tradition of the world is that wisdom abides with the One and not with the Many," wrote the Harvard classicist Irving Babbitt. "In seeking to persuade men of the contrary, M. Bergson is holding out to them the hope that they may become wise by following the line of the least resistance, that they may grow 'spiritual' by diving into the flux." Babbitt was not alone among conservatives in seeing Bergson as a symptom of cultural decline.

George Santayana took a similar view, but placed it in a larger and more flexible framework. For him the disease of "overcivilization" took on subtler symptoms than it had for most prophets of decline. Santayana, a rationalist but not a dogmatic one, reflected on the significance of the vitalist distrust of intelligence: "if life is better the more intense and concentrated it is, intelligence would seem to be the best form of life. But the degree of intelligence which this age possesses makes it so very uncomfortable that, in this instance, it asks for something less vital, and sighs for what evolution has left behind. In the presence of such cruelly distinct things as astronomy or such cruelly confused things as theology it feels *la nostalgie de la boue.*" Bergson's philosophy "brings relief to a stale imagination, an imagination from which religion has vanished and which is kept stretched on the machinery of business and society, or on small half-borrowed passions which we clothe in a mean rhetoric and dot with vulgar pleasures." Once things were different and better, Santayana believed—like so many of his contemporaries. "When life was really vigorous and young, in Homeric times, for instance . . . Life was like the light of day, something to use or to waste, or to enjoy. It was not a thing to worship," he wrote.

The cult of Bergson and the spread of life-worship were signs, Santayana believed, not of cultural vitality but of its lack. "Only when vitality is low do people find material things oppressive and ideal things unsubstantial. Now there is more motion than life, and more haste than force; we are driven to distraction by the ticking of the tiresome clocks, material and social, by which we are obliged to regulate our existence." Popular vitalism offered a restorative balm for sick souls. In our overcivilized state, "We must bathe in the currents of some nonhuman vital flood, like consumptives in their last extremity who must bask in the sunshine and breathe the mountain air; and our disease is not without its sophistry to convince that we were never so well before, or so mightily conscious of being alive." Behind the paeans to Energy, Force, and Life, Santayana shrewdly perceived a sense of panic.

"Another civilization" was indeed succeeding Christendom, or at least its nineteenth-century Protestant version, and only a few observers were attuned to its deeper rhythms. While Santayana glimpsed the anxiety accompanying the affirmations of perpetual progress, Babbitt recognized that the new vitalist currents could reinforce a new cultural style, more suited to emotional life under organized, corporate capitalism. The merger wave of 1897–1903 solidified the rising power of oligopolistic capital and created whole industries dominated by a handful of corporations. The emergence of national advertising cast a glamorous aura around the new world of corporate-sponsored abundance and the men who made it hum. Advertising reinforced a new image of male success—the paunchy bearded patriarch gave way to the trim, clean-shaven executive whose power derived more from physical and mental energy than from any pretensions to wisdom or moral stature. Bergson's celebration of diving into the flux could be easily assimilated to the new style, and could perhaps legitimate it, whether Bergson intended that outcome or not. "A man, we are to believe, may devote all his mental energy to the stock market, and yet be numbered with the sages," Babbitt wrote, "if only he succeeds in his odd moments in immersing himself in *la duree reelle* and listening, in M. Bergson's phrase, to the 'continuous melody of his inner life.'" At this point we are moving beyond Max Weber's Protestant ethic and catching sight of the faint outlines of a new spirit of capitalism—one epitomized in our own time by corporate appropriations of "mindfulness" and other efforts to colonize human subjectivity for purposes of maximizing profit. Bergson, no doubt, would be appalled.

THE INCORPORATION OF VITALISM

Through the 1910s, the assimilation of vitalism to institutional purposes proceeded apace. TR kept up a steady drumbeat of militarist rant, demanding the revitalization of national will through imperial adventure and eventually through entry into World War I. Lippmann put vitalism in the service of social engineering in *A Preface to Politics* (1913) when he criticized the Chicago Vice Commission's stance on prostitution: "for what might be called the *elan vital* of the problem they had no patience," he complained. He urged the channeling of lust into socially useful pursuits—canalizing the life force, in Bergson's terminology. This was the drift of things—the assimilation of vitalism into larger institutional agendas. The trend was apparent in the rise of national advertising, whose makers soon discovered that just about anything could be associated with sustained ecstasy—down to and including a bottle of soda pop.

The vitalist mood also enveloped exercises in national greatness, which often took the form of such gargantuan public projects as the Panama Canal. "With an explosion which shook the surrounding hills and threw huge rocks high into the air, eight tons of dynamite were set off this afternoon by President Wilson touching a button in Washington, more than 4,000 miles away. Gamboa dike, the last obstruction in the Canal, was swept away, and the dream of centuries became a reality," *The New York Times* reported. This was not the only burst of energy Wilson activated remotely in 1913: he also lit up the Woolworth Building, then the tallest one in the world, by pushing a button on his desk in the Oval Office. But skyscrapers were a dime a dozen by 1913; the canal was a thing unto itself. It marked a milestone in the developing manhood of the nation, according to the Progressive journalist Ray Stannard Baker: "Until we went to Panama, the nation was like a youth who first ventures upon feats of strength or daring; we did not realize how strong we were . . . We bungled to start with, doubtful of our own abilities, not trusting the new attitude toward public work which it seemed necessary to take." But "we finally succeeded in pointing the energies of the nation, and by arousing an 'irresistible and irrepressible spirit of enthusiasm,' discovered within ourselves hitherto untapped sources of power." Nations, especially those just entering the imperial arena, need untapped sources of power as much as men did.

The marriage of individual and national vitality, proposed by Progressives like Roosevelt and Baker, was consummated in Wilson's crusade to make the world "safe for democracy." American vitality (and even more European vitality) was quantified, harnessed to military discipline, and wasted on the battlefields of France. Bourne was appalled; for him the embrace of war as a source of revitalizing energy was a grotesque perversion of vitalist promise. For years he had seen that the pressures for "preparedness" were building inexorably toward military intervention. "We suddenly realize that if we are to defeat the militaristic trend which we loathe we shall have to offer some kind of action more stirring and creative," he wrote in 1916. "There looms up as a crucial need that 'moral equivalent of war' with which William James first aroused our imaginations. It no longer seems so academic a proposal. Confronted with the crisis, we see that he analyzed the situation with consummate accuracy." Still, Bourne wanted to expand James's vision of alternative service beyond the strenuous tasks of late-Victorian manhood. His "Moral Equivalent for Military Service" included necessary work of all kinds, done by girls as well as boys—caring for the old and sick, repairing roads, building playgrounds, cultivating gardens, destroying insect pests, inspecting food and factories. To those who might protest that this would not promote the stern heroism only war can bring out, Bourne said, "We want to turn the energies of our youth away from their squandering in mere defense or mere drudgery. Our need is to learn how to live rather than die; to be teachers and creators, not engines of destruction; to be inventors and pioneers, not mere defenders." Like his vision of a multiethnic "Trans-national America," this vision of service to the commonweal turned out to be a "wild hope," as he had feared.

That became apparent in April 1917, when Congress declared war. Woodrow Wilson's war aims were breathtaking: not only would the war make the world "safe for democracy"; it would also create an international organization that would make war obsolete. This would be a war to end war.

Bourne was bitter, especially toward his fellow intellectuals—led by Lippmann among others. They imagined themselves "gently guiding a nation" into "a war free from any taint of self-seeking, a war that will secure the triumph of democracy" while at the same time "talking of the rough rude currents of health and regeneration that war would send through the American body politic," Bourne wrote. All the while, they failed to provide any policy alternatives to the relentless buildup toward war. "Was the terrific bargaining power of a great neutral ever really used?" Bourne asked. Nor did they challenge the provincial Anglo-Saxonism that fed war fever. "Our intellectual class might have been occupied . . . in discovering a true Americanism which would not have been merely nebulous but might have federated the different ethnic groups and traditions," he wrote. "America might have been made a meeting ground for the different national attitudes." Instead it became just another breeding ground of jingoism and xenophobia. Even the League of Nations was designed to reaffirm existing imperial hierarchies. Its program, Bourne observed, "contains no provision for dynamic national growth or for international justice." Wilson's agenda was bound to end in disillusionment.

So why did intellectuals embrace it? Bourne's explanation caught the ironies at the core of military interventionism. American intellectuals, true to their activist traditions, did not want to be on the sidelines; they felt "the itch to be in the great experience which the rest of the world was having." Humanitarian sentiment, supposedly central to the pro-war cause, turned out to be curiously selective. "Numbers of intelligent people who had never been stirred by the horrors of capitalistic peace at home were shaken out of their slumber by the horrors of war in Belgium," Bourne observed. "Hearts that had felt only ugly contempt for democratic strivings at home beat in tune with the struggle for freedom abroad." The "primitive idea" of war for democracy, he concluded, was in the end little more than "a craving for action." But it was a craving for action in remote locales, nothing as banal as the local and familiar. The parallel with contemporary events could not be more apparent: too often, advocates of military intervention abroad seek support by shedding crocodile tears over the pain of Iraq and Afghanistan and (more recently) Ukraine, while ignoring the travails of Camden and Detroit. Bourne's critique reminds us that we have been here before.

In the pro-war rhetoric of his time as of ours, unthinking activism became translated into tough-minded realism. "The pacifist is roundly scolded for refusing to face the facts, and retiring into his own world of sentimental desire," Bourne wrote. "But is the realist, who refuses to challenge or criticize facts, entitled to any more credit than that which comes from following the line of least resistance?" Realism became a rationale for acquiescence in the plans of the powerful. "If we responsibly approve," the realist argument went, "we then retain our power for guiding. We will be listened to as responsible thinkers, while those who obstructed the coming of war have committed intellectual suicide and shall be cast into outer darkness." Bourne anticipated the pattern of foreign policy debate down to our own time—a time when those who advocated the invasion of Iraq (however mistakenly) preserve their status as "responsible thinkers," while those who opposed the war (however presciently) remain in "outer darkness." *Plus ça change, plus c'est la même chose.*

What was especially distressing to Bourne was the failure of John Dewey's version of pragmatism, which he had embraced as an undergraduate at Columbia, to provide any basis for a critical perspective on the war. "If William James were alive would he be accepting the war-situation so easily and completely?" Bourne wondered. Dewey had turned his philosophy into little more than a rationale for adjustment to the logic of events. As Bourne saw it, Dewey did not grasp "the sinister forces of war," its power to unleash fanatic intolerance; his belief in the pragmatist's power to control war, to mold it to his own liberal ends, overlooked "the mob-fanaticisms, the injustices and hatreds" that inevitably accompanied the mass mobilization of "the war-technique." Transcendence of the war technique required a return to the restless spirit of William James. As Bourne concluded:

> Malcontentedness may be the beginning of promise. That is why I evoked the spirit of William James, with its gay passion for ideas, and its freedom of speculation, when I felt the slightly pedestrian gait into which the war had brought pragmatism. It is the creative desire more than the creative intelligence that we shall need if we are ever to fly.

But we were not to fly in 1917, when vitalist sentiments were pressed into the service of the war effort. As always, naïve recruits were alleged to be champing at the bit to kill (in this case) Huns. Such sentiments soon dissipated under the stress of actual battle, but pro-war intellectuals still thought they saw a sacred lesson in the conflict. The psychologist G. Stanley Hall underscored the religious dimensions of the war when he imagined its chief achievement—at least on the domestic front—as the manufacture of what he called "morale." There is a chief goal of man, he told the *New-York Tribune* in 1920, though "it took the awful psychic earthquake of war to reveal it." During the war we learned "to keep ourselves, body and soul, and our environment, physical, social, industrial, etc. always at the very tip-top of condition. This super-hygiene is best described as morale." It was "the one and only true religion of the present and the future"—which we practice "when we thank whatever gods we believe in that we are alive, well, young, strong, buoyant, and exuberant with animal spirits at top notch," and which is most perfectly embodied in the ideal soldier, on alert and ready for action. Vitalist impulses could hardly have been more thoroughly integrated with the demands of the nation.

Still, the incorporation of vitalism remained a problematic project, especially given the unsettled state of popular science in the 1910s. It was all very well for Hall to harness animal spirits to military discipline, but by 1920 he was something of a relic of Victorian culture, and Roosevelt was dead. Outside of Hall's psychology, which he had long assimilated to moral concerns, science seemed less available than ever to the mobilization of any social endeavor.

This was largely due to the emergence of the new physics and the decomposition of familiar notions of matter. What had seemed like a liberation from mechanical determinism also opened new vistas of uncertainty. As Albert Gallatin wrote in the New York *Sun* in 1916: "Radioactivity and related phenomena have compelled us to modify our opinions of the doctrines of energy and of matter. Instability, impermanence, and decay seem to be the universal law of nature: matter in its simplest dissociated forms inevitably relates itself to and may be purely a manifestation of what is called energy." It was only a short step from uncertainty to unreality, and *Current Opinion* took it in 1917, announcing the possibility of the "unreality of all things in the light of modern knowledge." Citing George Bernard Shaw on the unavailability of any criterion for distinguishing real phenomena from "fancies of our too easily illusioned minds," the magazine observed, "The real in science takes on more and more, with the progress of knowledge, a quality of unreality . . . Who . . . has seen the ether or space or a wireless wave? Who has heard energy or put entropy into a vial to be smelled or tasted?" The specter of ultimate unreality could not be exorcised with mere injunctions to "real life."

But other forms of scientific knowledge, more easily popularized than post-Newtonian physics, were becoming resources for dispelling the demons of unreality and even uncertainty. None was more influential than statistics. The year 1913, the apex of the vitalist moment in America, was also when Robert Musil chose to set his novel *The Man Without Qualities*, in a thinly disguised Vienna he calls Kakania. It is the last year of the old order, before the proud tower of bourgeois civilization goes up in flames. Everyday Viennese life combines the commitment to calculation with the pursuit of spontaneity: it is the foundational dialectic of the emerging civilization that Santayana is trying to discern—numbers and flow. Musil's novel foreshadows their coexistence in the social world to come—a world where social scientists would seek to plumb and quantify dimensions of human experience that were previously thought immeasurable.

CALCULATING THE INCALCULABLE

Our days became numbered long before the rise of Big Data and algorithmic governance. Indeed, the creation of statistical selves in the service of state and corporate bureaucracies was well under way by the early twentieth century, in the midst of what U.S. historians still call the Progressive Era (in deference to the self-description of the reformers who dominated it). Eli Cook, Sarah Igo, Dan Bouk, and other gifted young historians have begun to explore sorting and categorizing institutions that branched out from their nineteenth-century predecessors, which had focused mainly on criminals and deviants. The new sorters were more catholic in their scope—life insurance actuaries quantifying the risks of insuring individual policyholders, pollsters using survey data in an attempt to construct a "majority man" or "average American"—with their efforts culminating in the most ambitious tabulating scheme of all, the Social Security system, in 1935. This was a program that assigned numbers to Americans for their own good, to help ensure their security in old age. Counting people and keeping tabs on them could underwrite benign government intentions.

Statistical selves emerged amid the cultural ferment around the turn of the nineteenth century. The overcivilized man of the 1880s was becoming the man without qualities of the 1910s, arising from his neurasthenic's bed to go out into the world, but lapsing into a kind of bland detachment when he did so. In Musil's novel, the first time we see the protagonist, Ulrich, he is looking out his window, "ticking off on his stopwatch the passing cars, trucks, trolleys and pedestrians . . . timing everything whirling past that he could catch in the net of his eye . . . calculating the incalculable." Later in the novel, the tables are turned: Ulrich becomes the object of calculation when he is arrested on a false charge of insulting a police officer. "He felt as if he had been sucked into a machine that was dismembering him into impersonal general components before the question of his guilt or innocence came up at all." Yet "he could, even at such a moment as this, himself appreciate this statistical demystification of his person and feel inspired by the quantitative and descriptive procedures applied to him by the police apparatus as if it were a love lyric invented by Satan. The most amazing thing about it was that the police could not only dismantle a man so that nothing was left of him, they could also put him together again, recognizably and unmistakably, out of the same worthless components." This recognition scene puts us on the cusp of our contemporary world.

One could hardly find a more appropriate slogan than "calculating the incalculable" for a historical moment when statistics have slipped the leash of social utility and become instruments for probing the public soul. The vitalist union of body and mind ironically promoted the belief that subjective states were measurable and quantifiable—subject to the tools of science. Ulrich, for his part, seems to have no subjective life at all. He is a professional mathematician, but not a practicing one; he has no sense of identity, individual, communal, or professional, no inner life, no convictions or even tastes ("he simply left the furnishing of his house to the genius of his suppliers, secure in the knowledge that he could safely leave the traditions, prejudices, and limitations to them")—not to mention no commitments outside the self, and no self.

Yet as Musil makes clear, the man without qualities inhabits Vienna at the very time, the aftermath of the *fin de siècle*, when artists and writers were obsessed with the creation of a vibrant free-floating self—with personal liberation from ossified cultural values, with spontaneous, overflowing vitality. But from the moment they were felt in public, the pulsing vibrations of energy were merged with the needs of big, emerging institutions—the national security state and the corporate capitalist economy. This was the development that culminated in Hall's celebration of "morale."

For decades, even vitalists themselves had recognized that spontaneous energies—animal spirits—were potentially disruptive to existing hierarchies and had to be harnessed to managerial ends. As early as 1844, the journalist Parke Godwin noted in the *New-York Daily Tribune* that while industrial leaders "have resorted to associated effort in the execution of almost every kind of enterprise, it has never occurred to them to organize the human forces, the vital energies by which alone all useful results are brought about." By the early twentieth century, industrial psychologists and personnel managers had finally begun to respond to Godwin's challenge. The task, as one of them, R. B. Wolf, noted in 1922, was "Making Men Like Their Jobs" (as he titled his contribution to the book *Practical Psychology for Business Executives*). "The only kind of an organization that will have a permanent esprit de corps is the kind where the creative spirit of the individual is free to express his real inner spirit," Wolf wrote. "Why not, then, pattern our system of control after the nervous system of the human body, through which the life impulses or vitalizing forces are distributed in the body structure?" Why not, indeed?

Progressive educators and social engineers had already come to this conclusion. They were committed to teaching children how to fit into an increasingly corporate society by allowing their animal spirits free play within carefully circumscribed limits. This was the rationale of the "play movement" during the Progressive Era—young ruffians would be transformed into useful citizens through the regular discharge of excess energies in harmless games and sports. With Lippmann's recommendation that prostitution could be managed by monitoring the life force and Hall's exaltation of the soldier ready for action, the incorporation of vitalism seemed complete—at least rhetorically.

Yet even among social engineers, calculation and spontaneity could coexist awkwardly. Perhaps the best way to show the uneasy cohabitation of those two modes of thought in one mind is to examine the most influential quantifying vitalist, the Yale economist Irving Fisher. More than anyone else, Fisher brought the emerging science of statistics into the arena where political economy and public policy meet. Fisher pioneered not just in categorizing people but in monetizing them, body and soul. He moved statistics from mere counting to cost accounting and cost-benefit analysis. Everything had its cash value; money could be used to measure the value of anything.

Fisher's views inspired *The New York Times* to publish a full-page article about him on January 30, 1910. It began: "An eight-pound baby, is worth, at birth, $362 a pound. That is a child's earning power as a potential wealth-producer. If he lives out the normal term of years, he can produce $2,900 more wealth than it costs to rear him and maintain him as an adult. The figures regarding earning capacity are given by Irving Fisher, Professor of Political Economy." Stunned by the inevitable outcry from outraged parents, Fisher tried to explain himself years later in another *Times* piece: "Human life is much more than a moneymaking machine, but it is only as a moneymaking machine that it has a calculable money value. The figures . . . were naturally not intended to include any sentimental human values in human life. What a baby is worth to its mother could never be calculated; but its value, or rather the value of the average baby as a prospective breadwinner, can be and has been calculated many times." As Eli Cook has argued, Fisher resorted to the pricing of everyday life in order to win the support of business, professional, and political elites for a larger program of promoting personal and national vitality. Cost-benefit analysis was a tool for putting across a utopian agenda of regeneration—one that also might increase productivity and therefore profits.

Fisher had always been a zealous quantifier. As an undergraduate at Yale, he was an ambitious young mathematician, confident in the capacity of numbers to explain the world. As a Yale graduate student in economics, he made calculating the incalculable the core of his dissertation. He focused on subjective desire as the basis for his version of marginal utility theory. For decades, he wrote, marginal utility theorists "have been taunted with the question: what is a unit of pleasure or utility?" His answer was consumer desire, which translated itself into the price the consumer was willing to pay for the desired object. As he later wrote, "Prices are determined by the actual desires of men." Value was, in effect, dependent entirely on price. Reducing consumer desire to quantifiable utility required Fisher to postulate an isolated, calculating, autonomous self, denuded of the dense network of social relations that Adam Smith and other classical economists had assumed surrounded all business transactions. This was how Fisher put the "neo" in neoclassical economics.

But Fisher was not just another Progressive bureaucrat, searching for order through managerial expertise; he also worshiped at the shrine of energy and vitality. A brush with tuberculosis when he was a young man had transformed him into a lifelong advocate of fresh air, exercise, and total abstention from all intoxicants and stimulants, down to and including a cup of tea. "To spread the gospel of good health became his guiding fetish," his son wrote years later. Fisher helped organize the Committees of 100 on National Health, which issued reports on national vitality; he won the ear of Roosevelt, who praised his work as a contribution to the critical work of revitalizing the American people. Like many other Progressives, Fisher became an enthusiastic advocate of eugenics, certain that "we are the trustees of the racial germ plasm that we carry," and committed to isolating "defectives" so that "we can save the bloodstream of our race from a tremendous amount of contamination." The path from eugenics to mass murder had not yet been cleared. In the 1910s and '20s, eugenics advocates were aiming at "perfecting the race." Whether it was the human race or merely the Anglo-Saxon one was an open question.

Fisher summed up his hygienic (and eugenic) wisdom in *How to Live* (1917, cowritten with Eugene Lyman Fisk), which sold more than 500,000 copies and was intended "to include every practical procedure that, according to the present state of our knowledge, an athlete needs to keep himself superbly 'fit,' or that a mental worker needs in order to keep his wits sharpened to razor-edge." This was a demanding goal, as Fisher and Fisk knew. "Our health ideals," they wrote, "should rise from the mere wish to keep out of a sick-bed to an eagerness to become a wellspring of energy." Here one can see the contemporary vogue of "wellness" in embryo.

But Fisher and Fisk did not stop there. Their highest and most fervent ambition was to overcome death itself. "So far as science can reveal, there seems to be no principle limiting life," they wrote in *How to Live.*

"There are many good and bad reasons why men die, but no underlying medical reason why they must die." When Fisher's daughter Margaret was diagnosed with schizophrenia, he had her treated at Trenton State Hospital by the psychiatrist Henry Cotton, who believed that mental illness resulted from bodily infection, and could be cured by surgical removal of infected tissue. Cotton removed sections of Margaret's bowel and colon, and she eventually died. Yet Fisher remained convinced of the rightness of Cotton's treatment. After Margaret's funeral he announced, "There aren't going to be any more deaths in this family!"—speaking with "fierce determination," as his son recalled. One can only imagine what he meant by this outburst, absurd on its face, yet revelatory of his deepest obsession—the conquest of death through the careful cultivation of spontaneous life.

Fisher believed he was an example of William James's "religion of healthy-mindedness," but his wife, Margaret, in moments of impatience, sometimes referred to him as a "health prude." He conceded the justice of this characterization: "As you say, it's all wrong to make a burden of Hygiene. True Hygiene means serenity and unconcern." Yet Fisher's quest for vitality never quite brought him serenity, despite his constant self-admonitions to cultivate it. He thought he was a Jamesian, but he clung to a monistic conception of the universe that James would have found profoundly unsatisfying. Whatever the meaning of life might be, Fisher wrote in 1903, "of one thing I am convinced: that it is for us to approve and not disapprove. It is perfect because it is impossible of variation by a hair's breadth. The wheels of time never jump the track . . . The program of Fate is never altered." Compare this assertion to one of James's own, that " 'ever not quite' has to be said of the best attempts made anywhere in the universe at attaining all-inclusiveness."

Two decades later, in 1924, Fisher wrote, in a letter to Margaret, "I've been reading a biography of Frederick Taylor and felt throughout as if I were reading my own biography." His affinity for the father of scientific management came from their shared anxieties and their common obsessive-compulsive tendencies, but also showed up in Fisher's Progressive prescription for ending the strife between capital and labor. The Industrial Workers of the World member, he wrote, was "the naughty boy of American industry"—healthy outlets should be found for his energies, so as to turn him from a potential hooligan into a model worker.

Fisher's social vision exalted superabundant vitality in the service of economic productivity and national greatness. This was Hall's "morale" but with a difference: Fisher's version of animal spirits could be quantified (not to mention monetized), hence rendered "scientific" and objective. In this it resembles the present-day efforts by behavioral economists and bankers to calculate the incalculable—such as Wells Fargo's quixotic "animal spirits index," which reduces the slipperiness of human motives to the parsimonious precision of numbers.

These gambits have the appeal statistics always have had: They seem to be objective, beyond politics, prejudice, and power—veritable messages from God, as Florence Nightingale believed. "To understand God's thoughts," she said, "we must study statistics, for these are the measure of His purpose." Nightingale wrote at a time when Providence and Progress moved forward hand in glove; some people think they still do. But if we were to replace Nightingale's God with the money god of capital, we would have a better sense of where we are today. It is, among other things, a world where quantified information serves the system Shoshana Zuboff has called "surveillance capitalism," and where human beings have been transformed into human capital—persons without qualities indeed. Irving Fisher is mostly remembered today as the man who, six days before the Great Crash of 1929, announced that the stock market had reached a permanently high plateau. But from our longer-range perspective, surrounded by signs and portents of monetized data, we can draw a different conclusion: Despite his defects as a short-term prognosticator, Irving Fisher had seen the future.

9

Race, Sex, and Power

DURING THE DECADE or so following the Armistice, animal spirits virtually disappeared from public discourse, even as vitalist currents coursed through popular culture. The reconfiguration of value intensified and spread; in some quarters—Harlem, for example—reconfiguration became reversal, as artists and writers of all hues exalted pulsating sensuality over puritanical restraint, while seldom if ever referring to animal spirits.

Harlem's cabarets throbbed with erotic promise, attracting a widening stream of white sensation-seekers. The white people would have swarmed less eagerly if they had not been primed with panting expectation by the idioms of primitivist vitalism that were spreading in literature, painting, and dance. At the National Theatre in Washington in 1921, an affluent white audience could witness the Russian ballerina Anna Pavlova's performance in "a wild 'goat dance' of sheer animal spirits," which *The Washington Post* reviewer described as "a mad bacchanal of sub-human species, recalling the diabolic pranks of Nijinsky years ago on this same stage." But by mid-decade, the reviewer's revulsion seemed a survival from another era. Primitivist vitalism was going mainstream, charged with a blend of racial and sexual energy, deploying stale essentialist tropes as if they were freshly minted.

GONE PRIMITIVE: SHERWOOD ANDERSON

No American author of the 1920s was more prone to primitivist vitalism than Sherwood Anderson. By his own account he was a clever and successful advertising copywriter, "a smooth son of a bitch." Rejecting the glib and superficial commercial culture he helped to create, Anderson embarked on a search for intense, authentic experience in the interstices of the emerging mass market society. Anderson's determination "to see beneath the surface of lives" led him at his best to transcend primitivist cliché. In *Winesburg, Ohio* (1919), he focused on the people he called "grotesques," outliers who were failures in the eyes of the smart and up-to-date—withered Victorian maidens disappointed in love, country doctors with pockets full of paper pills. This was the Anderson who inspired several generations of American writers, including William Faulkner, Thomas Wolfe, and Norman Mailer.

But the one work that truly resonated with a popular audience was *Dark Laughter* (1924), his only bestseller. The novel told the story of a man in flight from a pointless job and a loveless marriage who ends up in the arms of another restless seeker, the sex-starved wife of a boring factory owner. Black characters populate the edges of this conventional tale, brimming with sexual knowingness and posing a spontaneous alternative to the confused and self-deluding white folk.

Anderson was born in Camden, Ohio, in 1876. His family were of Presbyterian stock, but the Protestant ethic provided no path of success for them. His father was a harness maker and sign painter at a time when machines were putting harness makers out of business and commercial display was in its infancy. The son remembered the father as a windbag and a failure. Anderson's mother took in washing to support the struggling family and died of tuberculosis at forty-two. Out of this bleak background Anderson worked his way. He was a newsboy, a farmhand, a factory laborer, a soldier, and finally a crack copywriter at an advertising agency in Chicago, where he worked, on and off, from 1900 to 1922. He interspersed copywriting with entrepreneurial ventures that took him and his growing family to Cleveland and Elyria, Ohio.

Before long he was mixing business with pleasure in the acceptable ways—chasing golf balls over fields where he had once cut corn, arranging out-of-town trips as pretexts for picking up a little something on the side, phoning "Ed" to see if he could "manage" some women. "Sure, boys," the generic Ed would say when they arrived in town. "Let's have a shot or two. I can see that you boys are several shots to the good." As Anderson recalled the scene in 1933 he wrote: "God, why did we always have to call each other 'boys'?" To Anderson in retrospect, the pose of boyishness epitomized the dirty lies at the heart of American businessmen's social life—the lies of confidence men who feigned earnestness and innocence while they cut crooked deals and consorted with prostitutes.

Anderson glimpsed an alternative way of life one morning from his bedroom window, as he gazed out dazed and bleary after a night of false hilarity and drunken groping. In the yard of the house next door, an Italian man and his wife were laying out a garden with strings and wooden stakes. Their children joined them and "one of the children, a boy of nine or ten, suddenly began to dance. He threw up his arms and began whirling about the pile of dead weeds and vegetable stalks left from another year," while the younger children and eventually the parents stopped their labors, laughed and laughed. "Myself above . . . stale and dry-mouthed from my night of so-called 'fun.' American business men's fun." The Italian family's "dance of life," its pastoral celebration of vitality and fecundity, was nothing if not an outpouring of animal spirits, though the term was going out of fashion by the 1920s and Anderson did not use it.

He did later say that this glimpse of spontaneous joy focused his flight from a life of systematic deceit and self-hate toward a search for what he called "aliveness"—a quality he found increasingly elusive now that "the time of the wise-crackers" had come. The wisecrackers were often advertising men like Anderson himself, cooking up clever slogans to sell worthless products, cultivating a smart-ass ethos energized by the "effort to drag down, always to drag down, even life itself." For Anderson, as for other vitalists, the elusive phrase "life itself" signified a sense of pure being that came more easily to Italians of peasant stock as well as rural folk generally—indeed to anyone on the margins of modernity, especially people of color.

The search for "life itself" led him to quit advertising for good and head to Kentucky, where he began to feel rejuvenated. "I am myself as I was when I was a boy," he wrote to his confidante Harriet Finley. The trip to the rural South was for him "a kind of pilgrimage back into the realities of life." The product was *Dark Laughter.*

A century later, Anderson's views of black people make painful reading. He describes them as gods, monkeys, trees, colts, banana plants, children—anything but adult human beings. But this of course is precisely their appeal to the primitivist in Anderson.

Soon after he leaves his wife, Anderson's protagonist Bruce Dudley heads downriver toward New Orleans. En route he discovers a new, black world. "The niggers were something for Bruce to look at, think about," Anderson wrote. The men who worked on the docks had "faces like old monkeys—bodies like young gods." He watches a young black woman across the street, sometimes with her man, sometimes not. She knows Bruce is looking. "What does it matter? He is looking as he might look at trees, at young colts playing in a pasture." The woman's "slender, flexible body" reminds him of "the thick waving leaf of a young banana plant." He spends several months in New Orleans in a neighborhood populated mostly by African Americans, where he listens to their "dark laughter" and marvels at their ease and grace. Heading back up north, he arrives in Old Harbor, Indiana, on the Ohio River—the town where he grew up. He takes a job in a wheel factory. After days of routine physical labor, his nights are full of memory—opportunities for Anderson to indulge in his own racialized primitivist fantasies.

Bruce remembers the black workers he saw on the Ohio River when he was a boy. "Word-lovers, sound-lovers—the blacks seemed to hold a tone in some warm place, under their red tongues, perhaps. Their thick lips were walls under which the tone hid. Unconscious love of inanimate things lost to the whites—skies, the river, a moving boat—black mysticism never expressed except in song or in the movements of bodies. The bodies of the black workers belonged to each other as the sky belonged to the river." This was D. H. Lawrence with a racial twist—primitive Others in mystical union with one another and with the natural world.

Anderson's essentialist convictions were shared by leading black writers of the Harlem Renaissance. This outlook moved against the grain of the dominant trend in early twentieth-century thinking about race. The anthropologist Franz Boas had begun to emphasize the role of environmental influences on human development, and to deemphasize race—indeed to call into question its very existence as anything more than a cultural construction. But essentialism persisted. The writer Alain Locke kept alive the nineteenth-century black belief that white people were an especially brutal and predatory race, and even W. E. B. Du Bois slipped into essentialism occasionally, as when he wrote in 1915 that "[in] disposition the Negro is among the most lovable of men." The writers of the Harlem Renaissance were much less restrained. Among the most prominent was Claude McKay, a Jamaican immigrant to the United States whose career melded literature and politics, mixed race consciousness with class consciousness, and made McKay a celebrity among Soviet Communists as well as African Americans. His fictional celebration of the "Negro metropolis" relied heavily on essentialist tropes, even while he tried fitfully to transcend them.

THE SHEER RHYTHM OF DELIGHT: CLAUDE McKAY

McKay was born in 1889 or 1890 in Clarendon Parish, Jamaica. His parents were well-to-do farmers. His father was of Ashanti descent; his mother's people came from Madagascar; both were devout Baptists. When he was nine, Claude was sent to live with his oldest brother, a teacher who, his parents thought, would ensure that Claude was properly educated. The boy read widely in the English canon, developing a passion for Shakespeare and a determination to write poetry. By the time he was seventeen he had located a mentor, an English gentleman named Walter Jekyll, with whom he may have had a homosexual relationship.

(McKay's biographers agree that he was almost certainly bisexual.) Jekyll made his library available to McKay, everything from *Childe Harold* to *Paradise Lost* to *Leaves of Grass.* He also encouraged McKay to write in his native dialect and helped him get his first book of poetry, *Songs of Jamaica*, published in 1912.

That same year, McKay left for the United States to attend the Tuskegee Institute; he quickly developed a revulsion for the "semi-military, machine-like existence there," and fled to Kansas State University, to study agronomy. But reading W. E. B. Du Bois's *Souls of Black Folk* inspired him to combine poetry and politics. He headed for New York, where he married his childhood sweetheart Eulalie Lewars and fell in with the bohemian radicals around *The Seven Arts* and *The Liberator*, where some of his poetry was published. He also took a job as a dining-car waiter for the Pennsylvania Railroad, joined the Industrial Workers of the World, and co-founded the African Blood Brotherhood, a semisecret organization dedicated to black self-determination through socialist revolution.

It was 1919 and the postwar Red Scare was in full gallop—not a good time to be a political radical in America. McKay took off for London, where he quickly became involved in an internecine leftist dispute. The *Daily Herald*, a socialist paper, had published a racist article criticizing France's deployment of black troops in Europe and insinuating hypersexuality to black people in general. McKay responded in *The Workers' Dreadnought*, a rival leftist magazine:

> Why this obscene maniacal outburst about the sex vitality of black men in a proletarian paper? Rape is rape; the colour of the skin doesn't make it different. Negroes are no more over-sexed than Caucasians; mulatto children in the West Indies and America were not the result of parthenogenesis.

As a character in one of McKay's novels puts it, revealing a vernacular version of psychoanalytic insight: "You don't know why the white man put all his dirty jokes onto the race. It's because the white man is dirty in his heart and got to have dirt. But he covers it up in his race to show himself superior and put it onto us." It would be hard to find a more straightforward description of self-purgation through allegorical protection.

Yet despite these insights, McKay's fiction was full of "over-sexed" black people. Though he was not formally affiliated with the Negritude movement that inspired other Caribbean writers, like them he deployed what the literary critic Gayatri Spivak calls a kind of "strategic essentialism." In 1928, after two trips to the Soviet Union and years of contentious engagement with left-wing cultural politics in both Britain and the United States, McKay published *Home to Harlem*, a semi-autobiographical novel that celebrated Harlem as the place where black people could express their "sex vitality" more freely than anywhere else.

Sex is at the center of the book from the outset. Its protagonist, Jake Brown, has left the U.S. Army after the Great War and found his way back to Harlem, where one of his first social encounters is with the charming prostitute Felice. She likes him so much, she sleeps with him for free. Jake has concluded that women "were the real controlling force of life," as he remembers fights over women between white and black soldiers in France. "Victims of sex, the men seemed foolish, ape-like blunderers in their pools of blood." Self-contempt for his own sexual needs and resentment of women's capacity to exploit them sometimes float just beneath the surface of McKay's prose. Late in the novel, reflecting on his frustrations and obsessions, Jake imagines, "The wild, shrieking mad woman that is sex seemed jeering at him."

But this is only momentary. Jake thinks he knows a good woman when he sees one, and he spends much of the novel trying to reconnect with Felice after their first encounter. This leads him on a picaresque wander through bars, restaurants, cabarets, and whorehouses, not to mention multiple encounters with erotically adept women. Some do their best to keep him on the premises longer than a one-night stand. One of them, on the evening before Jake leaves her, "moved down on him like a panther, swinging her hips in a wonderful, rhythmical motion. She sprang upon his neck and brought him down." When Jake takes a job with the Pennsylvania Railroad, he has regular layovers in Pittsburgh; on one occasion he spots "a bouncing little chestnut-brown" in the doorway of a restaurant on Wiley Avenue, the main thoroughfare of the black neighborhood. "She rolled her eyes and worked her hips into delightful free-and-easy motions. Jake went in. He was not hungry for food."

From time to time, McKay sets his characters loose in a cabaret—a signature scene in the literature of the Harlem Renaissance, and an opportunity for racialized primitivist reveries: "The piano-player had wandered off into some dim, far-away, ancestral source of music . . . lost in some sensual dream of his own . . . Like a primitive dance of war or of love . . . the marshalling of spears or the sacred frenzy of a phallic celebration." The descriptions could also be more direct and immediate: "Brown bodies, caught up in the wild rhythm, wiggling and swaying in their seats." The music makes even sex workers forget they are on the job. "The women, carried away by the sheer rhythm of delight, had risen above their commercial instincts (a common trait of Negroes in emotional states) and abandoned themselves to pure voluptuous jazzing. They were gorgeous animals," McKay writes. To describe black prostitutes as "gorgeous animals," who abandoned mere monetary concerns in the throes of emotional ecstasy, may have been to indulge in primitivist, even racist cliché—certainly it could seem so from a contemporary perspective. Still, the primitivist clichés reflected a broader vitalist critique of capitalist modernity that often hit its target, and that McKay shared with Anderson, Lawrence, and other writers in the 1920s.

The most self-conscious critique is offered by Jake's friend Ray, another dining car waiter and something of a stand-in for the author. Ray is widely read and politically radical. His father was a government official in Haiti, who didn't want U.S. marines in his country and said so in public. When he refused to shut up, he was jailed. Ray's brother tried to organize a protest and the marines shot him in the street. There was no one to pay for the rest of Ray's time at university, so he became a waiter on the railroad. Waiting on white people isn't so bad, he tells Jake; once a big southern senator tipped him half a dollar. Such a life can be full of bruises and insults, Ray admits, but "when I have the blues I read Dr. Frank Crane." The reference to Crane, a syndicated advice columnist and professional positive thinker, was McKay's sly hint that even educated black workers could be attracted to the upbeat banalities of white popular culture.

Ray is a man between worlds. He recoils from nearly all his fellow dining car workers. "Intermittently the cooks broke their snoring with masticating noises of their fat lips, like animals eating," Ray observes in disgust. Indeed he "loathed every soul in that great barrack-room, except Jake." Why should he be lumped with these creatures in white people's minds, merely because they had race in common? "Race"—he ponders the word—"why should he have and love a race?" The very notion of race seemed a reified fetish.

Yet at the same time Ray recognizes that racial difference is impossible to ignore, and central to imperial domination. "Ray felt that if he was conscious of being black and impotent, so, correspondingly, each Marine down in Hayti [*sic*] must be conscious of being white and powerful. What a unique feeling of confidence about life the typical white youth of his age must have! Knowing that his skin-color was a passport to glory, making him one with tens of thousands like himself. All perfect Occidentals and investors in that grand business called Civilization." Many ordinary white soldiers may well have identified with the grandiose pretensions of empire, though some probably remained skeptical even as they clung to a sense of racial superiority. However precise or imprecise his perception, Ray is given to free-floating associations as he tosses on his bunk, reflecting on how his pride in Haiti's independence lifts him above North American Negroes, fearing that his servile occupation reduced him to their level.

Ray, like his creator, remains ambivalent toward "that grand business called Civilization." Advising Jake to use a condom, he says, "This is a new age with new methods of living. You can't just go on like a crazy ram-goat as if you were living in the Middle Ages." Yet he fears imprisonment in "that long red steel cage," the railroad, and marvels at "that great body of people who worked in nice cages: bank clerks in steel wire cages, others in wooden cages, salespeople behind counters, neat, dutiful, respectful, all of them. God! how could they carry it on from day to day and remain quietly obliging and sane?" The question transcended race and interrogated modernity itself. Was imprisonment, as Max Weber had suggested, an inescapable feature of the modern (capitalist) condition? Like Anderson recoiling from the docile impotence of the crowds on the Chicago streets, Ray longs for a life of more than mere compliance to routine.

> If the railroad had not been cacophonous and riotous enough to balance the dynamo roaring within him, he would have jumped it a long time ago. Life burned in Ray perhaps more intensely than in Jake . . . [Ray] drank in more of life than he could distill into active animal living. Maybe that was why he felt he had to write. He was a reservoir of that intense emotional energy so peculiar to his race.

Like Anderson's, McKay's vitalism drew strength from essentialist notions about race. The vitalist reconfiguration of value elevated dark skin over white, even as black intellectuals like Ray struggled to find a place in that reconfigured cultural universe. In McKay's next book, *Banjo* (1929), Ray reappears and is still struggling. "He was of course aware that whether the educated man be white or brown or black, he cannot, if he has more than animal desires, be irresponsibly happy like the ignorant man who lives simply by his instincts and appetites," McKay wrote. "But a black man, even though educated, was in closer biological kinship to the swell of primitive earth life." Despite his critical intellect, Ray still longs for "Peace and forgetfulness in the bosom of a brown woman. Warm brown body and restless dark body like a black root growing down into the soft brown earth." Civilization, McKay assumed, could not efface one's racial inheritance.

Jake is less ambivalent than Ray—"not raw animal enough to be undiscriminating, nor civilized enough to be cynical." He is certain that Felice is "a prize to hold," and that he wants "that little model of warm brown flesh." When he finally finds her again, they dance to a "haunting rhythm" in a Harlem cabaret where white people are devouring what they see as an exotic, vaguely threatening, but ultimately amusing spectacle: "now, like a jungle mask, strange, unfamiliar, disturbing, now plunging, headlong into the far, dim depths of profundity and rising out as suddenly with a simple, childish grin. And the white visitors laugh. They see the grin only." Jake persuades Felice to leave this stew of primitivist expectations and cross-racial confusions and head with him for Chicago; they must know they will find the same muddle of misunderstandings there, but Felice is game. En route to the train station, she runs back for her good-luck necklace—she couldn't leave without it. Through the bull market of the 1920s, African Americans remained immersed in the culture of chance; they didn't need Keynes to remind them that they were living lives of radical uncertainty.

As Felice's last-minute dash suggests, black women as well as black men needed to court the goddess Fortuna. Life was unpredictable and dangerous for both sexes. What made it even more complicated, for some, was the conflict created by mixed-race parentage in a society where respectable blacks and whites were equally insistent on patrolling the color line—and equally suspicious of the "mulattoes" whose parents had crossed it. Mixed-race people themselves were even more likely than educated blacks like Ray to feel trapped between two worlds, at home nowhere. No writer of the Harlem Renaissance experienced this sense of homelessness more deeply than Nella Larsen.

THE PROBLEM OF THE COLOR LINE: NELLA LARSEN

Larsen's mixed-race background gave her a "sense of partial invisibility" that was both "an affliction and a source of insight"—as her biographer George Hutchinson writes. Though Larsen supported the cause of black equality throughout her life, she resisted the notion that race was the defining force of personal identity. She wrote sympathetically about mixed-race women whose animal spirits took erotic form, clouding their judgment and undermining their ambitions. From her own experience she knew that sex, for women, had more complicated consequences—social as well as biological—than it did for men. Larsen's fiction provided convincing explorations of female sexual desire amid the ferment of the first "sexual revolution" in America.

Larsen was born in 1891 in a Chicago neighborhood known as "Satan's Mile"—State Street between Van Buren and 22nd. Her tenement birthplace was surrounded by burlesque houses, peep shows, and brothels. Her mother, Mary Hansen, had emigrated from Denmark in the 1880s; her father, Peter Walker, had come from St. Croix in the Danish West Indies. He disappeared from the family when Larsen was still very young. Mary took on work as a seamstress, married a teamster named Peter Larsen, and gave birth to Nella's white half sister. Through her autobiographical protagonist Helga Crane in *Quicksand* (1928), Larsen recalled her feelings about these changes as a child, and how she eventually came to terms with them as an adult. "That second marriage, to a man of her [mother's] own race but not of her own kind,—so passionately, so instinctively resented by Helga even at the trivial age of six—she now understood as a grievous necessity." For a cultivated Danish woman with a small child, marrying a working-class Scandinavian immigrant was a strategy for survival.

But the consequences for Larsen were disastrous. As the new white family gradually distanced themselves from her, she may well have felt "tangled feelings of love and abandonment, anger and self-loathing, empathy, shame, and powerlessness," as Hutchinson suggests. Even as a young child she was an outsider. En route to school she walked past drunks slouching outside saloons and whores soliciting clients. Her seamstress mother, straining for respectability, dressed her in fine fabrics, which Larsen loved. She would come to the conviction that a woman's choice of garments was an important sign of personal freedom. But at Wendell Phillips High School, she discovered that nice clothes could not ingratiate her with the children of the black bourgeoisie, who looked down on working-class immigrants, not to mention anyone of questionable paternity. As an adult, depending on the social setting, she remained sensitive to the stigma of blackness among white people, and of illegitimacy among respectable folk in general. She cultivated a diffident demeanor, remaining ready to reject friends before they rejected her. Helga Crane only gradually becomes aware of "that faint hint of offishness which hung about her and repelled advances, an arrogance that stirred in people a peculiar irritation."

Larsen's upbringing exacerbated her "offishness." Mary Larsen was attached to her mixed-race child but also embarrassed by her presence.

She wanted to meet Nella's needs but also keep her at a distance. So she sent her to Fisk University in Nashville, a magnet for respectable African Americans on the rise. Nella felt as separate from them as she had from her high school classmates. They were as proud of their families as old-stock white folk; she did not even know her father. After her freshman year, she was expelled for violating the school's prohibition of "extravagant and expensive dress." She spent the next several years with her mother's family in Copenhagen, enjoying but also resenting her role of exotic Other. She returned to the United States in 1912 and enrolled in the nursing school at Lincoln Hospital in New York. Upon graduation in 1915, she took a position as head nurse in the hospital at the Tuskegee Institute, where Claude McKay had been a student just a few years before.

She found the place even more repellent than he had, beginning with the drab uniforms the students were required to wear. As Larsen later wrote in *Quicksand* (where Tuskegee appears as Naxos): "Something intuitive, some unanalyzed driving spirit of loyalty to the great racial need for gorgeousness told her that bright colors *were* fitting and that dark-complexioned people *should* wear yellow, green, and red." The uniforms epitomized the conformist ethos of Tuskegee. Larsen felt suffocated by the endless talk of "teamwork" and "race consciousness," which seemed to her to stifle wayward impulses toward independent thought. This was the beginning of her lifelong revulsion from any form of racial uplift. Yet "it wasn't, she was suddenly aware, merely the school and its ways and its decorous stupid people that oppressed her," Helga realizes in retrospect. "There was something else, some other more ruthless force, a quality within herself, which was frustrating her, had always frustrated her, kept her from getting the things she wanted. Still wanted." She inhabited a soul divided against itself.

Fleeing Tuskegee, Larsen returned to New York, took a nursing job in the Bronx, and met the quintessential promising young man, Elmer Imes. The son of an Oberlin graduate and nonsectarian Protestant missionary, Imes was born in Memphis, went to Fisk, and later took a PhD in physics at the University of Michigan. Well connected with the black elite, an accomplished researcher in quantum physics who cultivated aesthetic and literary tastes, Imes was comfortable with white people and skilled at repartee. He and Larsen married in 1919.

About the same time, what became known as the Harlem Renaissance was beginning to hum, often at the interracial parties hosted by the writer James Weldon Johnson and his wife, Grace Nail Johnson, a daughter of the black elite and a prominent figure in the promotion of African American arts. The Imeses moved in the same circles. Larsen found the parties exciting, and began to create a social profile that fit them. She shifted from nursing to librarianship, focusing her ambition on the 135th Street branch of the New York Public Library, where the librarian Ernestine Rose was promoting a vision of cultural pluralism that involved exhibits of black artists' work and conversations with black writers.

It was a promising time for such projects, emerging in the wake of the vitalist moment. Walter White was promoting his Ethiopian Art Theatre in uptown Manhattan; female blues singers like Mamie Smith were reaching white audiences on Okeh Records and other crossover labels; Louis Armstrong was bringing the "Sugar Foot Stomp" from New Orleans to New York; Paul Robeson was performing Negro spirituals in Greenwich Village, abandoning pseudo-refinement, restoring evangelical energy. Black entertainment was about to go big-time. Within a few years the white journalist William Houghton could observe that "the negro" had acquired a kind of cultural hegemony:

> We talk his dialect, we sing his songs, we dance his dances. His drink, gin, is the national drink; his tempo, jazz, is the universal rhythm. Whenever we relax we fall under his spell; it is only in our tight working moments that we are free of it. And perhaps not entirely then. In the hum of the machinery that surrounds us, the click of the car rails, the rattle of typewriters, the rataplan of riveters, we are becoming increasingly conscious of the surging syncopation with which the negro, our former slave, has enslaved us.

However hyperbolic (and perhaps fearful) his claims, Houghton had captured a pervasive social trend: the Harlem Renaissance had attracted a huge white audience and, at least in certain circles, reversed the valuation of black and white. Nella Larsen was a beneficiary of this ferment: she was meeting a wider variety of people than she had ever known before, ranging from Anita Thompson, a seductress who moved easily between white and black worlds, to Jessie Fauset, a prim black novelist who believed the arc of enlightenment moved away from race-mixing. Thompson later chummed up with Man Ray in Paris; both she and Larsen would call him their "Dutch uncle." Fauset hosted afternoon teas like the one Helga found "boring beyond endurance"—Larsen's default-setting response to the conservative black bourgeoisie.

Like Thompson, Larsen actively sought white friends in the arts. The most important, for her, was Carl Van Vechten, an uncloseted gay man from Cedar Rapids, Iowa, who perfected the practice of camp before the idea had even been invented. Van Vechten was a generous friend and entertaining host who loved extravagant, self-parodic costumes. He was also a lifelong devotee of African American arts who embraced many primitivist clichés but eventually outgrew them. Harold Jackman, a gay black man who was also a vigorous promoter of African American arts, told Van Vechten: "You are the first white man with whom I ever felt perfectly at ease. You are just like a colored man!" To Van Vechten, it may have been the highest compliment he could have received.

But not all black people were as enthusiastic about him as Jackman. Van Vechten's roman à clef, *Nigger Heaven* (1926), provoked enormous controversy. Like the Harlem Renaissance it celebrated, *Nigger Heaven* was a product of the reconfiguration of value surrounding animal spirits, and a culmination of the vitalist moment. For a brief period, even the word "nigger"—now the very definition of unmentionable hate speech—became more than a mere insult; for some writers and intellectuals, at least, it had come to signify an authentic embodiment of vibrant life. Once at a dinner party attended by the Imeses and Van Vechten, the conversation turned to the question of whether "colored" or "Negro" should be the preferred racial designation. Overhearing, the kitchen maid piped up: "It don't matter what they call us . . . we're Niggers right on." The guests—white, black, and brown—erupted in laughter.

The significance of this scene is ambiguous. The maid may have been saying that no matter what label was applied to black people, they would still be considered by whites the bottom rail in the social order. Or she may have been suggesting that no matter how strenuously uplifters urged them to merge with bourgeois culture, they would remain attached to their own racial essence. Whatever she had in mind, the guests' bemusement reflected their sense of ironic distance and class superiority over the kitchen help, even as they admired her fresh eruption of feeling.

By the 1920s, the term "animal spirits" was rarely used by journalists popularizing science, perhaps because it was gradually becoming associated with an outmoded scientific concept. But it still evoked a familiar range of traits: warmth, spontaneity, humor, musicality, physical grace, in a word, vitality—especially but not exclusively sexual vitality. Van Vechten's novel showcased the varieties of black vitality on display in Harlem. He sympathetically addressed the conflicts that would be explored in greater depth by McKay in *Home to Harlem* and by Larsen in *Quicksand* (both of which appeared two years after *Nigger Heaven*)—the recoil from the notion that "race" lay at the core of one's very being; the tense ambivalence between an attraction toward a black racial inheritance and a desire to transcend it. Larsen loved the novel; James Weldon Johnson defended it publicly.

But Van Vechten was a white man, describing black lives from the outside in. However sympathetic his portrayal of Harlem street life, he could easily be seen as a slumming voyeur. Black leaders on the left were especially suspicious. Hubert Harrison, a leading Afro-Caribbean socialist, attacked Van Vechten as a literary "pansy" and dismissed the whole Harlem vogue as a production of poseurs. Du Bois, writing in *The Crisis*, was equally outraged: "Life to [Van Vechten] is one damned orgy after another, with hate, hurt, gin, and sadism," he complained. For him the book was a sign that white decadents were commandeering what had been a promising Negro Renaissance. Stung by the criticism, Van Vechten grew ambivalent about what he had written and regretful that he had written it—though ultimately he may have taken some comfort from the comparably hostile reaction provoked by McKay's *Home to Harlem*. Critics identified both books, oversimply, as paeans to the primitive.

While controversy swirled around Van Vechten, Larsen worked

away on the manuscript that became *Quicksand.* Van Vechten read it, made editorial suggestions, and promoted it with Alfred and Blanche Knopf, his own publishers. Eventually they accepted the novel, an extraordinarily sensitive account of a cultivated mixed-race woman caught between worlds—animated but ultimately undone by her own animal spirits, in particular her wayward erotic longings.

Quicksand opens in the elegant apartment of Helga Crane, a woman of taste and style who has been teaching English for two years at Naxos, a paramilitary institution in the Deep South committed to training young black people for success in a society dominated by white people. Helga feels isolated and unappreciated. Her aloof detachment is simply baffling to her colleagues, including the conventionally respectable young man she is engaged to marry. On the night in question, she has made up her mind to leave this place that has systematically suppressed her need for "individuality and beauty." The next morning, she meets with Dr. Anderson, the earnest gray-eyed brown man who has recently become principal, to tell him her decision. He launches into a sustained soliloquy aimed to dissuade her, invoking the school's noble mission and how he plans to enlarge it.

> Helga Crane was silent, feeling a mystifying yearning which sang and throbbed in her. She felt again the urge for service, not now for her people, but for this man who was talking so earnestly of his work, his plans, his hopes. An insistent need to be part of them sprang in her.

By the time Anderson is winding up his pitch, Helga realizes that "he had won her." But then he concludes by praising "an elusive something" in her. "Perhaps I can best explain it by the use of that trite phrase, 'You're a lady.' You have dignity and breeding." Helga abruptly rejects the compliment, telling him that she was born in a Chicago slum, that her father was a black gambler who deserted her "white immigrant" mother, and that the two may not even have been married. So much for "dignity and breeding." Despite Anderson's magnetic appeal, Helga is reminded that she does not belong at Naxos. Still, in the Jim Crow car on the train to Chicago, she remembers his "piercing gray eyes."

The city is indifferent to her economic plight. She tries to reconnect with her white uncle Peter, who had always been a benefactor, but is turned away by his new wife. She begins desperately seeking employment of any kind but is repeatedly told that she is too educated, too refined for domestic or even secretarial work. But finally she secures a temporary position as an assistant to Mrs. Hayes-Ross, the wealthy widow of a black politician. Hayes-Ross is traveling to New York to lecture on racial uplift, and when she discovers Helga has no prospects in Chicago, arranges for her to stay with her niece, Anne Grey, who is, in Helga's words, "almost too good to be true"—affluent, elegant, educated, "brownly beautiful." She scorns Naxos and its works, and she doesn't have much use for white people either. Within the black elite, she has been to the manner born.

Whatever their differences regarding white people, Anne brings Helga into her circle of black friends. Helga feels "that strange transforming experience . . . that magic sense of having come home. Harlem, teeming black Harlem, had welcomed her, and lulled her into something that was, she was certain, peace and contentment." The foundation of Harlem's appeal is its blackness. Helga realizes that "while the continuously gorgeous panorama of Harlem fascinated her, thrilled her, the sober mad rush of white New York failed entirely to stir her." Harlem is a refuge from self-important bustle.

But "peace and contentment" do not last. Spring comes, and with it, restlessness. "As the days multiplied, her need of something, something vaguely familiar, but which she could not put a name to and hold for definite examination, became almost intolerable." That "something vaguely familiar" soon assumes more palpable form. Mrs. Hayes-Ross has secured Helga a low-level administrative job with Mr. Darling's new Negro Insurance Company; she often has to substitute for her boss at boring "health and uplift" meetings, but at one of them she spots Dr. Anderson, in town on Naxos business.

He suggests they share a taxi and in the back seat they chat amiably. But "underneath the exchange of small talk lay another conversation of which Helga Crane was sharply aware. She was aware, too, of a strange ill-defined emotion, a vague yearning rising within her." When the cab pulls up to her door, she feels "consternation and regret" that the meeting is over so soon. When she bids him goodbye formally, he says,

"'You haven't changed. You're still seeking for something, I think.' At his speech there dropped from her that vague feeling of yearning, that longing for sympathy and understanding which his presence evoked. She felt a sharp stinging sensation and a recurrence of that anger and defiant desire which had so seared her on that morning in Naxos." He comes to call three days later; she puts him off, through Anne, with a suddenly unmissable engagement. Once again, Anderson has evoked an ambivalent mix of longing and revulsion in Helga.

In the midst of her disconsolate drifting, a deus ex machina appears—a check for $5,000 from her estranged uncle Peter, whose wife had sent her away a year earlier. The money could not have arrived at a more propitious time. Her delight in black Harlem has turned to "harrowing irritation" and ultimately "smoldering hatred." The feeling climaxes when she is on an errand in the company's general office and notices that "the inscrutability of the dozen or more brown faces, all cast from the same indefinite mold, and so like her own, seemed pressing forward against her . . . It was as if she were shut up, boxed up, with hundreds of her race, closed up with that something in the racial character which had always been, to her, inexplicable, alien. Why, she demanded in fierce rebellion, should she be yoked to these despised black folk?" Back in her cubicle, she feels self-loathing—"They're my own people, my own people"—but it was no good. She has to be excused, to get away, to run out into the heat of the street, where it's begun to rain. Outside, she concludes that "she didn't, in spite of her racial markings, belong to these dark segregated people. She was different. She felt it. It wasn't merely a matter of color. It was something broader, deeper, that made folk kin." Why, she wonders, had her mother not consented when her aunt Katrina begged for her to be allowed to stay with her in Denmark? Now the check from Uncle Peter made a return to Denmark possible.

But Harlem reasserts itself before she leaves. On a "thick, furry night" in late summer, after a dinner party in Anne's honor, the guests decide to go partying, and Larsen stages her own cabaret scene. It is, Helga realizes with bemusement, the sort of place characterized by the righteous as hell.

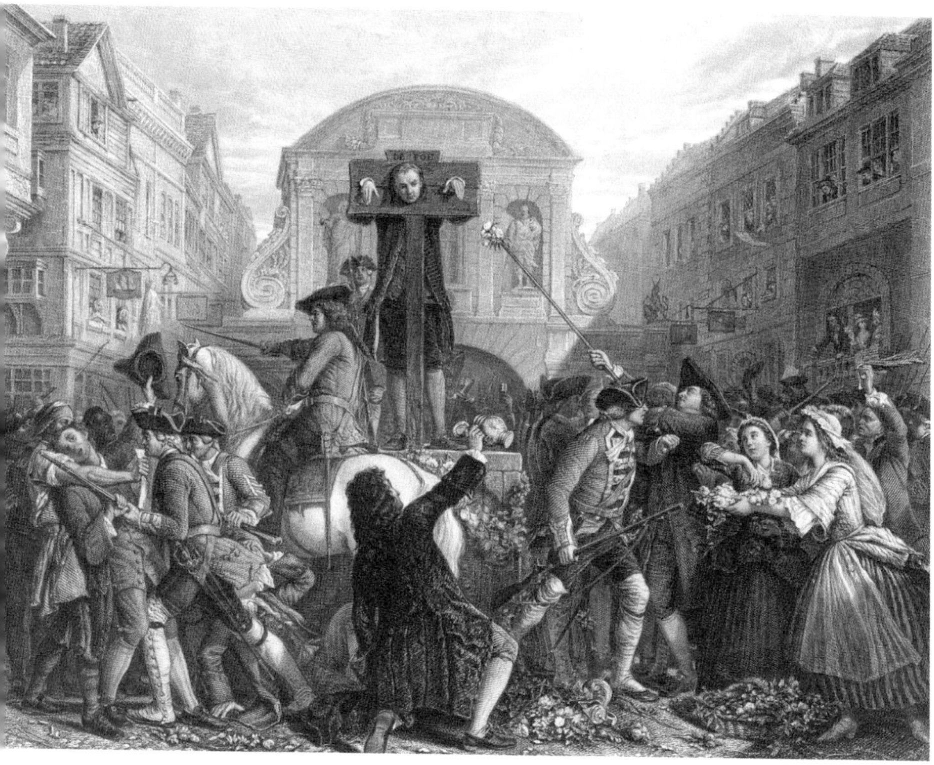

ABOVE: *Defoe in the Pillory*. Engraving by John Carr (or James Charles) Armytage, after Eyre Crowe, 1862 (© National Portrait Gallery, London)

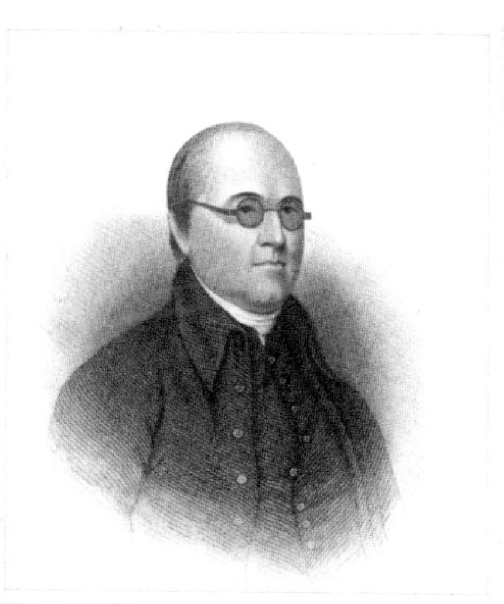

REV. TIMOTHY DWIGHT, S.T.D.LL.D.
PRESIDENT OF YALE COLLEGE
FROM 1795 TO 1817.
Timothy Dwight

LEFT: Timothy Dwight. Engraving, artist unknown, ca. 1820–1840 (The Miriam and Ira D. Wallach Division of Art, Prints and Photographs Collection, New York Public Library)

Camp Meeting, by Alexander Rider. Lithograph by Hugh Bridport for Kennedy & Lucas Lithography, ca. 1829 (Library of Congress Prints and Photographs Division)

Animal Magnetism. Lithograph published by T. McLean, June 14, 1838 (Images from the History of Medicine, National Library of Medicine)

ndrew Jackson Davis. Frontispiece
• *The Principles of Nature, Her Divine
evelations, and a Voice to Mankind,*
347 (The Miriam and Ira D. Wallach Division
Art, Prints and Photographs Collection, New
ork Public Library)

The Panic of 1873: Closing the Doors of the Stock Exchange on Its Members, Saturday, Sept. 20th. Wood engraving, 1873, from *Frank Leslie's Illustrated Newspaper*, no. 37 (October 4, 1873): 66. (Library of Congress Prints and Photographs Division)

yer's Sarsaparilla trade card. The inscription reads: "Purifies the Blood, Stimulates the
ital Functions, restores and preserves Health, and infuses New Life and Vigor throughout
ıe whole system." Dr. J.C. Ayer & Co., Lowell, MA, 1870–1890 (Museum of the City of
ew York)

Testimony in the Great Beecher-Tilton Scandal Case Illustrated. Lithograph designed by James E. Cook for Commercial Lithograph, ca. 1875 (Library of Congress Prints and Photographs Division)

Helen Wilmans Post (Frontispiece from Wilmans, *A Search for Freedom.* Sea Breeze, Florida: Freedom Publishing Company, 1898)

Professor William James, photographed in 1899 (The Miriam and Ira D. Wallach Division of Art, Prints and Photographs: Print Collection, The New York Public Library)

Wall Street Bubbles—Always the Same. A caricature of John Pierpont Morgan as a bull blowing bubbles, or "inflated values." From *Puck* no. 49, May 22, 1901. Lithograph by Udo J. Keppler for the J. Ottman Lithographic Company, 1901 (Library of Congress Prints and Photographs Division)

ABOVE: Mabel Dodge Luhan, photographed in 1912 at 23 Fifth Avenue (Mabel Dodge Luhan Papers. Yale Collection of American Literature, Beinecke Rare Book and Manuscript Library)

RIGHT: John Maynard Keynes and Lydia Lopokova. Photograph by Walter Benington for Elliott & Fry, 1920s (© National Portrait Gallery, London)

Claude McKay. Photograph by Carl Van Vechten, 1934 (Carl Van Vechten Papers Relating to African American Arts and Letters, Beinecke Rare Book and Manuscript Library, Yale University / © Van Vechten Trust)

Nella Larsen. Photograph by Carl Van Vechten, 1934 (Carl Van Vechten Papers Relating to African American Arts and Letters, Beinecke Rare Book and Manuscript Library, Yale University / © Van Vechten Trust)

Bryant Park. A Victim of the Depression. The inscription reads: "Out of a job, the attitude of utter dejection and submission to fate is all too strongly evident." Photograph by George Miller, Jr., ca. 1930 (Museum of the City of New York)

'he Durham Family of Brooklyn, New York, Practices Civil-Defense Drills. Photograph by ohn Vachon for *Look* magazine, 1951 (Museum of the City of New York)

Herman Kahn. Photograph by Thomas J. O'Halloran, 1965 (*U.S. News & World Report* Magazine Photograph Collection, Library of Congress Prints and Photographs Division)

Norman Mailer, writer, gliding. Photograph by Bernard Gotfryd, 1967 (Bernard Gotfryd photograph collection, Library of Congress Prints and Photographs Division)

> For the while Helga was oblivious of the reek of flesh, smoke, and alcohol; oblivious of the oblivion of other gyrating pairs, oblivious of the color, the noise, and the grand distorted childishness of it all. She was drugged, lifted, sustained by the extraordinary music, blown out, ripped out, beaten out, by the joyous, wild, murky orchestra. The essence of life seemed bodily motion. And when suddenly the music died, she dragged herself back to the present with a conscious effort, and a shameful certainty that not only had she been in the jungle, but that she had enjoyed it, began to taunt her. She hardened her determination to get away. She wasn't, she told herself, a jungle creature.

Helga pulls away from the crowd, looks around, then sees Dr. Anderson dancing with the light-skinned Audrey Denney (a thinly disguised version of Larsen's friend Anita Thompson). Helga watches Audrey dance "with grace and abandon, gravely, yet with obvious pleasure, her legs, her hips, her back, all swaying gently, swung by that wild music from the heart of the jungle." Forgetting her surroundings, Helga sees only two figures, clinging closely to each other. Head throbbing, she flees. She is off to Denmark on the next available ship.

She is embraced by her aunt, who immediately outfits her in bright new dresses, dangling earrings, and gold bracelets. While "she loved color with a passion that perhaps only Negroes and Gypsies know," she "felt like nothing so much as some new and strange species of pet dog being proudly exhibited." But gradually her perturbation gives way to pleasure. "She began to feel a little excited, incited. Incited. That was it, the guiding principle of her life in Copenhagen. She was incited to make an impression, a voluptuous impression." The point of this project, as Helga gradually discovers with some annoyance, is to attract suitors. Her aunt's particular favorite is Axel Olsen, a celebrity artist she hires to paint Helga's portrait. Meanwhile a letter from Anne Grey arrives, telling of her impending marriage to Dr. Anderson.

Helga continues to struggle with her racial ambivalence. Out with Axel and friends for an evening of black vaudeville, she is repelled by the African Americans capering about on stage—while the Danes love it.

"She felt shamed, betrayed, as if these pale pink and white people among whom she lived had suddenly been invited to look upon something in her which she had hidden away and wanted to forget." But later she realizes that the Danes "had divined its presence, had known that in her was something, some characteristic, different from any that they themselves possessed . . . And they hadn't despised it. No, they had admired it, rated it as a precious thing, a thing to be enhanced, preserved. Why?" The question persists in her mind. When Axel proposes marriage, she says, to his bafflement: "I couldn't marry a white man." She decides to return to America, telling herself, "I'm homesick, not for America, but for Negroes"—which she realized as "she mingled with people on the streets, meeting only pale serious faces when she longed for brown laughing ones."

But when she returns she must confront the awkwardness of Anne's marriage to Dr. Anderson. Anne knew her new husband felt something toward Helga that he didn't feel toward her: "a vagrant primitive groping toward something shocking and frightening to the cold asceticism of his reason . . . with her he had not had to struggle against that nameless and to him shameful impulse, that sheer delight, which ran through his nerves at mere proximity to Helga." When Anderson runs into Helga at a party, he finds her alone, upstairs, takes her in his arms, and kisses her: "She fought against him with all her might. Then, strangely, all power seemed to ebb away, and a long-hidden, half-understood desire welled up in her with the suddenness of a dream." But when "sudden anger seized her," she pushed him away and walked slowly down the stairs. "That night riotous and colorful dreams invaded Helga Crane's prim hotel bed. She woke in the morning weary and a bit shocked at the uncontrolled fancies which had visited her." For days, "she lived over those brief seconds, thinking not so much of the man whose arms had held her as of the ecstasy which had flooded her." She sees him again from time to time, even dances with him, silently and formally. Finally he asks to see her alone. She is elated but it turns out he only wants to apologize for "acting such a swine." She slaps him, storms off, and sinks into despair, foreseeing her future as "an endless stretch of dreary years."

The next day, wandering in the rain, Helga stumbles into a black church where the congregation sees her as a "scarlet'oman" [*sic*] and prays for her salvation. "There crept upon her an indistinct horror of an unknown world. She felt herself in the presence of a nameless people, observing rites of remote obscure origin." She yearns to leave but she cannot—"the horror held her," and "gradually a curious influence penetrated her; she felt an echo of the weird orgy resound in her heart; she felt herself possessed by the same madness; she felt a brutal desire to shout and fling herself about." Then "the thing became real. A miraculous calm came over her. Life seemed to expand and became very easy." To her amazement, Helga has had a conversion experience.

She finds herself strangely attracted to the fattish yellow man who had been standing next to her during her transformation and, thinking she was about to fall, had reached out his arms to her. He introduces himself as Rev. Mr. Pleasant Green, and he is powerfully drawn to her. Very soon, "in the confusion of seductive repentance," she marries him. Helga is off to Alabama to "labor in the vineyard of the Lord." As the preacher's wife, "in some strange way she was able to ignore the atmosphere of self-satisfaction which poured from him like gas from a leaking pipe." Part of the reason for this, Larsen implies, was what happened between them at night. "Emotional, palpitating, amorous, all that was living in her sprang like rank weeds at the tingling thought of night, with a vitality so strong that it devoured all shoots of reason." For a while, sex made the thousand daily annoyances—of housekeeping and child-rearing and conjugal life with a blowhard—somehow pale into insignificance.

But ultimately, "The children used her up." The weaker she became, the more faith appealed. "Her religion was to her a kind of protective coloring, shielding her from the cruel light of an unbearable reality." Recovering from her fourth pregnancy, which almost kills her, Helga asks her nurse to read Anatole France's "The Procurator of Judea." The urbane irony of the story, which imagines an aging Pontius Pilate unable to recall his encounter with Jesus, induces Helga's deconversion experience from "the white man's God." She decides to flee, recognizing that "this feeling of dissatisfaction, of asphyxiation, wasn't new." She had felt it at Naxos, in Copenhagen, and in New York. But now she is determined to leave—until she imagines her children crying for their mother. In the end, she cannot bring herself to leave them. She sinks into the quicksand that is suffocating her and ultimately burying her.

Quicksand is an incomparably rich revelation of the tensions between racism and primitivist vitalism in the 1920s. Not everyone grasped this at first. Most reviewers were relieved that—apart from the pivotal cabaret scene just before Helga departs for Denmark—*Quicksand* was not a "cabaret novel." Du Bois waxed ecstatic over it in *The Crisis*, praising its "subtle comprehension of the curious cross currents that swirl about the black American" and contrasting it with McKay's *Home to Harlem*, which he found little better than pornography. As he wrote, "after the dirtier parts of its filth I distinctly felt like taking a bath." Other reviewers acknowledged that sex was central to *Quicksand*, though not in the celebratory mode adopted by McKay. Eda Lou Walton, a white professor of English at New York University, was among the most discerning. Writing in *Opportunity*, the chief rival to *The Crisis*, she observed that "to tell the story of a cultivated and sensitive woman's defeat through her own sexual desire is a difficult task," and praised Larsen for accomplishing it—though she complained that Helga Crane's character did not cohere. Walton did not seem to realize that the incoherence of Helga's character was precisely her creator's point. Larsen's own character was no more coherent than her protagonist's. That was a consequence of the racial cross-currents identified by Du Bois.

Larsen enjoyed a few moments of fame after *Quicksand* and its successor novel, *Passing*, were published within two years of each other. In 1929 she was runner-up to McKay for the Harmon Foundation award, given to what the judges decided was the best black fiction of the year. She continued to be alternately bemused and fascinated by essentialist perspectives on blackness. In an interview with a journalist after *Quicksand*'s publication, as she later admitted, she descended to "twaddle concerning the inherent qualities of the Negro," which she had elsewhere scorned. On another occasion, after lunch with some fawning white people, she told Van Vechten: "I entertained them with quaint stories of my childhood in the bush, and my reaction to the tom-tom undertones in jazz. It was a *swell* luncheon." Yet she admitted to being "crazy about" the white journalist Willie Seabrook's *Jungle Ways* (1931), a preposterous pastiche of primitivist fantasies posing as "the unexpurgated truth" about cannibals, who in spite of "their seeming madness . . . yet believe in a religion of life and worship it after their fashion." The vitalist "religion of life" continued to evoke Larsen's ambivalent fascination, but she turned away from blackness in her subsequent fiction. After winning a Guggenheim Fellowship in 1930, she sailed off to Mallorca to write her next novel—a "white book," as she called it, about a philandering husband and jealous wife in the New Jersey suburbs. Even a friend who read the manuscript said "it was *rotten*," she told Van Vechten.

Larsen's choice of subject reflected her ambition to become more than a Negro novelist, but also her disintegrating marriage. The onset of the Great Depression had left Elmer jobless, but he soon found a faculty position at Fisk, where he began an affair with Ethel Gilbert, an administrator at the university who was everything Larsen was not—expansive, easygoing, adored by everyone, and white. The affair became increasingly hard to conceal, especially after Larsen started spending more time in Nashville. By the spring of 1933, she was emotionally unstrung, feeling betrayed by her husband in favor of a white woman who clearly belonged at Fisk—unlike Larsen, who never belonged anywhere. By the late 1930s, Larsen had divorced Elmer, returned to nursing in New York, and withdrawn from most of her old friends. Even her writing fell out of fashion, as critics denounced the decadence of the Jazz Age and embraced proletarian themes.

Times had changed. A new sobriety and earnestness pervaded literature. The Roaring Twenties had stopped roaring at about the same time the decade ended. Larsen's decline into obscurity coincided with the global collapse of capitalism.

Wall Street was a long way from Harlem, culturally if not geographically, but the two neighborhoods had more in common than might have been at first apparent. The "Negro Metropolis" offered far more than an erotic playground and a magnet for white voyeurs; it was the place for black people to cultivate style and grace. Standards were high: how one looked mattered. Skilled artisans, working-class aristocrats, wore business suits to work and carried their overalls and lunch in a briefcase. Like their white counterparts downtown, they found a stream of pleasurable sensations in taking risks with money. For the elegant strivers of Harlem, playing the numbers offered the same feverish excitement—the same daily frisson—as playing the market on Wall Street.

Gamblers had been playing versions of the numbers for decades, but the game took its Harlem form under the auspices of Casper Holstein, a black man born in 1876 in the Dutch West Indies. By the end of World War I, Holstein was working as a porter at a Fifth Avenue store. Unlike other porters, Saunders Redding wrote in 1934, Holstein combined "an eye for the stock market reports" with "the shrewdness of a race-track tout." Sitting in an "airless janitor's closet, surrounded by brooms and mops," he pored over the financial pages in the daily papers; again and again his eyes lit upon the New York banks' Clearing House Reports. "The thought that the figures differed each day played in his mind like a wasp in an empty room," said Redding.

Eventually Holstein came up with the concept of the daily number, based on the Clearing House Reports. The daily number, he decided, would be reached by combining the second and third digits from New York City bank clearings—say $5**89**,000,000—with the third digit from the Federal Reserve Bank's overall balance—say $11**6**,000,000. The daily number in that case would be 896. Any three numbers were a gig—winning was a one-in-a-thousand shot, but it paid off at 600:1.

The question, for ordinary folk, was how to dope it out. For the mathematically inclined, there were "systems" based on frequency or infrequency of a number's previous appearance. But in fact the odds never changed no matter how often or seldom a number had come up in the past, any more than five heads in a row make heads more or less likely on the next coin flip. More popular than systems, by far, were dream books, manuals of dream interpretation that deciphered messages from the unconscious, individual or collective. The interpretation always involved numerology—attaching particular numbers to particular dream subjects. So depending on what one dreamed about, one might play the

Washerwoman's Gig (4–11–44), the Police Gig (28–35–67), and the like. This was a science of subjective experience, indeed.

Dream books were rooted in a cosmos teeming with hidden indirect meanings; yet they were meanings that could take precise numerical form. This animistic worldview and the dream books it was based on flourished in rural hamlets as well as black districts of towns and cities all over the United States. Growing up in Oklahoma in the 1910s, the young Ralph Ellison bought Freud's *Interpretation of Dreams*, thinking it would help him win the lottery. But playing the numbers had a particular cultural resonance in Harlem, a mere subway ride from the New York Stock Exchange. The Harlem numbers game was an occult, "superstitious" version of what was happening on Wall Street, but a version nonetheless. Both were economic rituals that involved attaching numbers to products of the human imagination—dreams or share prices—attempting to quantify subjective experience, to calculate the incalculable. The speculative mania of the 1920s revealed the heights and depths that ritual could reach.

10

Numbers and Flow

BY THE 1920S, the notion of animal spirits was beginning to seem a touch archaic, amid emerging efforts to create a science of subjective experience—strategies that linked body and mind in new and systematic ways. In the popular discourse of the body, animal spirits had yielded to electricity as the carrier of nervous energy. "For many years the prevalent view was that the nerves were essentially tubes through which flows an exceedingly fine matter of the nature of air or gas, known as the animal spirits," Dr. Willam H. Howell, professor of physiology at Johns Hopkins, explained to readers of *The Washington Times* in 1922. Now we know that "it is more than possible that our nervous force is only electricity in a certain form. The nerves are as much wires along which current travels to the brain as are the wires between telephone and telegraph poles." So it may be that "the collection of the nerve energy in the wireless waves and its intelligent application to our bodies may very well amplify and tone up the natural nerve currents upon which so many of our bodily processes depend." Fat people might slim down, anxious people might calm down.

But the emerging science of the inner life had more ambitious aims:

its adherents, whatever theory they espoused, strained for complete illumination of hidden depths. The ambition was not new: mystics in many traditions had sought union with the deity in contemplative practice; Calvinists and Pietists had encouraged constant scrutiny of the soul for evidence of salvation or damnation. What was new in the early twentieth century was the belief that emotional depths could be measured or at least described with scientific precision. The project animated professional strategies for the systematic understanding of mental life and its connections with physical life. Everyone agreed that mind and body were linked; the question was how. Did mind influence body, or the other way around? Or did the two realms interact in subtler ways?

PLUMBING THE INNER LIFE

Psychologists posed rivalrous answers to those questions as they struggled to create legitimacy for their infant discipline. Psychotherapists sought insight through narratives, which became case histories. For therapists who were psychoanalytically inclined (as increasing numbers were), the task was to chart the workings of the "great unconscious force that exists within every person," as Anne Harrington writes, the force that George Groddeck called the It and that Freud rechristened the Id.

The psychoanalytic approach melded body and mind by showing how unarticulated emotional conflicts could generate physical as well as mental illness—and how both arose from that cauldron of contentious energies, the unconscious. Groddeck was a physician at the German health resort of Baden-Baden. He played a major role in the development of psychosomatic medicine, tracing all illness to the mysterious energy source he called the *Es*, or It. As he announced in *The Book of the It* (1923):

> I hold the view that man is animated by the Unknown, that there is within him an "Es," some wondrous force which directs what he himself does, and what happens to him. The affirmation "I live" is only conditionally correct, it expresses only a small and superficial part of a fundamental principle "Man is lived by the Es."

Freud wrote an appreciation, which Groddeck's American editor quoted in the English translation of 1927, affirming the core idea that "we are 'lived' by unknown and uncontrollable forces." Indeed, Freud may have acquired a useful metaphor from Groddeck's bubbling-cauldron notion of the Es. "The Es is always in eruption, and never for a second is there any peace," Groddeck wrote. "It bubbles and boils, and casts up now this bit of experience, now that." Groddeck avoided the stilted academicism of Freud's writing—or at least of James Strachey's English translation of it—by casting *The Book of the It* as *Psychoanalytic Letters to a Friend.*

Groddeck and Freud had much in common. Despite their insistence that the contents of the cauldron were "unknown," both claimed to know what the constantly erupting ferment was all about: sex. This was in keeping with what the historian Rochelle Gurstein aptly calls "the repeal of reticence": by the 1920s, whether or not people were actually having more sex, they were certainly talking about it more often and more openly. Defenders of the new openness characterized it as a turn toward honesty, and though this claim became a therapeutic cliché, it was sometimes true of the psychoanalytic point of view. There was something refreshingly candid, for example, about Groddeck's observation that dancing was "quite certainly a representation of sex, or at any rate of erotic behavior," despite his ridiculously overblown charge that those "who maintain that people dance merely for the sake of exercise" were "fanatical and pharisaical hypocrites."

What epitomized psychoanalysis at its self-parodic worst, though, was Groddeck's interpretation of what an earlier generation might have called animal spirits in one of his patients:

> During his mother's pregnancy, D. had been in the habit of lying in wait for hours at a time, near the outlet of a drain, in order to shoot the rats as they emerged. Boyish sport, you say. Certainly, but why do boys so much enjoy shooting and why did D. shoot rats coming out of a drain? Shooting . . . is the predominantly sexual urge of puberty, which finds vent in symbolic action. But the rat at which D. shoots is the sex organ of his father whom he punishes with death at the moment he emerges from the drain, the mother's body.

In this passage, as in many others in Groddeck's (and Freud's) work, the "wondrous force" of the It/Id is subjected to the arbitrary formula of the Oedipal theory, with its crude this-for-that symbolism and mechanical determinism. Despite Groddeck's occasional ascents into mystical rapture at the strangeness of the Es, he manages to reduce its explanatory power to predictable categories. The invocation of animal spirits, however superficial, at least did not pretend to explain their mysterious energy by resorting to spurious taxonomy.

The other main branch of psychology was based in the laboratory and made more conventional claims to scientific certainty. Like psychoanalysts, experimental psychologists aimed to provide precise information about subjective experience. Unlike psychoanalysts, they tended to define subjectivity as a mere expression of objectively measurable bodily processes. At their most dogmatic, in the behaviorist formulations of John B. Watson, they came close to denying independent subjectivity altogether, reducing consciousness to an assemblage of reflexes.

Rather than encouraging the subject to recover memories through free association, experimenters defined their task to be the search for physical signs that (they believed) would betray internal states of mind, using such instruments as the blood pressure cuff and later the lie detector. As the historian Michael Pettit has shown, when the American legal profession began to turn toward psychological expertise in the 1910s, the form of evidence lawyers sought gradually moved from narrative case studies to numbers. The case study method had been pioneered by William Healy at the Juvenile Psychopathic Institute in Chicago, but when his fellow psychologist Herman Adler reviewed Healy's book reporting his case studies of pathological liars, Adler dismissed the work as "literary rather than scientific" in its narrative form and its focus on individuals rather than statistical aggregates.

This was the historical moment when Irving Fisher had begun to price everyday life and quantify vitality. Statistics were starting to suffuse discussions of subjective life. The popular crime novelist Arthur Reeve introduced Craig Kennedy, a "scientific detective" who had supposedly been influenced by the psychologists Hugo Munsterberg and Walter Dill Scott. Kennedy used "psychometers" to solve crimes, identifying suspects by their altered emotional states during questioning. It was only a short step from the psychometer to the lie detector, the brainchild of George Moulton Marston, a psychologist who had been influenced by the Harvard physician Walter Cannon's research on blood pressure as a measure of fear. The lie detector, as Pettit writes, claimed to measure "the embodied fear generated by the anxiety of being caught in a lie." It was all very scientific, or seemed so, but the lie detector could never entirely escape Barnumesque associations, especially since Marston was as much showman as scientist. By 1928, he was orchestrating a demonstration of a lie detector detecting an answer to the question of who's more emotional, blondes or brunettes?—using Ziegfeld showgirls as his subjects.

While lie detection was easily reducible to the glib certainties of popularized science, psychoanalysis held more promising possibilities—intellectually if not therapeutically. In the work of Freud and his more sensitive interpreters, psychoanalytic thinking informed profound explorations of subjective experience. But less imaginative psychoanalysts transformed a rich tradition into a brittle taxonomy, which may have provided therapeutic answers to patients in search of simple explanations for their pain, but possessed no more value as a guide to the inner life than the crudest sorts of quantification. The problem for behaviorists, lie detectors, and orthodox psychoanalysts was a reductionist impulse to turn amorphous psychic energy into rigid categories and spurious certainties. When complex currents of mental and emotional life were channeled into a system, the resulting synthesis left little room for spontaneity, fluidity, or uncertainty. The older vernacular language of animal spirits and the larger tradition of vitalism created a more capacious intellectual space, where thinkers could speculate more creatively about the relationships between subjective experience and everyday life—including economic life. Few were more venturesome than John Maynard Keynes.

ENTER KEYNES: THE USES OF UNCERTAINTY

Keynes was born in 1883, to a comfortable upper-middle-class household in Cambridge, the son of an anxious university administrator who was more ambitious for his children than for himself, and a Nonconformist preacher's daughter with Liberal political inclinations. From about the time he was in short pants, young Maynard was being groomed for one examination or another, and to his parents' relief and delight won a scholarship to Eton. Keynes was housed with other "scholarship boys," and spared confrontation with the anti-intellectual aristocratic ethos that dominated much of the school population; his parents valued intellectual pursuits and he could freely indulge his own proclivities for them.

Numbers played a crucial contrapuntal role in Keynes's intellectual development. As an adolescent, he "had a passion for exact information, particularly when expressed in numerical form," his biographer Robert Skidelsky writes. This was what one would expect of a clever boy from a liberal household, raised with the conventional Victorian faith in quantifiable knowledge as a utilitarian instrument of progress. But as a Cambridge Apostle—confidant of Bertrand Russell, Lytton Strachey, and other luminaries—he came under the spell of the philosopher G. E. Moore, who inspired his young followers to spurn mundane utility in favor of more exalted notions of the good: the love of friends, the contemplation of beautiful objects, the pursuit of knowledge. Numbers continued to fascinate Keynes, and he manipulated them skillfully. But gradually he came to recognize their limits as a pathway to truth.

Upon graduation Keynes aced another examination and took a position in the India Office of the Treasury Department, which he soon left to return to Cambridge as a lecturer in economics. He championed better statistics and secured the appointment of a statistician to the department, but he also came to doubt the excessive claims statisticians made for quantitative knowledge. Too often, he thought, they slid unwittingly from precise description to sweeping interpretation. Numbers were essential to knowledge, but when they acquired a fetish-like quality they fostered intellectual laziness—creating an aura of precision around unwarranted claims, fostering fantasies of control over the future.

Early on, Keynes realized that statistics were strictly limited as a tool of prediction. He saw that relationships between variables in the present—interest rates, unemployment, copper prices—however precisely quantified, could not be used to predict those same relationships in the future. This recognition would be the basis, later in the century, for Keynes's skepticism toward the budding discipline of econometrics.

The heart of the matter was uncertainty, which in economic life (as in all life) was pervasive and inescapable. So the young Keynes came to believe. Even before the Great War had shattered the foundations of Victorian certitude, he questioned the implicitly positivist pillars of economic wisdom—especially the role that rational calculation was alleged to play in financial markets. "I lie in bed for hours in the morning reading treatises on the philosophy of probability by members of the Stock Exchange," he wrote to his father in 1908. "The soundest treatment so far is by the owner of a bucket shop." Keynes's bemusement was palpable: a bucket shop was a seedy backstreet operation where the desperate or the gullible could borrow dangerously large sums to gamble on share prices.

Modernist artists and writers, including Keynes's friend Virginia Woolf, were connoisseurs of uncertainty. But Keynes was the only one brave enough—or daft enough—to carry that connoisseurship into economic thought. By 1910, he was already bringing his awareness of uncertainty to bear on his view of investors' motives—to formulate the foundation of his insight into the centrality of animal spirits. The assumption that investors behaved like calculating "economic men" required overlooking the true nature of financial markets: what really made them hum was investors' willingness to make bets on a largely unknown future. As Keynes wrote, the investor "will be affected, as is obvious, not by the net income which he will actually receive from his investments in the long run, but by his expectations. These will often depend upon fashion, upon advertisement, or upon purely irrational waves of optimism or depression." Decisions were rooted in subjective experience, not objective data; to pretend otherwise was to try quixotically to calculate the incalculable.

The implications of this observation are vast. It contains the germ of Keynes's *General Theory*, of his critique of classical economics, and indeed of his larger contribution to twentieth-century social thought.

Economics was not a science depending on precise data, advancing through falsifiable hypotheses, and creating enduring laws; it was more like politics—"a flexible field of custom, rule of thumb, and adjustment," as Zachary Carter writes. Had politicians and economists themselves realized this, Keynes's impact on policy might have been greater and longer-lasting than it was.

Throughout his early career, Keynes inhabited a rarefied social world where young people—especially but not exclusively young men—were free to seek the ends elevated by Moore: love, art, knowledge. Among the Apostles, love meant the Higher Sodomy. Keynes pursued an active gay life for twenty years, in London and Cambridge, including a years-long affair with the painter Duncan Grant. Keynes, Grant, Lytton Strachey, and other Apostles migrated to Bloomsbury after graduation, where the Higher Sodomy competed and sometimes combined with heterosexual high jinks. The Bloomsbury set created an atmosphere of self-congratulation that could verge on self-parody, but also a community that sheltered the likes of Keynes, Strachey, and Virginia Woolf. For Keynes as well as others among a literate and prosperous minority, the prelude to the Great War was a golden moment. The war and especially its aftermath would darken and deepen his social vision.

He witnessed world events from an office in the Treasury. As a rising star in the economics profession, he had been an obvious early hire as a junior adviser. His first book, *Indian Currency and Finance* (1913), along with his articulate participation in government inquiries, had earned him a growing reputation. He was even called in to give expert advice to Prime Minister Lloyd George during the banking crisis at the beginning of August 1914, between the assassination at Sarajevo and the outbreak of hostilities.

Keynes was as indifferent to the war as the rest of Bloomsbury until November 1914, when a chatty letter he had written to a Cambridge friend in France came back with the word "Killed" scrawled across the envelope. In the months and years ahead, Keynes's outlook would become more attuned to chance and uncertainty, to the role of mere caprice in human affairs. He began by thinking the war a gigantic blunder, rather than a noble necessity, and gradually his views sharpened to an openly pacifist opposition. His friends in Cambridge and Bloomsbury were ferocious opponents of the war and conscription; and he did what he could from his Treasury post to push the legislation authorizing a draft in flexible and humane directions. He eventually received an exemption for doing work of "national importance," but he applied for conscientious objector status as a matter of principle. The principle was apparently all that mattered, as he never attended the hearing called to consider his application.

When the Armistice finally came and the carnage ended, Keynes felt a surge of relief and hope. While the bodies had been piling up he had become increasingly depressed, skeptical, and pacifistic, but Woodrow Wilson's vision of a postwar world stirred the liberal idealist in him. When the Peace Conference convened in 1919, the Treasury dispatched him as part of a deputation representing British interests. Keynes had an opportunity to observe the proceedings firsthand. The result was his most impassioned book.

The Economic Consequences of the Peace (1919) forcefully demonstrated the devastating impact of a punitive peace settlement on Germany and its allies. Expropriation of the defeated nations' assets, steep reparation payments for damages inflicted on the victors—all the treaty provisions were calculated to keep the Central Powers on their knees and unable to function as modern industrial societies. Keynes was appalled by Georges Clemenceau's vindictiveness, Wilson's ineffectual moralism, Lloyd George's chameleon-like manipulations. He drew portraits in acid of them all.

With equal precision he evoked the devastation wrought by the war in central and eastern Europe—and predicted the catastrophic consequences if no relief were provided to the suffering populations. "The danger confronting us," Keynes wrote, "is the rapid depression of the standard of life of the European populations to a point which will mean actual starvation for some (a point already reached in Russia and approximately reached in Austria). Men will not always die quietly. For starvation, which brings to some lethargy and a helpless despair, drives other temperaments to the nervous instability of hysteria and to a mad despair." In recognizing that "nervous instability" could animate lethargy into hysteria and helpless despair into mad despair, Keynes acknowledged the darker underside of animal spirits—"the spontaneous impulse toward action" could even be bred by starvation, and could lead to unlovely consequences.

Monetary instability, he believed, would further exacerbate mass hysteria. "Lenin was certainly right. There is no subtler, no surer way of overturning the existing basis of society than to debauch the currency," Keynes claimed, anticipating the financial disorder of the Weimar Republic: "As the inflation proceeds and the real value of the currency fluctuates wildly from month to month, all permanent relations between debtors and creditors, which form the ultimate foundation of capitalism, become so utterly disordered as to be almost meaningless, and the process of wealth getting degenerates into a gamble and a lottery." As a connoisseur of uncertainty, Keynes was a bit of a gambler himself, but he knew no organized society could long survive the constant "arbitrary rearrangement of riches" created by runaway inflation. Baffled and angry, ordinary citizens continue to believe in the value of their own currency long after it has depreciated. "To their minds it appears that value is inherent in money as such," Keynes observed. But he had come to understand that money's value resided in the labyrinth of the human imagination.

Ultimately the consequences of the treaty were about far more than monetary instability. The greatest dangers it posed lay in the human suffering it would cause, and the torrents of rage that suffering would unleash. Keynes put it succinctly: "If we aim deliberately at the impoverishment of Central Europe, vengeance, I dare predict, will not limp." In Russia, Hungary, and Austria, "the miseries of life and the disintegration of society are too notorious to require analysis, and these countries are already experiencing the actuality of what, for the rest of Europe is still in the realm of prediction," Keynes wrote: "they are the signal to us of how in the final catastrophe the malady of the body passes over into malady of the mind." Deprivation fostered derangement; whatever animal spirits remained available to desperate, starving people could be harnessed to destructive ends.

> Physical efficiency and resistance to disease slowly diminish, but life proceeds somehow, until the limit of human endurance is reached at last and counsels of despair and madness stir the sufferers from the lethargy which precedes the crisis. The man shakes himself, and the bonds of custom are loosed. The power of ideas is sovereign, and he listens to whatever instruction of hope, illusion, or revenge is carried to him on the air.

Keynes's prophecies were soon borne out. Across the ravaged post-war landscape of central Europe, the air was full of voices murmuring vague ideas of vengeance. Many were focused on a familiar, ancient target.

THE FOLK-STORM STIRS

On the same day the Jews of Vienna learned that the San Remo Conference had accepted the Balfour Declaration (authorizing the creation of a Jewish homeland in Palestine), "the Jew-hating ruffians of the city began to give expression to pogrom theory in terms of practical deeds," the Fort Worth–Dallas *Jewish Monitor* reported in 1920. For months "a certain personality" named Orel "has been carrying on fearful pogram propaganda in his filthy journal *Der Folks-Sturm.*" At an anti-Semitic meeting in the city hall, "German national students of both sexes" heard "an appeal for all elements of the German people to unite against the common enemy, the Jews, who it was claimed, committed many ritual murders during the Red revolutions in Russia, Germany and Hungary." The link between Bolshevism and Judaism was being forged in the anti-Semitic imagination.

Afterward, a crowd of anti-Semites attacked the "Kitchen for Jewish Students" that fed destitute Jewish, Czech, Polish, and German students. Twenty people there were beaten and the place smashed with damages of 100 kronen. Next day all the German students of the university and high school tried to drive Jews from the university halls, demanding their baptismal certificates. A "whole horde of the super-patriots" invaded the breakfast room run by English Quakers and drove out any Jewish students. When the university was closed for an investigation and to establish order, the Jewish students stayed off campus, disappointing the mob that had gathered to attack them, "but not finding any Jews to batter, the young brutes soon found another outlet for their animal spirits, by falling upon the group of international socialist students" in the neighborhood, as well as any passers-by who looked Jewish. Next day three hundred went to the Steftischen park and guarded the entrances to keep out Jews. Characteristically, the group only sang "the hymns of the old regime" like "The Watch on the Rhine": "Apparently, while ostentatiously it is the Jew who is being kicked, the blows are made to hit finally the recent republican government. The present seemingly unimportant student outbreaks may be but the harbinger of a reactionary wave to reestablish the monarchy."

By 1920, the merging of anti-Semitism with reactionary politics and of Jews with revolutionary socialists had become a characteristic pattern in right-wing rhetoric. But postwar impoverishment gave the rhetoric urgency and mass appeal. What fed the fire in the minds of men was the emptiness in their bellies. Mind and body were fused, as Keynes realized—and as Julien Benda, a more influential interpreter of fascism, did not. Like Keynes, Benda believed in the power of ideas; unlike Keynes, he detached those ideas from any grounding in everyday life.

For years Benda had been brooding about the eclipse of reason by a vitalist cult of irrationality. His *La Trahison des clercs* (1927)—*The Treason of the Intellectuals*—was a Cartesian rationalist's brief for transcendental truth and against what seemed to Benda to be the fashionable tendencies of the previous several decades—the worship of force, the elevation of experience over thought, the "adoration for the contingent, and scorn for the eternal," as well as "the thirst for immediate results, the exclusive preoccupation with the desired end." The clerks had betrayed their most sacred responsibility—to universal ideals—and the consequences were catastrophic: the "glorifying of national particularism," the aestheticizing of violence, the celebration of power. Benda's indictment was scattershot and sometimes wildly inaccurate (he labeled William James an imperialist); his chief villains, among many, were Bergson and Nietzsche, the second with more justification than the first. What was most important to Benda's later admirers was that he had foreseen Nazi storm troopers goose-stepping across Europe, in the name (among other things) of vital force.

Benda reduced the complex ferment of vitalism to a simple rejection of rationality; he also exaggerated the power of people like himself—other *clercs*—and overlooked the influence of mundane economic life (otherwise known as the struggle for survival). In 1924, the U.S. government instituted the Dawes Plan, a watered-down version of what Keynes had advocated at Versailles: the United States loaned Germany money to pay reparations and other war debts; the Allies used the reparations to pay down their own war debts, especially to the United States; and then the cycle would begin again. It was a rickety expedient, but it kept Germany from catastrophe until the global collapse of capitalism in the early 1930s. It also kept animal spirits flowing in benign channels, by preserving the web of creditworthiness and indebtedness—and this, one could say, kept vitalism from turning into fascism.

The exception was Italy, where the avant-garde had been extolling the "habit of energy and boldness" since the Futurist Manifesto of 1909, where Filippo Marinetti and other intellectuals fostered a cult of military valor, and where disgruntled nationalists encouraged the populace to believe that they had been betrayed by the Versailles Treaty, which had not delivered on land promised to Italy in the secret Treaty of London in 1915. The liberal government was corrupt, ineffectual, and ripe for takeover by a man promising national regeneration and a return to the greatness of the Roman Empire. Mussolini seized power in 1923, and soon won an appreciative audience on both sides of the Atlantic, including among American journalists.

Mussolini was a paragon of popular vitalism, a fount of energy that was fundamentally sexual. For Ida Tarbell, the Progressive muckraker famous for her crusade against Standard Oil, Mussolini was irresistible—"a despot with a dimple" who "kissed my hand in the gallant Italian fashion." His amorous escapades titillated prurient readers but also, as Alice Rohe noted, served political ends: "Duce knows how to get what he wants from women, whether it is a grand passion or a grand propaganda."

Some commentators wrapped Mussolini's sexual vitality in robes of righteousness. As would often happen in the emergent mass culture, piety and prurience cohabited. For the novelist Kenneth Roberts, Mussolini's movement was healthy, redemptive, and regenerative; the Duce's Spartan austerity was saving the virtuous middle class from the unspeakable evils of communism and the "mental perverts" who called themselves liberals. This regeneration, Roberts believed, resulted not from tedious parliamentary politics but through the "Ambush of Italy" by a man who embodied sheer physical force. Other journalists marveled at his coiled energy of body and mind—he was "built like a steel spring," they said, and there was "punch to his eyes, the darting thrust of a rapier." As Anne O'Hare McCormick wrote in *The New York Times* in 1923: "Direct action is intelligible in any language. A nation that thrilled to the Vigilantes and the Rough Riders rises to Mussolini and his Black Shirt army." A direct line of descent ran from Theodore Roosevelt to Benito Mussolini, in McCormick's eyes.

She was not alone in this view. When Irvin S. Cobb interviewed the "Big Little Man" for *Cosmopolitan* in 1927, he asked:

> "Do you know, your excellency, what a great many Americans call you? They call you the Italian Roosevelt."
>
> By this he was obviously gratified.
>
> "For that," he said, "I am very glad and proud. Roosevelt I greatly admired."
>
> He clenched his fists. "Roosevelt had strength—had the will to do what he thought should be done. He had greatness."

Henry Adams had called Theodore Roosevelt "pure act." The same phrase could apply to the Duce—also "a man of sheer will power" and an "anti-intellectual intellectual," as the historian John Patrick Diggins later observed. Though Roosevelt was a genuine liberal with a respect for constitutional constraints on power, he and Mussolini shared a similar bent for frenetic activism. Calling himself a pragmatist, Mussolini himself claimed inspiration from William James, but anyone even slightly acquainted with the humane depth of James's thought can recognize the thinness of this claim. If Mussolini had an American predecessor, it was TR.

Certainly, by the 1920s, TR was the last American president to embody vital energy. Wilson was a moralistic schoolmaster, and his successors in the 1920s ranged from handsome and ineffectual (Harding) to dour and ineffectual (Coolidge, Hoover). To some observers, American leaders were failing American youth, who still needed strong models for nurturing and channeling their animal spirits. One of the few venues where animal spirits were even mentioned in the 1920s was the popular discourse of youth and its problems. All the old tropes survived, as *The Washington Post* described "the healthy child" in 1927:

> He is usually happy and good-natured and he is full of life and animal spirits . . . He is, in short, what nature meant him to be before anything else—a healthy, happy young animal.
>
> The animal spirits natural to all healthy young are likely to be lacking in the malnourished child; he may be listless at play and work, not caring to romp and play like other children; he is likely to tire easily, and he may be regarded as lazy. He is likely to lack mental vigor also.

Animal spirits were also still thought to animate the mischievousness of the "bad boy," whose pranks were often the sign of just the traits he needed to succeed. The western farmer who told his eastern friends he wanted to hire bad boys "was after the energy and push which is often characteristic of badness," *The Philadelphia Inquirer* announced. "Most boys are mischievous from an overflow of animal spirits, and the old farmer knew that animal spirits is [*sic*] an excellent thing—in its place. A boy is never so bad that there is no good in him, and many a bad boy makes a good man."

Yet this conventional wisdom continued to be contested, perhaps more pervasively than in previous decades. The idea of the goodness of the bad boy, whose misbehavior was merely a consequence of overflowing animal spirits, began to seem a relic of Victorian sentimentality. In

1927, the Washington *Star* Sunday Supplement featured caricatures of types of public speeches, including one captioned, "The address to the jury. The lawyer for the defense, in summing up, is begging of the jury, with tears in his manly voice, that they consider the extreme youth of the prisoner. 'A young lad of 25, who had seldom been away from his mother's knee,' pleads the honest barrister. 'How could he foresee the outcome of what for him was a mere boyish prank due to animal spirits? How, I ask you, could he tell that a knock on the old man's head with a piece of lead pipe would result in a death blow?'" By the 1920s, the invocation of "mere animal spirits" as an excuse for boyish violence had been deployed often enough to become a self-parody. Sometimes bad boys really were bad.

The rejection of notions of childhood innocence accompanied the broader recoil from Victorian sentimentality. For those with time and resources to ponder larger questions, the determination to live without illusions sometimes created a dry, unsatisfying cultural atmosphere. A lingering world-weariness left the younger generation—especially the more sensitive upper-class males—adrift in bogs of uncertainty, yearning for release from cynicism and ennui into a more purposeful life, but clueless about how to seek it.

This might have been a recipe for fascism. In Britain, it was, but only for a while. The Great War bred widespread disillusionment with familiar notions of patriotism and duty. The rising generation was adrift and, according to its conservative critics, effeminate and soft. As the Washington *Star* reported, Sir Oswald Mosley tried to organize disaffected youth in his New Party "to rally youth against the effete and futile old gang of politicians in the best Mussolini manner. It had no use for politicians anyway, and little use for Parliament, which it dubbed the 'Talk shop.' Action, by youth, for youth—that was the motto of the Mosley New Party." The party's weekly *Action* encouraged youthful writers and readers "with plenty of stuff about hiking, opportunity, and the senility of everybody except the young." *Action* sold 160,000 copies of the first issue, but youth interest waned with subsequent issues, along with any interest in New Party candidates. "Youth is enigmatic, but one certain thing about it is that it will go Spartan and devote itself heart and soul to a cause if it can find a cause worthwhile and a leader who will give it something it can bite its teeth into."

The flare-up of interest in Spartan regeneration occurred against the British background of protracted economic stagnation. Britain's economy lurched about uncertainly after the war, and Keynes was called in frequently to minister to the nation's needs—though ultimately the men in charge never followed his advice. Still, the postwar decade was a crucial moment in Keynes's intellectual and emotional development. Throughout the 1920s, his skepticism toward statistics as a source of truth intensified. So did his appreciation for animal spirits, in economics and in everyday life.

KEYNES COMING INTO HIS OWN

By 1920, Keynes was a rich man, partly from the sales of *Economic Consequences of the Peace* and partly from successful investing in stocks. He acknowledged the "fun and mild excitement" to be had from either playing the ponies at the track or betting on stock prices, both of which he compared with the consumption of alcohol. All were pleasant pastimes that only occasionally led to ruinous outcomes. "It is agreeable to be habitually in the state of imagining all sorts of things are possible," he said. This sanguine point of view was underwritten by his new wealth and celebrity, which allowed him to take up foxhunting with the "kid gloves and tiara set"—a sport that lured him into awkward adventures as his horse wandered off from the pack.

After *Economic Consequences*, he turned to the completion of *A Treatise on Probability*, a book he had been writing and rewriting for over a decade. It was an argument against the reigning view that probability was an objective fact in the world, which could be statistically calculated with reference to frequency of occurrence: if one smoker in ten dies of cancer, according to this view, the probability of smoking causing cancer is 10 percent. But to identify probability with frequency, Keynes wrote, "excludes a great number of judgements which are generally believed to deal with probability." Probability judgments may depend in part on statistical data, but they are not reducible to the data—in fact they might have nothing to do with data at all.

Comparative judgments of probability are not numerical, Keynes observed; they are approximations, not precise calculations. And sometimes they are arbitrary. Consider the question of whether it is more or less likely to rain. There are times, he wrote, when "it will be an arbitrary matter to decide for or against the umbrella. If the barometer is high, but the clouds are black, it is not always rational that one should prevail over the other in our minds, or even that we should balance them—though it will be rational to allow caprice to determine us and to waste no time on the debate." Few devotees of reason were as willing as Keynes to grant so much space to caprice, even in trivial matters.

Keynes was groping toward his own version of a distinction between risk and uncertainty—one the Chicago economist Franklin Knight was already making in *Risk, Uncertainty and Profit* (1921) when he wrote: "A *measurable* uncertainty, or 'risk' proper . . . is far different from an *unmeasurable* one that it is not in effect an uncertainty at all." But Keynes was more doubtful than Knight that the probability of most events could ever be precisely measured.

Instead of a description of events in the world, Keynes argued, probability was a belief about those events, based on logical inference. This was a subjective process, but one that all rational beings shared. To make rational choices under conditions of uncertainty, one had to take into account what Keynes called "the weight of argument"—the amount and relevancy of evidence that an event is likely to occur—and the "moral risk"—the phrase that summarized his preference for choosing a smaller good with a higher possibility of attainment over a greater good with a lower possibility. The principle of moral risk underlay his choice of gradualist reform over socialist revolution. More broadly, the *Treatise* suggested the future direction of his economic thought—away from statistically based prediction and the spurious reduction of uncertainty to certainty, toward arguments that depended on persuasion rather than proof.

While Keynes's professional life prospered, his personal life swerved in a new direction. In December 1921, Sergei Diaghilev's Ballets Russes came to London, and Keynes saw an accomplished Russian ballerina called Lydia Lopokova dance a dual role as Aurora and the Lilac Fairy in Tchaikovsky's *Sleeping Beauty*. She was already a celebrity; the London papers waxed rhapsodic over her "exquisite plebian beauty," and "Lydia dolls" were flying off the shelves. Keynes found her performances hypnotic; he returned night after night, embracing the unfamiliar role of stage-door Johnnie. She was stirred by his cornucopian intelligence; he by her energy, vivacity, and talent. She invited him to tea on December 26; they were both already smitten.

By April, they were exchanging erotic notes. Hers were in the idiom Keynes and his friends later fondly dubbed Lydiaspeak: "I gobble you my dear Maynard"; "I place melodious strokes all over you"; "With caresses large as sea I stretch out to you." Keynes reciprocated: "I want to be . . . gobbled abundantly," he wrote. They kept this up well after they were married in 1925, though Keynes sometimes resorted to scholarly indirection. Researching Babylonian coins in 1926, he wrote to Lydia that he had found the earliest recorded "love poem"—"Come to me my Ishtavar and show your virile strength / Push out your member and touch with it my little place." Keynes's growing awareness of animal spirits in the 1920s was as much a matter of physical and emotional as of intellectual experience. Sex was at the heart of it.

Lydia was Maynard's first and only female lover. After twenty years in enthusiastic pursuit of gay sex, Keynes's heterosexual turn shocked his Bloomsbury friends, who gradually came to appreciate Lydia but for a long time viewed her with dismissive bemusement. Lydia did not cultivate the exquisite self-consciousness of the hypercivilized Bloomsbury set—indeed, that lack of self-consciousness was one source of her charm: Lydia and Duncan Grant, Keynes's other great love, were both "*uneducated*; their reactions were spontaneous, fresh, unexpected," as Skidelsky remarks, noting that despite Keynes's devotion to reasonableness, his "fancy could leap and soar over all rational obstacles. He was a gambler, and Lydia was his greatest gamble." It paid off. Keynes was already in high gear intellectually, but after taking up with Lydia, his engagement with public affairs was relieved at least occasionally by the peace and contentment he craved.

The British government continued to invite his advice, and Keynes continued to supply fresh ideas, which had little or no effect on policy. In his *Tract on Monetary Reform* (1924), he argued that the government had a responsibility to protect the population from the worst lurches of the business cycle—to stabilize prices rather than letting inflation or deflation burn itself out. Classical economists' resort to "the long run" was misplaced; we live our lives in the short run; while "in the long run, we are all dead." It was his most famous utterance, and it perfectly captured his preoccupation with lived experience over theoretical formula. He would find occasion to return to it.

Meanwhile Europe seemed to be falling apart. The young Weimar Republic was in a state of constant upheaval. In January 1923, when Germany failed to meet a reparations payment to France, the French army occupied the Ruhr Valley, home to much of German industry. The Versailles order crumbled, only to be restored by the American intervention of the Dawes Plan, a weaker version of what Keynes had suggested at the Peace Conference. The French withdrew in 1925.

Amid the intermittent chaos, Keynes began to write the lecture that would become *The End of Laissez-Faire.* Like almost everything else Keynes wrote in the 1920s, this pamphlet signaled an important new direction in Keynes's thought, as he urged that economists acknowledge the primacy of ethical concerns over technical economic efficiency. The mature Keynesian vision was coming into focus.

By the mid-1920s, Britain's stagnant economy was poised on the brink of prolonged depression. Winston Churchill's decision to stick to the gold standard at an overvalued exchange rate tipped it over the edge. Keynes was appalled by any contraction of the money supply in a depressed economy. "The proper object of dear money is to check an incipient boom," he wrote. "Woe to those whose faith leads them to use it to aggravate a depression!" Dear money was exacerbated by falling incomes. An overvalued pound sterling meant that British mine owners had to sell their coal abroad at reduced prices in order to compete in the world market; to make up the difference, mine owners imposed steep wage cuts. The miners struck to protect their wages, and soon the General Strike followed.

Amid spreading class war, Keynes wrote *Can Lloyd George Do It?* This proposed a preview of what Franklin Roosevelt would try during the New Deal—an ambitious public works program to counteract the looming depression, to combat collective gloom and to banish visions of a bleak, limited future. "There is no reason why we should not feel ourselves free to be bold, to be open, to experiment, to take action, to try the possibilities of things," Keynes wrote—the only obstacle was "a few old gentlemen in their frock coats, who need only to be treated with a little friendly disrespect and bowled over like ninepins." All of this was a valiant effort to rally the population. But the public was already convinced that laissez-faire was dead; class conflict was regnant. And Britain was not the United States, where a raging bull market provided a textbook example of animal spirits on the loose—and of the futility of attempting to quantify them.

QUANTIFYING VITALITY ON WALL STREET

The attempt to calculate the incalculable pervaded the bull market of the late 1920s. Fluctuations in asset prices reflected changes in investors' emotional temperature; numbers on the Big Board quantified the flow of animal spirits—a term not in use at the time that nevertheless aptly characterized what drove asset values up and down. When animal spirits roared like white water rushing through rapids, prices soared. When they ebbed, prices fell.

This incongruous use of objective numbers to characterize subjective feelings had characterized capital markets since Daniel Defoe's day. But the incongruity intensified in the United States during the decade aptly known as the Roaring Twenties, when bankers and brokers increasingly claimed that more sophisticated statistics and more systematic research had transformed investment into a science that could be mastered by skilled money managers—and perhaps even by the proverbial man on the street.

During the 1920s boom, celebrants of Wall Street liked to claim that the stock market had been democratized by attracting small investors—not only white-collar professionals but hairdressers, butlers, and elevator operators. Yet it was easy to exaggerate popular participation in the market. As John Kenneth Galbraith wrote in 1955, "to the great majority of all Americans, the stock market was a remote and vaguely ominous thing. Then, as now, not many people knew how one went about buying a security; the purchase of stocks on margin was in every respect as remote from life as the casino at Monte Carlo." To be sure, an unprecedented number of people were investing in stocks—but still no more than 10 percent of American households.

Yet the shift in public attitudes toward Wall Street was profound. Speculation, once condemned as a path to perdition, was now acclaimed as the chief instrument of wealth creation and modernization. It was no accident, apologists assumed, that the "high-stepping" equities were the high-tech sector of their day—Radio Corporation of America, Wright Aviation, General Motors. The speculator, at one time a diabolical, even Dionysian figure, was assimilated to a sanitized, techno-futurist vision of utopia, presided over by an elite corps of financial experts.

The science of money management was as fictional as the democratization of the stock exchange. Galbraith re-created a revelatory scene that occurred repeatedly at the height of the bull market—the reliance on local oracles. "At luncheon in downtown Scranton, the knowledgeable physician spoke of the impending split-up in the stock of Western Utility Investors and the effect on prices. Neither the doctor nor his listeners knew why there should be a split-up, why it should increase values, or even why Western Utility Investors should have any value. But neither the doctor nor his audience knew that he did not know."

Yet there were ways to paper over this pervasive ignorance. Writing in *Harper's* in April 1929, Charles Merz described "the rise of a new national literature," devoted to "the future achievements of an ascendant industry—its car loadings, bank clearings, stock dividends, and gold reserves—filtered through a medium of rich romanticism" and claiming to supply "accurate information regarding the intrinsic values behind various securities." But the search for "intrinsic values" was less beguiling than the codification of the gambler's hunch. At any newsstand in any large city, one could also find "a sudden horde of 'tipster sheets'" much like the racing forms that advised gamblers how to bet on horses.

By 1929, tipster sheets were outselling racing forms; as any news dealer would observe: "They ain't playing the ponies anymore." "Playing the market"—the phrase that came into vogue—was a more lucrative sport than the one taking place at the track.

Conceiving investment as sport was made easier by the tendency to quantify both realms of experience. As Merz wrote, playing the market "has fitted perfectly into the interests of a highly mathematical nation which can really give its heart to no sport which cannot be tallied in batting averages, fielding averages, goals per game, strokes per hole, team percentages, or stolen bases. Every night the American public knows precisely where it stands in this new contest. There are no uneven edges. Down to the last eighth the ticker posts the winners and the losers." Stock tickers were everywhere—in hotel lobbies and restaurants, barber shops and beauty parlors, and (by August 1929) on ships at sea. As Galbraith wrote, "even the person who was relying on hunches, incantations, or simple faith, as distinct from the effort to assess the efforts of the professionals, found it hard to be out of touch." The ubiquitous ticker spared the anxious investor the "nerve-wracking experience" of not knowing how his shares were doing.

It also underwrote the illusion of certainty by attaching precise numbers to asset values that were fluctuating in accordance with investors' emotional states, which in turn depended on more mysterious operations, often conducted out of public view. As the historian John Brooks wrote decades later: "'The [ticker] tape doesn't lie,' was the sucker's folk wisdom; but in fact, the tape could be made to lie." The most common method of making the tape lie was the pool, which brought a handful of high-rolling investors together behind closed doors to manipulate a given stock's price through what the historian Steve Fraser calls "carefully planted rumor and quick, concentrated infusions of cash." Under the direction of men like William Durant, the founder of General Motors who became known as the "poolmaster," pools could pump up a company's asset price to stratospheric levels, then sell it off at a precisely timed moment agreed upon by all the insiders. The suckers who were not part of the pool were left holding depreciated assets they had bought at inflated values. The numbers on the tape were anything but a stable indicator of share values.

Yet for a while, the quantified vitality of the stock market seemed an unalloyed engine of progress. Spokesmen for finance capital believed themselves to be the leading edge of modernity. Defining themselves against what they imagined to be the repressive xenophobia of provincial village life, they conjured a crowd of country bumpkins who supported the Ku Klux Klan, suppressed the teaching of evolutionary theory, and imposed the prohibition of alcohol on their sophisticated betters. This metropolitan snobbery constituted its own version of provincialism. William Jennings Bryan was a teetotaler who believed in biblical inerrancy, yet his closing statement at the Scopes trial contained an incisive critique of Social Darwinism as a sanctification of naked power. Cultural conflict in the 1920s was more complicated than a war between enlightenment and barbarism.

Still, acolytes of the New Era on Wall Street routinely posed as defenders of progress against the reactionary forces of the countryside. They combined anti-rural prejudice with anti-populist politics. In *Wall Street and Washington* (1929), the Princeton economist Joseph Stagg Lawrence dismissed Robert LaFollette and other Midwestern populists as "gentlemen of high moral voltage and abysmal prejudice," whose hatred for Wall Street was part of that "saturnine crusade" for purity that bred prohibition, isolationism, and "blatant bigotry." From the country's beginnings, Lawrence asserted, the "wealthy, cultured, and conservative settlements on the sea coast" had been pitted against "the poverty-stricken, illiterate, and radical pioneer communities of the interior." For decades those communities had demonized Wall Street and made war on it, but now they were about to be vanquished for good. Wall Street created unprecedented prosperity and provided crucial infusions of capital to "banking, finance, trade, commerce, agriculture, and to government itself. It has served intelligently and unostentatiously. It has maintained no lobbies. Its books have been open. It has enforced upon its members a code of ethics which it is well for the supreme legislative body of the land to emulate," Lawrence wrote. From his perspective, Senator Carter Glass's proposed

5 percent tax on stock purchases held less than sixty days (intended to slow down frenzied options trading) was nothing more than "vandalism" that would produce a destructive flurry of "bootleg finance."

Lawrence's reference to the effects of prohibition was deliberate: he wanted to connect efforts to regulate finance with the most glaring example of outmoded populism he could imagine. In the past, he said, a "fringe of fraud" had given a bad name to speculation; now we knew better. In fact, he claimed, "the investor and the professional speculator are infinitely better informed today than they were a generation ago and emotional typhoons are at least less probable than they have been at any time in the past." Information, it was assumed, stabilized uncertainty

Yet risk was unavoidable, and for Lawrence that was just fine. Risk and uncertainty were essential to most heroic achievements, indeed to life itself. "Christ himself took a chance," he wrote. "This world of ours would be a dreary place indeed if the element of risk were excluded from the market place." To be sure, the "prolific succession of uncertainties" offered by the stock market "constitutes a fertile hunting ground for those pure chances that the gambler finds necessary." But this no more justified government regulation of the stock market than it required "that coins should be minted with similar reliefs on both sides because men sometimes match them in what is undoubtedly a pure gamble."

For Lawrence, the centuries-old debate over the difference (if any) between gambling and speculation was mere Jesuitical casuistry, a remnant of outworn superstition. Condemning speculation as gambling was like condemning dancing, the Broadway theater, or smoking as antisocial. What we had learned since the war, Lawrence concluded, was that all pleasure was legitimate if it didn't harm others. Indeed, the "ultimate end of all economic activity" was "that pleasurable change in the state of feelings which we call psychic income. Many economists today define ultimate income as that stream of pleasurable sensations which accrues to us within a period of time."

By the summer of 1929, that stream had become a torrent. To take one example, the paper value of Samuel Insull's utility empire was appreciating at $7,000 a minute. Investing had acquired an erotic charge. "Sex has become so free and abundant that it no longer provides the thrill it once did," said the psychologist John B. Watson, who had fled Johns Hopkins for J. Walter Thompson in the wake of a sex scandal involving a colleague's wife: "gambling on Wall Street is about the only thrill we have left." Some American males saw "financial success, particularly success on the stock market . . . as evidence of virility," an English visitor observed, and they boasted about their adventures on Wall Street as a "primitive" might boast about sexual conquests. It was not only novelists like Theodore Dreiser and F. Scott Fitzgerald who recognized the erotic power of money.

A wide range of emotions characterized the bull market years of the 1920s. Life was not all beer and skittles for investors even at the height of the boom. "Seas of regret and remorse wash the land of purchase and sale," wrote the business journalist Bernie Winkelman. "Among considerable portions of the community the sale of securities or real estate at less than the highest attainable price is a major calamity to be regretted for the rest of one's life." And as Keynes observed, even the businessman who had made quick money from speculation might feel an unarticulated discomfort—a loss of self-confidence in his relation to society, of faith in his utility to the economic scheme of things. Yet these feelings could be dismissed by acolytes of the New Era as archaic relics of a bygone day. As share prices continued to climb, many people no doubt resembled the English visitor who found the atmosphere on Wall Street "savagely exciting" and felt a little wistful that he hadn't managed to get invited to the party. But the party would soon be over.

CRASH

As early as Labor Day 1929, signs of a market slowdown were unmistakable. Throughout the early fall, fitful sell-offs would course through the market, until they were stopped by a wave of buying. But the general tendency was down, and on Friday, October 24, the market opened with a broad sell-off that simply would not stop. By eleven thirty, Galbraith writes, "the market had surrendered to blind, relentless fear. This, indeed, was panic." Outside, on Broad Street, people's expressions showed "not so much suffering as a sort of horrified incredulity," according to a reporter from *The Saturday Evening Post.* After a noon meeting with other New York bankers, Thomas Lamont of J. P. Morgan admitted there was "a little distress" that morning on the floor of the exchange. After lunch, the bankers launched a classic rescue operation, much like the one J. P. Morgan had staged in 1907. As they bought millions of dollars' worth of shares, fear on the floor vanished. Prices boomed upward. Black Friday ended happily.

But the following Tuesday, October 29, did not have so cheerful a denouement. That Black Tuesday marked the end of organized support by the bankers. Panic selling began at the bell and persisted all day. The Governing Committee of the Stock Exchange met at noon. "The feeling of those present was revealed by their habit of continually lighting cigarettes, taking a puff or two, putting them out and lighting new ones—a practice which soon made the narrow room blue with smoke and extremely stuffy," President Richard Whitney reported. On the trading floor the mood was less restrained. When U.S. Steel—the ultimate blue chip—collapsed, brokers and speculators "hollered and screamed, they clawed at one another's collars. It was like a bunch of crazy men."

Outside the exchange a crowd gathered, emitting an "eerie roar." Said one eyewitness: "It wasn't an angry or hysterical sound. That was the most ominous thing about it. It was a kind of hopeless drone, a Greek dirge kind of thing. It was damned distracting, I must say." The crowd gathered there daily, for weeks. Mayor Jimmy Walker urged movie theaters "to show pictures that will reinstate courage and hope in the hearts of the people." Insurance policies were cashed in, college plans canceled. All through November, suddenly poor investors raced about trying to raise cash. "Never was there a time when more people wanted more money more urgently than in those days," Galbraith wrote. "The word that a man had 'got caught' by the market was the signal for his creditors to descend on him like locusts." Share prices kept falling. The drone continued.

Not everyone was dismayed. Edmund Wilson admitted that "the stock market crash was to count for us almost like a rending of the earth in preparation for the Day of Judgment." Yet, he added: "One couldn't help being exhilarated at the sudden and unexpected collapse of that stupid gigantic fraud." Keynes was far more engaged than Wilson with policy matters, but his first reaction to the crash was upbeat too, though for different reasons. There was, he announced in the *New York Post*, "an epoch of cheap money ahead." Britain had been struggling economically for years; there was no sense of sudden collapse there as there was in the United States, no sense that the bottom had fallen out. For Keynes, as for most Europeans, the sound of the Wall Street crash was muffled. He continued to produce work that laid the groundwork for the *General Theory*—arguing, for example, in his *Treatise on Money* (1930) that money and markets were the creation of the state, and not the other way around—and that the largest aim of public policy, the creation of a vibrant culture, was the consequence of lending and spending, and not the "voluntary abstinence of individuals from the immediate enjoyment of consumption which we call thrift." "Were the Seven Wonders of the World built by Thrift?" Keynes asked. "I deem it doubtful."

Keynes's buoyant sense of possibility contrasted sharply with the atmosphere of doom enveloping American society from boardrooms to breadlines. But when he visited the United States in spring 1931, he was reminded of what would become a key theme in the *General Theory*: the emotional basis of economic policy. He admitted what he had not earlier realized: "the anxiety of many banks and depositors throughout the country is a dominating factor." Economic recovery would not occur as long as the people were paralyzed by fear. On that key insight, Keynes and Franklin Roosevelt were united.

11

The Only Thing We Have to Fear

THE CRASH TOOK a while to make itself felt. "In small towns out West, we didn't know there was a Crash," a South Dakotan named Ed Paulsen remembered. "What did the stock market mean to us? Not a dang thing. If you were in Cut Bank, Montana, who owned stock? The farmer was a ping-pong ball in a very tough game." Farm country had been mired in depression all through the 1920s, and Paulsen had been hopping freight cars since he was fourteen. When he graduated from high school in 1930 there was no local work, so he and his two brothers "rode the freights" some more. They ended up in San Francisco in 1931.

By then the first long wave of bank failures had rolled through unlucky depositors' accounts; the banks were caught in a double bind: they needed liquidity but maintaining it contracted the money supply. The consequence was less capital for investment and fewer jobs, as the Paulsen brothers quickly discovered. Every morning they got up at five and headed out to look for work: maybe first to the waterfront, where a thousand men could be pressed against the Spreckels Sugar Refinery gates, hoping for one of three or four jobs; perhaps then to a construction site where the same thing would be happening. Paulsen remembered:

> We were a gentle crowd. These were fathers, eighty percent of them. They had held jobs and didn't want to kick society to pieces. They just wanted to go to work and they couldn't understand. There was a mysterious thing. You watched the papers, you listened to rumors, you'd get word somebody's gonna build a building.
>
> So the next morning you get up at five o'clock and you dash over there. You got a big tip. There's three thousand men there, carpenters, cement men, guys who knew machinery and everything else. The fellas always had faith that the job was gonna mature, somehow. More and more men were after fewer and fewer jobs. So San Francisco just ground to a halt. Nothing was moving.

Nearly every recollection of urban spaces in the early 1930s evokes a similar feeling: the slowing pace, the lengthening silences, and finally the standing still. What seemed to be happening was a collective withdrawal of energy from the atmosphere of everyday economic life—and an ebbing of spirits from the people, particularly the men, who had animated much of that life. Depending on personal temperament and circumstances, the emotional face of long-term unemployment ranged from desperation to denial. Behind those appearances lay bafflement, sometimes shame, often fear—which settled into constant dread.

The *élan vital* had seeped away from economic life, and Americans were experiencing a collective emotional breakdown. Anyone who had something to lose, however modest, feared losing it; anyone who had fallen a few rungs on the class ladder feared falling farther. The specter of starvation loomed. "Have you heard a hungry child cry?" the social worker Lillian Wald asked. "Have you seen the uncontrollable trembling of parents who have gone half-starved for weeks so that their children may have food?" Desperation drove many men to hit the road in search of work, even as many more sank into helpless passivity.

Anxiety crossed class lines, as foreboding about the future dampened investors' impulses toward risk-taking. John Dewey described what he called "The Collapse of the Romance"—by which he meant the romantic idea that gambling released human energies and hidden springs of good times. Prosperity had rested on confidence and confidence was gone. The entire society seemed bent on demonstrating the truth of Edmund Burke's axiom: "No power so effectually robs the mind of all its powers of acting and reasoning as fear."

FDR and Keynes shared this insight, and acted on it with uneven success. The fog of despair lifted and animal spirits revived, but only fitfully. Eventually fascism provided an energizing common foe, and after World War II Americans found relief from crippling anxieties in a new, broader-based sense of economic security.

Yet throughout the mid-century decades, fear remained a major feature of public discourse, refocused after the war on apocalyptic conflict with the Soviet Union and the prospect of nuclear annihilation. In the 1950s and '60s, quantitative models reassured policymakers by affirming that even nuclear war could be managed and controlled. The level of reassurance among the general population was another matter. Beneath the bland surfaces of postwar mass culture lay a longing for escape from cosmic dread. But this sort of fear had to be called into being by imagining future catastrophe. The dread that spread over the land in the early 1930s was more palpable, immediate, and immobilizing.

A STRANGE PARALYSIS

For Edmund Wilson and other left intellectuals, the first wave of exhilaration inspired by the Crash quickly gave way to hopes for socialist revolution—hopes soon disappointed when they went out into the countryside and encountered ordinary Americans. A sense that this was an unprecedented crisis sparked dozens of writers and photographers to document the common life under stress. Many were animated by radical visions that, like Wilson's, became clouded on contact with actuality.

Wilson returned from a trip to the heartland in 1931 and could report only "dreadful apathy, unsureness, and discouragement" among the people he encountered. "What we have lost," he wrote, is "not merely our way in the economic labyrinth but our conviction of the value of what [we] were doing. Money-making and the kind of advantages which a money-making society provides to buy are not enough to satisfy humanity—neither is a social system like our own where everyone is out for himself and the devil take the hindmost, with no common purpose and little common culture to give life stability and sense." Dazed and disoriented, most Americans were little inclined to participate in organized protest. Documentarians recorded "the look of pain, amazement, and resignation on faces of men and women trying desperately to survive," in the historian Richard Pells's words. "The amazing thing," wrote Sherwood Anderson, "is that there is so very little bitterness." Eager to find rage at the capitalist system, itinerant intellectuals instead found mostly a pervasive blankness. The Depression's victims "did not even know the name of the disease from which they'd been suffering, did not know its causes let alone its treatment and cure," James Rorty wrote. "The word 'despair' did not describe their condition. Despair implies consciousness and they were too far gone for that." This was hardly a seedbed of socialist revolution.

Documentarians detailed the psychic ravages of long-term unemployment. The novelist Louis Adamic was one of the most perceptive. "In Lowell I saw shabby men leaning against walls and lamp-posts, and standing on street corners singly or in twos or threes," he wrote in *Harper's* in 1931—"pathetic, silent, middle-aged men in torn, frayed overcoats or even without overcoats, broken shoes on their feet (in a town manufacturing shoes!), slumped in postures of hopeless discontent, their faces sunken and their eyes shifty and bewildered—men who winced and jerked queerly when they noticed me looking at them, and shuffled off uncertainly, wringing their hands in a mingling of vague desperation and of resentment at my gaze." The Marxist in Adamic could not resist noting the broken shoes of the poor in a shoe manufacturing town—the capitalist creation of scarcity amid plenty—while the novelist in him recorded the abject postures, gestures, and facial expressions of the long-term jobless. His assessment was sympathetic but unsparing. "Few of the unemployed . . . impressed me as competent people," he wrote. "They were willing, eager to work, but there was something dead in them, as from exhaustion or perhaps too much idleness, without any personal winsomeness or any power of demand. Lost, bewildered souls."

Bewilderment was especially epidemic among men. Anderson traced their psychic plight to their enforced passivity, their inability to act effectually (or at all) in the world. The consequence was "the breaking down of the moral fiber of the American man, through being out of a job, losing that sense of being some part of a moving world of activity, so essential to an American man's sense of his manhood—the loss of this essential something in the joblessness can never be measured in dollars." As survey research began to show, for many men paternal authority would never be the same. "When [the children] see me hanging around the house all the time and know that I can't find work, it has its effect all right," one man admitted ruefully. Self-blame was rampant, based on the conviction—despite all evidence—that unemployment was due to individual inadequacy. A survey of white Protestants near New York City concluded that the "hardest thing about unemployment" was the "humiliation within the family." A former breadwinner revealed that he felt "very useless to have his wife and daughter bring in money to the family while he does not contribute a nickel." Now he had "nothing to wake up for in the morning and nothing to live for." Going on the dole (if there was one) completed the humiliation, especially for white-collar men. "I simply had to murder my pride," an engineer in Birmingham told the journalist Lorena Hickock. And an insurance agent acknowledged, "We'd lived on bread and water three weeks before I could make myself do it." An inner struggle with shame produced an unsatisfying outcome: humiliated acquiescence.

By 1931, observers of various political persuasions recognized that the economic crisis of the Depression was enmeshed with an emotional crisis. "No economist doubts that the present depression has been prolonged and intensified by the fathomless pessimism which it has induced in the American people," Gerald Johnson wrote in *Harper's*. "The energy of the country has suffered a strange paralysis. We are in the doldrums, waiting not even hopefully for the wind which never comes." This condition required emotional as well as economic ministrations, and President Herbert Hoover was simply not up to the job. He was "constitutionally gloomy, a congenital pessimist who always saw the doleful side of any situation," the journalist William Allen White observed, and after meeting the president, the sculptor Gutzon Borglum agreed that "if you put a rose in Hoover's hand it would wilt." As a consequence of Hoover's dour temperament, his "appeals for good cheer came to seem feckless, even desperate," the historian John Kasson writes, "as helpful as tossing a drowning man a whoopee cushion instead of a life preserver." If smiles and frowns can be conceived as a medium of exchange, the Depression saw deflation of multiple currencies.

The wide spread of emotional stasis encouraged ambitious politicians to promise regeneration of the springs of vitality, the animal spirits that led to effective action in the world—sometimes action for its own sake, sometimes against internal or external enemies. Keynes sensed the darkening public mood when he visited Germany in January 1932. Amid appalling currency deflation, he noticed, "the reparations problem has become a matter of deep popular gusts of passion, and, consequently, of very simple reactions and decisions . . . If [the common man] is to think and feel about it at all, as today he must, he has to simplify it. And if he is determined on a 'change,' he can only demand what is concrete and appears to him to be within his power to effect." Soon a leader would arise to satisfy concrete demands and provide a sense of popular efficacy. Indeed, this was already happening by the time Keynes visited—the Nazis had received nearly 20 percent of the vote in 1930.

Perhaps even more explicitly than Hitler, Mussolini contrasted the efficiency of "Fascism in Action" with the dithering of liberal democracies. Fascism's strength lay in its completeness: "The Fascist conception of the state is all-embracing," he announced, "outside of it no human or spiritual values can exist, much less have value." Liberals winced at the rising tide of authoritarian rule, worrying along with Reinhold Niebuhr that a "crisis of democratic confidence" was under way. Anti-liberal governments, ironically echoing Americans' own providential faith in their nation's divinely ordained destiny, claimed to be "comprehending the tides of history"—and for a while it looked as if they were.

Into this morass stepped Franklin Roosevelt, projecting a preternatural sense of purpose and optimism. Like his cousin Theodore, Franklin was a descendant of the New York Anglo-Dutch elite; both got along fine with ordinary folk despite their sense of their own superiority. But

Franklin in particular was marked by what his biographer Robert Dallek calls "his capacity to charm people he wished to befriend, whatever his real feelings about them." This combination of geniality and duplicity served him well in private and public. He courted his future bride, Eleanor Hall Roosevelt (daughter of Theodore's brother), in secret, intending to present his possessive and suspicious mother, Sara, with a fait accompli—an engagement. This portended his MO in politics: "Never let the left hand know what the right is doing," he said. As editor of the Harvard *Crimson*, Roosevelt established a reputation for what his managing editor called "frictionless command" through suave conviviality. Cousin Theodore's command was rarely frictionless.

Yet the Republican Roosevelt exercised a profound influence on the Democratic one. When Franklin was at Groton, Theodore (who was president at the time) came to visit and scored a big hit with the students, who embraced TR's strenuous life as the model for right conduct. It was no accident that FDR's favorite charity became the Boy Scouts. Like TR, young Franklin pursued an ideal of virility through vigorous action and after he became an aspiring politician styled himself "an aristocrat at odds with the bosses" as well as a foe of men who cared only for money. A sense of noblesse oblige underlay both Roosevelts' commitments to what was increasingly called Progressive reform.

By the 1910s, Franklin was a handsome and dashing Democratic state senator who aimed to emulate his cousin's rapid ascent to the presidency. He was rewarded for his party loyalty, first with an appointment as assistant secretary of the navy during Wilson's administration (a post Theodore had held under McKinley) and then with the Democratic nomination for vice-president in 1920. By then FDR had shed any vestiges of patrician hauteur and learned how to perform enthusiasm and camaraderie convincingly, in ways that would advance his career by forging connections with public figures from a wide range of social backgrounds. Engulfed by a Republican landslide in the election of 1920, FDR nevertheless had shown himself to be a bright young man to watch.

Then polio felled him in August 1921. He became, in effect, a martyr to the strenuous life. Before he fell ill, despite exhaustion from the lingering demands of his Navy Department office, he threw himself into nonstop action at Campobello, the family retreat: fighting forest fires, running across the island's two-mile width, and swimming in water so cold it left him numb for hours. The overall effect, as Dallek suggests, may have been to compromise his immune system, rendering him more susceptible to the polio virus when it struck. Polio rarely had serious consequences for adults, but it devastated Franklin.

Eleanor, who had already discovered Franklin's affair with her social secretary Lucy Mercer, remained committed to his success in public life even while she refused him any further sexual intimacy. Unlike Franklin's mother, Sara, who wanted him to retire and become a country gentleman, Eleanor knew that public engagement was the key to her husband's well-being. Struggling to build upper-body strength through another strenuous program of swimming, weightlifting, and physical therapy, Roosevelt and his chief political adviser, Louis Howe, agreed that he must maintain a facade of physical vitality to ensure electoral success. This involved sustained denial of his actual disability. "You know that he has never said that he cannot walk," Eleanor marveled years later. FDR wasted no time in rejoining the political fray. He dragged himself to the 1924 Democratic convention—"an invalid on crutches, perhaps in pain, who conquered the frailties of body by sheer power of will," as one newspaper commentator wrote. It was a public relations triumph.

FDR's genius, as he restarted his pursuit of the presidency, lay in masking his grim determination with a display of ease and confidence. The economic collapse of the early 1930s presented him with the perfect opportunity to deploy this tactic. No personal style could have been more appealing to Americans than FDR's buoyancy, as they felt the bottom drop out and their security vanish. His ebullience ensured his easy victory over the dour incumbent.

During the four months between Roosevelt's election and his inauguration, the economic outlook worsened palpably. "Yes, we could smell the depression in the air," the New York theater director Harold Clurman remembered, "that historically cruel winter of 1932–3, which chilled so many of us like a world's end . . . It was like a raw wind; the very houses we lived in seemed to be shrinking, hopeless of real comfort." The president-elect concealed his private doubts and anxieties, saying "Fine! Fine! Fine!" to everyone who called on him, from the radical Huey Long of Louisiana to the conservative Joe Robinson of Arkansas. As he told Orson Welles: "Orson, you and I are the two greatest actors in America."

FDR's acting talents were quickly challenged by events. The sense of doom that gripped the Hoover administration during its last days spread to the country as a whole: banks failed by the dozen, downtowns were deserted, an ominous silence descended. By March 4, 1933, the banking system had stopped functioning altogether in most states, the New York Stock Exchange and the Chicago Board of Trade had closed, and the economic life of the nation had come to a standstill. In Washington, the skies were gray, and it was damp and chill when Roosevelt stood at the podium, rattling his notes. The nation waited.

THE TERROR LIFTS

All was quiet when Roosevelt began:

> I am certain that my fellow Americans expect that on my induction into the Presidency I will address them with a candor and a decision which the present situation of our Nation impels. This is preeminently the time to speak the truth, the whole truth, frankly and boldly. Nor need we shrink from honestly facing conditions in our country today. This great Nation will endure as it has endured, will revive and will prosper. So, first of all, let me assert my firm belief that the only thing we have to fear is fear itself—nameless, unreasoning, unjustified terror which paralyzes needed efforts to convert retreat into advance.

The man who had overcome his own paralysis to become president was now ministering to the nation's paralysis. Rejecting the fascist rhetoric of vengeful victimhood, Roosevelt rallied Americans to embrace a moral equivalent of war—a collective campaign against the Depression in the spirit of William James, rather than Benito Mussolini. Observers on the premises understood at once that the impact of FDR's speech was broader than politics: it replenished the springs of emotional vitality, the potential for spontaneity—including spontaneous laughter. "The new president's recurrent smile of confidence, his uplifted chin and the challenge of his voice did much to help the national sense of humor assert itself," *The New York Times* observed. To some he was a luminous figure; Lillian Gish said he seemed "dipped in phosphorous."

But one did not have to see the man to be inspired by him. Radio audiences were transfixed and transformed. "Today sitting among a gathering of all but 'forgotten men' during your inaugural address," a Cleveland man wrote to FDR, "I seen those worried looks replaced by smiles and confidence, eyes filled up with tears of gratitude, shoulders lifted and chest out." A woman from Des Moines reported shedding "tears of peaceful happiness despite the dreadful predicament the country is now in."

The president knew how to enact a positive-thinking emotional agenda. His first official act was a masterstroke of euphemistic spin—to prevent any more banks from failing, he closed the ones that remained open and called it a "Bank Holiday." By the time the "holiday" was over, he had held his first press conference, secured a bank bailout from Congress, and given his first "Fireside Chat," the intimate radio addresses that brought his calm, measured tones into millions of living rooms. The effect was electric. "You are bringing back confidence and driving out the fear that has been gripping the people for the last three years," a Chicagoan wrote, and a judge from Syracuse recalled being one of a bipartisan group of listeners worried about the banking crisis: after Roosevelt had finished speaking, they looked around and said, as if with one voice: "We are saved." When the banks reopened, depositors started putting their money back in them. In those days, before capital had become thoroughly globalized, it was possible to save the U.S. banking system (barely) by restoring domestic confidence.

Though FDR's campaign pledge of a "new deal for the American people" faced a bumpy path forward, the paralyzing terror had lifted. Within two weeks, Americans suddenly seemed to be back on their feet again, smiling, ready to work, invest, spend. All that mattered was action.

Charles Edison, son of the legendary inventor and president of Thomas Edison, Inc., posted placards on the company's walls that read:

> President Roosevelt has done his part; now you do something.
>
> Buy something—buy anything, anywhere, paint your kitchen, send a telegram, give a party, get a car, pay a bill, rent a flat, fix your roof, get a haircut, see a show, build a house, take a trip, sing a song, get married.
>
> It does not matter what you do—but get going and keep going. This old world is starting to move.

Edison's list of ways to "do something" was reassuringly domestic and ordinary. What was striking about it was its open-endedness, its celebration of action for its own sake. In other settings, this was the sort of sentiment that swept Fascist or Communist governments into power. And indeed, to *The New York Times*'s Anne O'Hare McCormick, the atmosphere in Washington in May 1933 seemed "strangely reminiscent of the atmosphere in Rome in the first weeks after the fall of the Blackshirts, or Moscow at the beginning of the [first] Five Year Plan." The American people "trust the discretion of the President more than they trust Congress," she wrote. "Nobody is much disturbed by the idea of dictatorship." Despite FDR's disavowal of fascist rhetoric, the allure of fascism persisted. The emotional ground remained well prepared. Recoiling from cowering in loneliness, many Americans yearned for effective group action, under the direction of a strong leader.

LONGING TO BELONG

During the early 1930s, Mussolini's corporatist state began to appeal to flattened American capitalists as an alternative to Communist planning. By the time Roosevelt took office, business leaders had decided that economic planning was a necessity: the question was who would do it. In 1934, during the early, corporatist phase of the New Deal, *Fortune* noted favorably the parallels between the wage and price codes of Roosevelt's National Recovery Administration and similar policies adopted by Italian labor and business syndicates. American businessmen turned against fascism only after they realized that it meant a regulatory state (like the later New Deal) rather than a business-government partnership.

As capitalism collapsed in the early 1930s, fascism stirred interest for political as well as economic reasons. Indeed, the structure of the Fascist system resembled what scholars would later call the "associative state" created by the New Deal. As the historian John Patrick Diggins observed, "A system based upon the guiding influence of a paternal state, a system that brought to the surface the subterranean struggles of classes and interest groups and harmonized those forces in official institutions, struck a positive note in the minds of those political thinkers tired of the old formulas and fictions of progressivism." For some, the leading fiction overdue for rethinking was "the public interest."

The New Deal's associative state frankly acknowledged the power of organized interest groups—farmers, laborers, consumers, businessmen—and created government agencies to regulate and represent that power. This reorganization replaced the Progressive model of everyone striving for a single public good with a broker state balancing the claims of, for example, the United Mine Workers, the National Association of Manufacturers, and the Grange, through the Departments of Labor, Commerce, and Agriculture. The developing network of bureaucratic procedures provided a barrier against both dictatorship and mob rule, allowing pluralistic democracy to flourish while "the social whole, and with it the idea of a common good based on shared goals, disappeared," as the political scientist Ira Katznelson writes. But while that may have been true in theory, at the level of lived experience bureaucratic procedures were not enough.

Americans battered by insecurities yearned for a sense of collective identity, of common purpose. Under dictatorial regimes, this longing to belong was addressed by Fascist or Communist ideology; in the United States, by a diffuse but pervasive cultural nationalism that took many forms. All helped to create a "we" by popularizing conceptions such the American People, the National Character, and the American Way of Life; many celebrated a new role for the federal government in creating a sense of community that spanned the continent—a role that provided unprecedented opportunities for state involvement in previously private matters.

One of the strangest and perhaps most revealing arguments for an intrusive state appeared in *Good Housekeeping* in 1935. "Uncle Sam Wants Your Mark," Vera Connolly wrote praising J. Edgar Hoover's plan to fingerprint all Americans. She urged voluntary compliance because, she believed, universal fingerprinting would end "a travesty on our modern civilization"—the anonymous burial of decent citizens in potter's fields. "Almost every 'unknown' is known to and loved by someone. Behind almost every commitment to that soil is family heartbreak somewhere. For it is chiefly the decent who are buried here. The criminal seldom is. His fingerprints are on file." By creating an enormous file of "the decent" as well as the criminal, fingerprinting would fashion a national community where no one was anonymous, in life or death. Connolly's argument revealed the depth and spread of longings to belong—even if the belonging was based on a common experience of bureaucratic surveillance.

Social Security posed a more benign and more numerically based opportunity for belonging through bureaucracy. Few phrases could more succinctly express the dominant desire of the '30s than what the program's title promised: "social security." It was collective, and it was solid. It epitomized the widespread popular recognition that under modern conditions "Life is safer, but living less secure," as a Social Security pamphlet put it in 1937. Improved medicine and hygiene had lengthened life spans, but maintaining a livelihood required more dependence on a certifiable social whole. Receiving a Social Security number certified one's membership in a secure national community, or so one could hope.

One famous Depression photograph captures that hope. Dorothea Lange gave it the flat caption "Unemployed lumber worker goes with his wife to the bean harvest." The setting is somewhere (unspecified by Lange) in Oregon. The gender distinctions are stark. The wife is peripheral, tired, receding into the background. The husband is out front, a well-built shirtless man with movie-star looks, smoking a pipe, smiling wryly—unemployed but brimming with self-confidence, or at least the appearance of it. He makes a sharp contrast with the cringing, twitching men in the Massachusetts mill towns of the early 1930s. But the most

striking feature of this portrait is the Social Security number tattooed and prominently displayed on the man's biceps. Thanks to this number, the historian Dan Bouk has discovered the couple's name: Thomas and Vivian Cave.

Within less than a decade, numbers tattooed on flesh would become fused in the popular imagination with horrific images of the Holocaust—the mass organization of mass extermination. But in 1937, despite the looming shadow of Nazism, the death camps were unimaginable to most Americans. The number on Thomas Cave's arm could have profoundly different associations, as Bouk observes: among migrant farmworkers, who were excluded from the Social Security program, it could have been a status symbol; it could also be useful for a lumberman who did dangerous work and might need to be identified after an accident. And it could numerically confirm a sense of belonging to a larger whole, a national community.

In this sense, Social Security was the public policy expression of the same sentiment that promoted fascination with opinion polls purporting to show what "the average American" thinks or what "we" believe. This was the era when pollsters began to take what George Gallup called "The Pulse of Democracy." The phrase suggests that public opinion polling, like lie detectors and blood-pressure cuffs, was another effort (on a mass rather than individual scale) to measure subjective experience—opinions and beliefs, anxieties and aspirations. By the 1930s, scientists of subjective experience claimed to quantify everything from human intelligence (even "genius") to what Irving Fisher called "the modern conception of death"—a death that could be planned for but also postponed, perhaps indefinitely, by careful attention to actuarial data. Numbers began to structure the terrors of the inner life.

Other, unquantified sources of reassurance flourished in popular media and entertainment. Animal spirits survived but were increasingly confined to children, athletes, entertainers, and innocent folk from the recent past. Newspaper advice columnists revealed a new sobriety regarding courtship, as the birth rate dropped and young people postponed marriage. "What chance do you think normal men of 35 to 40 have of ever marrying for love, especially if they are reasonably attractive to women?" a reader asked Dorothy Dix in 1931. Such a man's chances, she reassuringly replied, were simply "the best. For a man at that age is at the peak of his attractiveness to women," she wrote. "Of course, a little 19 or 20 year old flapper would prefer a boy of her own age who would want to jump around and dance endlessly and scream and make whoopee just as she does, because they are overflowing with animal spirits. To the flapper the man between 35 and 40 would seem positively decrepit with age, but I am not supposing that a man of that age would even want to be a cradle-robber." Marriage was for grown-ups. Animal spirits were for kids.

They were also for rural folk. During the early '30s, producers of Broadway musicals began to discover the potential of sanitized country settings, populated by "Cowboys and Farmers and Animal Spirits," as the *New York Times* drama critic Brooks Atkinson put it in a review of *Green Grow the Lilacs* in 1931. This show was what Atkinson called a "folk play"—"an artless play of native characters and customs." A world away from drawing room badinage, the characters' "talk has bravado and the smell of native soil." As Atkinson wrote: "These cowboys and farmers are all hearty people, coarse, natural and merry. After a decade of defeatist farm literature, it is refreshing to smell the healthy odors of the pioneer prairie." The desolate landscapes of Hamlin Garland and Sherwood Anderson were giving way to the more hopeful world of Rodgers and Hammerstein and Frank Capra. "Everyone in 'Green Grow the Lilacs' has so much animal good will that he feels like 'hollerin' and shoutin'—and most of them do," said Atkinson. For the next decade or more, hollerin' and shoutin' could be heard in almost any Broadway musical with a "folk play" feel.

Besides staging folk plays, Broadway and Hollywood producers addressed and reinforced popular longings to belong by sentimentalizing other settings associated with traditional, often hierarchical, community—the rural South, the military. African American reviewers recognized that the sanitized South of the movies offered career opportunities to black entertainers like the tap dancer Bill "Bojangles" Robinson. The *Chicago Defender* was delighted to see Shirley Temple "truckin' on down" with Robinson in *The Littlest Rebel*, as if fresh from a Cotton Club revue. In popular entertainment, animal spirits continued to flourish among familiar overlapping subgroups—African Americans, children, strapping young men on a ship at sea. "'Sailor, Beware!' is a bawdy prank," Atkinson reported in 1933. "It is one of the most outrageous bits of romantic buffoonery ever tossed about on Broadway. It is acted with robust animal spirits. Every one was vastly amused by it last evening. No doubt the United States Navy will use it for recruiting purposes when Broadway stops going to see it." Military comedy offered the potent combination of high jinks and hierarchy, animal spirits corralled by underlying discipline.

Big-time sports provided a similar mix. After Max Baer defeated Primo Carnera for the world heavyweight boxing title in 1934, *The Washington Post* listed the new champ's strengths: "He is young, full of animal spirits, can punch and, most important of all, he is smart. He behaves and trains with more care than most will believe." Championship boxing required energy and power but also brains and discipline.

This was how animal spirits were characteristically situated in the popular culture of the 1930s—a necessary ingredient for success that nevertheless had to be subordinated to an even more fundamental work ethic. In "Grandpa Jenkins' Gold: A Story of Two Young Prospectors," a story from "The Boys and Girls Page" of the Washington *Sunday Star*, Boyce Morgan describes Grandpa Jenkins's response to Fred and Tom's excited discovery that they have struck gold: "Grandpa watched them for a moment, then cut short the celebration. 'Enough of that dang foolishness,' he growled. 'Don't let a little bit of yellow metal put you plumb loco. Come on and eat your lunch now, and then get back to work. You can use all them animal spirits for turning over pay dirt.'" Animal spirits were best applied to work that paid. As a delight in playful energy gone "plumb loco," they belonged to irresponsible childhood or forms of popular entertainment that provided innocent escape.

Not too long ago, some said, even burlesque offered a kind of innocence. "Although a good many were offended by it and if periodically burlesque was the subject of sermons and proclamations, the vigor of its animal spirits contained little or nothing that in the light, say, of customs characteristic of the later prohibition era would be called sinister." This at least we could see now in retrospect, *The Wall Street Journal* reminisced in 1937. "Afterward, due to various causes, the institution of burlesque gradually lost its original, outrageous, slap-stick genius, began imitating first itself and then the Broadway revue and soon became effete. Following this in rapid order it became shabby, then nasty, then degenerate."

But fortunately for movie and theater fans, romantic comedy provided an alternative to degenerate burlesque. Consider *Happy Landing*, which according to the *Washington Post* reviewer was "made to order for the movie fans who love ice skating and the complications attendant upon the love life of a popular orchestra leader." Sonja Henie's skating is "superlative," and she and Don Ameche are "so cute and so sweet." Sports and sanitized sentiment played counterpoint to more forceful expressions of vital energy: "Ethel Merman is present, in better makeup than her last screen appearance, and with all her memorable animal spirits. The lady is exuberant, irrepressible, and if the ceiling is the limit, the good rafters must often quake a bit when she tempestuously hits a high note as only Merman can. She is the most persistent pursuer of the elegant Mr. [Cesar] Romero [the band leader], and causes much activity through her misbehaving." Cinematic conventions allowed actresses to express animal spirits in largely asexual comic roles—such as the one Bette Davis played in *The Bride Came C.O.D.* The question on viewers' minds, as the *New York Times* reviewer wrote, was what would happen on screen now that "Bette Davis, the Duse of Warners, had let her back hair down and given vent to the animal spirits repressed in a long line of lead-heavy roles. And the answer is that as the comic sparring partner of James Cagney, no slouch himself, Miss Davis has taken the bit in her teeth and flung her breathless way through a rough-and-tumble comedy with no gags barred . . . Let a lady have some fun." Throughout the Depression, Hollywood continued cranking out the upbeat fare Mayor Walker had begged for on Black Tuesday 1929.

Yet no matter how much fun Bette Davis and Ethel Merman were having on-screen, the public climate of fear persisted into the late 1930s and early '40s, intensified eventually by the specter of war abroad. Though paralysis lifted, economic stagnation and chronic insecurity persisted. In 1935, the sociologist Howard Odum recorded "widespread confusion, unrest, distrust, and despair" in his state of North Carolina and throughout much of rural America. FDR continued to talk a good game; in June 1936 he announced: "Today, my friends, we have won against the most dangerous of our foes—we have conquered fear." Yet the conquest proved temporary; fear remained an enemy, as FDR himself acknowledged when he made "Freedom from Fear" one of the bases of the Atlantic Charter in 1941. By summer 1938, according to Walter Lippmann, Americans were "seized by deep uncertainty" and "sick with nervous indecision" about how to respond (or not) to the rise of fascism in Europe. This may have been truer of East Coast Anglophiles than of most Americans, but those worried about war were a significant and growing minority. Interventionist academics argued that Americans must get over "the dominant mood that has possessed them since 1931," as Frederick Schumann of the University of Chicago said, "which has been one of fear and flight." Business leaders remained fearful too, as Alfred Sloan of General Motors remarked in 1938. Wondering at the slow pace of the American recovery, Sloan asked: "Why has it happened? Simply because of fear as to the future of American enterprise and the rules upon which it is to be conducted. In other words, our difficulties are political economic rather than purely economic." As Keynes recognized, investors could be terrified by the merest hint that the rules of enterprise might be changing—that the state might be sticking its nose more boldly into business affairs.

While the rules were indeed changing, it was not always clear how or in what direction. FDR was an inspiring leader, but he was largely innocent of economic theory. He clung to the conventional nostrum of the balanced budget, which left him largely unresponsive to Keynesian ideas. "I saw your friend Keynes," he wrote to his secretary of labor, Frances Perkins, after the British economist came to call in May 1934. "He left a whole rigmarole of figures. He must be a mathematician rather than a political economist." Though Keynes distrusted numbers as predictors, he no doubt used them to illustrate, for example, how public works projects could have what Keynes called a multiplier effect on aggregate demand. Building bridges provided cash to construction workers, whose families would spend it on consumer goods that would increase retail sales, which in turn would make more capital available to investors and contribute to a broader prosperity. Roosevelt, probably impatient and maybe a little confused, got Keynes exactly backward: Keynes was nothing if not a *political* economist, rather than a mathematician.

For his part, Keynes was equally underwhelmed with Roosevelt; he wrote to Perkins that he had "supposed the President was more literate, economically." Keynes emphasized the importance of raising purchasing power through government expenditures financed by loans; raising taxes to decrease the deficit, he argued, would be precisely the wrong thing to do in the depths of an economic downturn, because it would reduce purchasing power at the very moment when aggregate demand needed stimulating. Deficit financing could ultimately pay for itself by putting people back to work and getting more money in circulation. Wars had always been especially potent instruments for stimulating industry, Keynes told Roosevelt, noting that Hitler's rearmament program was already pushing Germany toward prosperity. James Rorty, after interviewing scores of ordinary Americans, recorded a vernacular version of Keynesian insight: "'I guess things won't get any better until we have another war.' How many times did I hear that all across the continent and back!"

Why not promote "intense industrial activity" through peaceful public works? FDR had begun such a program, but without a Keynesian justification. He simply wanted to put people back to work doing useful jobs. Puzzled by Keynesian concepts, he allowed deficit hawks in his administration, led by the treasury secretary, Henry Morgenthau, to continue to press for balanced budgets. The result was a steep business downturn in 1937–38.

Meanwhile Keynes had realized that bad theory—not simply bad policy—was the root of the Depression's intractability. He set out to address this problem by writing *The General Theory of Employment, Interest, and Money.* It was a summa of where his thinking had been headed for decades—away from the classical link between savings and investment and toward a connection between consumption and investment; away from probability and toward uncertainty; away from a focus on calculating utility and toward a recognition of animal spirits. The true investor, for Keynes, took long-term risks that resisted precise measurement, that arose from a spontaneous impulse to act, and that ultimately underwrote the common good. Investment could be actuated by motives as incalculable and heroic as those that inspired expeditions to the South Pole; both involved decisions made in the face of radical uncertainty. This is how Keynes came to use the concept of animal spirits, as the linchpin of his argument in the *General Theory.*

While few economists or politicians grasped the philosophical implications of the *General Theory*, its impact on public policy was ultimately profound. But it was only beginning to be felt in September 1938, when his old Bloomsbury friends' Memoir Club decamped from London to convene at Tilton, Keynes's crumbling country estate. He was the featured speaker of the evening, and was about to reveal how he had arrived at his contemporary worldview.

REENTER KEYNES: THE MATURATION OF THEORY

By 1938, Keynes was at the height of his fame. His *General Theory* had already provoked controversy far beyond the precincts of the economics profession. His ideas were to become the blueprint for managing wartime and postwar economies on both sides of the Atlantic. His career epitomized the fruitful merger of intellect and public policy, poised on the brink of practical achievement.

But his body was a wreck. He had suffered from chest pains and shortness of breath from time to time for years and in May 1937 he collapsed with a heart attack. His convalescence—devotedly overseen by Lydia—was long and slow. The doctors allowed him three hours of a work a day, in bed with his writing board. The biggest obstacle to his recovery was not work but worry.

There was plenty to fret about, especially for a public man like Keynes. "Lying in bed, I think a good deal about foreign policy," he wrote to the chancellor of the exchequer in July 1937. An article in the *New Statesman* soon followed. Alarmed by the rise of the "brigand nations" of Germany and Italy and recoiling from the Soviet alternative, Keynes argued that liberal democracy was under siege and continued to believe that maintaining peace was Britain's primary responsibility. "It is our duty to prolong peace, hour by hour, day by day, for as long as we can," he wrote. "I have said in another context that . . . in the long run we are all dead. But I could have said equally well that . . . in the short run we are still alive. Life and history are made up of short runs." He concluded that "Britain should build up its naval strength and wait for the dictators *to make mistakes.*"

Closer to home, there were more immediate causes for anxiety. After a brief market upturn, Keynes's financial position shrank alarmingly during 1937 and 1938. His net worth and his income both dropped by nearly two thirds over twenty-four months. His wealth and his health slumped together. The steep decline in share prices slowed his own recovery; his body and mind roiled with the uncertain political economy, prolonging his invalidism.

But after nearly a year and a half of convalescence, Keynes was finally ready to rise from his invalid's bed to address the assembled Bloomsberries. In Virginia Woolf's account, he read a "a very packed, profound and impressive paper," then had to "be slowly conveyed to his ground floor bedroom for a rest, while Lydia chirpily fed them ham sandwiches and hot cakes." Keynes's talk was indeed full of substance. Reflecting in "My Early Beliefs," he melded his own biography with a diffuse but inescapable shift in British intellectual life—from utilitarian faith in rational choice toward recognition of the irrational springs of human conduct.

Keynes begins by recalling D. H. Lawrence's visit to Cambridge in 1914. The occasion was a breakfast party in Bertrand Russell's rooms. Lawrence sat awkwardly apart; Keynes assumed he found "Cambridge rationalism and cynicism, then at their height," to be "repulsive." In recalling the shallowness of his younger self and his fellow rational cynics, the older Keynes wonders: "was there something true and right in what Lawrence felt?" Keynes's attempt to answer that question illuminates his own intellectual odyssey from the self-satisfactions of Bloomsbury to a more complex and capacious vision of human experience—the worldview that gave rise to his appreciation of animal spirits.

Keynes arrived at Cambridge in the Michaelmas term of 1902. Not long afterward, the Cambridge philosopher G. E. Moore published his *Principia Ethica*; its effect on young Maynard and his classmates was electric and enduring. "We were at an age when our beliefs still influenced our behaviour, a characteristic of the young which it is easy for the middle-aged to forget, and the habits of feeling formed then still persist in a recognizable degree," Keynes said. Moore was an unlikely object of an undergraduate cult. He was "a puritan and a precisian," Keynes said; he believed in careful language as the avenue to truth, and in the value of custom and convention as sources of morality. Yet his influence on the young was "exciting, exhilarating, the beginning of a renaissance, the opening of a new heaven on a new earth, we were the forerunners of a new dispensation, we were not afraid of anything."

The key to Moore's impact was that he combined his conventional morality—which the Cambridge lads largely ignored—with an exalted conception of an ideal life, which became a kind of religion for them. "Nothing mattered except states of mind, our own and other people's of course, but chiefly our own," Keynes remembered. "One's prime objects in life were love, the creation and enjoyment of aesthetic experience, and the pursuit of knowledge." There was a suspicion that doing good might interfere with being good, and the Cambridge outlook remained "altogether otherworldly—with wealth, power, popularity or success it had no concern whatever, they were thoroughly despised." Moore's followers regarded this otherworldliness as "entirely rational and scientific in character." One apprehended "good" just as one apprehended "green," as a simple indefinable entity, identifiable only by intuition or direct inspection. All of this apprehension occurred "under the influence of Moore's method, according to which you could hope to make essentially vague notions clear by using precise language about them and asking precise questions," said Keynes. For Keynes, the Mooreite dispensation exuded "a purer sweeter air by far than Freud cum Marx . . . It is still my religion under the surface," he admitted.

Moore was the first significant force pulling the young Keynes away from conventional utilitarian thought, despite the older man's own attachment to it. In the undergraduate version of Moore's creed, "the life of passionate contemplation and communion was supposed to oust all other purposes whatever." Given such an imperative, there was no room for a Benthamite hedonistic calculus or "its *reduction ad absurdum*, Marxism," Keynes observed—both worldviews placed far too much emphasis on economic concerns for Moore's followers: "We repudiated entirely customary morals, conventions, and traditional wisdom," Keynes said. "We were, that is to say, in the strict sense of the word, immoralists."

Yet they clung uncritically to one set of conventional beliefs. Keynes recalled his own and his contemporaries' faith in "continuing moral progress" through the pursuit of "rational self-interest" by "reliable, rational, decent people, influenced by truth and objective standards"—people like themselves, who could be exempted from traditional rules of conduct due to their superiority to the common herd. This was a fair description of the prewar Bloomsbury creed. Vitalists like Lawrence found it repulsive at the time, and the older Keynes now acknowledged that Lawrence's visceral reaction depended on a deeper truth: that the veneration for "rational self-interest" rested on a vacuous conception of human nature. As Keynes recalled:

> We repudiated all versions of the doctrine of original sin, of there being insane and irrational springs of wickedness in most men. We were not aware that civilization was a thin and precarious crust erected by the personality and the will of a very few, and only maintained by rules and conventions skilfully put across and guilefully preserved. We had no respect for traditional wisdom or the restraints of custom. We lacked reverence, as Lawrence observed and as Ludwig [Wittgenstein] with justice also used to say—for everything and everyone.

Keynes could justly imagine that he was one of "the very few" who constructed and maintained that "thin and precarious crust." Yet his views were more complex than those of a comfortable meritocrat. By acknowledging the centrality of torrential irrational forces in human affairs, his emerging outlook resonated with the musings of Freud, Conrad, Bergson, and other Modernists. Lawrence and Wittgenstein had indeed shared an important insight: Cambridge rationalism was a superficial, trivializing mode of thought. As Keynes said, "the attribution of rationality to human nature, instead of enriching it, now seems to me to have impoverished it." It ignored not only "powerful and irrational springs of wickedness" but also more benign and necessary "springs of feeling" that were "more various, and also much richer, than we allowed for."

Keynes's public tribute to emotional life was rooted in personal and intellectual experience. For more than a decade, his marriage to Lydia had allowed his own springs of feeling to flow more freely. By 1938, he had been reading Freud for years, and though he did not embrace psychoanalysis tout court, he did believe that it was impossible to understand human experience without considering the buried life of unconscious thoughts and feelings. For all their pretensions to profundity, Keynes admitted, the Cambridge undergraduates were "water-spiders, gracefully skimming, as light and reasonable as air, the surface of the stream without any contact at all with the eddies and currents underneath . . . that is why I say that there may have been just a grain of truth when Lawrence said in 1914 that we were 'done for.'"

This was a major admission from a major public figure. Keynes was not disavowing reasonableness as a criterion of worth, nor the value of analytic intellect applied to public policy—his entire career was a vindication of that value. But he was confessing that his youthful faith in human rationality was vastly overblown, sadly misplaced, and wholly unable to encompass the darker dimensions of life—which were more apparent in 1938 than they were in 1914.

Yet the difficulty was not only the absence of darkness: springs of feeling generally were missing from Cambridge rationalism. Keynes's growing recognition of irrationality in public life melded his personal odyssey with his perceptions of world-historical catastrophe: the collapse of capital markets and the long depression that followed it, the rise of the dictators in Europe. But Keynes was not a Julien Benda, not a rationalist lamenting the descent of the intellectuals into irrationalism and of the masses into madness. Keynes had a sense of how spontaneous emotional impulses could serve an infinite variety of purposes, from the monstrous to the sublime, and that rationality and irrationality could coexist interdependently, especially in the realm of political economy. Beneath the rhetoric of capitalist rationality, the proliferating numbers and the appearance of precision, Keynes detected depths of fantasy and fear.

All his observation and experience came together in the *General Theory.* The emphasis should be on "General" rather than "Theory," as the author himself said at the outset. Keynes made conceptual breakthroughs of interest to policymakers and academic economists, but he also developed a broader theme of cultural criticism. He questioned a cornerstone of bourgeois culture—what Keynes's biographer Robert Skidelsky calls "the abstinence theory of progress"—by arguing that saving was not the virtue it was cracked up to be, as it withheld money from the larger social purposes that could be served by the multiplier effects of consumer demand. The urge to consume, not the urge to save, Keynes argued, underwrote investment in enterprise and created prosperity. These assumptions would guide the management of economies on both sides of the Atlantic during the comparatively prosperous mid-century decades—the Keynesian era. Keynes did not foresee the aesthetic and environmental damage that would be done by rampant consumption, but he would have likely proposed policy measures to contain its destructive effects. He was a flexible thinker, responsive to changing historical conditions.

The *General Theory* was about more than policy. Though Keynes was a thoroughly secular man, beneath the equations and formulas his theory resonated with a subversive strain of Christianity: the celebration of reckless generosity over careful frugality, of losing all to gain all. This tradition was articulated in a vernacular idiom by an author who called himself Harlem Pete, in a dream book published in Philadelphia in 1949. "If you want to be rich, Give! If you want to be poor, Grasp! If you want abundance, Scatter! If you want to be needy, Hoard!" he wrote. Keynes was no ordinary economist; he and Harlem Pete were brothers under the skin.

THE ECONOMIST AS MODERNIST

The *General Theory* is a scattering of gems, separated by stretches of dense technical argument. The gems include fanciful examples and playful thought experiments, the most famous of which was meant to show the efficacy of government-sponsored public works to promote prosperity:

> If the Treasury were to fill old bottles with bank-notes, bury them at suitable depths in disused coal mines which are then filled up to the surface with town rubbish, and leave it to private enterprise on well-tried principles of laissez-faire to dig the notes up again . . . there need be no more unemployment and, with the help of the repercussions, the real income of the community, and its capital wealth also, would probably become a good deal greater than it actually is. It would, indeed, be more sensible to build houses and the like; but if there are political and practical difficulties in the way of this, the above would be better than nothing.

Decades later, Keynes's Cambridge colleague Joan Robinson charged self-described Keynesian economists with, in effect, taking the thought experiment literally as a policy proposal by treating military spending as if it were like any other kind of public spending. "Keynes did not *want* anyone to dig holes and fill them," an exasperated Robinson told the American Economic Association in 1970. Nor did he want governments to promote prosperity by buying (or building) things that blow up. But that is in fact what happened in the United States of the post–World War II decades.

Keynes himself was a social democrat who believed that policy should be made to serve the public interest. Ordinary people, through their representatives, would decide how public investment would be allocated; with any luck the representatives would be advised by clever people like Keynes himself. Keynes was by no means an uncritical advocate of top-down planning, but he distrusted speculative capitalists' capacity to allocate resources in ways that would promote the common good. "When the capital development of a country is the by-product of the activities of a casino," he wrote, "the job is likely to be ill done."

Yet Keynes was also a gambler, a risk-taking investor, and a connoisseur of chance. Next to William James, he was perhaps the greatest philosopher of uncertainty in the twentieth-century Anglophone world. At the heart of the *General Theory* was a sweeping revision of the ontological foundation underlying classical economics—its ability to formulate enduring laws that would apply as certainly to the future as to the present and past, even with respect to the chaotic movements of finance capital. Daily trading on the stock exchange depended on investors' shifting expectations of movements in asset prices. "How then are these highly significant daily, even hourly re-evaluations of existing investments carried out in practice?" Keynes asked. His answer subverted a century or more of economic orthodoxy: "In practice," said Keynes, we have tacitly been "assuming that the existing state of affairs will continue indefinitely, except in so far as we have specific reasons to expect a change." Rarely if ever was this assumption stated explicitly, but it undergirded the calculations that supposedly guided every investment decision.

The rational actor was the central figure in the morality play staged by conventional economic thought. Behind the drama of calculating choice lay decades of utilitarian tradition—the tradition Keynes had learned to reject as an undergraduate at Cambridge. Jeremy Bentham as well as Adam Smith were the presiding spirits of classical economics, and their influence had long-term consequences. For more than a century, among professional economists, "risks . . . were supposed to be capable of an exact actuarial computation. The calculus of probability . . . was supposed to be capable of reducing uncertainty to the same calculable status as that of certainty itself; just as in the Benthamite calculus of pains and pleasures or of advantage and disadvantage, by which the Benthamite philosophy assumed men to be influenced in their general ethical behaviour," Keynes wrote.

But this assumption was fundamentally flawed. "Actually, we have, as a rule, only the vaguest idea of any but the most direct consequences of our acts," Keynes observed in a follow-up article. This vagueness was especially the case with respect to financial affairs: "The whole object of the accumulation of Wealth is to produce results, or potential results, at a comparatively distant, and sometimes at an *indefinitely* distant, date." Since "our knowledge of the future is fluctuating, vague, and uncertain," wealth is "a peculiarly unsuitable subject for the methods of the classical economic theory." Keynes was not ruling out risk management through probabilistic calculations, as he made clear:

> By "uncertain" knowledge . . . I do not mean to distinguish what is known from what is only probable. The game of roulette is not subject, in this sense, to uncertainty, nor is the prospect of a Victory bond being drawn. Or again, the expectation of life is only slightly uncertain. Even the weather is only moderately uncertain. The sense in which I am using the term is that in which the prospect of a European war is uncertain, or the price of copper and the rate of interest twenty years hence, or the obsolescence of a new invention, or the position of private wealth-owners in the social system in 1970. About these matters there is no scientific basis on which to form any calculable probability whatever. We simply do not know.

Risk could be measured in mathematical probabilities with objective standards; uncertainty could not. Under conditions of uncertainty, decisions often must be made straight from the gut—hence the opening for animal spirits, the core of Keynes's brief against exaggerated claims for rational self-interest. Most investment decisions, he argued, were "a result of animal spirits—of a spontaneous urge to action rather than inaction," rather than "an exact calculation of benefits to come." Venturesome enterprise was rooted in visceral feelings and only a little more rationally motivated than "an expedition to the South Pole."

And venturesome enterprise required long-term investors, not the sort who primarily counted on short-term gains. They were mere speculators, though their activities were shrouded in a mystifying web of quantitative expertise that gave them the aura of investments. "The actual, private object of the most skilled investment to-day is 'to beat the gun,' as the Americans so well express it, to outwit the crowd, and to pass the bad, or depreciating, half-crown to the other fellow," Keynes wrote. Despite the skills involved in options or commodity futures trading, these forms of speculation (among others) reduced investment to "a game of snap, of Old Maid, of Musical Chairs—a pastime in which he is victor who says Snap neither too soon nor too late, who passes the Old Maid to his neighbor before the game is over, and who secures a chair for himself when the music stops."

Keynes's ideal investor, like the entrepreneurs he backed, was engaged in a far more useful, maybe even heroic enterprise—one that required generosity and magnanimity and vision, to be sure, but also perhaps energy, risk, resilience, and endurance. Not to mention a tolerance for radical uncertainty, from the outset. It all sounds a little like an expedition to the South Pole. Such were the possibilities of enterprise animated by animal spirits.

Keynes's discussion of animal spirits and long-term investment reveals him to be far more philosophically and psychologically interesting than Joseph Schumpeter, the economist who in recent years has been credited with displacing him as the presiding spirit of our entrepreneurial age. Schumpeter's ideal entrepreneur turns out to be little more than a capitalist embodiment of conventional male will, spearheading the relentless forward march of technological innovation, leaving a trail of "creative destruction" in his wake. Keynes's ideas led in far more humane directions, toward a utopian future, created by "science and compound interest," when people no longer need to work more than five hours a day, with the rest of the time left open to creative leisure. This was the future he imagined in "Economic Prospects for Our Grandchildren" (1930). Keynes's rosy scenario overlooked its prerequisite: a broad redistribution of wealth. But his vision of a steady-state economy constituted one of the few enduring intellectual alternatives to the repeated catastrophes created by creative destruction. The concept of creative destruction has in fact become a capitalist version of Providence, assuring us that the most apparently calamitous developments will somehow all work out for the best. Keynes knew better.

Keynes's *General Theory* was an especially sophisticated example of a characteristic Modernist project—uncovering the role of subjective, even irrational experience in the apparently rational realm of human will and choice. Unlike neoclassical economists, he made no attempt to calculate the incalculable; he was willing to rest content with radical uncertainty, and remained closer kin to William James than to Irving Fisher.

In principle the *General Theory* could have provided an opportunity for fundamentally rethinking the received principles of political economy. But few economists or policymakers took advantage of it. Most commonly, Keynes's ideas were reduced to mere tools and assimilated to utilitarian ethics, which he had aimed to transcend. The concept of animal spirits was at the heart of that aim: it is about far more than investors' motives; for Keynes it embodied a recoil from a bloodless utilitarian ethos and a yearning to recover deeper "springs of feeling." Similar yearnings pervaded the Modernist maelstrom that swept up thinkers as different as Lawrence and Wittgenstein.

As Edmund Wilson wrote, Modernism was a "second flood" of the same Romantic tide that produced Blake, Wordsworth, and Coleridge. Like the first flood, it included a vitalist strain. The resurgence of literary vitalism lay behind James Joyce's cultivation of openness to epiphanies of sudden insight, and Walter Pater's warning against the danger of habit, which (he claimed) inured one to the ecstasy of such intense moments—the moments of vision that Virginia Woolf called the "little daily miracles, illuminations, matches struck unexpectedly in the dark." The Christian version of vitalist illumination was explored a few decades earlier by Gerard Manley Hopkins in his poems of "inscape." A stale phenomenon abruptly "will flame out, like shining from shook foil" to reveal "the dearest freshness deep down things," which in turn reflects the glory of Our Lord. "He fathers forth whose beauty is past change. Praise him." This was a powerful idiom in many religious traditions—the song of praise for God's creation—and it shows how a vitalist vision of an animated universe could flourish in varying idioms at different historical moments.

Keynes seems a long way from Hopkins (or Lawrence), but appearances can be deceiving. What all had in common was a reverence for the miraculous force at the core of lived experience. Keynes was the latest blooming and the least rhapsodic vitalist among these modernists. Yet by the time he wrote the *General Theory*, as Jon Levy observes, Keynes had come to see capital as at least in part an expression of undifferentiated libidinal energy—though this energy was closer, perhaps, to Jung's conception of libido than to Freud's. Keynes's emphasis on the economic importance of "the spontaneous urge to action" at moments of radical uncertainty—and on the centrality of animal spirits to investment decisions at all times—brought vitalism into the realm of public policy (whether economists knew it or not) in the United States as well as Great Britain. The coming of World War II licensed Keynesian ideas for practical use, and ultimately created a postwar economy where animal spirits were harnessed, however fitfully, by managerial expertise. But the triumph of management did not mean the defeat of fear.

12

The Triumph and Failure of Management

GREAT THINKERS SOMETIMES acquire reputations for the wrong reasons; Keynes met this fate. The prosperity of the postwar decades was Keynesian, but only in a superficial and misleading sense; it was based on what Zachary Carter calls "reactionary Keynesianism"—creating aggregate demand through military spending and tax cuts rather than through deficit financing for the public good. It was real prosperity, broadly if not evenly distributed, and it made Keynes a name to conjure with in policy circles. But it was not what Keynes had in mind.

En route to its enthronement as public policy during the 1950s and '60s, the Keynesian tradition lost touch with its founder's larger social vision. Keynesian economics became a species of technocratic wizardry, a tool kit of monetary and fiscal techniques used to smooth out the rough spots in the business cycle by balancing inflation and unemployment. When the tools seemed inadequate to the stagflation of the 1970s, policymakers began abandoning the tradition altogether. But meanwhile they had built an enormous warfare state. Unlike the rudimentary welfare state enacted by Roosevelt, the warfare state turned out to be impossible to challenge successfully, or even to debate seriously.

Part of the reason for its persistence was the continued prominence of fear in public discourse. The rapid mobilization for war in the early 1940s brought an end to the Great Depression but not to popular anxieties. Even as the Allies seemed to be moving toward victory in 1945, ordinary Americans wondered: Would there be another depression when military spending contracted? But the destruction of Hiroshima and Nagasaki gave birth to a profounder ambivalence—relief at the war's end but also a haunting fear that, in unleashing the apparently limitless power of atomic energy, Americans had created a Frankenstein's monster that could be turned against themselves and indeed could reduce the entire planet to smoldering ruin. Yet popular fear of a holocaust had next to no impact on military policymakers, who behind walls of official secrecy continued to develop ever more powerful nuclear weapons. FDR's death had brought Truman to power, ensuring that foreign policy would be conducted in a spirit of adolescent pugnacity and exceptionalist hubris. Within just a few years, the Truman administration managed to redirect popular anxiety from nuclear catastrophe to Soviet communism. Nuclear fear never disappeared, and resurfaced at several critical points in subsequent decades, but nothing slowed the inexorable progress of the emergent national security state as it produced an enormous stockpile of weapons and an out-of-control arms race with the Soviet Union.

Postwar fear eventually produced rage against yet another foreign foe, but more commonly it fed feelings of helplessness and fretful compliance with government policy. In the mid-century political economy, animal spirits would play a limited role. But they had already been marginalized during the war itself. It was a different kind of war from those in the past, and it would be a different kind of peace.

WAR AND THE RECALIBRATION OF FEAR

In earlier conflicts, the imagery of preparation for combat featured young men spilling out of troop transports, itching for a crack at the enemy. But after the United States had been drawn into World War II, such scenes were rarely enacted in the American press. Among soldiers and the journalists who reported on them, the dominant wartime sentiment seemed guided mostly by a desire to avoid jejune posturing and idealistic cant. In military humor and newspaper dispatches as well as book-length journalistic accounts such as John Hersey's *Guadalcanal Diary*, the prevailing mood of the fighting men came across as unillusioned realism: we've got a dirty job to do, let's get it over with. Animal spirits, when they appeared at all in wartime public discourse, tended to be defined as a love of danger—and that sentiment could easily be associated with the Fascist cult of war for its own sake.

This connection became apparent in January 1944, when the ABC radio commentator H. R. Baukhage reported on the status of Fascism in Spain. Baukhage traced its origins to misdirected animal spirits. Try denying "the hardboiled youth" access to "decent outlets for his animal spirits—on the ball field, in the school yard, anywhere where he can whoop and holler and be himself—and what happens?" he asked. "A terrific, pent-up force, all the primitive emotions seeking an outlet." This was the moment of opportunity for Nazis and Fascists. They knew the power of those "primitive emotions" and derived their strength from "the strength of the youth they perverted: the primal instincts of the caveman, which lurk within all of us, turned to the base uses of the party." But those instincts were drying up in Spain:

> Spanish fascismo is almost an empty shell. It is an axiom that fascism can only live on blood, the blood of its enemies and when they are not within reach, their own people. It has no other sustenance—it represents the group which, in the lower animals, produces the outlawed, the locoed, the mad. We have these phenomena among the wolves, among elephants, even among horses—the "bad elephant"—the tiger which kills for pleasure and not for food. Spanish fascism has been starved to death and the essential, decent instincts of civilized man are again coming to the surface.

Baukhage was one of many observers (Keynes was another) who recognized the powerful links among animal spirits, madness, and Fascism.

The amorality of vitality, its status as pure potentiality, made it susceptible to service in destructive causes. The quest to energize emotional experience led to the Fascist cult of death; the effort to unleash the primal energy of the cosmos led to the atomic bomb and the subsequent nuclear arms race. On August 6, 1945, the apotheosis of Energy would enter a new phase.

Early reports were sobering rather than triumphant. At noon eastern time, the radio newsman Don Goddard announced: "Without qualification, the president has said that Allied scientists have harnessed the basic power of the universe. They have harnessed the atom." That same evening, Goddard had already begun to imagine what it would mean for such a weapon to be used on the American population: "It would be the same as Denver, Colorado, with a population of 350 thousand persons, being there one moment, and wiped out the next." Two days after the news of Hiroshima hit the headlines, a letter to *The New York Times* reported "a creeping feeling of apprehension" seeping across the city and its surroundings. "We have sowed the whirlwind," Hanson Baldwin had already concluded in a *Times* editorial on August 7. On August 8, *The Milwaukee Journal* published what would become an iconic journalistic form in the nuclear age: a map of the paper's own city as an A-bomb target, with concentric circles of damage and death radiating outward from a downtown ground zero—showing what would happen if the chickens came home to roost. As the *New York Herald Tribune* admitted, it was easy to forget the bomb's effect on Japan "as one senses the foundations of one's own universe trembling." For many Americans, this was an ontological crisis.

But not for President Truman. On August 9, after the bomb fell on Nagasaki, he announced: "We thank God that it has come to us instead of to our enemies, and we pray that He may guide us to use it in His ways and for His purposes." The notion that God had granted the United States sole access to the bomb was rooted in exceptionalist and providentialist assumptions dating back to Timothy Dwight's time. The Cold War and the War on Terror would resurrect this pseudo-religion of American Destiny, and keep it alive for decades to come.

Not everyone was comfortable with the God-anointed role. Even Henry Luce's *Life* preferred a more tempered and secular idiom, expressing relief that "Prometheus, the subtle artificer and friend of man, is still an American citizen" but warning Prometheus not to play Jove—or God. By August 12, Edward R. Murrow concluded: "Seldom, if ever, has a war ended leaving the victors with such a sense of uncertainty and fear, with such a realization that the future is obscure and survival not assured." Certainly this was true of journalists, academics, and intellectuals; but survey results indicated a steadily growing concern among ordinary Americans, too—about the bomb's threat to their own safety and security.

For months after the war's end, commentators struggled to imagine the extent of cataclysmic destruction in the next world war. J. W. Campbell, Jr., the editor of *Astounding Science Fiction*, predicted that "every major city will be wiped out in 30 minutes," that "New York will be a slag heap," and that "radioactive energy will leave the land uninhabitable for periods ranging from 10 months to 500 years, depending on the size of the bomb." Another observer forecast "a barren waste, in which the survivors of the raid will live in caves or hide among ruins." Well into the summer of 1946, many Americans still felt haunted by what the sociologist W. F. Ogburn called "paralyzing fear." Then John Hersey's searing and detailed report from Hiroshima burned into American public consciousness, first as a *New Yorker* article and then as a bestselling book—also distributed free by the Book-of-the-Month Club. It was the most detailed account yet of what happened on the ground in Hiroshima. Resolutely avoiding sensationalism or melodrama, Hersey chronicled the cataclysmic erupting into the ordinary. He described, among other things, a little girl playing with her cat on the sofa when the bomb fell, and the liquefied eyeballs of the observers who looked directly at the blast.

After decades of fascination with Energy and Force, Americans were suddenly required to confront the consequences of the vitalist quest when it was pressed into the service of total war. In the ultimate act of self-destructive Promethean mastery, physicists had created a weapon that could annihilate thousands of people in a single flash. The dawning prospect of Armageddon shook the ground of being. In 1946, the poet Hermann Hagedorn wrote that the atomic bomb had made well-paved

Main Street come to seem "a kind of vast jelly, quivering and dividing underfoot." Fundamental uncertainty fed feelings of futility.

Public figures struggled for words to describe the significance of this new kind of weapon. According to Secretary of War Henry Stimson, the atomic bomb would cause "a revolutionary change in the relation of man to the universe." As Ira Katznelson writes, for many, "fear became permanent." Some policymakers found this frustrating. David Lilienthal, head of the Atomic Energy Commission, complained in 1947 that "public thinking is dominated by fear," that "fear is brother to panic," and that "unreasoning fear is not going to get us anywhere . . . we want to go." But it was not always clear who "we" were, nor where "we want to go." Already, a mere two years after Hiroshima, atomic strategists were discussing the possibility of strategic bombing with atomic weapons. According to an official government account in 1948, the legislative process that created the Atomic Energy Commission was suffused with "emotions of fear and awe"—not the emotions that usually animated debate in the U.S. Capitol. "There is much to fear in the atomic age," the historian Clinton Rossiter observed, "and our fear is the more naked because it touches on the unknown."

Fear could induce paralysis, as Ogburn noted, but it could also energize political activism in behalf of international control of atomic weapons and a "One World" organization to back it up. The United Nations, it was hoped, could fill the bill. Among the most committed One World advocates were atomic scientists themselves, veterans of the Manhattan Project who founded the *Bulletin of the Atomic Scientists* and set its doomsday clock at seven minutes to midnight. Their method was plain: they wanted to "scare the pants off" the American people. "Only one tactic is dependable—the preaching of doom," one scientist advised. "Anything else induces yawns." The aim of the *Bulletin*, said the physicist Eugene Rabinowitch, was "to preserve our civilization by scaring men into rationality." The question was how to define "rationality."

The rise of dictatorships abroad had encouraged Americans to find signs of madness in foreign leaders. Hitler's frenetic posturing made him and his followers seem deranged. But the men who were building and testing atomic weapons introduced a new kind of madness into public policy. In March 1946, on hearing of the plan to test two atomic bombs on Bikini Atoll, Lewis Mumford announced: "Gentlemen, you are mad!" The gentlemen in question were the strategists planning the tests, and the "fatal symptom of their madness," Mumford wrote, was "the solemn conviction that they are normal, responsible people, living sane lives, working for reasonable ends. Soberly, day after day, the madmen continue to go through the undeviating motions of madness: motions so stereotyped, so commonplace, that they seem the normal motions of normal men, not the mass compulsions of people bent on total death." This was what was new about the madness of the atomic age: it was enveloped in the language of technocratic rationality. This was what produced what Hannah Arendt would later call (in connection with the Nazi Holocaust) "the banality of evil." A focus on technique rather than consequences concealed the real significance of weapons research from the technicians themselves, throwing a blanket of normality over the whole enterprise.

Meanwhile, atomic scientists and one-worlders were not the only public figures seeking to galvanize support for their agenda by stoking up fear. Truman was planning to announce a major arms buildup and a reorganization of the executive branch to create the foundations of the national security state—including the euphemizing of the War Department into the Defense Department and the creation of the CIA. Senator Arthur Vandenberg of Michigan advised the president that he had to "scare hell out of the American people" to win support for such an ambitious program. The result was the speech that originated the Truman Doctrine by invoking the threat of a Soviet Union bent on world domination and avowing U.S. determination to fight communism wherever it reared its head. This was a blank check for the protracted Cold War, punctuated by hot ones when and where they were alleged to be needed.

To focus fear on the Soviets, the Truman administration had to turn it away from bombs—which was a tricky business since the bombs kept getting more powerful. Yet during the months and years following the Truman Doctrine speech, at least for a compliant press, events abroad seemed to confirm the wisdom of the president's bellicose stance: Mao Zedong established Communist rule in China and the Soviet Union successfully tested its first atomic bomb. Truman was determined to stay ahead, and soon authorized the development of a hydrogen bomb, based on nuclear fusion rather than nuclear fission, and a thousand times more powerful than the bombs dropped on Hiroshima and Nagasaki. Atomic bombs began to be rechristened "nuclear weapons."

Meanwhile Lilienthal was rolling out a fresh propaganda offensive, focusing on "Atoms for Peace." It was part of a broad effort to normalize atomic energy and make the threat of radiation sickness seem just another routine hazard of modern life. Allied with this campaign was the rise of civil defense and the routinization of air raid drills. The effect of such exercises was to encourage the assumption that the atomic bomb was a weapon like any other, and could be survived.

The propaganda offensive quickly seemed to be having an impact. "The atom bomb, and all it means, does not appear to have sunk in at all," the British writer Wyndham Lewis observed on a visit to the United States in 1949. "It has bounced off, or been mentally repelled as a tactless intruder." Survey research appeared to confirm this observation. "I know the bomb can wipe out cities, but I let the government worry about it," one informant told a pollster. Those more inclined to worry could turn to the latest version of positive thinking, promoted by Rev. Norman Vincent Peale. His motto, repeated by millions, was "Through God's help and simple techniques I will be free from fear."

Yet freedom from fear remained more an aspiration than an accomplishment. What really redirected popular anxiety away from nuclear war and toward the Soviet Union was not upbeat propaganda but the secrecy surrounding weapons development. Telford Taylor, chief U.S. counsel at the Nuremberg War Crimes Tribunal, had reason to want to know about the plans of nuclear strategists but was constantly frustrated in his efforts to find out anything. As Taylor wrote, "the journalist must write his newspaper column on the basis of a guess and a whisper; the rest of us can only grope blindly in an oppressive and baffling murk." Taylor put his finger on the fundamental threat posed by the national security state to the creation of a well-informed citizenry.

Secrecy kept the specter of nuclear annihilation at bay. Focusing on the Red Menace, abroad and at home, made it easier to forget altogether about burgeoning weapons stockpiles, and to satisfy the need to fit into a safe and secure society. Quantitative surveys continued to address that need by creating numerical bases for social identities—incomes, education levels, political affiliations, religious preferences. Whether numbers could actually measure subjective experience remained an unanswered (and unasked) question. But statistics became the lingua franca of a developing public policy consensus.

TECHNOCRATIC RATIONALITY REGNANT

The boldest effort to map intimate behavior was the Kinsey Report, *Sexual Behavior in the Human Male*, which quickly became a bestseller when it was published in 1948. (*Sexual Behavior in the Human Female* appeared five years later.) Popular journalistic accounts stressed the sensational findings of the Kinsey Report, particularly its confirmation of the large number of men who had homosexual experiences. Yet as Lionel Trilling noticed, the report revealed how human experience was impoverished when it was rendered in strictly quantitative terms.

That was not the only thing he noticed. To Trilling, the report was both therapeutic and symptomatic. Its therapeutic dimension lay in its "permissive effect"—its tendency to render behavior acceptable that had previously been considered pathological. This group therapy went "a long way," Trilling observed, "toward establishing the *community* of sexuality." Meanwhile, its symptomatic significance lay in "the fact that the report was felt to be needed at all, that the community of sexuality requires now to be established in explicit quantitative terms." Having cast countless people into solitude by defining their practices as perverted, popular sexual science was now moving to relieve that sense of isolation, simply by counting. "We must assure ourselves by statistical science that the solitude is imaginary," Trilling wrote. Statistics created a new sense of belonging, attenuated but genuine.

What made the report different from other imaginative interpretations of sex (stretching back to Aristophanes, as Trilling remarked) was its claim to be scientific—and its authors' definition of science in reductionist, behaviorist terms. As Trilling observed, "we are led to see that their whole definition of a sexual experience is comprised by the physical act and that their principles of evidence are entirely quantitative." Counting orgasms, ignoring any larger context outside "the physical act," the report reduced sexual experience to mechanical repetition. The more orgasms, the better, period. While its title announced its male-centered approach, the report's denial that there was any such thing as premature ejaculation combined male-centeredness with a focus on quantity rather than quality. Entirely quantitative standards excluded any consideration of sex as social intimacy. As Trilling observed, "It is striking how small a role woman plays in *Sexual Behavior in the Human Male*." Neither disappointed nor satisfied partners were on the premises. Sex was a one-man show. As the Kinsey Report revealed, the connections supposedly created by statistics could be incomplete, unsatisfying, and misleading.

Yet numbers remained at the core of technocratic thinking and the management of fear. Reliance on quantification was the cognitive style of policymakers who claimed to tame the vagaries of the business cycle—and even the threat of nuclear war—through various forms of rationality. But these kinds of rationality had little to do with classical ideas of reason; they eschewed subjective discernment, reflection, and judgment in favor of techniques and rules that transcended human imperfection.

The limitations of this rationalizing project only gradually became apparent. For two decades, a managerial consensus dominated Washington, promoting an implicit acceptance of technocratic rationality but undergirded by a sense of righteous community and reinforced at its margins by outbursts of red-baiting. This consensus survived business downturns and even brushes with nuclear catastrophe; it only began to fall apart as the Vietnam War revealed the hubris at its heart.

But until the mid-1960s, conventional wisdom held that a "mixed economy"—based on a partnership between corporate capital and the federal government—had transformed politics from traditional right-left conflicts to disagreements between rival teams of experts. The emergence of a new governing class of salaried managers and technicians meant the toning-down of political debate, perhaps even "the end of ideology," as the sociologist Daniel Bell predicted in 1960. Technocratic rationality had little need for spontaneous popular energy—though there was an abundance of it outside big business and big government (in rock 'n' roll, blues, and country music, for example). The apparent triumph of management meant the consignment of animal spirits to the margins of public discourse and public policy, into the zanier versions of television comedy (Lucille Ball, Ernie Kovacs), and onto the dance floor, where young people gyrated to the rhythms of Little Richard and Elvis Presley.

THE FATE OF ANIMAL SPIRITS IN A MANAGERIAL AGE

As the notion of animal spirits seemed more archaic than ever, it was increasingly confined to animals themselves. In 1950, *The New York Times* titled a compendium of notable doings by animals "Animal Spirits." These included a story of a puppy in Brockton, Massachusetts, who had been peeking into a woman's bedroom every night, provoking her to call the dogcatcher; the adventure of "a Detroit pet monkey, rescued by his master from a fire, [who] rushed back and came out safely with his favorite toy, a wooly lamb"; and the research of the psychologists at the Bronx Zoo, who discovered that "the gorillas there were suffering from melancholia" and who "recommended that keepers should force themselves to act jolly and so deceive the apes into a state of happiness." (Apparently it never occurred to anyone that the gorillas' imprisonment might have had something to do with their sadness.) In these examples, "animal spirits" had become a phrase to describe animals when they most resembled humans—albeit in quirky and amusing ways.

There seemed little need for animal spirits in economic life at this mid-century moment, as industrial capital reasserted its central role in sustaining prosperity. In popular imagery, the massive, hierarchically organized corporation, not the stock exchange, became the characteristic institution of American capitalism. The Street lacked magnetism for decades after the Crash; the volume of shares traded did not reach 1929 levels until 1961. With some maverick exceptions, both parties agreed that prosperity depended on Keynesian techniques for fine-tuning the business cycle, particularly the relationship between inflation and unemployment. The domestication of Keynes reduced animal spirits to "confidence," which became the subject of regular statistical surveys—more contributions to the quantitative science of subjective experience. Under the regime of reactionary Keynesianism, fiscal policy fed the coffers of military hardware manufacturers, while monetary policy tamped down confidence to keep it from spiraling into a speculative orgy. The Crash cast a long shadow.

Even pared-down Keynesian techniques provoked suspicion among conservative economists, who thought Keynes's focus on maintaining investor confidence was overly psychological, insufficiently quantitative, and insensitive to the need for balancing the budget. "The real test will come in 1964 when animal spirits and the economy may both need a lift," a business columnist predicted in *The New York Times* in 1963. Keynesian technique passed the test: investment surged when a tax cut proposed by John F. Kennedy and pushed through Congress by Lyndon Johnson took effect the following year. It was a victory for Keynesian monetary policy—promoting prosperity, not by public spending but by putting more money in the hands of private lenders, investors, and consumers.

The limited nature of the role played by Keynesianism in mid-century public policy became clear in the discussion of the Federal Reserve Board's margin requirements—the percentage of cash up front required to purchase securities on credit. *The Washington Post* doubted "that a limitation in the amount of credit which brokers make available to their customers can sober a public that is intoxicated with a speculative zeal." As late as the early 1960s, everything was still about sustaining sobriety on the post-Crash financial sector. "In attempting to protect investors against the consequences of their own folly and the economy against the advent of rude shock, the Board runs the risk of dampening confidence and making those who suffer real or paper losses less eager to spend on goods and services," the *Post* admitted. "But if past experience is any guide, it is better to err on the side of caution in coping with the animal spirits that pervade the market place." Among investors, the longing for a grounding in stability and certainty survived for decades; even as they rejected central planning, they recoiled from too much risk. And as the *Post*'s financial advice columnist observed a few weeks later, despite the proliferation of statistical forecasts, "the uncertainty which has always beclouded our economic future has not been dispelled." Keynes would not have been surprised. For him, uncertainty was not a passing cloud but an inescapable feature of the human condition.

But Keynes was idiosyncratic. Technocratic management of chance became the dominant mode of discourse in governance, from fiscal policy to nuclear strategy. The attempt to impose a spurious "rationality" on apocalyptic war was even more challenging than the attempt to impose it on the business cycle. Yet the managers of the arms race, seeking a "balance of terror" between the United States and the Soviet Union, faced the challenge of unthinkable calamity with calm algorithmic certainty.

Through the 1950s, scientists and policymakers predicted higher and higher casualty rates as they projected the costs of a nuclear exchange. In 1955, the physicist Ralph Lapp constructed this scenario in the *Bulletin of the Atomic Scientists*, and it was reprinted in *Time* magazine:

> A single superbomb, exploded close to the ground, can contaminate a state the size of Maryland with lethal radioactivity. A "small-scale" attack [on the U.S.] with 28 bombs restricted to the industrial heart of America could produce an inverted L-shaped pattern over the northeastern states and an irregular fallout bracketing much of Indiana, Ohio, Michigan, New York and Pennsylvania. The "atomized" area would be occupied by 50 million Americans. Over two-thirds of the U.S. industrial production centers in the same areas.

By July 1961, a subcommittee of the National Security Council was reporting to President Kennedy that 48 to 71 million Americans would be quickly killed in a nuclear exchange with the USSR and China, while 45 to 71 percent of the nation's residences would be blanketed by radioactive fallout. Meanwhile, 67 million Russians and 76 million Chinese would have died. Trying to measure the costs of nuclear war was truly an exercise in calculating the incalculable.

Still, the effort to manage uncertainty with numbers proceeded apace among the experts advising the U.S. government. Their faith in algorithms soared as they imagined a winnable nuclear war. As projected casualty figures rose alarmingly with each technological advance, nuclear strategists still appeared to derive some reassurance from the capacity of quantification to cast an aura of rationality onto a thoroughly irrational enterprise.

The emergence of a nuclear arms race posed the constant danger of accidental—or intentional—world conflagration. The stakes of the policy game had been raised since the Depression, but the players' quantitative agenda was similar. The numbers increasingly took the form of algorithmic rules as well as statistical compilations, but their cultural work was still comparable to what it had been during the Depression. Numerical calculation remained part of an effort to manage public anxieties by invoking the authority of quantitative expertise. Yet what was being counted was no longer boarded-up stores and millions of unemployed, but ruined cities and millions of dead bodies—or estimated projections of them. Numbers ultimately failed to provide emotional insurance against uncertainty, and managerial hubris continued to provoke restive animal spirits—which erupted, from time to time, in mass protest.

FROM CALCULATING THE INCALCULABLE TO THINKING THE UNTHINKABLE

After 1960, the USSR and the USA had built enough missiles to destroy each other and much of the rest of the world. The arms race from this point forward could only seem a kind of madness. "Why make the rubble bounce?" as Churchill asked (ignoring the economic interests invested in making it bounce). Yet the madness was covered by a veneer of "Cold War rationality," as Lorraine Daston and other historians of science have called it in a pathbreaking study. As estimated casualty numbers ascended into meaninglessness, Daston and her colleagues write, "strategists widened their view to absorb human interactions as well as the megatonnage of bombs and the trajectory of missiles. The world on the brink became personalized, 'a war of nerves, like the wrestling bout on the brink of the cliff in so many Old Western movies.' Within the framework of Cold War rationality, the hot-headed cowboys became cold-blooded calculators, intelligent, implacable, and symmetric." Thus began one of the strangest episodes in American intellectual history.

Rationality, from the strategic perspective, was not to be confused with traditional notions of reason, which involved deliberation and judgment, and which took complexity and contingency into account. On the contrary: strategic rationality, like its technocratic kin in economics and other social sciences, involved a quest for parsimony—a reduction of complexity through the stripping away of all but the essential elements of a problem (as in a mathematical model) or through the shrinking of the issue to dimensions small enough to be observed under controlled circumstances (as in a laboratory experiment). Game theory, which became increasingly fashionable in the 1960s, reflected the core epistemology of Cold War rationality, with its dependence on the assumption that rational actors sought to maximize utility through rules-based decisions made under conditions of uncertainty. The project was inherently reductionist.

It was also post-human—an effort to transcend the vagaries of animal spirits altogether. Cold War rationalists looked to computers to protect us from the "Stone Age mentality" of ordinary human beings in stressful confrontation, whose aggressive instincts might lead us over the brink. This was a reasonable enough fear, but the strategists' mode of responding to it was fundamentally flawed. With decision-making reduced to algorithmic rules obeyed by compliant machines, human perversity was removed from the process, but so was any room for human deliberation or reflection. And machines, no matter how sophisticated, could malfunction or make mistakes just as humans could.

Transforming reason into rationality meant departing from materiality and humanity altogether, creating the rule of rules. As the computer scientist Jerome Weizenbaum said, "The rule that such a device [as a computer used for guiding missiles] is to follow the law of which it is to be an embodiment, is an abstract idea. It is independent of matter, of material embodiment, in short of everything except thought and reason." Reason in this case, Weizenbaum added, meant "formal thinking, calculation, and systematic rationality." Whatever rationality was, it could be expressed in algorithmic rules, though experts disagreed about what specific form those rules should take—strategies in game theory or utility maximization, actuarial formulas, cognitive representations. The important thing was that the rules be universal and unvarying.

The men who pursued the grail of Cold War rationality, as Theodore White wrote approvingly in *Life* in 1967, constituted "a new priesthood, unique to this country and this time, of American action intellectuals." Despite their commitment to abstract thought, they were "husky, wiry, physically attractive men who, by and large, are married to exceptionally pretty women." The most prominent action intellectuals clustered at the RAND Corporation in Santa Monica, California. Among them was Albert Wohlstetter, who coined the phrase "the delicate balance of terror" in a RAND policy paper of 1958, and who consulted with John F. Kennedy during the Cuban Missile Crisis.

The man who most fully elaborated the balance of terror was the RAND analyst Herman Kahn. His enormous girth made him anything but "wiry," and he remained uncharacteristically confident (even among Cold War rationalists) about using rationality to manage the run-up to nuclear war—with the avowed purpose of ultimately preventing it. Others, such as Oskar Morgenstern, acknowledged the inevitability of computer error (as well as the dreaded "human error") in what he called a "stochastic universe," which was characterized at best by probability, if not outright uncertainty. But Kahn's more insistent rationality, coupled with his brash style, attracted media attention and made him a Cold War celebrity. In *On Thermonuclear War* (1960) and *On Escalation* (1965), Kahn claimed that both sides, out of self-interest, would produce decisions through algorithmic rules—every step up the ladder of escalation would be taken in accordance with axiomatic, formal rationality. (As in free-market ideology, self-interest became the stabilizing force that somehow automatically kept the delicate mechanism of decision-making from flying apart.) To make deterrence work, Kahn insisted, the threat of escalation had to be credible: this meant inching as close as possible to the nuclear brink. What he did not say was that the logic of deterrence required the arms race to continue, by implicitly ruling out alternatives such as reduction or abolition of nuclear weapons.

With his argument for brinkmanship, Kahn attempted to refute critics like Bertrand Russell, who claimed that the attempt to maintain a balance of terror during a nuclear confrontation boiled down to little more than a game of "chicken" between rich boys facing off in high-powered cars—the consequences of which could prove fatal to either or both. Cold War rationalists tried to replace this analogy by claiming that any president involved in a nuclear confrontation must deploy "a cool and clear-headed means-ends calculation," as the political scientist Sidney Verba wrote in 1961. "He uses the best information available and chooses from the universe of possible responses that alternative most likely to maximize his goals." There were many problems with using this formalist fantasy as a guide to policy, but the most potentially disastrous was its tendency to encourage escalating a nuclear confrontation by making it seem like cool and clearheaded strategy. A year after Verba wrote those words, Cold War rationality legitimated Kennedy's public confrontation with Khrushchev over Soviet missiles in Cuba.

What was striking about the American response to the Cuban Missile Crisis was the broad acceptance of Kennedy's brinkmanship—even, or perhaps especially, among intellectuals. The absence of critical views was partly due to the chattering classes' infatuation with JFK but also to changes in the tenor of political discourse since World War II. The triumph of technocratic rationality had transformed much political debate into disagreements over technique, easing the shift of formerly radical critics into a more appreciative stance toward American politics and society.

As early as 1952, much of this appreciation was on display in a *Partisan Review* symposium, "Our Country and Our Culture," which asked twenty-five intellectuals (including Trilling, David Riesman, and Margaret Mead) to comment on the new and positive relationship between American intellectuals and mass democratic culture. With Trilling, they celebrated the emergence of new alliances between wealth and intellect in the world of universities and foundations. Only a very few participants registered any dissent from the roseate views of the majority. One of them was Norman Mailer, who declared that he was "in almost total disagreement with the assumptions of this symposium," and insisted on the value of an oppositional stance, rather than "a strapping participation in the vigors of American life." There were plenty of reasons, he believed, to continue to cultivate alienation. Mailer's effort to sustain this stance led him to create his own vitalist critique of mid-century American culture. Like other intellectuals, he was blinded by Kennedy's charismatic style, and his revulsion from "technology land" was rooted in a familiar melodrama of beleaguered masculinity. But as the Vietnam War provoked new varieties of countercultural protest, his perspective broadened and deepened.

MANHOOD AT MID-CENTURY: NORMAN MAILER

Mailer had first won notice in 1946, with his great war novel *The Naked and the Dead*. It captured the futility, stupidity, and brutality of war with elegant precision. Mailer evoked a male world of competition, careerism, and fitful camaraderie, detailing an infantry platoon on a grim slog through the jungles of a South Pacific island in obedience to confused, contradictory, and constantly changing orders. There was no room in this world for the spontaneous energy of animal spirits or the swaggering masculinity epitomized by Theodore Roosevelt. Those who swaggered, for the young Mailer, were likely to be careerist pricks.

Yet Mailer would be swaggering in print before too long. Impatient with the complacency of the PR crowd and the compliant red-baiting of the publishing industry, Mailer joined other intellectuals in turning from politics to cultural criticism. Dwight Macdonald, who wrote the searching essay "The Responsibility of Peoples," in the wake of Hiroshima and Nagasaki, offered a model of the swerve from politics to culture in 1953, when he addressed the rise of middlebrow culture in "A Theory of Mass Culture." Macdonald appropriated the apocalyptic mode, which might have been appropriate with respect to foreign policy, for a discussion of taste and style. He announced somberly: "there is slowly emerging a tepid, flaccid middlebrow culture that threatens to engulf everything in its spreading ooze." Here the fear of an asphyxiating, homogenous culture veers into the murky waters of absurdity: the "spreading ooze" that was going to "engulf everything" was being promoted by the Book-of-the-Month Club. But Mailer's own fears of suffocation, combined with his obsessive masculinity, led him into murky waters, too.

After the smashing success of *The Naked and the Dead*, Mailer spent a decade wandering in the literary wilderness. His anarcho-socialist politics made him a pariah in Cold War publishing circles; his writing became erratic and uneven. Like Macdonald and other intellectuals, as well as a broad swath of the bohemian avant-garde, he was increasingly repelled by what he felt to be the stifling banality of American middle-class life. And like others before him he began to seek a vital alternative. His search revealed the shortcomings of vitalist cultural criticism, as well as—eventually—some of its strengths.

Finally, in 1957, he found his vitalist formula when he published "The White Negro" in *Dissent*. It was a paean to the rebellious, violent, and sexually emancipated life that Mailer associated with black people, and to the white hipster's effort to emulate that life through his own pursuit of intense experience. The hipster lived "the life where a man must go until he is beat, where he must gamble through all his energies, through all those small or large crises which beset his day, where he must be with it or be doomed not to swing." Assuming Mailer is dead serious—and I think he is—here we have clearly entered the terrain of unwitting self-parody. "The White Negro" was a locus classicus of imperial primitivism; Mailer joined Sherwood Anderson, Carl Van Vechten, and other white men in identifying black people with primal, spontaneous vitality—pressing them to play a narrowly scripted role in the drama of the white imagination.

But what really pushed Mailer over the edge into prolonged vitalist fantasy was the Democrats' nomination of John Kennedy for president in 1960, which inspired his ode to JFK's masculine mystique, "Superman Comes to the Supermarket." This was the clearest evidence yet of Mailer's new preoccupation with cultural criticism, rather than politics or fiction. A self-proclaimed anarcho-socialist who backed JFK had a lot of explaining to do. Mailer evaded the task by ignoring JFK's politics altogether, and for good reason. During the 1960 campaign, JFK attacked Nixon from the right, asserting that the Republican administration had "lost" Cuba to communism and promising a more confrontational approach to the Soviet Union. The latter involved the invention of a "missile gap" between the two nations as an excuse for accelerating the nuclear arms race and extending an already considerable U.S. advantage. There was little to choose from, as I. F. Stone realized, between Kennedy and Nixon with respect to policy matters—especially foreign policy. But style was another matter. And Mailer was concerned with nothing if not taste and style. Like other American intellectuals suffering from suffocation at that historical moment, he failed to realize that the task of resuscitation involved more than a breath of fresh air from Camelot.

Mailer's tribute began by assuming that America was mired in a swamp of mediocrity and in desperate need of redemption by a hero on the order of FDR or Churchill—an assumption he shared with many conventional liberals. Arthur Schlesinger, Jr., for one, had published "The Decline of Greatness" just two years earlier in *The Saturday Evening Post.* Lamentations over declining greatness could be pressed into the service of various ideologies, as Mailer's preamble made clear. "It was a hero America needed, a hero central to his time, a man whose personality might suggest contradiction and mysteries which could reach into the alienated circuits of the underground, because only a hero can capture the secret imagination of a people, and so be good for the vitality of his nation; a hero embodies the fantasy and so allows each private mind the liberty to consider its fantasy and find a way to grow. Each mind can become more conscious of its desire and waste less strength in hiding from itself." The language was a muddle of populist vitalism and libertarian existentialism—a vision of the hero as regenerator of the nation and liberator of private fantasy.

Presently JFK would make an appearance, but first Mailer wanted to make clear that the regeneration he wanted had to come from the city—not from the country and (still less) from the small town. (For some reason he left out the suburb—always a convenient whipping boy for critics of banality.) "In American life, the unspoken war of the century has taken place between the city and the small town; the city which is dynamic, orgiastic, unsettling, explosive and accelerating to the psyche; the small town which is rooted, narrow, cautious and planted in the life-logic of the family," Mailer wrote. "The need of the city is to accelerate growth; the pride of the small town is to retard it." As in his musings on heroism, Mailer deemed "growth" a sine qua non of authentic selfhood and sign of psychic health, or at least his own idiosyncratic version of it. Infatuated with jazz, he overlooked entirely the restive energies in other forms of popular music—blues, rockabilly, rock 'n' roll—which emanated from allegedly backward rural areas throughout the 1950s. He was a true urban provincial.

Mailer revered a frenetic activism, recoiling from the life of stability and security that was sponsored (however inadequately) by the American corporation. Despite his self-professed socialist principles, Mailer joined many of his intellectual contemporaries in ignoring political economy and viewing America's ills as at bottom a matter of taste. He announced, "the incredible dullness wreaked upon the American landscape in Eisenhower's eight years has been the triumph of the corporation. A tasteless, sexless, odorless sanctity in architecture, manners, modes, styles has been the result. Eisenhower embodied half the needs of the nation, the needs of the timid, the petrified, the sanctimonious, and the sluggish." Eisenhower may have been a war hero—the Supreme Commander on D-Day, no less—but he was an old man incapable of any longer embodying the physical vigor and courage epitomized by Jack Kennedy's PT boat exploits.

Even after JFK's serious back injury, Mailer wrote, he asked to go back on duty and became so bold in the attacks he made with his PT boat "that the crew didn't like to go out with him because he took so many chances." How this made him a desirable presidential candidate, let alone a good naval officer, Mailer left unsaid, preferring instead to conduct his readers into the labyrinth of his own portentous musings: "Like Brando, Kennedy's most characteristic quality is the remote and private air of a man who has traversed some lonely terrain of experience, of loss and gain, of nearness to death, which leaves him isolated from the mass of others." Ultimately, Mailer made Kennedy bear the burden of the novelist's own longings for personal regeneration, which he conflated with national regeneration.

The stakes in an American presidential election, Mailer believed, had never been so high—they melded aesthetics and authentic selfhood: "So, finally, would come a choice which history had never presented to a nation before—one could vote for glamour or for ugliness, a staggering and most stunning choice—would the nation be brave enough to enlist the romantic dream of itself, would it vote for the image in the mirror of its unconscious?" For this to happen, "mass man might now have to dare again," otherwise "the undetermined would go out in the morning to vote for the psychic security of Nixon the way a middle-aged man past adventure holds to the stale bread of his marriage." This was boilerplate postwar misogyny—the revulsion from domesticity, the fear of middle age, the determination not to be "past adventure," all recalled the huffings of Hugh Hefner on similar subjects. Mailer's self-absorption allowed him to enshroud public policy in private fantasy. He had nothing to say about what Kennedy might actually do in office.

What Kennedy did do, at least in foreign policy, consistently reflected the dangerous heroic posturing that Mailer found so attractive. In keeping with his promise to close the nonexistent "missile gap," Kennedy authorized the largest peacetime military buildup in U.S. history, with special attention to enlarging the already huge nuclear arsenal. The latter project included the deployment of intermediate-range Jupiter missiles in Turkey, not far from the Soviet border. The Jupiter missiles were immobile and aboveground; they required lengthy preparations before they were ready to launch. With little use as deterrents, they appeared far better suited to a preemptive first strike (which the Kennedy administration had considered during the Berlin crisis of 1961). U.S. strategists perceived the Jupiter missiles as powerful destabilizers of the arms race—potential provocations, in fact, of a Soviet first strike.

Kennedy's aggressive nuclear policy, combined with his administration's determination to topple the Castro regime, put Nikita Khrushchev in a tight place. He needed to disarm his rivals and critics within his own country. Deploying the missiles in Cuba, he later told the journalist Strobe Talbott, ensured that Americans "would learn just what it feels like to have enemy missiles pointing at you; we'd be doing nothing more than giving them a little of their own medicine." Kennedy and his advisers agreed that the Cuban missiles had no real military significance, no impact on either country's strategic advantage; despite his public claim that they menaced "the peace and security of all the Americas," he made it clear in private, as Robert McNamara recalled, that their main importance was political rather than military. Allowing them to stay would look weak, supposedly to allies and (more important) to voters.

This was the reasoning behind Kennedy's public ultimatum to Khrushchev and implementation of an illegal blockade—two moves that brought the superpowers within a hairsbreadth of conflagration. Eventually Kennedy won plaudits for resisting the crazier militarists in his own administration and accepting Khrushchev's proposal to withdraw the Cuban missiles in exchange for the United States removing the ones in Turkey—though that agreement had to be kept secret, again to avoid the appearance of weakness.

Kennedy's subsequent conduct during his final year in office suggests that he may have learned something from his brush with Armageddon—beginning with his sponsorship of an atmospheric-test-ban treaty and including other gestures toward peaceful coexistence. It may be that Kennedy became smarter, more diplomatically adept, and ultimately more humane than Mailer's pop-existentialist caricature—at least after he recoiled from the brinkmanship of the Cuban Missile Crisis. Maybe, as some of his defenders claim, had he lived he might even have realized the folly of trying to crush Vietnamese nationalism with the resources of technocratic rationality.

By the later 1960s, the moral and strategic failures of the U.S. war in Vietnam had become impossible to ignore. The parade of statistics and slogans—kill ratios, body counts, clearing and holding, winning hearts and minds—told a story of futility and mendacity. Mailer had developed a more politically grounded perspective on war-making, if not on the martyred Kennedy. Still, he preferred to stay in the realm of style and taste.

In *The Armies of the Night*, his arresting account of his own participation in an antiwar march on Washington, he set an early scene on the eve of the march at a party hosted by a professor-and-wife team of liberal Democrats. As in his earlier writing, aesthetic taste and political inclinations were twinned. Mailer began by casting a gimlet eye about the couple's apartment: "The furnishings are functional, the prevailing hues of wall and carpet and cloth are institutional brown and library gray, the paintings and sculpture are stylized, abstract, hopeless imitation." The blandness and drabness, the absence of any hint of idiosyncrasy or surprise, let alone beauty—all of this suggested the liberal academic's acquiescence to a sterile technocratic way of life. In many ways this critique continued the worst excesses of 1950s mass-culture criticism—its disdain for the ordinary, its reliance on superficial social cues as a key to moral worth. This couple, however predictable their tastes, were giving over their home to the effort to end a vile and apparently endless war. Mailer's claim to glimpse their inner lives, based on their carpets and furnishings, strikes a false note.

Still, there was more to this book than mere snobbery. Like the Frankfurt School Marxists, Mailer viewed liberal technocrats as social engineers in the service of managerial capitalism, collaborators in the creation of a mass culture that persuaded its audience to embrace catastrophic imperial adventure as patriotic duty. "If the republic was now managing to convert the citizenry to a plastic mass, ready to be attached to any manipulative gung-ho," Mailer wrote, "the author [Mailer himself] was ready to cast much of the blame for such success into the undernourished lap, the overpsychologized loins, of the liberal academic intelligentsia." Their opposition to the Vietnam War was merely "a quarrel among engineers. Liberal academics had no root of a real war with technology land itself, no, in all likelihood, they were the natural managers of that air-conditioned vault where the last of human life would still exist . . . They were servants of that social machine of the future in which all irrational human conflict would be resolved, all conflicts of interest negotiated, and nature's resonance condensed into frequencies which could comfortably phase nature in or out as you please." This glimpse of a mechanized future was an updated version of the mildly degrading despotism Tocqueville had envisioned as the dark underside of democracy over a century before. Mass-culture critics of the 1950s, reviving Tocqueville, saw his vision realized in the standardized tract housing of the postwar suburbs, whose inhabitants supposedly sat stupefied in front of their telescreens. The critique of monolithic suburban banality depended on a gross simplification of a complex social reality that most intellectuals had never seen, and soon it became as standardized as the houses supposedly were. But Mailer did his best to revive it and give it a political edge.

When he joined his fellow peace marchers the next morning, Mailer discovered what he felt might be a vital alternative to the death-dealing banality of "technology land." Not the New Leftists trailing clouds of Old Left righteousness, but the ragged and strange gatherings of people who seemed to depart from conventional politics altogether—and who, despite maintaining a wide variety of esoteric beliefs, were conventionally lumped together as "hippies." Observing their rituals, Mailer wrote, one began to feel "the unspoken happy confidence that politics had again become mysterious, had begun to partake of Mystery; that gave life to a thought the gods were back in human affairs." What he thought he was witnessing was not a protest against "technology" per se, but a challenge to the collective mentality and social agenda conventionally associated with it—the effort to make a whole society conform to technical imperatives of efficient productivity. The enemy, in short, was not technology but technocracy, though Mailer never used that word. The clash of worldviews surfaced vividly when hippies surrounded the Pentagon, chanting "Om" as they attempted to levitate it.

What Mailer failed to see was what many chroniclers of the antiwar counterculture have also missed—the spread of the protest against technocracy beyond a scruffy crowd of hippies to include Americans of various ages, races, and classes. Like other journalists, he focused on "the new generation," which "had no respect whatsoever for the unassailable logic of the next step; belief was reserved for the revelatory mystery of the happening where you did not know what was going to happen next; that was what was good about it." "The unassailable logic of the next step" was the stuff of rational argument and political debate, the language of certain conclusions and predictable outcomes—the worldview of managerial technocrats. Mailer preferred the hippies because (he believed) they relished chance, not knowing what was going to happen next. While Keynes simply acknowledged uncertainty as an inescapable part of life, Mailer celebrated it as a portal to personal liberation from domestic or bureaucratic routine. This intellectual stance depended on economic security; for people on the margins of prosperity, uncertainty was a threat to be minimized if possible. For Mailer, the equation of chance with liberation was the pose of an affluent mid-century white male writer, annoyed by the comfort and predictability that he imagined all around him and may have felt himself.

Mailer celebrated countercultural rebels' witness against "technology land" and its imperatives. But it was left to Theodore Roszak to probe the larger significance of the counterculture as an episode in U.S. intellectual history. In *The Making of a Counterculture* (1969), Roszak joined Mailer in reasserting the value of spontaneous vital energy against the regime of rationality. But he went beyond that reflex to recognize that the technocratic claim to plumb subjective experience and quantify vital needs was misleading and menacing. Quantification of subjective experience, he argued, was a way of hollowing out our inner life and ultimately denying its very existence. The perfect psychology for technocrats was behaviorism, which reduced the stream of consciousness to a series of observable acts; Kinsey's claim to have explained men's sex lives by counting their orgasms typified the method at work. The synthesis of numbers and flow, of discontinuous quantification and continuous human experience, was specious. Eventually that merger would be trotted out again, as counterculture gave way to cyberculture, and Silicon Valley appropriated the rhetoric of rebellion to underwrite a hip new version of technocratic domination. But no one could see that outcome on the horizon in 1969.

RETHINKING THE UNTHINKABLE

Roszak was one of the few interpreters of the antiwar counterculture to explore its moral and even religious seriousness, though like Mailer he treated it too narrowly as a generational phenomenon rather than a broad, heterogenous movement. For Roszak, the counterculture's greatest significance lay in its challenge to technocratic thinking, a challenge articulated by intellectuals from Herbert Marcuse and Norman O. Brown to Paul Goodman and Alan Watts (all of whom Roszak discussed) and enacted by countercultural dissenters. They resurrected what the technocracy deemed "a purely negative catch-all category"—subjective experience, which included not only private thoughts and feelings but also a variety of mental states beyond normal waking consciousness. And they explored that realm in search of alternative way of knowing and being.

Roszak recognized that the eclectic jumble of countercultural tendencies derived coherence from a common rejection of technocracy—a word that, for Roszak, melded political, military, and economic power structures with fundamental ways of knowing and being. Technocracy transcended economic systems like capitalism and socialism, shaping our very sense of what it meant to be human. Countercultural rebels who challenged this Moloch were playing for high stakes. According to Roszak, technocracy was "a grand cultural imperative which is beyond question, beyond discussion." It depended on a regime of experts who aim not to coerce but "to charm conformity from us by exploiting our deep-seated commitment to the scientific world view and by manipulating the securities and creature comforts of the industrial affluence which science has given us." Assuming that the vital needs of humankind were purely technical, the technocrat was certain that more is always better, posing this "fanatically quantitative ethos" against the "qualitative life-needs of the person."

Roszak's sweeping condemnations of "scientists," "science," and "the scientific world view" left him vulnerable to charges of anti-intellectualism. He neglected to make clear that his real focus was on scientism—the belief that a reified "science" had answered (or was about to answer) all the questions we could possibly pose to the cosmos. This outlook, which is completely at odds with the scientific method, has always been more prominent among journalistic popularizers than among scientists themselves.

Yet despite Roszak's imprecise aim at "science," he recognized that elevation of quantity over quality—like the technocratic worldview it enabled—depended on a dualistic Cartesian ontology. Though Roszak never referred to Descartes, he focused on "the myth of objective consciousness" as the intellectual foundation of technocracy. "There is but one way of gaining access to reality—so the myth holds—and this is to cultivate a state of consciousness cleansed of all subjective distortion, all personal involvement," he wrote. The stance of objectivity, according to Roszak, required a sharp distinction between In-Here (the conscious, observing mind) and Out-There (the inert, manipulatable world that lies beyond our heads). The consequence was the "subordination of the particular and immediate experience to a statistical generalization."

The spread of behaviorist assumptions was the largest symptom of the rule of technocracy. As Roszak observed, quoting the psychiatrist R. D. Laing, "we are so estranged from the inner world that there are many arguing that it does not exist, and that even if it does exist, it does not matter." By diminishing, devaluing, or even denying subjective experience, behaviorism facilitated the rise of algorithmic decision-making.

However restricted the observer's role, there was always the danger that he might fall victim to subjective impulses. Computers could prevent that from happening. In this task the clock was their precursor. Clocks calculated the incalculable human experience of time, bypassing how the experience of time actually *felt*, as John Donne had recognized centuries before. Bergson had challenged this quantified regime by substituting the idea of duration—what Roszak called "the living experience of life itself"—for "the rigid rhythms of clock time." Though Roszak dismissed George Bernard Shaw's vitalism as a boutique worldview held by "alienated artists, eccentric psychiatrists, and assorted cranks," he embraced Bergson's vitalist critique of clock time as a prescient protest against a hyperorganized life.

Technocratic thinkers, led by nuclear strategists, had embraced computerized algorithms as a hedge against human caprice, maybe even a substitute for all subjective decision-making. Within the technocracy the computer had become "an electronic nervous system" that takes over when its operator fails to maintain a completely impersonal stance. As Roszak recognized, artificial intelligence was the telos of objective consciousness—a notion of intelligence reduced to problem-solving, based on behaviorist assumptions. If problems proved resistant to algorithmic solutions, they were redefined so that computers could solve them—so that human well-being, for example, could be measured by quantifiable indices. The notion of knowledge itself was being pared down to fit reductionist imperatives.

Roszak's critique of the mind-set behind technocracy derived its immediate urgency from Cold War military policy. Cognitive styles had cataclysmic consequences; apparently abstract ideas bred palpable, fleshly suffering. Objective consciousness fed the ability to contemplate inflicting mass death with equanimity, as many scientists and military men were being trained to do. The shadow that hovered over *Making* was less the war in Vietnam—though that technocratic adventure was pervasively present in Roszak's book—than the threat of nuclear war. It was, he wrote, "an evil which is not defined by the sheer *fact* of the bomb, but by the total *ethos* of the bomb, in which our politics, our public morality, our economic life, our intellectual endeavor are now embedded with a wealth of ingenious rationalization." For Roszak, "the decisive measure of the technocracy's essential criminality" was "the extent to which it insists, in the name of progress, in the name of reason, that the unthinkable become thinkable and the intolerable become tolerable." A particular, historically shaped way of thinking had enshrined madness as a form of rationality.

Romantic poets, as Roszak observed, had anticipated the critique of technocratic rationality. He provided a deep genealogy of the 1960s counterculture, citing Shelley's influential announcement that in defense of poetry we must invoke "light and fire from those eternal regions where the owl-winged faculty of calculation dare not ever soar." The assumption that the free play of imagination required the rejection of calculation was itself a failure of imagination; numbers can stir fresh thought as well as stabilize uncertainty and provide necessarily precise knowledge. Still, Shelley's pursuit of "light and fire" in "eternal regions" resonated with countercultural longings to embark on inner quests for authentic selfhood.

Trips inward posed the prospect of getting lost in the labyrinth of subjective experience, as Roszak acknowledged when he decried the "counterfeit infinity" offered by psychedelic drugs. The specter of self-absorption loomed, as did the reverence for raw force that had haunted the vitalist tradition for decades. While Roszak applauded the "cultivation of a feminine softness among [countercultural] males," he deplored the masculine worship of force that he found in a review of a Seattle concert by the Doors: "'if they leave us crotch-raw and exhausted, at least they leave us aware of our aliveness,' the *Helix* reported. 'And of our destiny . . . We want the world and we want it . . . NOW!'" Like vitality, subjectivity was a neutral concept that could lead in sinister directions: Roszak was not uncritically celebrating subjective experience, but challenging a worldview that denied it. And he was trying to restore it to our sense of what it meant to be a conscious human being.

Fortunately, the masculine worship of force was overbalanced by more benign countercultural tendencies, in Roszak's account. One was the burgeoning interest in Zen Buddhism and other Eastern religions, with their "heritage of gentle, tranquil, and thoroughly civilized contemplativeness," their recognition that "analysis and debate must finally yield to the claims of ineffable experience," and their validation of a place for silence. The counterculture's improvised rituals were hopeful signs as well—the rituals celebrating "something postulated as sacred . . . the magnificence of the season, the joy of being the human animal so vividly alive to the world." The rhetoric of vitalism flourished amid countercultural ferment.

Soon enough the ferment would subside and what was left of countercultural protest would be absorbed into the newer, hipper technocracy pioneered in Stewart Brand's *Whole Earth Catalog* and brought to fulfillment in Silicon Valley. Tracy Kidder's *The Soul of a New Machine* (1980) signaled a new sort of technophilic mysticism, well suited to the mass distribution of personal computers. Hip capitalist advertisers helped to channel countercultural impulses toward the creation of "alternative lifestyles" through the assemblage of consumer goods—including expensive gear that could make the purchaser feel and look like an outdoorsman even if he spent sixteen hours a day staring at a screen.

The political promise of the early '70s—the pioneering environmental legislation, the critique of the intelligence agencies' illegal spying—was stillborn. By the end of that decade, Ronald Reagan was dismissing Jimmy Carter's warnings about limits to growth and removing the solar panels from the White House. "America is back," he declared—which meant a return to unfettered economic expansion and unapologetic accumulation.

REAGAN'S LEGACY: REGENERATIVE WAR AND IRRATIONAL EXUBERANCE

Reagan's victory also meant a return to unabashed saber-rattling, though Carter had done his share. Reagan spent much of his first term denouncing the Soviets' "Evil Empire," deploying Pershing missiles in West Germany and England, and promoting the Strategic Defense Initiative, a Rube Goldberg boondoggle that proposed to shoot down incoming missiles in outer space. But in 1985, Reagan began yielding to the diplomatic charms of Mikhail Gorbachev as well as the citizen diplomacy of the nuclear freeze movement and came within an ace of abolishing nuclear weapons outright. Gorbachev must have known what had happened on September 26, 1983, when a Soviet early warning system mistook the sun's reflection off clouds for five incoming Minuteman missiles. Lt. Col. Stanislav Petrov and his staff, under unimaginable pressure, correctly concluded that the system flashing "LAUNCH" had raised a false alarm; Petrov did not report the incoming missiles to his superior officers, who would have immediately ordered a full-scale nuclear attack on the United States. This was the sort of incident (and there have been more on both sides) that would have inspired a thoughtful leader like Gorbachev to urge the abolition of nuclear weapons. Reagan was nearly persuaded, but in the end he simply could not give up his quixotic dream of the Strategic Defense Initiative. Despite warming relations between the superpowers and a few substantial arms-control treaties, the dream of abolition—or even significant cuts in the nuclear arsenals—disappeared.

As a result, the nuclear arms race has continued. The *Bulletin of the Atomic Scientists* has set its doomsday clock to one hundred seconds before midnight, closer than ever due to deteriorating U.S. relations with Russia and China, the scrapping of arms-control agreements, and the renewed determination of nuclear powers—led by the United States—to modernize their nuclear arsenals. Of course, the latest technological developments remain shrouded in secrecy, but we can be sure that artificial intelligence remains near the center of strategic research, and with it the possibility of caprice and mistake—human or post-human.

Despite his rapprochement with Gorbachev and his brief flirtation with nuclear pacifism, Reagan's impact on foreign policy was ultimately calamitous. Apart from covert interventions in Nicaragua and elsewhere in Latin America, Reagan's long-term influence was subtler: it centered on his triumphalist resurrection of American power and virtue, after the shameful loss in Vietnam. Red-baiting his way through his campaign and first term, he allowed the militarist narrative of the Vietnam catastrophe to seep into the corridors of power and poison the political atmosphere by reviving the idea of regenerative war. According to this tale, faint-hearted politicians, abetted by their allies in the media and on campus, had forced American soldiers to fight with one hand tied behind their backs. Having failed to support the troops adequately, American policy-makers had fallen victim to a "Vietnam syndrome," which rendered them unable to act forcefully when it was necessary; the population itself, in its growing reluctance to go to war, had collaborated in this cowardice. The stage was being set for the revival of militaristic vitalism; no wonder the ghost of Theodore Roosevelt seemed to stalk the streets of Washington, as presidents from both parties identified him as their model, and admiring biographies of him filled bookstores.

Gradually the notion of regenerative war began to regain some legitimacy, especially among the policy intellectuals who called themselves "Vulcans"—Condoleezza Rice, Paul Wolfowitz, Donald Rumsfeld, and Dick Cheney, among others. Cheney in particular had been traumatized by the defeat in Vietnam, the disgrace of Nixon, and the decline (however temporary) of executive power. Throughout the 1990s, the Vulcans discussed how to reassert U.S. military power abroad, especially in the Middle East but also in eastern Europe, through the expansion of NATO—this last would eventually provoke the proxy war with Russia over Ukraine. More immediately, the Vulcans remained fixated on finishing the job they imagined had been begun in the Gulf War: regime change in Iraq.

The terrorist attacks of September 11, 2001, gave them their opportunity. Intellectuals, including self-proclaimed liberals, played an important supporting role in legitimating the Vulcans' plans—in large part by resurrecting faith in regenerative war. Less than a month after the attacks, George Packer praised Americans—and fellow liberals in particular—for "recapturing the flag," for refusing any longer to leave patriotism solely to working-class folk. The problem was that what he called patriotism turned out, on closer examination, to be something more akin to militarism. Packer admitted that as a child he had secretly chafed under the sappy slogans of the peace movement, such as "War Is Not Healthy for Children and Other Living Things." "No, war was not healthy," wrote Packer, "but it was more exciting than anything else I could think of." Eventually, he recalled, "the part of me that craved danger and commitment and sacrifice had to find an outlet in not quite satisfying alternatives like the Peace Corps." But now, in the wake of 9/11, we had a genuine national emergency, and even liberal intellectuals were swept up in a surge of collective virtue. "What I dread now," he wrote, "is a return to the normality we're all supposed to seek: instead of public memorials, private consumption; instead of lines to give blood, restaurant lines."

Packer was quick to deny that he was celebrating war, but he left no doubt about its tonic effects. "I don't desire war," he concluded, "but I know that patriotic feeling makes individuals exceed themselves as the bland comforts of peace cannot . . . I've lived through this state, and I like it." Here again, as in earlier versions of militarist vitalism, an intellectual's inner state took precedence over the actual devastations of war. How easy it was to prefer the excitement of war fever (not to mention "danger and commitment and sacrifice") over the "bland comforts of peace" when one was seated comfortably at one's keyboard. Citing William James on the need for a "moral equivalent of war," Packer failed to follow James's anti-imperialist example. He supported the Iraq invasion on the assumption that it would benefit the Iraqi people, and while this belief proved illusory, it legitimated the war among liberals and moderates who might otherwise have been more suspicious of the Bush administration's global War on Terror—an open-ended crusade whose very name revealed its emotional underpinnings.

The declared intent of the War on Terror was to "exterminate all the brutes" (as Conrad's Kurtz put it)—to vanquish the source of popular fear while keeping that fear at white heat as long as possible. When asked by Bob Woodward when the War on Terror would end, Vice-President Cheney said, "Not in our lifetime." One could imagine his lips quivering with excitement. America was back, indeed. Reagan would have approved. From his campaign well into his presidency, he sanctioned a strutting militarism that laid the emotional foundation for a series of imperial misadventures in the Middle East. His shadow stretched well into the twenty-first century.

Reagan had an equally lasting impact on political economy. The genial demagogue with the lemon-twist smile and the twinkle in his eye ushered in a new era that celebrated entrepreneurial risk-taking (especially among those most insulated from its downside) and reanimated the flow of animal spirits on Wall Street. Reagan's successors, Democrats and Republicans alike, followed his lead in deregulating finance capital and participating in its renewed potency.

Reagan's ascendancy reinforced the emergence of a new ideological consensus. Democrats and Republicans joined in hollowing out the discourse of liberal democracy and transforming it into a language of managerial technique—a technocratic jargon used to legitimate the spread of free-flowing capital. Within this discourse, freedom was reduced to market behavior, citizenship to voting, efficiency for the public good to efficiency for profit. The return of nineteenth-century slogans and pieties, combined with a twenty-first-century veneer of neutral expertise, have inspired many observers to call this new consensus "neoliberalism."

The term had been in use in various ideological settings for decades, and its most recent meaning is equally rooted in a particular historical moment. It captures what distinguishes contemporary mainstream politics from the mid-century marriage of big business and big government—the arrangement underlying the technocracy challenged by Roszak. The "neo" in the neoliberal outlook involves the merger of technocratic expertise and market fundamentalism. The results are all around us: the privatization of areas previously protected from market discipline, mainly health care and education; the reliance on economic utility as the sole criterion of worth; the reverence for quantitative data as a guarantor of certainty and source of social value; the indifference to the fate of the millions of people ignored or left behind in the wake of the "creative destruction" caused by capitalist development. Neoliberal policies have dominated the received political wisdom from the Reagan administration down to the present, surviving the financial crisis of 2008 as well as challenges from the populist left and right. Whether it will survive the crises induced by the COVID pandemic and the war in Ukraine remains to be seen, but it has been a resilient ideology. If it is crumbling, chunks of it will no doubt remain in Washington for a long time, deflecting policy debate away from humane agendas.

The resilience of neoliberalism is rooted in its very nature. It is about more than mere policy making. It is a way of thinking and being, an ethos or structure of feeling, with the capacity to reshape subjective experience by redefining the self. Under the neoliberal regime, each person becomes a piece of "human capital"—a little firm with assets, debts, and a credit score anxiously scrutinized for signs of success or failure, much as Calvinists scrutinized their souls for evidence of salvation or damnation. The neoliberal self intrudes instrumentalist market assumptions into every corner of human experience, accelerating the pricing of everyday life—down to and including the calculation of a human being's monetary value. Irving Fisher would be pleased. What was eccentric in the 1910s has become mainstream in our own time.

The capitalization of the self has had wide and deep impact. An hour's worth of NPR commercials suggests the emergence of a new model psyche, reflected in the current obsession with behavioral economics and neuroscience generally. These enterprises claim to point the way beyond old, static, rational-actor models while at the same time encouraging self-modification to conform to the ever more pervasive and relentless demands of market rationality. The cultivation of expertise becomes essential—not merely to the management of corporations and governments but also to the management of personal identity.

Contemporary policy expertise depends on unprecedented deference to data, with respect to all areas of human existence, the inner life of mind and emotion as well as economic and bodily functions. The reliance on numbers as the key to understanding subjective experience characterizes all sorts of enterprises from happiness surveys to opinion polling; it has spread to the citadels of numerology on Wall Street, where soothsayers deploy quantitative methods to penetrate (or claim to penetrate) the mysteries of capital markets.

Perhaps the greatest mystery remains the ebb and flow of animal spirits. The phrase itself has reentered public discourse since the crash of 2008—though a dozen years earlier, Alan Greenspan's caution against "irrational exuberance" was a warning against animal spirits run amok. As in the post–World War II era, financial policymakers sought to conjure animal spirits, but also to keep them moving in the right direction by systematically deploying statistics, as Wells Fargo does in its animal spirits index. Such exercises have led observers to discern a contemporary revival of Keynes's ideas.

In 2009, two behavioral economists, George Akerlof and Robert Shiller, appeared to signal the return of Keynes when they published *Animal Spirits: How Human Psychology Drives the Economy, and Why It Matters for Global Capitalism*. But they defanged animal spirits, reducing them to mere confidence—the sort of emotion that seems quantifiable in surveys, not to mention assimilable to neoclassical economic assumptions. Like previous mainstream economists, Shiller and Akerlof turned Keynesianism into mere technique. In fact, Keynes's ideas remained profoundly at odds with contemporary policy assumptions.

Keynes would undoubtedly take issue with the consensus faith in quantitative expertise, which has been fed by popularizing journalists. Ignoring the experimental cast of mind at the heart of the scientific method, they have made a reified "science" the repository of absolute truth. Behind this enterprise lies the reductionist assumption that science has answered (or is about to answer) all ultimate questions with quantifiable precision. The determination to calculate the incalculable has accelerated, promoting "happiness studies" and other forms of survey research that purport to plumb the depths of subjective experience on the dubious basis of self-reporting.

All of this suggests a resurgence of positivist faith in quantification, down to and including the quantification of animal spirits. But vitalist tendencies have resurfaced as well, even in places where one would least expect them, such as the life sciences. A vision of universal animacy, once considered a vestige of primitive superstation, has miraculously come to seem scientific again.

The welcome resurgence of serious animistic thinking takes place amid what can only be called an epistemological and ontological crisis. Long-standing sources of authority—including positivist science—are being widely called into question and insistently reasserted. Polarizing points of view are rooted in colliding moral certainties. Reality itself is up for grabs, and rival versions confront one another fiercely. Scapegoating and banishment flourish in political rhetoric and practice.

So does apocalyptic thinking, often with sound evidence of imminent catastrophe—arising from climate change, global war, or both. Given that evidence, it is hard to imagine a more urgent human task than honoring our kinship with other living things, unlike us in many ways but like us in our common residency on earth. A revived vision of universal animacy, equipped with scientific legitimacy, could rekindle a fresh engagement with the natural world. And that, we have reason to hope, is already happening.

Epilogue: A Fierce Green Fire

Soon after he graduated from the Yale Forestry School in 1909, Aldo Leopold headed for Arizona to take a job with the U.S. Forest Service—the new federal agency charged with the (equally new) task of "wildlife management." Theodore Roosevelt had just left the White House and embarked on a big-game hunt in Africa, but his presence could still be felt in government policies toward wild nature.

For Leopold and his contemporaries in the Forest Service, managing wildlife meant, among other things, killing creatures deemed undesirable by ranchers, farmers, and hunters. Few were deemed more undesirable than wolves, or were more exciting targets for young men with guns. "In those days we had never heard of passing up a chance to kill a wolf," Leopold remembered some decades later in *A Sand County Almanac.* This was an exterminationist ethic in action, folded into the dictates of official policy.

So when Leopold and his companion spotted an old she-wolf and her six grown pups tangling playfully on a steep hillside, the men quickly started "pumping lead into the pack, but with more excitement than accuracy . . . When our rifles were empty, the old wolf was down, and a pup was dragging a leg into impassable slide-rocks." As the men moved closer to size up what they had done, something unexpected and arresting happened. As Leopold recalled:

> We reached the old wolf in time to watch a fierce green fire dying in her eyes. I realized then, and have known ever since, that there was something new to me in those eyes—something known only to her and to the mountain. I was young then, and full of trigger-itch; I thought that because fewer wolves meant more deer, that no wolves would mean hunters' paradise. But after seeing the green fire die, I sensed that neither the wolf nor the mountain agreed with such a view.

This gaze into the eyes of the other, this glimpse of an animal's spirit, became an archetypal moment in the history of ecological consciousness. Leopold's account of the dying wolf went on to describe the calamitous consequences of exterminating the entire species—mountains denuded of every edible tree and bush by proliferating deer, rangeland turned into a dust bowl by overgrazing cattle. The eradication of the wolf upset the balance of nature, which the mountain embodied before it was ravaged by deer (and men). The rancher, like the wolf exterminator, "has not learned to think like a mountain," Leopold concluded.

The attribution of sentience and thought to wolves and even mountains—the reanimation of the world—was a portal of discovery for Leopold. It led him eventually to leave the Forest Service and conduct his own experiment in conservation on a farm situated among the agriculturally unpromising "sand counties" of south-central Wisconsin. It also made *A Sand County Almanac* a bible for American environmentalists.

But that did not start to happen until the late 1960s, when visions of a reanimated universe began appearing amid countercultural ferment. The critique of technocratic domination; the rejection of an ethos of human mastery over manipulatable nature; the recovery of respect for nonhuman creatures—all the countercultural impulses celebrated by Roszak (and Mailer) found a home in the emerging environmental movement. Not many environmentalists were genuine animists in any strict sense. They did not believe in either a single spirit animating nature or a multitude of lesser spirits animating living creatures. Yet the movement revalued animistic traditions, recognizing their resonance with ecological notions of the earth as a living organism composed of countless smaller interdependent organisms. This was the cultural moment when *A Sand County Almanac*, first published in 1949, was reissued—in 1970. The time was temporarily ripe for Leopold's vision of a sentient natural world, full of creatures who could feel and think in ways comparable if not identical to human ways.

Rising respect for nonhuman nature fostered renewed interest in the deeper meanings of animal spirits, though the term itself was seldom used. Yearnings to reconnect body and mind resurfaced—as fervent as Donne's need to connect body and soul, and often as imbued with spiritual longing. Many of these impulses animated holistic medicine, flowing from Groddeck's postulate of the It to contemporary explorations of *qi*—which resonate strikingly with Andrew Jackson Davis's vision of a vital spiritual force that needs to flow freely to maintain a healthy organism. Holistic conceptions of the self melded with ecological awareness to spawn a strain of vitalist feminism—prominent in the early novels of Margaret Atwood and the eco-feminist histories of Carolyn Merchant, among other significant works. Eco-feminism made its critique of patriarchy part of a broader challenge to human domination of the nonhuman world.

But all this occurred within a brief historical moment. To be sure, holistic medicine has thrived and Leopold's book has continued to sell well; his vision of universal animacy has influenced many people's personal commitments, swelling the ranks of vegetarians and vegans and advocates of animal rights. While the yearning to feel some political efficacy has led many people to focus on areas of experience they can actually control, such as diet, mainstream politics has remained beyond popular control or even influence—stuck in stale debates, impervious to pervasive needs, with both sides subservient to corporate interests that are at best indifferent to environmental concerns.

What is happening as I write may alter or even transform this situation. Out-of-control wildfires, smoke-filled skies, melting icecaps, and rising sea levels—these signs of global warming have become impossible to ignore, and may be reigniting a politically effective ecological consciousness, a recognition that humans share the earth with other inspirited species, which depend on one another and on a habitable, living earth.

The resurgence of environmentalist thought is accompanied by a parallel resurgence of vitalist tendencies in geology, physics, botany, and epigenetics. These intellectual developments pose a potential challenge to the technocratic assumption that nature is merely an inert "resource" to be plundered for human use; indeed, they point to a renewed and widening vision of universal animacy—a growing awareness that not only living organisms but even apparently solid materials such as lumber, steel, and granite are a ferment of microscopic motion.

We are beginning to learn a great deal about the vibrancy of matter. More than a decade ago, in *Vibrant Matter*, the philosopher Jane Bennett posed the ontological questions raised by the concept: "Does life only make sense as one side of a life-matter binary, or is there such a thing as a mineral or metallic life, or a life of the it in 'it rains'?" she wondered. Offering her "vital materialism" as an alternative to teleological visions of a purposive Nature and mechanistic visions of blind fate, she challenged the notion of a human self that can somehow be set apart from nonhuman nature. As she wrote, the recognition that "we are made up of its"—the countless bacteria that populate our bodies—ought to be a key to "the newish self that needs to emerge" in an "onto-tale" where "everything is, in a sense, alive."

Since *Vibrant Matter* was published, scientists have been creating a broader foundation for Bennett's speculation. Robert Macfarlane converses with some of them in his remarkable book *Underland*. One is a physicist studying the collisions of dark matter. During a lull in their conversation, "he pauses. I wait," Macfarlane writes. "Trillions of neutrinos pass through our bodies and on through the earth's bedrock, its mantle, its liquid innards, its solid core." Then the physicist says, "as if the phrase has just entered his head without warning, scoring a trace as it passes through—'Everything causes a scintillation.'" "Scintillation" becomes a key word for Macfarlane as he comes to understand the constant movement within apparently solid organisms and objects.

The question is: How do human thoughts and feelings apprehend this world? "Does it change the way the world feels," Macfarlane asks the physicist, "knowing that 100 trillion neutrinos pass through your body every second, that countless such particles perforate our brains and hearts? Does it change the way you feel about matter—about what matters? Are you surprised we don't fall through each surface of our world at every step, push through it with every touch?'" His interlocutor pauses to ponder, then says: "'I know our bodies are wide-meshed nets, and the cliffs we're walking on are nets too, and sometimes it seems, yes, as miraculous as if in our everyday world we suddenly found ourselves walking on water, or air."

Everywhere he looks, Macfarlane finds evidence of vibrant matter. With the botanist Merlin Sheldrake in Epping Forest, he discovers, "Living wood, left long enough, behaves as a slow-moving fluid like the halite down in the darkness of Boulby mine, like the calcite I had seen beneath the Mendips, like glacial ice drawing itself over topsoil and bedrock, living wood flows, given time." From another botanist, Lynn Margulis, he learns about holobionts—"collaborative compound organisms, ecological units 'consisting of millions of bacteria, viruses, and fungi that collaborate in the task of living together and sharing a common life,' in the philosopher Glenn Albrecht's words." None of this would be news, Macfarlane notes, to indigenous peoples, whose animistic traditions postulate a conversational relationship with the jungle or woodland they inhabit.

A big part of our problem in the industrialized West, Macfarlane observes, is that (unlike Native Americans or other indigenous peoples) we have neither the grammar nor the vocabulary to represent animacy. Consider the Potawatomi word *puhpowee*—"the force which causes mushrooms to push up from the earth overnight"—or *wikwegamaa*—"to be a bay." We have no language to express these ways of seeing and being.

But maybe we could develop one. The recovery of a "grammar of animacy" would challenge the reductionist imperative at the heart of technocratic rationality, which requires its devotees to reject any vestiges of vitalism they can sniff in the cultural atmosphere. As Steven Pinker says, "Intelligence . . . has often been attributed to some kind of energy flow or force field"—a point of view he derides as little more than "spiritualism, pseudo-science, and sci-fi kitsch." Pinker is here playing the classic custodian of conventional wisdom, policing the boundaries of responsible opinion with any ideological weapons available, including the rhetoric of scientific expertise.

But among scientists themselves, there is more controversy than Pinker acknowledges. One reason he disdains the vitalist view may be that it violates the taken-for-granted reluctance to acknowledge that organisms help make their environments, as opposed to merely adapting to them. The idea that organisms can participate in their own evolution has been developed by a number of influential biologists, including Richard Lewontin. It has come to be known as "niche construction" and it challenges the strict adaptationist view with a revived and implicitly Lamarckian emphasis on the ways that ancestral organisms' modifications of their environment can affect subsequent generations.

The Viennese physicist Erwin Schrodinger pointed the way toward "niche construction" in 1944 by asking, "What is life?" He proposed a quantum theory of evolution, and speculated that mutations were "quantum jumps in the gene molecule," rather than the millions of tiny accidents imagined by conventional neo-Darwinians. In this version of evolution, natural selection worked in collaboration with the behavior of individual organisms, which would reinforce and enhance the usefulness of the mutation, leading to further physical change. Natural selection was "aided all along by the organism's making appropriate use" of the mutation, Schrodinger insisted. Selection and use "go quite parallel and are . . . fixed genetically as one thing: a used organ—as if Lamarck were right." For Schrodinger, genetic mutations interacted with the organism's own tendency to use what it had—its capacity to shape its own surroundings, creating its own ecological niche rather than simply adapting to an existing one. The consequences, some theorists subsequently claimed, could shape the development of the organism's descendants. From this view there are two kinds of inheritances, genetic and environmental.

Schrodinger's phrase "as if Lamarck were right" has acquired more palpable meaning in recent decades, with the rise of epigenetics. This field makes more ambitious claims than niche construction theory, suggesting that changes in an organism's environment may actually change its DNA. Epigeneticists emphasize the whole context in which genetic material functions, from the cell to the organism and its environment. Several decades ago, the biologist Barbara McClintock discovered what she called "transposons": mobile elements in a cell's genome that respond to stress such as starvation or sudden temperature changes by rearranging the cell's DNA. McClintock first found transposition in maize, but it has turned out to be important in other organisms as well. Current research suggests that bacteria develop resistance to antibiotics, "not through a purely random process of mutation followed by natural selection, but in important part by moving their DNA around," as Jessica Riskin writes. James Shapiro, a bacterial geneticist at the University of Chicago, has extended McClintock's work by showing that nearly all cells possess the biochemical tools for changing their DNA, and they use them "responsively, not purely randomly," in Riskin's words.

Other examples of epigenetic research offer a compelling variety of evidence. The British geneticist Marcus Pembrey found that the malnutrition of Swedish villagers in one generation could lower life expectancy in a following generation that was itself better nourished. Michael Skinner studied exposure to fungicide in one generation of rats and its continuing effects on several subsequent unexposed generations. No gene, it has begun to appear, is an island; it is part of a multidimensional main. The boundaries of our genetic identity are beginning to seem more porous than strict adaptationist Darwinism would allow.

Nothing has been settled, and none of this theoretical controversy means a new evolutionary synthesis is on the horizon. But what has been the conventional Darwinian view for more than a century is being called into question. From this established perspective, genetic change occurs through random mutations, some of which survive the process of natural selection and are passed along to subsequent generations as species adapt to their environments. In the newer view, whether articulated in the idiom of niche construction or epigenetics, an organism can respond to environmental challenges in ways that permanently alter the inheritance—ecological or genetic—that it passes along to future generations. The epigenetic version of this idea violates the orthodox assumption that changes in the body cannot influence the genes. This heresy, in Richard Dawkins's view, will open the floodgates of "fanaticism" and "zealotry"—by which he means Lamarckism. Somewhere, Lamarck is smiling.

The philosophical implications of this scientific ferment are fundamental. Emphasizing what humans have in common with the rest of the natural world allows for our participation alongside other creatures in an interdependent, animated universe. And a clearer understanding of our relationship to nature demands a sensitivity to the ways that organisms engage with the contingent circumstances of their environment in historical time. For humans, that environment includes religions and ideologies and economic systems as well as air and soil and water. Who knows? Maybe scientists will have something to learn from historians, as well as the other way around.

The consequences of a more capacious "grammar of animacy" might be political and moral as well as intellectual. A full recognition of an animated material world could well trigger a deeper mode of environmental reform, a more sane and equitable model of economic growth, even religious precepts that challenge the ethos of market utility and mastery over nature. Schrodinger's question—what is life?—leads us to reconsider what it means to be in the world with other beings, like but also unlike ourselves.

The task could not be more timely or more urgent. This book has highlighted two great vitalist thinkers in Anglo-American cultural history, William James and John Maynard Keynes. Though they never used the term "vitalism," they embodied the tradition's most humane meanings and possibilities. Both men celebrated spontaneous vitality while recognizing its darker possibilities, above all the delusion of regenerative war. We now live in a very dark time, when that delusion has once again been unleashed upon the world.

Remembering James and Keynes offers a way to reassert the benign and necessary claims of animal spirits on the conduct of our lives—a capacity for spontaneous feeling and sheer exuberance, but also a tolerance for uncertainty and an awareness of the ubiquity of caprice, for good or ill. All these qualities of mind foster resistance to militarist rant, which begins its ideological work by manipulating the more sinister potential of animal spirits. The opening rhetorical moves are all too familiar: incite rage and fear to a fever pitch, evoke the excitement of chaos on the assumption it can be managed—or at least can generate unforeseen possibilities. Whatever happens, from the militarist view, decisive action will bring relief from uncertainty and drift.

The ultimate expression of this fantasy is the dream of a winnable nuclear exchange, which has now resurfaced in certain circles of public discourse. As policy elites reshape the world into hostile blocs, bristling with sophisticated weaponry, the unthinkable has once again become thinkable. James and Keynes would be appalled. For the sake of planetary survival, the hubris of militarism requires the kind of counterweight their sensibility embodies—a reverence for life itself, a respect for the centrality of chance in human affairs, a reminder that every new deal contains the possibility of a wild card.

In 1929, a year after Aldo Leopold left the Forest Service, Ludwig Wittgenstein returned to Cambridge—the first time he had been there since before the war. Keynes was tense but glad. To Lydia, he wrote: "Well, God has arrived. I met him on the 5:15 train." Wittgenstein proceeded to complete his degree (the *Tractatus*) and join the philosophy faculty. But what is most interesting to me about Wittgenstein's return is that in November 1929 he gave a lecture on ethics that marked a decisive turn in his own thought and may have decisively influenced Keynes's thinking as well.

Wittgenstein began by dismissing the idea that there could ever be a science of ethics, because "no statement of fact can ever be, or imply, a judgment of absolute value." This was familiar enough territory; Hume had made a similar claim nearly two centuries before. Yet Wittgenstein pushed forward to a paradox, observing that we all have certain experiences that are undeniably facts ("they have taken place then and there, lasted a certain definite time, and consequently are describable")—and that these experiences seem to us to embody absolute value. He was not sure how to describe his own most insistent version of such an experience except to say, "when I have it I wonder at the existence of the world. And I am then inclined to use such phrases as 'how extraordinary that anything should exist' or 'how extraordinary that the world should exist.'"

The sentiments recall Jonathan Edwards, seeing "images or shadows of divine things" in the meadows and woods outside Northampton, marveling at the continuous creation of the deity. Wittgenstein himself realized that what he was trying to describe was an experience of the sacred. Ethics was entangled with some form of religious belief, however heterodox or idiosyncratic, and that entanglement made it impossible to talk about ethics in the familiar idioms of sense and nonsense. "My whole tendency and, I believe, the tendency of all men who ever tried to write or talk Ethics or Religion was to run against the boundaries of language," he said. "This running against the walls of our cage is perfectly, absolutely hopeless," though the Sisyphean impulse (he thought) is an admirable "tendency of the human mind." Despite Wittgenstein's efforts to describe it, his own experience of absolute value remains ineffable: "It is the experience of seeing the world as a miracle."

We are back with the core of the vitalist tradition—the dearest freshness deep-down things, the miraculous aliveness of the world. In this fraught and fateful historical moment, there is no more compelling affirmative vision.

Notes

INTRODUCTION

4 *"the spontaneous urge to action"*: John Maynard Keynes, *The General Theory of Employment, Interest, and Money* [1936] (reprint, 1964), 161.

6 *"a pantheon of animal spirits"*: Paul Shepard, *The Others: How Animals Made Us Human* (1996), 206.

7 *"What shall happen"*: E. Benton-Benai, *The Mishomis Book: The Voice of the Ojibway* (1979), cited in Raymond Pierotti and Brandy R. Fogg, *The First Domestication: How Wolves and Humans Co-evolved* (2017), 156.

7 *"When a bowl"*: Hopi informant, cited by Mark Tomas Bahti, "Animals in Hopi Duality," in *Signifying Animals: Human Meaning in the Natural World*, ed. R. G. Willis (1990), 135. Italics in original.

7 *"the unseen people"*: Ibid.

8 *"just the same"*: Ibid.

8 *"snake people"*: Ibid., 137–38.

8 *"spirits that can help us" . . . "sent home"*: Ibid., 138.

8 *"the reality of the unseen"*: William James, title of lecture 3 in his *The Varieties of Religious Experience* (1902).

10 *"that, beneath the masks"*: Shepard, *Others*, 240.

10 *"wild men"*: Michael Palencia-Roth, "Enemies of God: Monsters and the Theology of Conquest," in *Monsters, Tricksters, and Sacred Cows: Animal Tales and American Identities*, ed. A. James Arnold (1996), 23–24.

11 *the differences were more important than the similarities*: This theme is ably developed by Virginia DeJohn Anderson in *Creatures of Empire: How Domestic Animals Transformed Early America* (2004).

12 *"the meretricious ontology"*: Eugene McCarraher, *The Enchantments of Mammon: How Capitalism Became the Religion of Modernity* (2019), 5–6.

13 *"His intellect is not replenished"*: William Shakespeare, *Love's Labour's Lost* (1598), IV.ii.27.

13 *"subtil, aiery substance"*: Bartolomeus Anglicus, *De proprietatibus rerum* (1240), trans. as *On the Properties of Things* by John Trevisa (1397), cited in Simon Kemp, *Medieval Psychology* (1990), 20.

1. BETWEEN BODY AND SOUL

15 *"He which at one o'clock"*: F. J. Snell, *The Chronicles of Twyford* (c. 1893), cited in Keith Thomas, *Religion and the Decline of Magic* (1971), 20–21.

16 *"Whence it cometh"*: H. Holland, *Spiritual Preservatives Against the Pestilence* (1603), 20, cited in ibid., 11.

16 *"A plague o' both"*: William Shakespeare, *Romeo and Juliet* (1597), III.i, 111–12.

16 *"doth comfort"*: John Taylor, quoted in W. T. Marchant, *In Praise of Ale* (1888), 57, cited in Thomas, *Religion*, 23.

18–19 *The common practice of baptizing puppies*: Thomas, ibid., 41, and on "the magic of the medieval church" in general see his chap. 2.

19 *The most popular repetitive ritual*: On the history of the rosary, see Garry Wills, *The Rosary: Prayer Come Round* (2006), chap. 1.

20 *"mare will make"*: Wells Diocesan Records, A22, cited in Thomas, *Religion*, 86.

21 *"altered the intrinsic value"*: John Locke, *Second Treatise of Government* (1690), cited in McCarraher, *Enchantments*, 38.

22 *Weber's ideal type*: Max Weber, *The Protestant Ethic and the Spirit of Capitalism* [1904], trans. Talcott Parsons (1958).

22 *"as immediately as the colour"*: T. S. Eliot, "The Metaphysical Poets," in his *Selected Essays* (1999), 287–88.

23 *"hydroptique immoderate desire"*: John Donne, *Letters to Certain Persons of Honour* (1651), 51, cited in John Stubbs, *John Donne: The Reformed Soul* (2006), 17. I am deeply indebted to Stubbs's thorough and penetrating scholarship.

23 *"Though like the Pestilence"*: John Donne, "Satyre II," 7–8, cited in Stubbs, ibid., 28.

23 *"matters of the heart"*: Stubbs, ibid., 30.

24 *"years, since yesterday"*: "The Computation," line 1, in *John Donne: The Complete English Poems* (Penguin Books ed., 1996), 49.

24 *"Full nakedness, all joys"*: "To His Mistress Going to Bed," lines 34–36, in ibid., 124.

24 *"cherishing fyre"*: "To Mr. R. W.," lines 5–6, cited in Stubbs, *Donne*, 43.

25 *"a rotten state"*: "The Calme," line 7, cited in ibid., 72.

25 *"England, to whome"*: "The Storme," line 9, cited in ibid., 72.

25 *"When my grave"*: "The Relic," lines 1–11, in Donne, *Poems*, 75–76.

27 *"For love, all love"*: "The Good Morrow," lines 9–10, cited in Stubbs, *Donne*, 185.

27 *"Pregnante Bank"*: "The Extasie," line 2, in Donne, *Poems*, 53.

27 *"As our blood labours to beget"*: "The Extasie," lines 61–72, in ibid., 55.

28 *"In the constitution and making"*: *Sermons*, II, 161, cited in John Carey, *John Donne: Life, Mind, and Art* (1981), 267.

28 *"idolatrous"* . . . *"profane mistresses"*: "Holy Sonnet XIII," lines 9–10, cited in Stubbs, *Donne*, 263.

28 *"Our two souls, therefore"*: "A Valediction: Forbidding Mourning," lines 21–25, in Donne, *Poems*, 85.
29 *"She of whose soul"*: "Of the Progress of the Soul: The Second Anniversary," lines 241–46, 451–55, in ibid., 293–94, 299.
29 *"raging fever"*: Stubbs, *Donne*, 318.
30 *"Every man is a little* Church*"*: *Sermons*, IV, 7, cited in Stubbs, *Donne*, 323.
30 *"marriage is but a continual fornication"*: *Sermons*, II, 17, cited in ibid., 350.
30 *"I said to all"*: "Holy Sonnet XIII," lines 10, 12–14, in Donne, *Poems*, 314.
30 *"Batter my heart"*: "Holy Sonnet XIV," lines 1, 12–14, in ibid., 314–15.
30 *"All that the soule does"*: *Sermons*, IV, 358 (Easter 1623), cited in David L. Edwards, *John Donne: Man of Flesh and Spirit* (2001), 289.
30 *"sacred Art and Courtship"*: Izaak Walton, cited in Edwards, ibid., 306.
30 *"to share in an ecstasy"*: Stubbs, *Donne*, 431.
31 *"burn always"*: Walter Pater, *The Renaissance* (1873), "Conclusion," 236.
31 *"animist materialism"*: Stephen Fallon, *Milton Among the Philosophers: Poetry and Materialism in Seventeenth-Century England* (2007), 79–110.
31 *"one first substance"*: Ibid.
31 *"Thus God the heav'n created"*: John Milton, *Paradise Lost* (1667), bk. 7, lines 232–39.
31 *"Instead of being"*: Fallon, *Milton*, 79–110.
32 *"extremely small bodies"*: René Descartes, cited in John Sutton, *Philosophy and Memory Traces: Descartes to Connectionism* (1998), 103.
33 *"always include a force"*: Pierre Gassendi, cited in Jonathan Sheehan and Dror Wahrman, *Invisible Hands: Self-Organization and the Eighteenth Century* (2015), 28.
33 *"moving animal spirits"*: Thomas Willis, *The Practice of Physick* (1684), 36.
33 "Magically *and* Sympathetically": Ralph Cudworth, *The True Intellectual System of the Universe* (1678), 162.
33 "there must be something more": Sheehan and Wahrman, *Invisible Hands*, 168.
34 *declared the only legitimate prayer to be spontaneous*: Lori Branch, *Rituals of Spontaneity: Sentiment and Secularism from Free Prayer to Wordsworth* (2006), chap. 1.
34 *"Hark! He talks of a Sensible New Birth"*: *Anglican Weekly Miscellany*, cited in Harry S. Stout, *The Divine Dramatist: George Whitefield and the Rise of Modern Evangelicalism* (1991), 40.
34 *"tears, trembling, groans"*: Jonathan Edwards, "The Marks of a Work of the True Spirit," in *The Works of Jonathan Edwards, A. M.* (1835), 261.
34 *"a kind of ecstasy"*: Ibid., 263.
35 *"the best Observer doubtless"*: George Cheyne, *The English Malady* (1733), 79.
36 *"appear solid, transparent"*: Ibid.
36 *"of the same Leaven"*: Ibid., 85.
36 *"in* Substances *of all Kinds"*: Ibid., 87.
36 *"the same (for ought I know)"*: Ibid.
36 *"extremely subtile fluid"*: Richard Mead, *Medical Precepts and Cautions* (1755), 2.
36 *"make that great engine"*: Ibid., 272–73.
36 *"to asswage these swelling surges"*: Ibid., 273–74.

2. THE MADNESS AND MILDNESS OF MONEY

39 *"one very often trades"*: Commercial writer, cited in James Buchan, *John Law: A Scottish Adventurer of the Eighteenth Century* (2018), 58.

39 *"a Money'd Man"*: *A Familiar Epistle to Mr. Mitchell Containing a Seasonable SATIRE, Written in the Style of Modern Poetic Beggars* (1720), 8.

39 *"visionary ideas"*: Charles MacKay, *Extraordinary Popular Delusions and the Madness of Crowds* (1841), 46–47.

39 *"calculate the movement"*: Isaac Newton, cited in Andrew Odlyzko, "Newton's Financial Misadventures in the South Sea Bubble," *Notes and Records: The Royal Society Journal of the History of Science* (2018), doi.org/10.1098/rsnr.2018.0018.

40 *"How from all Corners"*: *A Familiar Epistle*, 4–5.

40 *"invincible patience"*: Paula Backscheider, *Daniel Defoe: His Life* (1989), 11.

41 *"there was not less gaged"*: Daniel Defoe, *An Essay on Projects* (1697), 60.

41 *"weake and Leakey"*: Defoe, cited in Backscheider, *Defoe*, 51.

42 *"Projects and Undertakings"*: Defoe, cited in ibid., 496.

42 *"the Infinite Mazes"*: *Defoe's Review* 3 (1706), 85. Italics in original.

42 *"Men whose Affairs are declining"*: Daniel Defoe, *Remarks on the Bill to Prevent Frauds Committed by Bankrupts* (1706), cited in Backscheider, *Defoe*, 202. Italics in original.

42 *"the miserable, anxious, perplexed life"*: Daniel Defoe, *The Complete English Tradesman* 1 (1727), 79.

43 *"If the Pulse of the Trade"*: Defoe, cited in Backscheider, *Defoe*, 69.

43 *"This substantial Non-Entity called CREDIT"*: *Defoe's Review* 9 (1709), 122.

44 *"Why do East India Company's stocks rise"*: *Defoe's Review* 3 (1706), 502–3.

44 *"It's a shame really"*: Epigraph in Buchan, *Law*, n.p.

44 *"Trade is a Mystery"*: *Defoe's Review* 3 (1706), 645.

45 *"The bank[er] is impressive"*: Fortia de Piles, cited in Buchan, *Law*, 221.

45 *"The madness of stock-jobbing"*: Robert Harley's son, cited in Sheehan and Wahrman, *Invisible Hands*, 102.

46 *"City gamblers"*: Defoe, cited in Backscheider, *Defoe*, 452.

46 *"Extravagant gamesters"*: Defoe, cited in ibid., 454.

46 *"What makes a homely woman fair?"*: Defoe, cited in ibid., 473.

46 *thinkers in Britain and on the Continent*: A. O. Hirschman, *The Passions and the Interests: Political Arguments Over Capitalism Before Its Triumph* (1977).

47 "to set affection against affection": Machiavelli, cited in ibid., 22.

47 *"to the position of the privileged passion"*: Ibid., 38.

48 *"the industrious professions"*: David Hume, cited in ibid., 66.

48 *"immediate sense and feeling"*: Adam Smith, *The Theory of Moral Sentiments* (1759), part 7, section 3, chap. 2, 285.

49 *"mere inventions of the imagination"*: Adam Smith, cited in Dennis C. Rasmussen, *The Infidel and the Professor: David Hume, Adam Smith, and the Friendship That Shaped Modern Thought* (2017), 41.

49 *"the lowest and most pusillanimous superstition"*: Ibid.

49 *"all trades and places"*: Bernard Mandeville, *The Fable of the Bees, or Private Vices, Public Benefits* [1714] (reprint, 2017), 5.

50 *"Then leave complaints"*: Ibid., 12.

50 *"falls short of that complete self-denial"*: Smith, *Theory*, 277.

50 *"whatever other passions"*: Hume, cited in Rasmussen, *Infidel*, 90–91.
50 *"we feel emotions"*: Smith, cited in ibid., 92.
51 *"impertinent jealousy"*: Adam Smith, *The Wealth of Nations* (2000), 646.
51 *"mean rapacity"*: Ibid., 647.
51 *"interested sophistry"*: Ibid.
51 *"Invention is kept alive"*: Adam Smith, *An Inquiry into the Nature and Causes of the Wealth of Nations* (Modern Library ed., 1994), 840.
51 *"By preferring the support"*: Smith, *Wealth of Nations*, 593–94.
52 *"The rich . . . divide with the poor"*: Smith, *Theory*, 164.
53 *"the uniform, constant, and uninterrupted effort"*: Smith, *Wealth of Nations*, 373.
53 *"the most Absent Man that ever was"*: Rasmussen, *Infidel*, 147.
53 *"as dull a dog"*: James Boswell, cited in ibid., 156.
53 *"a professed infidel"*: Samuel Johnson, cited in ibid.
54 *"impartial spectator" . . . "Highest Tribunal" . . . "the man within the breast"*: Smith, *Theory*, 115.
54 *"so as to deserve applause"*: Ibid., 170.
55 *"tranquility of the mind"*: Ibid., 116.
55 *"a world to come"*: Ibid., 117.
55 *"agony can never be permanent"*: Ibid., 130.
55 *"frequent visits and odious examination"*: Smith, *Wealth of Nations*, 889–90.
55 *"exact propriety and perfection"*: Smith, *Theory*, 221.
56 *"the great antidote to the poison"*: Smith, *Wealth of Nations*, 855.
57 *"infinity of oddities"*: Laurence Sterne, *Tristram Shandy* [1759] (Dover Thrift ed., 2007) V, xxiv, 382.
58 *"You have all, I dare say"*: Ibid., 1.
59 *"My Tristram's misfortunes"*: Ibid., 3.
59 *"a very unseasonable question"*: Ibid., 2.
59 *"his own animal spirits"*: Ibid., 3.
59 *"I have been the continual sport"*: Ibid., 6.
59 *"the few animal spirits I was worth"*: Ibid., 236.
60 *"the thought floated"*: Ibid., 132.
60 *"poured down warm as each of us could bear it"*: Ibid., 154.
60 *"What confusion!—what mistakes!"*: Ibid., 157.
61 *"I would remind him"*: Ibid., 80.
62 *"People are said"*: *Federal Spy*, Oct. 2, 1794, 4.
62 *"a wonderful connexion"*: "On the Sympathy Between the Breeches Pocket and the Animal Spirits," *New York Magazine; or, Literary Repository* (Nov. 1, 1792), 646.
63 *"latent force of life"*: Ibid., 647.
64 *"He maintained to all"*: MacKay, *Extraordinary Popular Delusions*, 321–22.
65 *"Then came in the assistant magnetisers"*: Ibid., 324.
66 *"Electricity defied"*: James Delbourgo, *A Most Amazing Scene of Wonders: Electricity and Enlightenment in Early America* (2006), 8.
66 *"spiritual fire"*: Ibid., 214.
66 *"the medium of passion"*: Théophile Gautier, cited in Robert Darnton, *Mesmerism and the End of the Enlightenment in France* (1968), 152.
66 *"electric fire"*: Archibald Spencer, cited in Delbourgo, *Amazing Scene*, 29.

66 *"all the phenomena"*: Joseph Macrery, cited in ibid., 255.
67 *"that things change, and that nothing"*: Benjamin Waterhouse, *A Discourse on the Principle of Vitality* (1790), 2–3.
67 *"Full fathom five thy father lies"*: William Shakespeare, *The Tempest*, I:ii.
68 *"the union of soul with body"*: Waterhouse, *Discourse*, 18–19.
68 *"would often land"*: George Makari, *Soul Machine: The Invention of the Modern Mind* (2015), 63.
68 *"Go, proud reasoner"*: Erasmus Darwin, *Zoonomia* (1801 ed.), 141.
68 *"all alive / The world"*: William Blake, *Europe: A Prophecy*, cited in M. H. Abrams, *Natural Supernaturalism: Tradition and Revolution in Romantic Literature* (1969), 435.
68 *"even the gorgeous"*: William Blake, *Milton* (1810), cited in ibid.
69 *"he was a chosen son"*: William Wordsworth, "The Ruined Cottage," cited in ibid., 103.
69 *"Ye motions of delight"*: William Wordsworth, *The Prelude: The Four Texts*, ed. Jonathan Wordsworth (2004), 464.
69 *"we murder to dissect"*: William Wordsworth, "The Tables Turned" (1798), line 28, https://www.poetryfoundation.org/poems/45557/the-tables-turned.
69–70 *"I am that I am"*: Samuel Taylor Coleridge, cited in Jack H. Haeger, "Samuel Taylor Coleridge and the Romantic Background to Bergson," in *The Crisis in Modernism: Bergson and the Vitalist Controversy* ed. Frederick Burwick and Paul Douglass (1992), 99.
70 *"incalculable series of centuries"*: Jean-Baptiste Lamarck, The Crisis in Modernism cited in Jessica Riskin, *The Restless Clock: A History of the Centuries-long Argument over What Makes Living Things Tick* (2016), 199.
70 *"The brain of a man of labor"*: Lamarck, cited in ibid., 177–78.
71 "generative variability": Charles Darwin, cited in ibid., 231. Italics in original.
72 *"a small drop"*: Joshua Smith, *Divine Hymns* (1803), cited in Brett Malcolm Grainger, *Church in the Wild: Evangelicals in Antebellum America* (2019), 81.
72 *"bowed her knees and cowered down on the ground"*: Zilpha Elaw, "Memoirs of the Life, Religious Experience, Ministerial Travels, and Labors of Mrs. Zilpha Elaw," in *Sisters of the Spirit: Three Black Women's Autobiographies of the Nineteenth Century*, ed. William Andrews (1986), 56–57.
72 *"quiet vegetable creation"*: Thomas Coke, *Journals*, 170, cited in Grainger, *Church*, 121.
72 *"the creation's state of unceasing prayer"*: Ibid., 129.
72 *"sweet meltings"*: Francis Asbury, *Journal*, I, 460, cited in ibid., 121.
72 *"the very soul of the universe"*: T. Gale, *Electricity, or Ethereal Fire, Considered* (1802), 7. Delbourgo, *Amazing Scene*, chap. 6, contains an illuminating discussion of this text.
73 *"like an electric shock"*: Robert Patterson, "Extract from a letter from Col. Robert Patterson, of Lexington, Ky., to the Rev. Dr. John King, of Chambersburgh, Penn., dated Nov. 18, 1801," *Zion's Herald* 3, no. 26 (1825), 1.
73 *"like a wave of electricity"*: Charles Grandison Finney, *Memoirs of the Rev. Charles G. Finney, Written by Himself* (1876), 20, cited in Grainger, *Church*, 179.
73 "enkindler" . . . "vital flame": "God in Christ," *Massachusetts Missionary Magazine* 4 (1806), 79.

3. TOWARD A PULSATING UNIVERSE

78 *"common sense of the entire society"*: Antonio Gramsci, *The Modern Prince and Other Writings*, trans. Louis Marks (1972), 58–75.
79 *"He preached incessantly"*: Lyman Beecher, *The Autobiography of Lyman Beecher* (1961), ed. Barbara Cross, I, 27.
80 *"the immediate continued creation"*: Jonathan Edwards, *The Works of Jonathan Edwards*, vol. 3, *Original Sin* (1972), 401.
81 *"one blood, one kindred"*: Timothy Dwight, "Greenfield Hill" (1788), cited in John R. Fitzmier, *New England's Moral Legislator: Timothy Dwight, 1752–1817* (1998), 43.
81 *"Address to Ministers of Every Denomination"*: Timothy Dwight, cited in ibid., 51.
82 *"nothing enthusiastic"*: Timothy Dwight, cited in ibid., 100.
82 *"it was impossible for him"*: Benjamin Dwight, cited in ibid., 102.
83 *"If there are certain principles"*: Terence Cuneo and Rene von Woudenberg, eds., *The Cambridge Companion to Thomas Reid* (2004), 85.
83 *"a man who thinks a horse running"*: James Beattie, cited in Fitzmier, *Dwight*, 86.
83 *"so high, and so vast"*: Timothy Dwight, cited in ibid., 117.
83 *"Hail land of Light and Joy!"*: Timothy Dwight, "America" (1780), cited in ibid., 144.
84 *"a corpulent man"*: Timothy Dwight, *Travels in New England and New York* (1818), 4 vols., I, 308.
84 *"state of nature"*: Ibid.
84 *"labor is the only source"*: Ibid., III, 17.
84 *"Mere wanderers"*: Ibid., II, 34.
85 *"people of fashion"*: Ibid., I, 370ff.
85 *"industry, regularity, and exactness"*: Ibid., II, 13.
85 *"the increase of wealth, the influx of strangers"*: Ibid., I, 240.
85 *"scattered plantations"*: Ibid., 244.
85 *"the gross amusement"*: Ibid., III, 42.
86 *"good music"*: "Music," *Yale Literary Magazine* 5 (Jan. 1840), 132.
86 *"Christian Joy"*: Wm. Jones, "Christian Joy," *New York Evangelist* 11 (March 14, 1840), 44.
86 *"the all-powerful faculties"*: "Elements of Success in Business," *Merchants' Magazine and Commercial Review* 30 (June 1, 1854), 778.
87 *"He touches no subject"*: H. J., "Goethe and His Morality," *New-York Daily Tribune*, Jan. 15, 1856, 3.
87 *"a visible or invisible intention"*: This and other quotations in this paragraph cited in Edmund Reiss, "Whitman's Debt to Animal Magnetism," *PMLA* (1963), 80–88.
88 *"Does the earth gravitate?"*: Walt Whitman, "I Am He That Aches with Love," in *Leaves of Grass* (Norton ed., 1965), eds. Harold Blodgett and Sculley Bradley, 109.
88 *"Mine is no callous shell"*: Walt Whitman, "Song of Myself," in ibid., 57.
89 *"a vast lottery"*: Alexis de Tocqueville, *Democracy in America* [1835], 2 vols., ed. and trans. Phillips Bradley (1945), II, 168.
90 *"That there is a hidden"*: Elisha North, M.D., "Desultory Outlines of Animal Life," *New England Journal of Medicine and Surgery* 15 (Jan. 1826), 2–3.
90 *"the principle of* Vitality": The Secretary, "Lecture Delivered at the Free Press As-

sociation: On the Vital Principle," *Correspondent* 3 (May 19, 1828), 247. Italics in original.

91 *"In the estimation of the Psalmist"*: John Harris, "Testimony of the Material World," *Millennial Harbinger* 4, no. 12 (1840).

92 *"human bodies were surrounded"*: Grainger, *Church*, 161.

92 *"a power in* the ends of his fingers": Catharine Beecher, cited in ibid.

93 *"nearly certain that electricity"*: Edward Hitchcock, *Religious Truth Illustrated from Science* (1857), 152.

94 *"she could hear the desert wind"*: Nathaniel Hawthorne, *The Blithedale Romance* [1842] (Oxford World's Classics ed., 2009), 202.

95 *"He spoke of a new era"*: Ibid., 200.

95 *"there is an elastic"*: "A Practical Magnetizer," *The History and Philosophy of Animal Magnetism, with Practical Instructions for the Exercise of This Power* (1843), 15.

96 "poured out and exhausted": Ibid., 17.

96 *"a very simple application"*: Cited in S. B. Brittan and B. W. Richmond, *A Discussion of the Facts and Philosophy of Ancient and Modern Spiritualism* (1853), 132.

97 *"a certain isolated, unpainted, unfinished dwelling"*: Andrew Jackson Davis, *The Magic Staff; An Autobiography* [1857], 24.

97 *"The heavy chains of poverty"*: Ibid., 25.

97 *"Sylvanus will soon leave us"*: Ibid., 35.

97 *"nothin' but worms"*: Ibid., 49.

98 *"organ of* marvellousness": Ibid., 59.

98 *"vigilant incredulity"*: Ibid., 65.

98 *"In their graves laid low"*: Ibid., 191.

98 *"A soft breathing"*: Ibid., 199.

99 *"vitalic force"*: Andrew Jackson Davis, *Arabula; or, The Divine Guest* (1867), 386.

99 *"magnetic buffoonery"*: Davis, *Magic Staff*, 201.

99 *"the mystic magnetic state"*: Ibid., 214.

100 *"I not only beheld"*: Ibid., 215.

100 *"Thus I saw not only"*: Ibid., 217.

100 *"I saw the many and various forms"*: Ibid., 219.

100 *"My ties and ballasts leave me"*: Whitman, "Song of Myself," in *Leaves of Grass*, book 3, section 33.

100 *"The various salts in the sea"*: Davis, *Magic Staff*, 220.

100–101 *"to revere, obey, and depend"*: Ibid., 233.

101 *"And—mark this fact!"*: Ibid., 221, 223.

101 *"the unknown attraction"*: Ibid., 226.

102 *"a man of ordinary stature"*: Ibid., 238–39.

102 *"a staff, far exceeding in beauty"*: Ibid., 240.

102 *"in a due season thou shalt return"*: Ibid., 245.

103 *"I soon ascertained Disease"*: Ibid., 252.

103 *"Here is thy magic staff"*: Ibid., 263.

103 *"an unconquerable repugnance"*: Ibid., 266.

103 *"flippant levity"*: Ibid., 270.

104 *"ministerial-looking stranger"*: Ibid.

104 *"that morceau of the Spirit of Nature"*: Ibid., 288–90.

104 *"magical spell"*: Ibid., 297.
104 *"physical indispositions"*: Ibid., 327.
104 *"The God of eternal destinies"*: Ibid., 328.
104 *"unpolished mechanics and ungloved merchants"*: Ibid., 440.
105 *"witty burlesque"*: Ibid., 523–27.
105 *"all speculation is wrong"*: Ibid., 352.
105 *"the things which are seen"*: Ibid., 360.
105 *"Oh, I am wholly awake!"*: Ibid., 366.
105 *"Matter and Mind have heretofore"*: Andrew Jackson Davis, *The Great Harmonia* [1850–1861], 6 vols. (1890), III, 15.
106 *"the fundamental principle of all Life"*: Ibid., IV, 280.
106 *"the relations and dependencies"*: Ibid., III, 86.
106 *"Every fiber of the wild flower"*: Ibid., 117.
106 *"broom-riding witches"*: Davis, cited in Robert Delp, "Andrew Jackson Davis: Prophet of American Spiritualism," *Journal of American History* (1967), 51.
106 *"magnetic healing"*: Ibid., 54.
107 *"The animal spirits cannot"*: "Moral," *Connecticut Spectator* 8 (June 8, 1814), 4.
107 *"holy boldness"*: "A Call to the Christian Ministry," *Religious Intelligencer* 19, no. 29 (Dec. 13, 1834), 457.
108 *"When from some inexplicable cause"*: "The 'Blue Devils,'" *Rutland Herald*, April 27, 1841, 2.
109 *animal spirits buoyed up*: "The Victory of Mrs. Gaines," *New York Times*, March 15, 1861, 4.
109 *"high principle and extraordinary force of will"*: "William Hickling Prescott," *New York Times*, Feb. 20, 1864, 4.
109 *"the clubbable man"*: "Clubbable Men," *Harper's Bazaar* 2 (Feb. 13, 1869), 98.
109 *"When the spark of life"*: "Moffat's Life Medicines," *Burlington Free Press*, Jan. 18, 1839, 3.
109 *"the strengthening, life-giving"*: "Dr. Christie's Galvanic Belt, Bracelets, Necklace and Magnetic Fluid," *Staunton Spectator*, March 19, 1851, 4.
110 *"The stomach being disordered"*: "Much Truth in a Small Compass," *Jeffersonian*, Aug. 5, 1858, 2.
110 *Hostetter's Stomach Bitters*: See, e.g., *New Orleans Daily Crescent*, March 8, 1858, 3.
110 *Tarrant's Seltzer Aperient*: See, e.g., *Memphis Daily Appeal*, July 12, 1871, 4.
110 *"imparts a much greater degree"*: "Ripe Bread," *Christian Reflector* 10 (May 13, 1847), 76.
110 *"The mind is like"*: Willis, *Somerset Herald and Farmers' and Mechanics' Register*, Oct. 12, 1847, 3.
110 *"of a nature calculated"*: Lindley Murray, "Employment Essential to Health," *Clarksville Chronicle*, March 9, 1860, 1.
110 *"A cold, sluggish blood"*: Ralph Waldo Emerson, *Society and Solitude: Twelve Chapters* (1870), 11.
111 *"something invisible"*: Johan Huizinga, *Homo Ludens: A Study of the Play-Element in Culture* (Beacon Press, ed. 1955), 14.
111 *"I am too old"*: Horace Smith, "The Wisdom of Laughter," *Evergreen* 1 (Jan. 1, 1840), 24.

4. FEVERISH FINANCE, REVIVAL RELIGION, AND WAR

113 *"a houseful, a hole full"*: Frederick Jackson, cited in Ann Fabian, "Speculation on Distress: The Popular Discourse of the Panics of 1837 and 1857," *Yale Journal of Criticism* (1989), 135.

114 *"keep his system"*: "Confidential," *New Mirror* 1 (July 22, 1843), 256.

114 *"Adventures of a Bank Note"*: Cited in Jose R. Torre, *The Political Economy of Sentiment* (2007), 59.

115 *"destroying that confidence"*: James Madison, cited in Andrew H. Browning, *The Panic of 1819: The First Great Depression* (2019), 128.

117 *"The* Alabama Feaver": James Graham, cited in ibid., 103.

117 *"I have been trying"*: James Henry Hammond, cited in ibid., 104.

117 *the "fevers" of migration and land investment*: John Quincy Adams, cited in ibid., 187.

117 *"presents a dull and uncheery spectacle"*: Boston *Patriot*, cited in ibid., 189.

118 *"keen sharp features"*: Andrew Combe, *The Principles of Physiology Applied to the Preservation of Health, and to the Improvement of Physical and Mental Education* (1834), 163.

118 *"that mysterious invisible energy"*: Jessica Lepler, *The Many Panics of 1837: People, Politics, and the Creation of a Transatlantic Financial Crisis* (2013), 9.

118 *"titanic and unnatural power"*: Andrew Jackson, cited in ibid., 19.

118–119 *"confidence performed"*: Ibid., 28.

119 *"a very considerable advance"*: Asa Greene, *The Perils of Pearl Street, Including a Taste of the Dangers of Wall Street* (1834), 162–63.

119 *"sudden changes of fortune"*: Andrew Combe, cited in Lepler, *Many Panics*, 81.

119 *"speculators went to bed"*: Alastair Roberts, *America's First Great Depression: Economic Crisis and Political Disorder After the Panic of 1837* (2012), 33.

120 *"infused a species of confidence" . . . "people losing their senses"*: New York *Herald*, cited in Lepler, *Many Panics*, 64.

120 *"The care-clouded countenance"*: Jason Whitman, *The Hard Times: A Discourse Delivered to the Second Unitarian Church, and also to the First Parish Church, Portland, Maine, January 1, 1837*, cited in ibid., 71.

121 *"everybody is afraid"*: Condy Raguet, cited in Roberts, *America's First Great Depression*, 85.

121 *"In one word, excitement"*: "Correspondence of the Courier and Enquirer, New Orleans, 26 April, 1837," *National Intelligencer*, April 27, 1837, cited in Lepler, *Many Panics*, 3.

121 *"general wreck"*: Joseph Shipley, cited in ibid., 205.

121 *"credit, a mere* creature": Rev. Andrew Preston Peabody, cited in ibid., 148.

122 *"Increase not a general panic by unreal terrors"*: Ibid., 147.

122 *"Andrews is a very timid man"*: Testimony of Joseph Wood, in *Andrews vs. His Creditors*, 11 Louisana 464 (1838), cited in ibid., 127.

122 *"load of disappointment and remorse"*: *Gravillon vs. Richard's Executor, et al.*, 13 Louisiana 293 (1839), cited in ibid., 139.

122 *"a mire of debt and fear"*: Ibid., 140.

122 *"The merchants are the most excitable class"*: Diary of Philip Hone, May 11, 1837, cited in ibid., 209.

122 *"It is a dangerous time"*: Diary of Philip Hone, May 6, 1837, cited in ibid., 188.

122 *class blinders*: Ibid., 197.

123 *"a much more tranquil feeling"*: "Money Market and City Intelligence," *Times* (London), June 7, 1837.
123 *"from the summit of hope to the lowest abyss"*: James Kirke Paulding, cited in Mentor Williams, "A Tour of Illinois in 1842," *Journal of the Illinois State Historical Society* (1949), 292–312.
123 *"The Capitalist is the most easily frightened"*: Sidney George Fisher, "The Diaries of Sidney George Fisher," *Pennsylvania Magazine of History and Biography* (1952), 215.
123 *"speculation itself"*: Orville Dewey, "The Moral Ends of Business," in *Works of Orville Dewey*, 196–97, cited in Stewart Davenport, *Friends of the Unrighteous Mammon: Northern Christians and Market Capitalism, 1815–1860* (2008), 199.
124 *"must necessarily regard everyone around him with a jealous eye"*: Henry Boardman, *The Bible in the Counting House: A Course of Lectures to Merchants* (1853), 138–39.
124 *"bold and restless spirits"*: *American Review* (1845), cited in Roberts, *America's First Great Depression*, 189.
124 *"springs from directly opposite"*: "The Present Crisis," New York *Herald*, Aug. 25, 1845, 2.
125 *"The world has become stale"*: Reprinted as "Let Us Go to War," *Portland Daily Advertiser*, May 27, 1845, 2.
125 *"people here are all in a state of delirium"*: Herman Melville, quoted in Hershel Parker, *Herman Melville: A Biography, 1819–1851* (1996), 421.
126 *"Are we not also"*: Caleb Cushing, quoted in "General Caleb Cushing," *Anti-Slavery Bugle*, Nov. 12, 1847, 1.
126 *Wright's Indian Vegetable Pills*: "Relief Notes," *Tarboro Press*, Feb. 19, 1848, 2.
126 *"Now, every human being"*: S. O. Gleason, "Who Kills Us?," *Water-Cure Journal* 10 (Dec. 1850), 223.
127 *"Labor is the yeast"*: Karl Marx, cited in Dipesh Chakrabarty, *Provincializing Europe: Postcolonial Thought and Historical Difference* (2000), 60.
127 *"It is precisely the genius"*: David Harvey, *The Enigma of Capital* (2010), 160.
128 *"the effect of his labor"*: "Brain and Muscle Market: Journeymen Shoemakers," *New York Times*, Sept. 18, 1857, 3.
128 *"All active occupations"*: "Brain and Muscle Market: Tailors and Tailoresses," *New York Times*, Sept. 9, 1857, 2.
128 *"is a constant drain"*: "Brain and Muscle Market: Journeymen Shoemakers," *New York Times*, Sept. 18, 1857, 3.
129 *"In the inordinate hope"*: Kit Kelvin, "Mania: Its Progress," *Knickerbocker* 34 (July 1849), 22.
129 *"Mania's haggard face"*: Ibid., 24.
129 *"bird of passage"*: Ibid., 25.
130 *"There are many new trades"*: Edward Jarvis, "Causes of Insanity," *Boston Medical and Surgical Journal* 45, no. 15 (Nov. 12, 1851), 304.
130 *"We exhaust our energies"*: "Are We a Happy People?," *Harper's New Monthly* 14 (Jan. 1857), 208.
131 *"men, especially in banking circles"*: James L. Huston, *The Panic of 1857 and the Coming of the Civil War* (1987), 19–20.
131 "without either real or apparent cause": Napoleon III, cited in "Foreign Intelligence," *Reynolds's Newspaper* (London), Nov. 15, 1857. Italics in original.

131 *"The remedy for this crisis must be psychological"*: Allan Nevins and Milton Harvey Thomas, eds., *The Diary of George Templeton Strong* (1952), II, 359.

131 *"Truly it may be said"*: Fernando Wood, quoted in *New York Times*, Oct. 23, 1857.

132 *"ravenous intensity"*: *Harper's Monthly* 16 (Dec. 1858), 694.

132 *"fast living"*: Cleveland *Plain Dealer*, Oct. 24, 1857.

132 *"these vampyres"*: *Mississippi Free Trader*, cited in Huston, *Panic*, 39.

132 *"poverty is a crime"*: Louis Wigfall in *Southern Planter* (1859), cited in Huston, *Panic*, 89.

132 *"trembles and staggers"*: Henry Ward Beecher, *A Discourse on the Present Fearful Commercial Pressure* (1857), 4–7. Italics in original.

133 *"The Evangel of Christ"*: Gilbert Haven, *National Sermons* (1869), 144.

133 *"[Wednesday] prayer meeting"*: Samuel Prime, *The Power of Prayer Illustrated in the Wonderful Displays of Divine Grace at the Fulton Street and Other Meetings in New York and Elsewhere, in 1857 and 1858* (1859), 7–8.

134 *"by the ploughshare of his judgments"*: James Waddell Alexander, *The Revival and Its Lessons* (1858), 6.

134 *"still, solemn, and tender"*: James Waddell Alexander, *Letters II* (1860), 275–277, cited in Timothy L. Smith, *Revivalism and Social Reform* (2004), 69.

134 *"What Shall I Do to Be Saved?"*: *Christian Register*, April 3, 1858, cited in Smith, ibid., 71.

135 *"'ecstatic enjoyment'"*: Phoebe Palmer, cited in Smith, ibid., 158.

135 *"Ten days have passed"*: "Life in the Camp: No. XXX," *Fayetteville Observer*, May 2, 1861, 2.

135 *"the men were in the highest"*: "Our Citizen Military: Departure of the Firemen Zouaves," *New York Times*, April 30, 1861, 1.

135 *"The Red, White, and Blue"*: Ibid., 8.

136 *"Most Yankees"*: William Freehling, *The Road to Disunion*, vol. 2, *Secessionists Triumphant, 1854–1861* (2007), xii–xiii.

136 *"only marginally related to race"*: Eric Foner, *The Fiery Trial: Abraham Lincoln and American Slavery* (2007), 120.

137 *"yankee marauders"*: Edward Ayers, *In the Presence of Mine Enemies* (2003), 390.

137 *"What are you fighting for anyhow?"*: Union soldiers, cited in Shelby Foote, *The Civil War: A Narrative*, vol. 1, *Fort Sumter to Perryville* (1958), 65.

137 *"Thirty Thousand"*: *Memorial of Thirty Thousand Disfranchised Citizens of Philadelphia to the Honorable Senate and House of Representatives* (1855), 13.

137 *"the negroes of the South"*: "By One Who Has Seen It," "The Southern Rebellion," *Burlington Free Press*, May 9, 1862, 1.

138 *"are said to have a fine"*: "By a well-known Medical Author in the Phrenological Journal," "Sudden Death: An Interesting Treatise on Apoplexy," *Wheeling Daily Intelligencer*, Aug. 24, 1869, 3.

139 *"mesmeric healer, who had assumed"*: "Mrs. Eddy Descended from Puritan Stock," *New-York Tribune*, Dec. 5, 1910, 2.

139 *"His theory is"*: "A New Doctrine of Health and Disease," *Bangor Jeffersonian* (1857), quoted in Annetta Dresser, *The Philosophy of P. P. Quimby* (1895), 22–25.

140 *"As indicating a force"*: "Is Vitality Vital?," *Scientific American* 30 (Feb. 7, 1874), 80.

5. THE RECONFIGURATION OF VALUE

141 *Thus were the ideas of Providence*: I am indebted to Jessica Riskin's lucid discussion of these issues in *The Restless Clock.*

144 *"a gradual and sure revival"*: "Physical Amusement and Culture," *Evening Telegraph*, July 28, 1868, 2.

144 *"from theological barns"*: Ibid., 2.

144 *"American ladies"*: Ibid., 2.

145 *"The American people"*: "Address of Prof. W. T. Thurmond," *Troy Herald*, Oct. 9, 1873, 1.

145 *"The animal spirits"*: Ibid., 1.

145 *"Fun, mirth, real animal spirits"*: Henry Barton Baker, "Theodore Hook," *Frank Leslie's Popular Monthly* 5 (May 1878), 610. Italics in original.

146 *"The dependence of health"*: Charles Eliot Norton, "Harvard University in 1890," *Harper's Monthly* 31 (Sept. 1890), 586.

146 *"the pleasures of animal existence"*: Charles W. Eliot, "The Happy Life," *Independent* 47 (Dec. 19, 1895), 5.

146 *"It is a happy thing"*: Charles W. Eliot, "The Durable Satisfactions of Life," an address to new students at Harvard, Oct. 3, 1905, *McClure's Magazine* 26 (Jan. 1906), 339.

146 *"students work off their excess"*: Henry Wade Rogers, "Athletics as a Factor in College Education," *Belford's Monthly* 11 (June 1893), 22.

147 *"cure our American nervousness"*: "Ethics of the Wheel," *San Francisco Call*, June 22, 1896, 11.

147 *"neurasthenia"*: George Miller Beard, *A Practical Treatise on Nervous Exhaustion (Neurasthenia): Its Symptoms, Nature, Sequences, Treatment* (1880).

147 *"a desirable step"*: "Ethics of the Wheel," 11.

147 *"The ordinary youth"*: Ernest Hamlin Abbott, "Christian Pagans," *Outlook* 81 (Dec. 16, 1905), 919.

147 *"a new interpretation"*: Ibid., 911.

148 *"there is no fundamental difference"*: Charles Darwin, *The Descent of Man* [1871] (reprint, 1981), 34–35.

148 *"Ironically, by becoming animals"*: Harriet Ritvo, *The Animal Estate: The English and Other Creatures in the Victorian Age* (1987), 40.

149 *"Descartes said"*: T. H. Huxley, "Are Animals Automatons?," *Popular Science Monthly* 5 (Oct. 1, 1874), 726.

149 *"though they feel as we do"*: T. H. Huxley, "On the Hypothesis That Animals Are Automata, and Its History," *Eclectic Magazine* (1875), 61.

149 *"our mental conditions"*: Ibid., 63.

150 *"the brutes"*: Ibid., 61.

150 *"never use the words"*: Charles Darwin (c. 1845), note written on the margin of his copy of Robert Chambers's 1844 *Vestiges of The Natural History of Creation*, www.eoht.info/page/Darwin%20on%20higher%20and%20lower. Italics in original.

150 *"one can hardly avoid"*: Charles Darwin, "Appendix," in George John Romanes, *Mental Evolution in Animals* (1883), 379.

150 *"the grossest utilitarianism"*: Ibid., 383.

150 *"for satisfaction is an attribute"*: George Cary, "The Mental Faculties of Brutes," *North American Review* 108 (Jan. 1869), 41.

151 *"The pride and beauty"*: Philip Gilbert Hamerton, *Chapters on Animals* (1877), 2.

151 *"The brute creation"*: Ibid., 2–3.

151 *"The gladness that we seek"*: Ibid., 3.

151 *"none of us"*: Ibid., 11.

151 *"This impossibility of knowing"*: Ibid., 12.

152 *"Do the lower animals"*: "Animal Intelligence," *Westminster Review* 57 (April 1880), 449.

152 *"no grander sight in nature"*: Paul Du Chaillu, quoted in "A Sign of the Times," *Salt Lake Herald*, Feb. 25, 1883, 12.

152 *"throughout the animal world"*: "Animal Spirits," *Wichita Daily Eagle*, May 8, 1887, 9.

152 *"Keep the doctor"*: Olive Thorne Miller, *Our Home Pets: How to Keep Them Well and Happy* (1894), 196.

153 *"The more exact"*: E. P. Evans, *Evolutional Ethics and Animal Psychology* (1898), 167.

153 *"If we could trace"*: Ibid., 167–68.

153 *"that loses nothing"*: Ibid., 168.

154 *"I think I could turn and live awhile"*: Whitman, "Song of Myself," in *Leaves of Grass*, 60.

154 *"a splendid thing"*: William J. Long, *School of the Woods: Some Life Studies of Animal Instincts and Animal Training* (1902), 314.

155 *"I had never yet met"*: Ibid., 316.

155 *"never a one"*: Ibid., 317.

155 *"the animal has no great mentality"*: Ibid., 329.

155 *"they do, in fact, share"*: C. J. Cornish, *Animals at Work and Play: Their Activities and Emotions* (1904), 85–86.

156 *"the simple gladness"*: William J. Long, "The Question of Animal Reason," *Harper's Monthly*, Sept. 1905, 588.

156 *"If the subconscious self"*: Ibid., 588.

156–57 *"With the animal's instinct"*: Ibid., 593.

158 *"It is an arbitrary line"*: Henry Jacob Bigelow, *Surgical Anaesthesia: Addresses and Other Papers* (1900), 374.

158 *"If the harmony or concord"*: E. P. Evans, "The Aesthetic Sense and Religious Sentiment in Animals," *Popular Science Monthly* 42 (Feb. 1893), 475.

158 *"The terror of the dog"*: Ibid., 478.

160 *"The adherents of both"*: "Chicago! The Great Convention," *Evening Star*, June 5, 1880, 9.

160 *"new virtual world"*: Richard White, *Railroaded: The Transcontinentals and the Making of Modern America* (2011), 68.

161 *"from nowhere to nowhere"*: Cornelius Vanderbilt, cited in M. John Lubetkin, *Jay Cooke's Gamble: The Northern Pacific Railroad, the Sioux, and the Panic of 1873* (2006), 287.

162 *"Gradually fevered blood commenced"*: A journalist, *History of the Terrible Panic of 1873* (1873), 5.

163 *"Thus, while men rushed wildly"*: Ibid., 14.

164 *"life itself is* essentially *appropriation"*: Friedrich Nietzsche, *Beyond Good and Evil*, cited and translated in Frederick Amrine, "'The Triumph of Life': Nietzsche's

Verbicide," in Burwick and Douglass, *The Crisis in Modernism*, 146. For a brilliant overview of Nietzsche's importance in late nineteenth- and earlier twentieth-century American culture, see Jennifer Ratner-Rosenhagen, *American Nietzsche: A History of an Icon and His Ideas* (2011).

164 *"wonderful wit"*: "Good Natured Scoundrels," *Burlington Free Press*, Dec. 22, 1871, 2.

165 *"why in the name of God' "*: "That Awful State Department," *Stark County Democrat*, July 24, 1879, 4.

166 *"emotional soul baring"*: Debby Applegate, *The Most Famous Man in America: The Biography of Henry Ward Beecher*, 212.

166 *"mental* dishabille": Thomas Knox, *Life and Work of Henry Ward Beecher* (1887), cited in ibid. Italics in original.

166 *"such* manliness": Undated clipping in Beecher Family Papers, Yale University, cited in ibid. Italics in original.

166 *"The slightest pathos"*: Ibid.

166 *"boils with earnestness" and "bubbles with playfulness"*: Henry Bellows to Eliza T. Bellows, Oct. 10, 1855, Bellows Papers, Massachusetts Historical Society, cited in ibid., 212–13.

166 *"The Unitarians like him"*: Susan Howe, in John Raymond Howard, *Remembrance of Things Past* (1925), cited in ibid., 215.

167 *"the* doing *of good"*: Brooklyn *Eagle*, Aug. 22, 1848, cited in ibid., 217.

167 *"man was made for enjoyment"*: Brooklyn *Eagle*, Dec. 27, 1848, cited in ibid.

167 *"The public began to take"*: Eunice Beecher, quoted in *Ladies' Home Journal* (1891), cited in ibid., 217.

167 *"It is perfect"*: Henry Ward Beecher, *Yale Lectures on Preaching* (1872), I, 73–74.

167 *"Mary Hallock, sit still!"*: Mary Hallock Foote, *A Victorian Gentlewoman in the Far West* (1972), cited in Applegate, *Beecher*, 366.

168 *"men who are self-trusting"*: Ralph Waldo Emerson, cited by Rutherford B. Hayes, *Diary and Letters*, I, 301–3, cited in ibid.

168 *"The greatest part of a seed"*: Henry Ward Beecher, "The Life of Christ:—Within," preached Oct. 8, 1865, in *Sermons*, vol. 1 (1869), 141.

169 *"this vitality of a Christian soul"*: Henry Ward Beecher, "Sermon: The Life Force in Men," *Christian Union* 15 (April 4, 1877), 305.

169 *"It is said that a dollar a day"*: Henry Ward Beecher, cited in Henry May, *Protestant Churches and Industrial America* (1949), 94.

169 *"In a word, Charlie"*: Herman Melville, *The Confidence Man* [1857] (Signet Classics ed., 1964), 174.

170 *"Conviviality is one good thing"*: Ibid., 184.

170 *"By the way, talking of geniality"*: Ibid.

170 *"'like a humbug'"*: Joseph Twichell's Journal, Feb. 23, 1876, cited in Applegate, *Beecher*, 453.

171 *"perfectly transparent"*: Elizabeth Tilton to Theodore Tilton, Dec. 1866, cited in Applegate, *Beecher*, 366–67.

172 *"I found him"*: Moses Coit Tyler, *Moses Coit Tyler, 1835–1900: Selections from His Letters and Diaries*, ed. Jessica Tyler Austen (1911), 77.

172 *"I had seldom seen"*: Ibid., 78.

172 *Rev. Leonard Bacon denounced Theodore Tilton*: Hugh Davis, *Leonard Bacon: New England Reformer and Antislavery Moderate* (1998), 235.

172 *"Mr. Beecher, so say his friends"*: "Editorial Article," *New York Times*, Aug. 25, 1874, 4.
172 *"the torments of the damned"*: Henry Ward Beecher, cited in "The Psychology of Beecher's Case," *Wheeling Daily Intelligencer*, Dec. 5, 1874, 1.
173 *"We respected her"*: Frank Moulton in *Chicago Tribune*, Aug. 23, 1874, cited in Applegate, *Beecher*, 445.
173 *"great animal spirits"*: "The Beecher-Tilton Trial," *New-York Tribune*, March 8, 1875, 2.
173 *"That an excess of animal spirits"*: "Tilton Against Beecher," *Nation* 21 (July 8, 1875), 23.
173 *"psychological phenomena"*: Nevins and Thomas, *The Diary of George Templeton Strong*, IV, 422.
174 *"Nothing seems to be able"*: "Beecher," *Iola Register* 9 (Nov. 27, 1875), 1.

6. THE APOTHEOSIS OF ENERGY

176 *"the dynamo became a symbol"*: Henry Adams, *The Education of Henry Adams*, in *Henry Adams: Novels, Mont Saint Michel, The Education* (1983), 1067.
176 *"the child of incalculable"*: Ibid., 1174.
176 *"As he grew accustomed"*: Ibid., 1067.
177 *"the automatic genius"*: "The Savior of Florida," *Washington Times*, May 30, 1895, 4.
177 *"He is composed"*: Ibid., 4.
177–78 *"a new efflorescence"*: Henry Tyrrell, "Edison," *Frank Leslie's Popular Monthly* 39 (March 1895), 2.
178 *"As a perambulating"*: Ibid., 6.
178 *"sparks of sanity"*: Ibid., 11.
178 *"It is energy of will"*: "Energy of Will," *Vermont Watchman and State Journal*, Sept. 27, 1871, 1.
179 *"What looks like self-conceit"*: "Self-Praise," *Staunton Spectator*, Jan. 29, 1884, 1.
179 *"the first was high animal spirits"*: "The Bar as a Profession I," *Saturday Review*, Feb. 9, 1889, 159.
180 *"the sustaining of a thought"*: William James Diary I, April 30, 1870, quoted in Robert D. Richardson, *William James in the Maelstrom of American Modernism* (2006), 120.
180 *"The Right to Believe"*: William James, *The Correspondence of William James*, ed. Ignas K. Skrupskelis and Elizabeth M. Berkeley, 12 vols. (1992–2004; electronic ed., 2008), 10:449.
181 *"matter and mind were interdependent"*: Beryl Satter, *Each Mind a Kingdom: American Women, Sexual Purity, and the New Thought Movement, 1875–1920* (1999), 254.
182 *"To succeed in any undertaking"*: Prentice Mulford, *Thoughts Are Things* [1889] (reprint, 1908), 97.
182 *"thought structure"*: Ibid., 108.
182 *"In time to come"*: Prentice Mulford, *Your Forces and How to Use Them* (1904), IV, 182.
183 *"by the very force"*: Ralph Waldo Trine, *In Tune with the Infinite* (1897), 154.
183 *"take the attitude of mind"*: Ibid., 180. Italics in original.
183 *"Never give a moment"*: Ibid., 181.
183 *"is just so much"*: Ibid., 184.
183 *"desire, matter, and the animal will"*: Satter, *Kingdom*, 152.

183 *"And oh! a wonderful thing"*: Helen Wilmans, *A Search for Freedom* (1898), 9.
184 *"When an 'I' shall stand"*: Ibid., 202.
184 *"complete control"*: Ibid., 28.
184 *"There was always the pressure"*: Ibid., 32.
184 *"The aptest word"*: Ibid., 88.
185 *"Mother was decidedly"*: Ibid., 147.
185 *"Mother soon manifested"*: Ibid., 89.
185 *"I did not fully comprehend"*: Ibid., 142.
185 *"damn the devil"*: Ibid., 41.
185 *"sheer force of animal will"*: Ibid., 206.
186 *"I felt sure I had something"*: Ibid., 210.
186 *"intentness of purpose"*: Ibid., 35ff.
186 *"I did not know"*: Ibid., 44.
186 *"The very moment"*: Ibid., 285.
187 *"but there was an undercurrent"*: Ibid., 236.
187 *"Upon being put to bed"*: Ibid., 92.
187 *"a machine for photographing thought"*: Ibid., 97.
187 *Louis Darget*: www.bbc.com/future/article/20170116-the-man-who-tried-to-photograph-thoughts-and-dreams.
188 *"there is no real happiness"*: Wilmans, *Search for Freedom*, 183.
188 *"the ordinary animal marriage"*: Ibid.
188 *"soul [was] ground into the dust daily"*: Ibid., 293.
188 *"a veritable product of earth"*: Ibid., 347.
188 *In 1877*: Satter, *Kingdom*, 154–62, provides a detailed account of Wilmans's marriage and early career in journalism, which Wilmans glides over in her autobiography in the interest of creating a forward-thrusting narrative of self-development.
189 *"The slaves of capital"*: Helen Wilmans, *The Conquest of Poverty* (1899), 39.
189 *"were dead to any sense of power"*: Ibid., 42.
189 *"On the road to progress"*: Ibid., 46.
189 *"declaration of individuality"*: Ibid., 50.
189 *"universal reaching out for money"*: Ibid., 85.
190 *"The supply of money"*: Ibid., 106.
190 *"these positive thought currents"*: Ibid., 111.
190 *"The man who mentally"*: Ibid., 123.
190 *"Fear is the only thing"*: Ibid., 65.
190 *"Every thought a man can have"*: Ibid., 82.
191 *"thought is an actual substance"*: Ibid., 112.
191 *"all substance is, fundamentally"*: Ibid., 114.
191 *"correlation of forces"*: Ibid., 50.
191 *"thought was a force"*: Ibid., 56.
191 *"disease is simply"*: Ibid., 126.
191 *"for hope and faith do project"*: Ibid., 151.
192 *"I am not sick"*: Wilmans quoted by Elizabeth, "Editorials: 'Vale et Ave,'" *Nautilus* 10 (Nov. 1907), 11.
193 *"It is one thing"*: G. Stanley Hall, "Boys Who Should Not Go to College," *Youth's Companion*, March 15, 1894, 119.
193 *"The pure animal spirits"*: "Theodosia Burr," *Harper's Monthly* 29 (Aug. 1864), 297.

193 *"from sheer excess"*: "Wild Girls," *Memphis Daily Appeal*, Aug. 23, 1868, 1.
193 *"precocious girls"*: "Precocious Girls," *Youth's Companion* (July 19, 1883), 294.
194 *"There are nations"*: "Animal Spirits," *St. Johnsbury Caledonian*, April 16, 1885, 2.
194 *"quick, springy"*: "New Feminine Style in Gait," *Evening Star*, Nov. 3, 1885, 6.
194 *"The metropolitan girl"*: "An Artistic Conclusion," *Salt Lake Herald*, Feb. 28, 1886, 11.
194 *"Give the girls exercises"*: "In Woman's Behalf," *Maryville Times*, June 3, 1891, 7.
194 *"She never calculates"*: "Keyed to Happiness," *Arizona Republican*, Aug. 23, 1892, 4.
194 *"They are brown"*: "Woman's Beauty," *Evening Star*, May 4, 1895, 16.
194 *"overflowing with animal spirits"*: Katherine Morton, "The Quest of Beauty," *Evening Star*, July 12, 1902, 20.
195 *"The athletic summer girl"*: "The Athletic Summer Girl and What She Wears," *Minneapolis Journal*, August 2, 1902, 17.
195 *"as pretty a collection of girls"*: "The Cowgirl," *Palestine* (Texas) *Daily Herald*, November 18, 1908, 3.
195 *"aggressive, fun-loving pluck"*: Samuel Osgood, "Boys, Read This," *Highland Weekly News*, Jan. 30, 1868, 1.
196 *"In the first place"*: "The Ideal Boy," *Vermont Phoenix*, Oct. 2, 1891, 2.
196 *"Without any hesitancy"*: "A Boy's Surplus Energy," *Wichita Daily Eagle*, Feb. 6, 1898, 11.
196 *"In short, in life"*: Theodore Roosevelt, "What We Can Expect of the American Boy," *St. Nicholas* 27 (May 1900), 583.
197 *"the floor might have passed"*: An unidentified observer, cited in Jack White, *The Edge of Anarchy: The Railroad Barons, the Gilded Age, and the Greatest Labor Uprising in America* (2018), 13.
197 *"a strange and curious magnetism"*: "Bryan in the Field: Scenes of Crazy Enthusiasm," *Washington Post*, July 10, 1896, 1.
197 *"A Wild, Raging"*: "The Silver Fanatics Are Invincible," *New York Times*, July 7, 1896, 1.
198 *"Virile, strong, healthy"*: "Wonderful Californians," *Wichita Daily Eagle*, Oct. 5, 1892, 3.
199 *"Do these savage views"*: Edward B. Tylor, "The Philosophy of Religion Among the Lower Races of Mankind," *Journal of the Ethnological Society of London* 2 (1870), 379.
199 *"the difference between"*: Ibid., 371.
199 *"who scarcely distinguishes"*: Ibid., 372.
199 *"has its roots in"*: Theodore Achelis, "Animal Worship from the Standpoint of Ethnic Psychology," *Open Court* 11 (Dec. 1897), 716.
200 *"The two criminals"*: "Six Traps Sprung," *Memphis Daily Appeal*, June 22, 1878, 1.
200 *"every face wore a look"*: Fannie B. Ward, "In Yucatan," *Sacramento Record-Union*, May 19, 1888, 2.
201 *"was a wild beast caged"*: "Dies with a Devisive [*sic*] Laugh," *Daily Telegraph*, April 19, 1886, 1.
202 *"He is a negro"*: "Local News: Tom," *Evening Star*, Dec. 12, 1860, 3.
202 *"no boisterous fun"*: "Men in Better Spirits," *Sun*, Aug. 26, 1898, 2.
202 *"negro regiments"*: "Rough Riders at Play," *Sun*, Aug. 28, 1898, 2.
202 *"The young negro"*: "The Negro Soldier," *Kinsley Graphic*, Oct. 13, 1899, 7.
203 *"When the Indian goes"*: "The Indian Religious Outbreak," *Pittsburg Dispatch*, Nov. 23, 1890, 4.

203 *"to undergo the tortures"*: "Mooney to Report on Sun Dance Incident," *Washington Times*, Aug. 6, 1903, 3.

204 *"The average church-going"*: William James, "A Strong Note of Warning Regarding the Lynching Epidemic," *Springfield Republican*, July 23, 1903, 11.

204 *"the water-tight compartment"*: Ibid., 11.

204 *"moral equivalent of war"*: William James, "The Moral Equivalent of War" [1910], in *William James, Writings 1902–1910* (1987), 1281–93.

7. ANOTHER CIVILIZATION

206 *"The fiddles are tuning up"*: John Butler Yeats, cited in John Lukacs, *A New Republic: A History of the United States in the 20th Century* (2004), 23n.

206 *"The present age is a critical one"*: George Santayana, "The Intellectual Temper of the Age," in his *Winds of Doctrine* (1913), 1.

207 *"For fifty years"*: Charles Moore, "The Return of the Gods," *Dial* 53 (Nov. 16, 1912), 371.

207 *"blooming, buzzing confusion"*: William James, *Psychology: Briefer Course* in *William James; Writings 1878–1899* (1992), 24.

208 *"Certainty is the root"*: Benjamin Paul Blood, quoted in William James, "A Pluralistic Mystic," *Hibbert Journal* 8 (July 1910), 758.

208 *"the lyrical left"*: This useful phrase was introduced by John Patrick Diggins in *The American Left in the Twentieth Century* (1973).

208 *"the subjective necessity of social settlements"*: Jane Addams, title of essay in *Twenty Years at Hull House* (1910).

209 *"Empty 'being' but not full and green 'life'"*: Friedrich Nietzsche, cited and translated in Amrine, "'The Triumph of Life,'" 135.

209 *"One only acts perfectly when one acts instinctively"*: Friedrich Nietzsche, *The Will to Power, Books I and II* [1914] (Project Gutenberg, 2016), 364.

210 *"In the sex relation"*: George Bernard Shaw, *Man and Superman* (1903), act 3.

210 *"Why are you trying to fascinate me"*: Ibid., act 4.

211 *"to explain some"*: John Haldane, "Vitalism," *Eclectic Magazine* 68 (Oct. 1898), 509.

212 *"whatever is the result"*: Wilhelm Ostwald, quoted in John Grier Hibben, "The Theory of Energetics and Its Philosophical Bearings," *Open Court* 13 (April 1903), 2.

212 *"said that science"*: "Old Argument Still Valid," *Independent* 55 (May 7, 1903), 1109.

213 *"Man is ceasing"*: D. B. Potter, "The Life Force," *Health* 61 (Dec. 1911), 267.

213 *"We need to recognize"*: William E. Ritter, "The Controversy Between Materialism and Vitalism: Can It Be Ended?," *Science* 33 (March 21, 1911), 439.

213 *"the sophisticated thinker"*: Ibid., 440.

214 *"how futile is"*: Ibid., 441.

214 *"There is something"*: John Burroughs, "The Problem of Living Things," *Independent* 76 (Oct. 2, 1913), 21.

214 *"The world of complex"*: Ibid., 22.

214 *"In all ages"*: Herbert Quick, "'On Board the Good Ship Earth': The Only Thing Worth Worshiping—Force," *Tacoma Times*, Jan. 23, 1913, 8.

215 *Bergson was the consummate*: My discussion of Bergson is indebted to Thomas Quirk's pathbreaking "Bergson in America," *Prospects* (1986), 453–80, especially his account and examples of Bergson's aphoristic style.

215 *"Real duration"*: Henri Bergson, *Creative Evolution*, trans. Arthur Mitchell (1911), 46.

215 *"idea of regulating life"*: Henri Bergson, *Laughter: An Essay on the Meaning of the Comic*, trans. Cloudesly Brereton and Fred Rothwell (2008), 29.
215 *"The role of life"*: Bergson, *Creative Evolution*, 126. Italics Bergson's.
215 "There are things that intelligence": Ibid., 151. Italics Bergson's.
216 "The intellect is characterized": Ibid., 165. Italics Bergson's.
216 *"You must take things"*: Ibid., 193.
216 *"transcends finality"*: Ibid., 265.
216 *"I believe electricity"*: "Ophelia," *McCook Weekly Tribune*, July 3, 1884, 6.
217 *"the animal spirits of Galen"*: "Animal Spirits—Nervous Impulses," *Journal of the American Medical Association* 62 (Feb. 14, 1914), 542.
217 *"The human body"*: John Francis Byrnes, "The Secret of Success Is Nervous Energy," *Los Angeles Herald*, March 11, 1906, 10.
217 *"Look around you"*: William Walker Atkinson, *Thought-Force in Business and Everyday Life* (1901), 13.
217 *"nothing is a happier"*: "The Sense of Humor," *Crittenden Press*, April 24, 1902, 3.
218 *"The sick look"*: George F. Shears, "Making a Choice of a Profession. IV. Medicine," *Cosmopolitan* 34 (April 1903), 655.
218 *"A single successful effort"*: William James, "The Energies of Men," *Philosophical Review* 16 (Jan. 1907), 9.
218 *"The need of feeling responsible"*: William James, "The Gospel of Relaxation," in *Talks to Teachers and Students* (1900), 227.
219 *"a right royal rough housing"*: Frank Waugh, "Rough-Housing," *Independent* 72 (Jan. 25, 1912), 183.
219 *"The whole essence"*: Ibid., 184.
219 *"should have a bright, cheerful"*: M. M. K., "The Ideal Lady Typewriter," *Stenographer* 9 (March 1896), 84.
219 *"Law stenographers"*: Caroline A. Huling, *Letters of a Business Woman to Her Niece* (1906), 96.
219 *"Remember that you"*: Ibid., 97.
219 *"The sensible girl"*: Ibid., 102–3.
220 *"Your face is constantly clouded"*: Quoted in William Thomas McElroy, "The Value of Cheerfulness," *New York Observer and Chronicle* 89 (Nov. 9, 1911), 589.
220 *"I became accustomed"*: "A Business Woman," "How Love Passed Me By: The Confessions of a Business Woman," *Harper's Bazaar* 46 (June 1912), 277.
220 *"I allowed myself"*: Ibid.
220 *"Of vital force"*: John James Ingalls, "The Extinction of Leisure," *Forum*, Aug. 1889, 685.
220 *"the great American idol"*: "An American Idol," *Pittsburg Dispatch*, March 21, 1891, 10.
221 *"the typical American"*: H. D. Sedgwick, Jr., "Certain Aspects of America," *Atlantic Monthly* 90 (July 1908), 7.
221 *"This neglect betrays"*: Ibid., 8.
221 *"either to make up"*: Ibid.
221 *"In nature, of course"*: C. G. Jung, *Jung Contra Freud: The 1912 New York Lectures on the Theory of Psychoanalysis* [1961] (reprint, 2012), 47.
221 *"is not only not concrete"*: Ibid., 48.
222 *"almost entirely on his business"*: Jung, quoted in "'America Facing Its Most Tragic Moment'—Dr. Carl Jung," *New York Times*, Sept. 29, 1912, SM2.

222 *"It takes much"*: Ibid.
222 *holds you [Americans] together*: Ibid.
222 *"cautioned his hearers"*: "How to Train the Young," *Kansas City Journal*, Oct. 24, 1899, 4.
222 *"the president was"*: "Merry Chase at Sight of a Herd," *Butte Inter Mountain*, April 9, 1903, 3.
223 *"He is full of electricity"*: "Home Again," *New York Sun*, June 7, 1903, 8.
223 *"Familiar only with"*: "Achates Abroad," *St. Paul Globe*, June 19, 1904, 32.
223 *"President Roosevelt has"*: "The President's Peculiarities," *Indianapolis Journal*, Aug. 23, 1903, 2.
223 *"A few years ago"*: Annie Russell Marble, "The Gospel of Vitality in Current Literature," *Congregationalist*, Dec. 7, 1899, 864.
223 *"this last decade"*: Ibid., 865.
224 *"the animal spirits"*: Rev. Calvin W. Laufer, "Watchwords for the Fireside: Buoyancy—That's It!," *New York Observer and Chronicle* 88 (April 21, 1910), 495.
224 *"the messenger and missionary"*: Edwin Björkman, "Art, Life and Criticism," *Forum*, Dec. 1911, 686.
224 *"submit to no other"*: Ibid., 687.
224 *"which demands that"*: Ibid., 689.
224 *"She swaggers"*: Octavius Cohen, "Ta-Ra-Ra Boom-De-Ay," *Times*, Oct. 2, 1892, 13.
225 *"Animal spirits, and not to be"*: Katherine Pope, "Youth in the City," *Virginia* (Minnesota) *Enterprise*, Feb. 10, 1905, 7.
225 *"We moderns like"*: "Tango Is Inherited from the Savages," *Anaconda Standard*, Feb. 15, 1914, 13.
225 *"Any locomotive boiler"*: Parkhurst, cited in "Dr. Parkhurst Discusses the Giving of Dances by a Church," *El Paso Herald*, Jan. 29, 1912, 8.
226 *"I never could see"*: Eis, cited in "'Crude and Vulgar' Says Miss Eis of Tango as Danced Here," *Sun*, June 8, 1913, 8.
226 *"the universal human expression"*: Harold J. Howland, "What Shall We Do with the Turkey Trot?," *Suburban Life* 17 (Oct. 1913), 199.

8. THE VITALIST MOMENT: 1913 AND AFTER

226 *"agnostic-and-water"*: Cornelia Comer, "A Letter to the Rising Generation," *Atlantic Monthly* 107 (1911), 145–54.
229 *"It is the glory"*: Randolph Bourne, *Youth and Life* (1911), 25.
229 *"The secret of life"*: Ibid., 26–27.
229 *"Most of these professors"*: Ibid., 24.
229 *"a vivid and intense feeling"*: Ibid., 103.
230 *"The ironist is the only man"*: Ibid., 111.
230 *"There is but one"*: Ibid., 130.
230 *"For Margaret Sanger to attempt"*: Mabel Dodge Luhan, *Intimate Memories: The Autobiography of Mabel Dodge Luhan* (1999), ed. Louise Palken Rudnick, 119–20.
231 *"One must just let life"*: Ibid., 122.
231 *"They have only invited"*: Mabel Dodge to Gertrude Stein, Jan. 24, 1913, in *A History of Having a Great Many Times Not Continued to Be Friends: The Correspondence Between Mabel Dodge and Gertrude Stein, 1911–1934* (1996), ed. Patricia R. Everett, 158.

231 *"Many roads are being broken"*: Dodge to Stein, quoting *Art and Decoration*, March 1913, in ibid., 273.
231 *"the sound of breaking"*: Virginia Woolf, "Mrs. Bennett and Mrs. Brown" [1926], in her *The Captain's Deathbed and Other Essays* (1956), 115–17.
231 *"And out of the shattering"*: Dodge to Stein, in *A History*, 273.
232 *"creative destruction"*: Joseph Schumpeter, *Capitalism, Socialism, and Democracy* [1942] (third ed., 1950), 81.
232 *"I felt as though"*: Luhan, *Intimate Memories*, 112.
233 *"Imagine suddenly"*: Ibid., 134.
233 *"He is the most natural"*: John Reed, "With Villa in Mexico," *Metropolitan* 39 (Feb. 1914) 72.
233 "Darktown Follies *drew space"*: James Weldon Johnson, *Black Manhattan* (1930), 192.
234 *"Nine out of ten"*: Carl Van Vechten, *In the Garret* (1920), 316–17.
234 *"there has been a spiritual expansion"*: Bourne, *Youth and Life*, 179.
234 *"Five hundred"*: "Bergson Fills Hall at First Lecture," *Sun*, Feb. 4, 1913, 7.
235 *"two thousand students"*: "Professor Bergson at the City College," *Outlook*, March 1, 1913, 467.
235 *"M. Bergson has"*: Arthur O. Lovejoy, "The Metaphysician of the Life-force," *Nation* 89 (Sept. 30, 1909), 301.
235 *"He offers men again"*: Louise Collier Willcox, "Impressions of M. Bergson," *Harper's Weekly* 57 (March 8, 1913), 6.
236 *"There is nothing conservative"*: "Henri Bergson, 'Intellectual Bottle of Smelling Salts,'" *New-York Tribune*, March 23, 1913, 5.
236 *"The world was"*: Walter Lippmann, "The Most Dangerous Man in the World," *Everybody's Magazine* 26 (July 1912), 100.
236 *"And if I were interested"*: Ibid., 101.
237 *"Imagine a Broadway"*: "5,000 Women March, Beset by Crowds," *New York Times*, March 4, 1913, 5.
237 "the greatest event": Louise Collier Wilcox, "Impressions of M. Bergson," *Harper's Weekly*, March 8, 1913, 6. Italics in original.
237 *"his insistent demand"*: Marian Cox, "Bergson's Message to Feminism," *Forum*, May 1913, 548. Italics Cox's.
237 *"the subconsciousness of every"*: Edwin E. Slosson, introduction to Henri Bergson, *Dreams* (1914), 7.
238 *"Americans have discovered"*: "Rudolf Eucken," *Outlook*, March 22, 1913, 601.
238 *"To fight hard"*: "A Philosopher of the Modern Spirit," *Evening Post*, Feb. 4, 1913, 8.
239 *"Because the microscope"*: Ibid., 8.
239 *"the sentiment of rationality"*: William James, "The Sentiment of Rationality," in *William James: Writings 1878–1899* (Library of America ed., 1992), 950–85.
240 *"I believe the tendency"*: William Thomson, Thomson Collection, University of Cambridge Library, quoted in Crosbie Smith, *The Science of Energy: A Cultural History of Energy Physics in Victorian Britain* (1998), 111.
240 *"One evening Roelker"*: A. R. Macdonough, "The Century Club," *Century Magazine* 41 (March 1891), 682–83.
241 *"running down like a clock"*: Edwin E. Slosson, "This Changing World III: Man and His Mill-Race," *Independent* 105 (March 19, 1921), 285.

241 *"a world of order"*: Charles Nordmann, "The Death of the Universe," *El Paso Herald*, March 2, 1912, 3.
241 *"Reasons for Believing"*: "Reasons for Believing in the Eternal Duration of the Universe," *Current Literature* 39 (Aug. 1905), 183–84.
242 *"It is very strange"*: Charles Nordmann, "The Death of the Universe," *El Paso Herald*, March 2, 1912, 3.
242 *"a great historical date"*: Robert Kennedy Duncan, "Some Unsolved Problems in Science," *Harper's Monthly* 125 (June 1, 1912), 31.
242 *"the transcendent energies"*: Ibid., 32.
242 *"God made it"*: Robert Kennedy Duncan, *The New Knowledge* (1905), 245.
242 *"The need for a new"*: Arthur O. Lovejoy, "The Practical Tendencies of Bergsonism I," *International Journal of Ethics* 23 (April 1913), 254–55.
243 *"a resemblance to features"*: Arthur O. Lovejoy, "The Metaphysician of the Life-Force," *Nation* 89 (Sept. 30, 1909), 299.
243 *"The ancient tradition"*: Irving Babbitt, "Bergson and Rousseau," *Nation* 95 (Nov. 14, 1912), 455.
243 *"if life is better"*: George Santayana, "The Intellectual Temper of the Age," in his *Winds of Doctrine* (1913), 13–14. Italics in original.
244 *"Only when vitality is low"*: Ibid., 14.
245 *"A man, we are to believe"*: Babbitt, 455.
245 *"for what might be"*: Walter Lippmann, *A Preface to Politics* (1913), 135. Italics in original.
246 *"With an explosion"*: "Canal Is Opened by Wilson's Finger," *New York Times*, Oct. 11, 1913, 9.
246 *"Until we went"*: Ray Stannard Baker, "The Glory of Panama," *American Magazine* 76 (Nov. 1913), 33.
246 *"We suddenly realize"*: Randolph Bourne, "A Moral Equivalent for Universal Military Service" [1916], in his *War and the Intellectuals: Collected Essays, 1915–1919* (1964), 142, 146.
247 *"gently guiding a nation"*: Randolph Bourne, "War and the Intellectuals" [1917], in ibid., 3, 4, 6, 8.
248 *"the itch to be"*: Ibid., 10, 11.
248 *"The pacifist is roundly scolded"*: Ibid., 12, 13.
249 *"If William James were alive"*: Randolph Bourne, "Twilight of Idols" [1917], in ibid., 33, 54.
249 *"Malcontentedness may be"*: Ibid., 64.
249 *"it took the awful"*: G. Stanley Hall, quoted in "The Supreme Standard of Life," *New-York Tribune*, Aug. 29, 1920, 11.
250 *"Radioactivity and related phenomena"*: Albert Gallatin, "The Range of Reason," *Sun* 83 (March 9, 1916), 6.
250 *"fancies of our too easily"*: "Unreality of All Things in the Light of Modern Knowledge," *Current Opinion* 63 (Nov. 1917), 325.
251 *Our days became numbered*: Eli Cook, *The Pricing of Progress: Economic Indicators and the Capitalization of American Life* (2017); Sarah E. Igo, *The Averaged American: Surveys, Citizens, and the Making of a Mass Public* (2007); Dan Bouk, *How Our Days Became Numbered: Risk and the Rise of the Statistical Individual* (2015).

252 *"ticking off on his stopwatch"*: Robert Musil, *The Man Without Qualities* [1930–1943], trans. Sophie Wilkens (Picador ed., 2017), 6–7, 168–69.
252 *"he simply left"*: Ibid., 16.
253 *"have resorted to"*: Parke Godwin, "What Is This Association?" *New-York Daily Tribune*, March 16, 1844, 2.
253 *"The only kind"*: R. B. Wolf, "Making Men Like Their Jobs," in *Practical Psychology for Business Executives*, ed. Lionel D. Eddie (1922), 110–13.
254 *"An eight-pound baby"*: "What the Baby Is Worth as a National Asset," *New York Times*, Jan. 30, 1910, 1.
254 *"Human life"*: Irving Fisher, "The Money Value of Human Beings," *New York Times*, March 19, 1916.
254 *As Eli Cook has argued*: Eli Cook, "The Neoclassical Club: Irving Fisher and the Progressive Origins of Neoliberalism," *Journal of the Gilded Age and Progressive Era* 15 (2016), 255.
254 *"have been taunted"*: Fisher, cited in Cook, "Neoclassical Club," 251.
255 *"To spread the gospel"*: Irving Norton Fisher, *My Father Irving Fisher* (1956), 82.
255 *"we are the trustees"*: Irving Fisher and Eugene Lyman Fisk, *How to Live* (1917), 165, 300, 322.
255 *"to include every practical procedure"*: Fisher and Fisk, *How to Live*, x, 5.
255 *"So far as science can reveal"*: Ibid., 142, 114.
256 *"There aren't going to be"*: Fisher, *My Father*, 181–82. On Cotton's treatment, see Andrew Scull, *Madhouse: A Tragic Tale of Megalomania and Modern Medicine* (2005).
256 *"As you say"*: Irving Fisher to Margaret Hazard Fisher, from Dresden, 1911, in Fisher, *My Father*, 151–52.
256 *"of one thing"*: Irving Fisher to Margaret Hazard Fisher, from Peacedale, R.I., 1903, in ibid., 86.
256 *"'ever not quite'"*: William James, *A Pluralistic Universe* (1909), 321–24.
256 *"I've been reading"*: Irving Fisher to Margaret Hazard Fisher, from Minneapolis, Sept. 27, 1924, in Fisher, *My Father*, 214.
256 *"the naughty boy"*: Irving Fisher, "Humanizing Industry," *Annals of the American Academy of Political and Social Science* 82 (March 1919), 85.
257 *"animal spirits index"*: Wells Fargo Securities Economics Group, "The Roar of the Animal Spirits: A New Index," Jan. 18, 2018. I am indebted to Joe Davis of the Institute for Advanced Studies in Culture for this reference.
257 *"To understand God's thoughts"*: Eileen Magnello, "Florence Nightingale: The Compassionate Statistician," *Plus*, plus.maths.org/content/florence-nightingale-compassionate-statistician.
257 *"surveillance capitalism"*: Shoshana Zuboff, *The Age of Surveillance Capitalism: The Fight for a Human Future at the New Frontier of Power* (2019).

9. RACE, SEX, AND POWER

258 *"a wild 'goat dance'"*: "Pavlowa in 'Goat Dance,'" *Washington Post*, Nov. 2, 1921, 26.
259 *"a smooth son of a bitch"*: Sherwood Anderson to Floyd Dell, cited in Malcolm Cowley, introduction to Sherwood Anderson, *Winesburg, Ohio* [1919] (Viking Press ed., 1964), 3.
259 *"to see beneath the surface of lives"*: Anderson, *Winesburg*, frontispiece.

260 *"Sure, boys"*: Sherwood Anderson, *Sherwood Anderson's Memoirs* (1969), 263–64.
260 *"one of the children"*: Ibid., 265–66.
260 *"the time of the wise-crackers"*: Ibid., 387.
261 *"I am myself"*: Anderson to Finley, June 14, 1922, in William A. Sutton, ed., *Letters to Bab: Sherwood Anderson to Marietta D. Finley, 1916–1933* (1985), 183.
261 *"The niggers were something"*: Sherwood Anderson, *Dark Laughter* (1924), 77.
261 *"What does it matter?"*: Ibid., 80–81.
261 *"Word-lovers, sound-lovers"*: Ibid., 106–7.
262 *"[in] disposition the Negro"*: W. E. B. Du Bois, *The Negro* (1915), cited in Mia Bay, *The White Image in the Black Mind: African-American Ideas About White People, 1830–1925* (2000), 200.
263 *"semi-military, machine-like"*: Claude McKay, "Claude McKay Describes His Own Life," *Manoa* 31, no. 2 (2019), 105.
263 *"Why this obscene"*: McKay, cited in Robert Reindeers, "Racialism on the Left: E. D. Morel and the 'Black Horror on the Rhine,'" *International Review of Social History* (1968), 17.
263 *"You don't know"*: Claude McKay, *Banjo: A Story Without a Plot* [1929] (reprint, 1957), 182.
264 *"strategic essentialism"*: Sara Danius, Stefan Jonsson, and Gayatri Chakravorty Spivak, "Interview with Gayatri Spivak," *boundary 2* (Summer 1993), esp. 45–50.
264 *"the real controlling force"*: Claude McKay, *Home to Harlem* [1928] (reprint, 1987), 70.
264 *"The wild, shrieking"*: Ibid., 328.
264 *"moved down on him"*: Ibid., 118.
264 *"a bouncing little chestnut-brown"*: Ibid., 141.
265 *"The piano-player"*: Ibid., 196.
265 *"Brown bodies"*: Ibid., 94.
265 *"The women, carried away"*: Ibid., 108.
265 *"when I have the blues"*: Ibid., 139.
266 *"Intermittently the cooks"*: Ibid., 153.
266 *"Ray felt"*: Ibid., 154.
266 *"This is a new age"*: Ibid., 206.
266 *"that long red steel cage"*: Ibid., 264.
267 *"If the railroad had not been"*: Ibid.
267 *"He was of course aware"*: McKay, *Banjo*, 323.
267 *"Peace and forgetfulness"*: Ibid., 283.
267 *"not raw animal"*: McKay, *Home to Harlem*, 311.
267 *"now, like a jungle mask"*: Ibid., 337.
268 *"sense of partial invisibility"*: George Hutchinson, *In Search of Nella Larsen: A Biography of the Color Line* (2006), 25.
269 *"That second marriage"*: Nella Larsen, *Quicksand* [1928], in *The Complete Fiction of Nella Larsen* (2001), 56.
269 *"tangled feelings"*: Hutchinson, *Larsen*, 25.
269 *"that faint hint"*: Larsen, *Quicksand*.
270 *"extravagant and expensive"*: Hutchinson, *Larsen*, 63.
270 *"Something intuitive"*: Larsen, *Quicksand*, 51. Italics in original.
270 *"it wasn't, she was suddenly"*: Ibid., 44.

271 *"We talk his dialect"*: William Houghton, "Color Notes," March 18, 1927, cited in Jayna Brown, *Babylon Girls: Black Woman Performers and the Shaping of the Modern* (2008), 218.
272 *"boring beyond endurance"*: Larsen, *Quicksand*, 83.
272 *"You are the first white man"*: Harold Jackman, cited in Hutchinson, *Larsen*, 179.
272 *"It don't matter"*: Anecdote from unpublished "Reminiscences of Carl Van Vechten," Columbia University, cited in ibid., 190.
273 *"pansy"*: Hubert Harrison, cited in ibid., 214.
273 *"Life to [Van Vechten]"*: W. E. B. Du Bois, cited in ibid., 220.
274 *"individuality and beauty"*: Larsen, *Quicksand*, 53.
274 *"Helga Crane was silent"*: Ibid., 54.
274 *"an elusive something"*: Ibid.
274 *"piercing gray eyes"*: Ibid., 55.
275 *"almost too good"*: Ibid., 76.
275 *"that strange transforming experience"*: Ibid., 75.
275 *"while the continuously gorgeous"*: Ibid., 77.
275 *"As the days multiplied"*: Ibid., 78.
275 *"underneath the exchange of small talk"*: Ibid., 82.
276 *"harrowing irritation" . . . "smoldering hatred"*: Ibid., 86.
276 *"the inscrutability of the dozen"*: Ibid., 85–86.
276 *"thick, furry night"*: Ibid., 88.
277 *"For the while Helga"*: Ibid., 89.
277 *"with grace and abandon"*: Ibid., 92.
277 *"she loved color"*: Ibid., 99.
277 *"felt like nothing so much"*: Ibid., 100.
277 *"She began to feel"*: Ibid., 103–104.
278 *"She felt shamed"*: Ibid., 112–13.
278 *"I couldn't marry"*: Ibid., 118.
278 *"I'm homesick"*: Ibid., 122.
278 *"a vagrant primitive"*: Ibid., 124.
278 *"She fought against"*: Ibid., 133.
278 *"acting such a swine"*: Ibid., 135.
278 *"an endless stretch"*: Ibid., 137.
279 *"scarlet'oman"*: Ibid., 141.
279 *"There crept upon her"*: Ibid., 141–42.
279 *"in the confusion"*: Ibid., 145.
279 *"labor in the vineyard"*: Ibid., 146.
279 *"in some strange way"*: Ibid., 149–50.
279 *"The children used her up"*: Ibid., 150.
279 *"Her religion was to her"*: Ibid. 153.
279 *"the white man's God"*: Ibid., 160.
280 *"this feeling of dissatisfaction"*: Ibid.
280 *"subtle comprehension"*: W. E. B. Du Bois, cited in Hutchinson, *Larsen*, 284.
280 *"to tell the story"*: Eda Lou Walton, cited in ibid., 285.
280 *"twaddle concerning"*: Nella Larsen, review of T. Bowyer Campbell, *Black Sadie, Opportunity* (1929), cited in ibid., 311.

280 *"I entertained them"*: Nella Larsen to Carl Van Vechten, June 1929, cited in ibid., 352.
280 *"crazy about"*: Larsen to Van Vechten, June 4, 1931, cited in ibid., 388.
281 *"white book"*: Larsen to Henry Allen Moe, Oct. 1930, cited in ibid., 367.
281 *"it was* rotten": Larsen to Van Vechten, April 7, 1931, cited in ibid., 377. Italics in original.
282 *"an eye for the stock market reports"*: J. Saunders Redding, "Playing the Numbers," *North American Review* (1934), 534–35. For useful background, see Shane White, Stephen Carton, Stephen Robertson, and Graham White, *Playing the Numbers: Gambling in Harlem Between the Wars* (2020).

10. NUMBERS AND FLOW

284 *"For many years"*: William H. Howell, cited in "Wireless Treatment at Home for Obesity and Nerves?," *Washington Times*, May 14, 1922, 6.
285 *"great unconscious force"*: Anne Harrington, *The Cure Within: A History of Mind-Body Medicine* (2008), 82.
285 *"I hold the view"*: George Groddeck, *The Book of the It: Psychoanalytic Letters to a Friend*, trans. by the author (1927), 9.
286 *"we are 'lived'"*: L. Pierce Clark, citing Freud in introduction to ibid.
286 *"The Es is always"*: Ibid., 115.
286 *"the repeal of reticence"*: Rochelle Gurstein, *The Repeal of Reticence* (1996).
286 *"quite certainly"*: Groddeck, *The Book*, 149.
286 *"During his mother's"*: Ibid., 104.
287 *"literary rather than scientific"*: Herman Adler, review of William Healy and Mary Healy, *Pathological Lying*, in *Harvard Law Review* (1915), 347, cited in Michael Pettit, *The Science of Deception: Psychology and Commerce in America* (2013).
287 *"scientific detective" . . . "psychometers"*: Arthur Reeve, cited in ibid., 177.
288 *"the embodied fear"*: Ibid., 180.
288 *who's more emotional*: Ibid., 184.
289 *"had a passion"*: Robert Skidelsky, *John Maynard Keynes: I, Hopes Betrayed, 1883–1920* (1983), 83–84.
290 *"I lie in bed"*: Keynes to his father (1908), cited in ibid., 208.
290 *"will be affected"*: Keynes, 1910, cited in ibid.
291 *"a flexible field"*: Zachary Carter, *The Price of Peace: Money, Democracy, and the Life of John Maynard Keynes* (2021), 18.
291 *Keynes was as indifferent*: The anecdote is told by Skidelsky, *Hopes Betrayed*, 296.
292 *"The danger confronting us"*: John Maynard Keynes, *The End of Laissez-Faire* [1926] *and The Economic Consequences of the Peace* [1919] (reprint, 2012), 241.
293 *"Lenin was certainly right"*: Ibid., 247.
293 *"To their minds"*: Ibid., 250.
293 *"If we aim deliberately"*: Ibid., 273.
293 *"the miseries of life"*: Ibid., 258.
294 *"Physical efficiency"*: Ibid., 258–60.
294 *"the Jew-hating ruffians"*: Lobel Taubes, "The Pogroms in Vienna," *Jewish Monitor* (June 4, 1920), 7, 9.
295 *"adoration for the contingent"*: Julien Benda, *The Treason of the Intellectuals* [1927], trans. Richard Aldington (Transaction Books ed., 2007), 61.
295 *"thirst for immediate results"*: Ibid., 29.

295 *"glorifying of national particularism"*: Ibid., 52.
296 *"habit of energy and boldness"*: Filippo Marinetti, "Futurist Manifesto," cited in Alastair Hamilton, *The Appeal of Fascism: A Study of Intellectuals and Fascism, 1919–1945* (1971), 3.
296 *"despot with a dimple"*: Ida Tarbell, *All in the Day's Work* (1939), 380–84.
296 *"Duce knows how to get"*: Alice Rohe, cited in "Mussolini, Lady Killer," *Literary Digest* (July 31, 1937), 37.
297 *"mental perverts"*: Kenneth Roberts, "The Ambush of Italy," *Saturday Evening Post*, Feb. 24, 1923, 34–38.
297 *"built like a steel spring"*: John Gunther, *Inside Europe* (1938), 194.
297 *"punch to his eyes"*: Clarence Streit in *New York Evening Post*, Nov. 22, 1922.
297 *"Direct action"*: Anne O'Hare McCormick in *New York Times*, July 15, 1923.
297 *"Do you know, your excellency"*: Irvin S. Cobb, "A Big Little Man," *Cosmopolitan* (Jan. 1927), 145–46.
297 *"a man of sheer will power" and an "anti-intellectual intellectual"*: John Patrick Diggins, *Mussolini and Fascism: The View from America* (1970), 63, 62.
298 *"He is usually happy"*: W. A. Evans, "How to Keep Well: Latest U.S. Bulletin on Malnutrition," *Washington Post*, May 25, 1927, 10.
298 *"the energy and push"*: "Bad Boys Wanted," *Philadelphia Inquirer*, July 22, 1928, 112.
299 *"The address to the jury"*: W. E. Hill, "The Public Speaker," *Washington Sunday Star* (April 10, 1927), Gravure Section.
299 *"to rally youth"*: C. Patrick Thompson, "Britain's Call to Youth," *Sunday Star Magazine* (Feb. 14, 1932), 1–2.
300 *"fun and mild excitement"*: John Maynard Keynes, cited in Carter, *Price of Peace*, 116.
300 *"It is agreeable"*: Keynes, cited in ibid., 117.
300 *"kid gloves and tiara set"*: Keynes, cited in ibid., 119.
300 *"excludes a great number"*: Keynes, cited in Robert Skidelsky, *John Maynard Keynes: II, The Economist as Savior, 1920–1937* (1992), 59.
301 *"it will be an arbitrary"*: Keynes, cited in ibid.
301 "A measurable *uncertainty"*: Frank H. Knight, *Risk, Uncertainty and Profit* (1921), 20. Italics in original.
301 *"the weight of argument" . . . "moral risk"*: Keynes, cited in Skidelsky, *Savior*, 60.
302 *"exquisite plebian beauty," and "Lydia dolls"*: Carter, *Price of Peace*, 119.
302 *"I gobble you"*: Lydia Lopokova to Keynes, cited in ibid., 121.
302 *"I want to be"*: Keynes to Lopokova, cited in ibid.
302 "uneducated; *their reactions"*: Skidelsky, *Savior*, 101.
303 *"the long run"*: Keynes, cited in ibid., 62, 153–54.
303 *"The proper object"*: Keynes, cited in ibid., 203.
304 *"There is no reason"*: Keynes, cited in Carter, *Price of Peace*, 173.
305 *"to the great majority"*: John Kenneth Galbraith, *The Great Crash: 1929* (1955), 77.
305 *"At luncheon in downtown"*: Ibid., 77.
305 *"the rise of a new national literature"*: Charles Merz, "Bull Market," *Harper's*, April 1929, 644.
306 *"has fitted perfectly"*: Ibid., 645.
306 *"even the person"*: Galbraith, *Great Crash*, 80.
306 *"'The [ticker] tape doesn't lie'"*: John Brooks, *Once in Golconda: A True Drama of Wall Street, 1920–1938* (1968), 60.

306 *"carefully planted rumor"*: Steve Fraser, *Every Man a Speculator: A History of Wall Street in American Life* (2005), 307. I am indebted to Fraser's shrewd and searching account of the bull market and the crash.
307 *"gentlemen of high moral"*: Joseph Stagg Lawrence, *Wall Street and Washington* (1929), 14, 3, 7.
308 *"fringe of fraud"*: Ibid., 133, 151.
308 *"Christ himself"*: Ibid., 139, 142.
308 *"ultimate end"*: Ibid., 144–45.
308 *"Sex has become"*: John B. Watson, cited in Fraser, *Every Man*, 395.
309 *"financial success"*: English visitor, cited in Brooks, *Golconda*, 107.
309 *"Seas of regret"*: Bernie Winkelman, cited in ibid., 84.
309 *"the market had surrendered"*: Galbraith, *Great Crash*, 99.
309 *"not so much"*: Edwin Lefevre, "The Little Fellow in Wall Street," *Saturday Evening Post*, Jan. 4, 1930, cited in ibid., 100.
310 *"a little distress"*: Thomas Lamont, cited in ibid., 101.
310 *"The feeling of those present"*: Richard Whitney, *The Work of the Stock Exchange in the Panic of 1929*, an address before the Boston Association of Stock Exchange Firms (1930), 16–17ff.
310 *"hollered and screamed"*: Eyewitness, cited in Fraser, *Every Man*, 416.
310 *"eerie roar"*: Eyewitness, cited in Brooks, *Golconda*, 119.
310 *"to show pictures"*: Mayor Jimmy Walker, cited in Galbraith, *Great Crash*, 115.
310 *"Never was there a time"*: Ibid., 123.
310 *"the stock market"*: Edmund Wilson, *The Thirties* (1980), 65–66.
311 *"an epoch of cheap money"*: Keynes to *New York Post*, cited in Carter, *Price of Peace*, 163.
311 *"voluntary abstinence"*: John Maynard Keynes, *Treatise on Money* (1930), vol. 2, 148–50.
311 *"the anxiety of many banks"*: Keynes, cited in Carter, *Price of Peace*, 208.

11. THE ONLY THING WE HAVE TO FEAR

312 *"In small towns"*: Ed Paulsen, quoted in Studs Terkel, *Hard Times: An Oral History of the Great Depression* (1970), 30.
313 *"We were a gentle crowd"*: Ibid., 31.
313 *"Have you heard a hungry child"*: Lillian Wald, cited in Arthur M. Schlesinger, Jr., *The Crisis of the Old Order, 1919–1933* (1957), 171.
313 *"The Collapse of the Romance"*: John Dewey, cited in Fraser, *Every Man*, 423.
314 *"No power so effectually"*: Edmund Burke, cited in Ira Katznelson, *Fear Itself: The New Deal and the Origins of Our Time* (2013), 29.
314 *"dreadful apathy"*: Edmund Wilson, "An Appeal to Progressives," *New Republic* (Jan. 14, 1931), 235–36.
315 *"the look of pain"*: Richard Pells, *Radical Visions and American Dreams: Culture and Social Thought in the Depression Years* (1973), 196.
315 *"The amazing thing"*: Sherwood Anderson, *Puzzled America* (1935), ix.
315 *"did not even know"*: James Rorty, *Where Life Is Better* (1936), 117.
315 *"In Lowell I saw"*: Louis Adamic, "Tragic Towns of New England," *Harper's* 162 (May 1931), 752.
315 *"Few of the unemployed"*: Ibid., 755.
316 *"the breaking down"*: Anderson, *Puzzled America*, 161–62.

316 *"When [the children] see me"*: Quoted in Mirra Komarovsky, *The Unemployed Man and His Family* (1940), 98.
316 *"hardest thing"*: Quoted in ibid., 27.
316 *"I simply had"*: Engineer, quoted in Lorena Hickock to Harry Hopkins, April 2, 1934, in Hickock, *One Third of a Nation* (1981), 206.
316 *"We'd lived on bread"*: Insurance agent, quoted in ibid.
316 *"No economist doubts"*: Gerald W. Johnson, "Bryan, Thou Shouldst Be Living," *Harper's*, Sept. 1931, 388.
316 *"constitutionally gloomy"*: William Allen White, cited in John Kasson, *The Little Girl Who Fought the Great Depression: Shirley Temple and 1930s America* (2014), 15.
316–17 *"if you put a rose"*: Gutzon Borglum, cited in ibid.
317 *"appeals for good cheer"*: Ibid., 17.
317 *"the reparations problem"*: Keynes, cited in Carter, *Price of Peace*, 217.
317 *"Fascism in Action"*: Mussolini, cited in Katznelson, *Fear*, 112–13.
317 *"crisis of democratic confidence"*: Katznelson paraphrasing Niebuhr in ibid., 115.
317 *"comprehending the tides of history"*: Ibid., 116.
318 *"his capacity to charm"*: Robert Dallek, *Franklin D. Roosevelt: A Political Life* (2017), 20.
318 *"Never let the left"*: FDR, cited in ibid., 35.
318 *"frictionless command"*: Harvard *Crimson* managing editor, cited in ibid., 32.
318 *"an aristocrat at odds with the bosses"*: Ibid., 44.
319 *his immune system*: Ibid., chap. 3.
319 *"You know that he has never"*: Eleanor Roosevelt, cited in Kasson, *Little Girl*, 24.
319 *"an invalid on crutches"*: A "typical newspaper assessment," cited in Dallek, *Roosevelt*, 91.
319 *"Yes, we could smell"*: Harold Clurman, *Fervent Years* (1957), 107, 112.
320 *"Fine! Fine! Fine!"*: FDR, cited in Dallek, *Roosevelt*, 128.
320 *"Orson, you and I"*: FDR, cited in ibid., 129.
320 *"I am certain"*: FDR inaugural address: avalon.law.yale.edu/20th_century/froos1.asp.
321 *"The new president's recurrent smile"*: "500,000 in Streets Cheer Roosevelt," *New York Times*, March 5, 1933, 1.
321 *"dipped in phosphorous"*: Lillian Gish, cited in Kasson, *Little Girl*, 31.
321 *"Today sitting"*: Cleveland man, cited in ibid., 35.
321 *"tears of peaceful happiness"*: Des Moines woman, cited in ibid.
321 *"You are bringing back"*: Chicagoan, cited in ibid., 37.
321 *"We are saved"*: Syracuse judge, cited in ibid., 38.
321 *"new deal"*: FDR, acceptance speech to Democratic Convention, July 2, 1932, www.presidency.ucsb.edu/documents/address-accepting-the-presidential-nomination-the-democratic-national-convention-chicago-1.
322 *"President Roosevelt has"*: *Time*, April 3, 1933, 43.
322 *"strangely reminiscent"*: Anne O'Hare McCormick, "Vast Tides That Stir the Capital," *New York Times Magazine*, May 7, 1993, 1–3.
323 *"A system based upon"*: Diggins, *Mussolini and Fascism*, 225.
323 *"the social whole"*: Katznelson, *Fear*, 478.
323 *"Uncle Sam"*: Vera Connolly, "Uncle Sam Wants Your Mark," *Good Housekeeping*, Dec. 1935, 24–25.

324 *"Life is safer"*: Social Security Board, "Why Social Security?" (1937), cited in Bouk, *How Our Days Became Numbered*, 216.
324 *"Unemployed lumber worker"*: Ibid., 209–11.
326 *"the modern conception of death"*: Irving Fisher, cited in ibid., 115.
326 *"What chance do you"*: "Dorothy Dix's Letter Box," *Washington Evening Star*, March 19, 1931, C-10.
326 *"folk play"*: J. Brooks Atkinson, "A-Hollerin': 'Green Grow the Lilacs' with Cowboys and Farmers and Animal Spirits," *New York Times*, Feb. 8, 1931, 106.
327 *"truckin' on down"*: "Shirley Goes Harlem—Learns to Truck," *Chicago Defender*, Jan. 11, 1936, 8.
327 *"'Sailor Beware!' is a bawdy"*: Brooks Atkinson, "Limitations of the United States Navy in a Comedy Entitled 'Sailor, Beware!'" *New York Times*, Sept. 29, 1933, 24.
327 *"He is young"*: Bill McCormick, "Around the Ring . . ." *Washington Post*, June 17, 1934: 17.
328 *"Grandpa watched them"*: W. Boyce Morgan, "Grandpa Jenkins' Gold: A Story of Two Young Prospectors. Installment V," *Sunday Star*, March 18, 1934, 14.
328 *"Although a good many"*: "The Theatre: Succeeding Burlesque," *Wall Street Journal*, July 14, 1937, 13.
328 *"made to order for the movie fans"*: "Sonja Henie Is Skating Again at the Palace," *Washington Post*, March 5, 1938, X10.
329 *"Bette Davis, the Duse of Warner's"*: T.S., "Bette Davis Tries Comedy in 'The Bride Came C.O.D.' at the Strand," *New York Times*, July 26, 1941: 18.
329 *"widespread confusion"*: Howard Odum, cited in Katznelson, *Fear*, 43.
329 *"Today, my friends"*: FDR, cited in ibid., 35.
329 *"seized by deep"*: Walter Lippmann, cited in ibid., 298.
329 *"the dominant mood"*: Frederick Schumann, cited in ibid.
330 *"Why has it happened?"*: "Sloan Finds Recession Influenced by Fear, 'Political-Economic' Ills Halting Recovery," *New York Times*, Jan. 3, 1938, 34.
330 *"I saw your friend"*: FDR to Frances Perkins, May 1934, cited in Dallek, *Roosevelt*, ibid.
330 *"supposed the President"*: Keynes to Perkins, cited in ibid.
331 *"'I guess things'"*: Cited in Rorty, *Where Life Is Better*, 31.
332 *"Lying in bed"*: Keynes to Kingsley Martin, July 1, 1937, cited in Robert Skidelsky, *John Maynard Keynes: III, Fighting for Britain, 1937–1946* (2000), 7.
332 *"It is our duty"*: Keynes, cited in ibid., 33. Italics in original.
333 *"a very packed"*: *Diary of Virginia Woolf*, ed. A. G. Bell, v, 128–29.
333 *"Cambridge rationalism"*: Keynes, "My Early Beliefs," in *The Collected Writings of John Maynard Keynes*, X, 434.
333 *"We were at an age"*: Ibid., 435.
334 *"Nothing mattered"*: Ibid., 436, 438, 442.
334 *"the life of passionate"*: Ibid., 445, 446. Italics in original.
334 *"continuing moral progress"*: Ibid., 447.
335 *"We repudiated all versions"*: Ibid.
335 *"the attribution of rationality"*: Ibid., 448.
335 *"water-spiders"*: Ibid., 450.
336 *"the abstinence theory of progress"*: Skidelsky, *Savior*, 541.

337 *"If you want to be rich"*: *Watch Your Dreams with Harlem Pete Dream Book* (1949), 2, in University of Michigan Library, Special Collections.
337 *"If the Treasury"*: Keynes, *General Theory*, 129.
338 *"Keynes did not* want": Joan Robinson to American Economic Association, cited in Carter, *Price of Peace*, 456. Italics in original.
338 *"When the capital"*: Keynes, *General Theory*, 159.
338 *"How then are these"*: Ibid., 151–52.
339 *"risks . . . were supposed"*: Keynes, "The General Theory of Employment," *Quarterly Journal of Economics* (1937), 213.
339 *"Actually, we have"*: Ibid. Italics in original.
339 *"By 'uncertain' knowledge"*: Ibid., 213–14.
340 *"a result of animal spirits"*: Keynes, *General Theory*, 161.
340 *"The actual, private object"*: Ibid., 155.
341 *"science and compound interest"*: Keynes, "Economic Prospects for Our Grandchildren" (1930), in his *Essays in Persuasion* (reprint, 2010), 321–32.
341 *a capitalist version of Providence*: See the probing remarks in White, *Railroaded*, xxv.
341 *"second flood"*: Edmund Wilson, *Axel's Castle: A Study in the Imaginative Literature of 1870–1930* [1931] (reprint, 1969), 2.
342 *"little daily miracles"*: Virginia Woolf, *To the Lighthouse*, ed. David Bradshaw (2006), 133.
342 *"will flame out"*: Gerard Manley Hopkins, "God's Grandeur" [1877, first pub. 1918], lines 2, 10, https://www.poetryfoundation.org/poems/44395/gods-grandeur.
342 *as Jon Levy observes*: My thinking on these matters has been freshened and sharpened by Jon Levy's brilliant essay "Primal Capital," *Critical Historical Studies* 6, no. 2 (Fall 2019), 161–93.

12. THE TRIUMPH AND FAILURE OF MANAGEMENT

343 *"reactionary Keynesianism"*: Carter, *Price of Peace*, passim.
345 *"the hardboiled youth"*: H. R. Baukhage, "Washington Digest: Status of Fascism in Spain," *Midland Journal*, Jan. 14, 1944, 2.
346 *"Without qualification"*: Don Goddard, cited in Paul Boyer, *By the Bomb's Early Light: American Thought and Culture at the Dawn of the Nuclear Age* (1994), 4, 5.
346 *"a creeping feeling of apprehension"*: A. Garcia Diaz to *New York Times*, Aug. 9, 1945, 20.
346 *"We have sowed the whirlwind"*: Hanson Baldwin, "The Atomic Weapon," *New York Times*, Aug. 7, 1945, 10.
346 *an iconic journalistic form*: "News of the Week in Review," *Milwaukee Journal*, Aug. 8, 1945, 12.
346 *"as one senses the foundations"*: "The Atomic Bomb," *New York Herald Tribune*, Aug. 7, 1945, 22.
346 *"We thank God"*: Truman, cited in Boyer, *Bomb's Early Light*, 6.
347 *"Prometheus, the subtle artificer"*: "The Atomic Age," *Life*, Aug. 20, 1945, 32.
347 *"Seldom, if ever"*: *In Search of Light: The Broadcasts of Edward R. Murrow, 1938–1961* (1967), 102.
347 *"every major city"*: J. W. Campbell, interview in *The New Yorker*, Aug. 25, 1945, 16.

347 *"a barren waste"*: *Chicago Tribune*, cited in Boyer, *Bomb's Early Light*, 15.
347 *"paralyzing fear"*: W. F. Ogburn, "Sociology and the Atom," *American Journal of Sociology* 31 (Jan. 1946), 269.
348 *"a kind of vast jelly"*: Hermann Hagedorn, cited in Boyer, *Bomb's Early Light*, 280.
348 *"a revolutionary change"*: Henry Stimson, cited in Katznelson, *Fear*, 349.
348 *"fear became permanent"*: Ibid.
348 *"public thinking"*: David Lilienthal, cited in ibid., 416.
348 *"emotions of fear"*: Government review of congressional debate, cited in ibid., 432.
348 *"There is much to fear"*: Clinton Rossiter, "Constitutional Dictatorship in an Atomic Age," *Review of Politics* 2 (1949), 418.
348 *"scare the pants off"*: Cited in Boyer, *Bomb's Early Light*, 70.
348 *"to preserve our civilization"*: Eugene Rabinowitch, "Five Years After," *Bulletin of the Atomic Scientists* 7, no. 1 (Jan. 1951), 3.
349 *"Gentlemen, you are mad!"*: Lewis Mumford, "Gentlemen, You Are Mad!" *Saturday Review of Literature*, March 2, 1946, 5, 6.
349 *"scare hell out of the American people"*: Arthur Vandenberg, cited in Greg Herken, *Shattered Peace: The Origins of the Cold War and the National Security State* (1977), 282–84.
350 *"The atom bomb"*: Wyndham Lewis, *America and Cosmic Man* (1949), 244.
350 *"I know the bomb"*: Survey respondent, cited in Boyer, *Bomb's Early Light*, 23.
350 *"Through God's help"*: Norman Vincent Peale, *A Guide to Confident Living* (1948), 146.
350 *"the journalist must write"*: Telford Taylor, "The Trouble Is Fear," *The Nation*, May 20, 1950, 507.
351 *"permissive effect"*: Lionel Trilling, "The Kinsey Report," *Partisan Review*, April 1948.
352 *"the end of ideology"*: Daniel Bell, *The End of Ideology* (1960).
353 *"a Detroit pet monkey"*: Paul Steiner, "Animal Spirits," *New York Times*, April 2, 1950, 172.
354 *"The real test will come"*: M. J. Rossant, "Crisis of Confidence: A View of the Spirits of Businessmen and How They May Affect the Economy," *New York Times*, April 15, 1963, 46.
354 *"that a limitation"*: "Tightening Up on Margins," *Washington Post*, Nov. 8, 1963, A22.
354 *"the uncertainty which has"*: Harvey H. Segal, "Investment View: The Incest Impact on Forecast Crop," *Washington Post*, Dec. 23, 1963, A22.
355 *"A single superbomb"*: Ralph Lapp, "Civil Defenses Outmoded by New H-bomb," *Time*, Feb. 21, 1955, content.time.com/time/subscriber/article/0,33009,892974,00.html.
356 *"Why make the rubble bounce?"*: Churchill, quoted in James Reston, "'Why Make the Rubble Bounce?,'" *New York Times*, March 31, 1976.
356 *"strategists widened"*: Paul Erickson, Judy Klein, Lorraine Daston, Rebecca Lemov, Thomas Sturm, and Michael D. Gordon, *How Reason Almost Lost Its Mind: The Strange Career of Cold War Rationality* (2013), 6.
357 *"Stone Age mentality"*: Ibid., 16.
357 *"The rule that such a device"*: Jerome Weizenbaum, cited in ibid., 29.
358 *"a new priesthood"*: Theodore White, "The Action Intellectuals," *Life* (June 9, 1967), 3.

358 *"the delicate balance of terror"*: Albert Wohlstetter, cited in Erickson et al., *How Reason*, 13.

358 *"stochastic universe"*: Oskar Morgenstern, cited in Erickson et al., *How Reason*, 48.

359 *"a cool and clear-headed"*: Sidney Verba, cited in ibid., 83.

359 *"in almost total disagreement"*: Norman Mailer, contribution to "Our Country and Our Culture," *Partisan Review* (May–June 1952), 298–301.

360 *"there is slowly emerging"*: Dwight Macdonald, "A Theory of Mass Culture," in *Mass Culture: The Popular Arts in America*, ed. Bernard Rosenberg and David Manning White (1957), 59–73.

361 *"the life where a man must go"*: Mailer, "The White Negro" [1957], in his *Advertisements for Myself* (1959), 313.

362 *"The Decline of Greatness"*: Arthur Schlesinger, Jr., "The Decline of Greatness" [1958], *Saturday Evening Post*, Nov. 1, 1958, reprinted in his *Kennedy or Nixon: Does It Make Any Difference?* (1960).

362 *"It was a hero"*: Mailer, "Superman Comes to the Supermarket," *Esquire*, Nov. 1960.

364 *Kennedy's aggressive nuclear policy*: My interpretation of the Cuban Missile Crisis is based on Sheldon M. Stern, *The Cuban Missile Crisis in American Memory* (2012), which is ably summarized by Benjamin Schwarz, "The Real Cuban Missile Crisis," *The Atlantic* (2013), www.theatlantic.com/magazine/archive/2013/01/the-real-cuban-missile-crisis/309190/.

364 *"would learn just"*: Khrushchev to Strobe Talbott, cited in Schwarz, "Real Cuban Missile Crisis," 3.

365 *"the peace and security"*: Kennedy, television address to the nation, Oct. 22, 1962, cited in ibid.

366 *"The furnishings are functional"*: Norman Mailer, *The Armies of the Night* (Signet Books ed., 1968), 25–26, 27.

366 *"If the republic was now"*: Mailer, *Armies*, 110, 103.

369 *"a purely negative"*: Theodore Roszak, *The Making of a Counterculture: Reflections on a Technocratic Society and Its Youthful Opposition* [1969] (reprint, 1994), 53, 9, 198.

370 *"There is but one way"*: Ibid., 208, 218, 120.

371 *"the living experience"*: Ibid., 228, 140, 227.

371 *"an evil which is not"*: Ibid., 47, 55.

372 *"cultivation of a feminine"*: Ibid., 74–75, 82, 149–50.

372 *Soon enough the ferment would subside*: The best interpretation of this subsidence is Fred Turner, *From Counterculture to Cyberculture: Stewart Brand, the Whole Earth Network, and the Rise of Digital Utopianism* (2006).

375 *"recapturing the flag"*: George Packer, "Recapturing the Flag," *New York Times Magazine*, Sept. 30, 2001, www.nytimes.com/2001/09/30/magazine/the-way-we-live-now-9–30–01-recapturing-the-flag.html.

376 *"exterminate all the brutes"*: Joseph Conrad, *The Heart of Darkness* [1899] (Penguin ed., 2017), 57.

376 *"Not in our lifetime"*: Cheney, cited in Bob Woodward, "CIA Told to Do 'Whatever Necessary' to Kill Bin Laden," *Washington Post*, October 21, 2001, www.washingtonpost.com/archive/politics/2001/10/21/cia-told-to-do-whatever necessary-to-kill-bin-laden/19d0e8f1-dbe5–4b07–9c47–44c5b4328f1f/.

378 *"irrational exuberance"*: Alan Greenspan, "The Challenge of Central Banking in a Democratic Society," speech to American Enterprise Institute, Dec. 5, 1996, www.federalreserve.gov/boarddocs/speeches/1996/19961205.htm.

EPILOGUE: A FIERCE GREEN FIRE

382 *"We reached the old wolf"*: Aldo Leopold, *A Sand County Almanac* [1949] (reprint, 2020), 121–22.

384 *"Does life only make sense"*: Jane Bennett, *Vibrant Matter* (2010), 53, 113, 119.

384 *"he pauses. I wait"*: Robert McFarlane, *Underland* (2019), 65, 67.

385 *"Does it change the way"*: Ibid., 69.

385 *"Living wood, left long"*: Ibid., 92, 104.

385 *"the force which causes"*: Ibid., 112.

385 *"grammar of animacy"*: Ibid.

385 *"Intelligence . . . has often been"*: Steven Pinker, cited in Riskin, *The Restless Clock*, 347.

386 *"niche construction"*: Kevin Laland, Blake Matthews, and Marcus Feldman, "An Introduction to Niche Construction Theory," *Evolutionary Ecology* 30 (2016), 191–202.

386 *"quantum jumps"*: Erwin Schrodinger, *What Is Life?* [1944] (Canto Classics ed., 2012), 34, 113.

387 *"not through a purely random"*: Riskin, *The Restless Clock*, 357.

388 *"fanaticism" and "zealotry"*: Richard Dawkins, cited in ibid., 364.

389 *"Well, God has arrived"*: Keynes to Lopokova, cited in Skidelsky, *Savior*, 291.

389 *"no statement of fact"*: Ludwig Wittgenstein, "A Lecture on Ethics" [1929], 2, 3, 5, 6, sackett.net/WittgensteinEthics.pdf.

Acknowledgments

AT THE END of a long slog of writing a book, it's always a pleasure to recall the generosity and support that made it happen. Once again, I have been lucky.

Rutgers University provided a crucial institutional foundation for my work, as it has for nearly forty years. The staff at Alexander Library was top-notch and reliable as always. The staff at *Raritan*—Donna Green, Michael Van Unen, Julie Meidlinger, and Stephanie Volmer—held down the fort, even during the trying times of the Covid pandemic. My colleagues in history engaged intelligently with this project as it took shape. In particular, James Delbourgo, Jamie Pietruska, Seth Koven, Johan Mathew, Camilla Townsend, David Greenberg, Tom Figueira, and Toby Craig Jones helped me clarify larger concepts in ways they may not have realized at the time. Pat McGrath provided stellar research and playful intellect. The students in my undergraduate seminar "Humans and Animals in the Western Imagination" offered fresh insights into large issues—especially Giuseppe Lazzarotti, in his passionate and incisive work on wolves.

I have also depended heavily on the work of other historians, biographers, and critics, with admiration and gratitude—as I trust my endnotes indicate. David Bromwich and Richard Moser are not mentioned in the endnotes, but they have provided crucial intellectual companionship in dark times. Invitations to speak at Virginia Tech, Cornell, Northwestern, the University of Tel Aviv, the University of Liverpool in London, the Italian Institute of American Studies in Rome, the Einstein Forum in Potsdam, and the University of California at Santa Barbara gave me opportunities to sharpen my ideas and extend their reach. Among many lively interlocutors, Giles Gunn, Nelson Lichtenstein, Eileen Boris, Ed Gitre, Jon Levy, Michael Kramer, Amy Dru Stanley, Michael Zakim, and Dror Wahrman offered especially shrewd insights that helped me realize I was writing (among other things) a history of capitalism and emotional life.

I owe a huge debt of gratitude to the Institute of Advanced Studies in Culture at the University of Virginia, where I wrote the first draft of this book. Its founder and executive director, James Davison Hunter, and its director, Ryan Olson, provided solid material support; James also offered a model of creative involvement with broad cultural issues—not to mention his friendship. Matt Crawford, Joe Davis, Tal Brewer, Rachel Wahl, Andrew Lynn, Kyle Williams, James Mumford, Paul Nedelisky, Chris Yates, Garnette Cadogan, Jennifer Geddes, Isaac Reed, Olivier Zunz, and many other Institute Fellows created a challenging and rewarding intellectual community. Jay Tolson was in a class by himself, encouraging me at every turn, nudging my research in fruitful directions, reading the entire manuscript with a critical but sympathetic eye.

My dear daughters, Rachel and Adin, provided stirring inspiration in their own creative work, Rachel as a documentary filmmaker and Adin as a scholar of medieval literature. Both of them, in very different ways, have kept me mindful of the need to address urgent contemporary concerns. Adin was engaged with *Animal Spirits* from the start; she generously shared her understanding of medieval bodies and souls, how they interacted, and how they resurfaced in modernist guise.

A number of generous, competent people provided assistance at critical moments. Jackie Ko of the Wylie Agency and Ian Van Wye of FSG deserve particular mention in this regard.

As in the past, Virginia Gilmartin provided superb research assistance. She found mountains of newspaper and magazine articles, located the most important quotations in them, and deftly paraphrased the rest. She is an energetic, conscientious, and imaginative reader—not to mention an eagle-eyed fact-checker. I could not have written this book without her.

Nor could I have written it without Alex Star, my editor at FSG. Long before I ever signed a contract, he was deeply enough immersed in this project to write extended, searching critiques of grant proposals and other summaries I had written. When I started work on the manuscript, he encouraged me to think ambitiously and range widely, and when he started to read it, he gave me just the kind of encouragement I needed, even while he cautioned me not to enter blind alleys and pointed me toward promising topics, based on his own wide learning and his grounded knowledge of literature and history. Alex has been truly indispensable.

My largest debt is acknowledged, however inadequately, in the dedication. Karen Parker Lears took essential time from her own artistic work to read the manuscript with the sharp perception and exceptional care that she is uniquely capable of providing. Crucial as that reading was, her contributions to my writing and thinking are even deeper and wider. For decades, she has been engaged in much of her own work (albeit in very different forms and idioms) with many of the concerns that drive this book—above all with the conviction that we inhabit an animated, scintillating cosmos. During our innumerable discussions about *Animal Spirits* (and the books that preceded it), Karen constantly articulated the most significant questions and urged me to explore them. She has always been there, seeing through to the heart of the matter. I have been lucky in many things, but most of all in having this extraordinary person for my life companion.

Furman's Corner, New Jersey
Starr Hill, Virginia
November 6, 2022

Index

Page numbers in *italics* refer to illustrations.

A Note About the Author

Jackson Lears is a Board of Governors Distinguished Professor of history at Rutgers University and the editor of *Raritan*. His books include *Rebirth of a Nation: The Making of Modern America, 1877–1920*; *Something for Nothing: Luck in America*; *Fables of Abundance: A Cultural History of Advertising in America*; and *No Place of Grace: Antimodernism and the Transformation of American Culture, 1880–1920.*